T0315812

Women and Psychiatric Treatment

Women and Psychiatric Treatment provides a practical guide to the challenge of preserving fairness in access and quality of provision of health care and argues that equity is only achievable through greater recognition of gender differences.

Taking into account the main variables which influence treatment, such as setting, age and culture, clear suggestions are given for the reform of training, research and provision of services according to gender differences. Divided into seven sections, the book discusses the following subjects:

- The background
- Treatment settings
- Treatment of particular groups
- Specific disorders
- Managing the sequelae of trauma
- Therapies
- The future

This comprehensive and practical text offers a thorough investigation of the issues surrounding the treatment of women with mental health problems. It will be welcomed by psychiatrists, clinical psychologists and other mental health workers.

Claire Henderson is Attending Psychiatrist, Bronx Psychiatric Center, Assertive Community Treatment team and Adjunct Associate Research Scientist, Joseph L. Mailman School of Public Health, Columbia University, New York, USA.

Catherine Smith is a Specialist Registrar in General Psychiatry and Psychotherapy with West Hampshire NHS Trust.

Shubulade Smith is a Clinical Senior Lecturer and Honorary Consultant Psychiatrist at the Institute of Psychiatry and the South London and Maudsley NHS Trust.

Angela Stevens is a Specialist Registrar in Child and Adolescent Psychiatry at the South London and Maudsley NHS Trust.

Contributors: Jennifer Bearn, Kay Beaumont, Mary Burd, Marta Buszewicz, Sue Conroy, Cathy Cox, Joanne Godley, Penny Cutting, Judith Erskine, Jo Evans, Claire Henderson, Louise Howard, Sonia Johnson, Dora Kohen, Sarah Majid, Jane Marshall, Shirley McNicholas, Penny Mostyn, Eleni Palazidou, Ulrike Schmidt, Trudi Seneviratne, Bart Sheehan, Catherine Smith, Shubulade Smith, Angela Stevens, Lynda Todd, Ray Travers, Ruth Williams, Charlotte Wilson-Jones

Women and Psychiatric Treatment

A comprehensive text and practical guide

**Edited by
Claire Henderson, Catherine Smith,
Shubulade Smith & Angela Stevens**

Routledge
Taylor & Francis Group

LONDON AND NEW YORK

First published 2006
by Routledge
27 Church Road, Hove, East Sussex, BN3 2FA

Simultaneously published in the USA and Canada
by Routledge
711 Third Avenue, New York, NY 10017, USA

*Routledge is an imprint of the Taylor & Francis Group,
an informa business*

Typeset in Times by RefineCatch Ltd, Bungay, Suffolk

Paperback cover design by Hybert Design

British Library Cataloguing in Publication Data
A catalogue record for this book is available from the British Library

Library of Congress Cataloging-in-Publication Data
A catalog record has been requested

ISBN 13: 978-0-415-2194-3 hbk

ISBN 10: 0-415-21394-0 hbk

Contents

Acknowledgements

We should like to thank all organisers of previous conferences on women and mental health at the Institute of Psychiatry, who inspired and advised us during the organisation of the conference that led to this book.

Preface

The production of this book follows the sixth conference on Women and Mental Health held at the Institute of Psychiatry, organised by the editors. Many of the chapters have been written by people who spoke at the conference, while others have been commissioned to fill important gaps. Nevertheless we are aware of still further gaps caused by our decision to focus on the area of psychiatry in which we were all working at the time we proposed the book, i.e. general adult psychiatry. There is no chapter on the treatment of psychiatric problems in women with learning disabilities, and no section on the treatment of female children and adolescents.

The extent to which feminism as a theoretical perspective informs the content of the book varies from chapter to chapter. In this sense it is reflective of the whole series of conferences mentioned above, and is thus likely to draw similar criticisms from those who think it too feminist and from others who think it is insufficiently so. In drawing together this variety of perspectives, our overriding aim has been to make the book useful to practitioners working with women with mental health problems. To the same end we have also included details at the end of most chapters of relevant organisations, mostly national ones, which can provide further assistance to women with mental health problems.

Foreword

This book should be welcomed by all those involved in the provision of mental health services for women.

My profession of medicine has not had a good record in distinguishing sufficiently between women and men in how an individual develops and maintains mental health. Nor, with some notable exceptions, have those who research causal and precipitating factors for mental illness, or its effective treatment, whether that is socio-psychological or bio-pharmacological.

Women and Psychiatric Treatment contributes to addressing the particular features of why women develop mental health problems, and how they can most effectively helped. It is a practical book, full of observations based on experience, with references to additional reading, and descriptions of promising new developments.

It can be read from the logical beginning of the 'Background' which includes some recent history of these issues in the twentieth century.

Alternatively, the reader may turn immediately to their area of particular interest whether it be an age group, a diagnosis, treatment relevant to one of these, or grouped into modality in the section on therapies, and finally a number of different treatment settings.

The latter are particularly helpful in describing the aspects of service provision from primary care, through adult services in the community and in hospital, and in forensic services that have special significance for the effective care of female patients.

The chapters on community and out-patient services, and on in-patient services, are particularly illuminating, the latter graphically describing how female patients have been disadvantaged, or even abused, in conventional 'mixed sex' wards. The lack of serious attention to complaints from women on 'mixed sex' wards is another disadvantaging phenomenon that should be addressed much more vigorously and consistently than hitherto.

The contribution of several chapters on the treatment of specific groups, and on individual disorders, is particularly helpful in updating understanding from recent research on gender differences.

There is a theme of disadvantage and neglect of women, who need help with mental health problems, running through the book, from the study of eating disorders (much more prevalent in women), the lack of attention of the pharmaceutical industry to the teratogenicity of drugs and their differential impact on sexual functioning in women and men, the differences between male and female drug addicts, and our shameful lack of understanding of ethnic differences, particularly when combined with those of gender.

The relative under funding of provision for the mentally ill, and their continuing stigmatisation has contributed to widespread failure to ensure that current services meet the needs of those who present to them. Where both genders are concerned, there is evidence that individuals resist availing themselves of the help that is provided, e.g. women resisting the prescription of psychotropic medication, as part of the medicalisation of psycho-social difficulties.

Books such as this, and the conference from which it derives, will do much to ensure that those with mental health problems receive appropriate care, as near to their home as possible, with the most suitable and effective treatment for that individual being made easily available.

That will be 'a giant step forward' for woman kind.

Fiona Caldicott DBE, MA, BM, BCh, FRCPsych, FRCP

Contributors

Jennifer Bearn, Consultant Psychiatrist, South London and Maudsley NHS Trust, Bethlem Royal Hospital, Monks Orchard Road, Beckenham, Kent BR3 3BX

Kay Beaumont, Forensic Services Development Manager, Lambeth Southwark and Lewisham Health Authority (formerly Team Manager, Southwark Social Services)

Mary Burd, Royal Free and University College Medical School, Gower Street, London WC1E 6BT

Marta Buszewicz, Department of Primary Care and Population Sciences, Royal Free and University College Medical School, Gower Street, London WC1E 6BT

Sue Conroy, Research Officer, Section of Perinatal Psychiatry, Institute of Psychiatry, De Crespigny Park, London SE5 8AF

Cathy Cox, Clinical Nurse Specialist in Deliberate Self Harm, South London and Maudsley NHS Trust, Bethlem Royal Hospital, Monks Orchard Road, Beckenham, Kent BR3 3BX

Penny Cutting, Manager, Croydon Women's Service, South London and Maudsley NHS Trust, 158 Foxley Lane, Purley, Surrey CR8 3NF

Jo Evans, Homeopath, Lifeworks, 92–94 Drummond Street, London NW1

Joanne Godley, Research Assistant, Department of Psychological Medicine, King's College Hospital, Denmark Hill, London SE5 9RS

Claire Henderson, MRC Special Training Fellow in Health Services Research, Health Services Research Department, Institute of Psychiatry, and Honorary Specialist Registrar in Psychiatry South London and Maudsley NHS Trust, London

Louise Howard, Wellcome Research Training Fellow, Institute of Psychiatry and Honorary Specialist Registrar, South London and Maudsley NHS Trust, London

Sonia Johnson, Senior Lecturer in Social and Community Psychiatry, Department of Psychiatry and Behavioural Sciences, Royal Free and University College London Medical Schools, University College London, Gower Street, London WC1E 6BT

Judith Erskine, Registered general nurse, registered mental nurse and psychoanalytical psychotherapist, Traumatic Stress Service, South London and Maudsley NHS Trust, Bethlem Royal Hospital, Monks Orchard Road, Beckenham, Kent BR3 3BX

Dora Kohen, Professor of Psychiatry, Lancashire Postgraduate School of Medicine, Leigh Infirmary, The Avenue, Leigh WN7 1HS, Lancashire

Shirley McNicholas, Manager, Drayton Park residential crisis project for women, London

Sarah Majid, Specialist Registrar in Psychotherapy at the Tavistock and Portman NHS Trust, Tavistock Centre, 120 Belsize Lane, London NW3 5BA

E. Jane Marshall, Senior Lecturer in the Addictions and Consultant Psychiatrist, National Alcohol Unit and South London and Maudsley NHS Trust, Maudsley Hospital, Denmark Hill, London SE5 8A2

Penny Mostyn, Associate Specialist in Psychosexual Medicine, Department of Sexual Health, Kings College Hospital, Denmark Hill, London SE5 9RS

Eleni Palazidou, Consultant Psychiatrist at the Royal London Hospital and Honorary Senior Lecturer at Queen Mary and Westfield University (Dept of Psychological Medicine) London and the Institute of Psychiatry (MRC Psychopharmacology Unit) London

Ray Travers, Consultant Forensic Psychiatrist, Ashworth Hospital, Maghull

Lynda Todd, Clinical Research Worker, Eating Disorders Unit, South London and Maudsley NHS Trust, Bethlem Royal Hospital, Monks Orchard Road, Beckenham, Kent BR3 3BX

Ulrike Schmidt, Consultant Psychiatrist, Eating Disorders Unit; South London and Maudsley NHS Trust, Bethlem Royal Hospital, Monks Orchard Road, Beckenham, Kent BR3 3BX

Trudi Seneviratne, Lecturer in Perinatal Psychiatry, Institute of Psychiatry, De Crespigny Park, Camberwell, London SE5 8AF

Jenny Sargeant, Occupational Therapist, South London and Maudsley NHS Trust, Bethlem Royal Hospital, Monks Orchard Road, Beckenham, Kent BR3 3BX

Catherine Smith, Specialist Registrar in General Psychiatry and Psychotherapy, Hampshire Partnership, Southampton NHS Trust

Shubulade Smith, Consultant Psychiatrist and Honorary Senior Lecturer, North East Lambeth Sector, South London and Maudsley NHS Trust and Institute of Psychiatry, London

Bart Sheehan, Senior Clinical Lecturer in Old Age Psychiatry, Health Sciences Research Institute, Medical School Building, Gibbet Hill Campus, University of Warwick, Coventry CV4 7AL

Ruth M. Williams, Senior Lecturer in Clinical Psychology, Institute of Psychiatry, De Crespigny Park, Camberwell, London SE5 8AF

Charlotte Wilson-Jones, Consultant Liaison Psychiatrist, Department of Psychological Medicine, The Maudsley and Kings College Hospital, Denmark Hill, London SE5 9RS

Introduction

Claire Henderson, Shubulade Smith,
Catherine Smith and Angela Stevens

The goal of equity or fairness in access and quality of provision in health care is a challenge to all providers. The size of this challenge increases with the extent to which the population served comprises diverse groups with differing needs. The editors of this book are all female psychiatrists working within the National Health Service in the UK, a service that is used by the entire population. Within the NHS, equity was once thought to be achievable by adopting a 'blind' approach to difference, whether in gender, ethnicity or any other demographic characteristic that influences health and health-related behaviour. This approach has been widely criticised by those who have identified discrimination within the NHS on the basis of gender, race, age, intellectual ability and social class. As in many other countries, this view has now been largely replaced by the recognition that equity is only achievable if differences that affect health and health-related behaviour are identified and addressed by providers and policy makers.

This book is written either for those working within the health service in any country or for agencies whose clients may require care for mental health problems. Although some might debate the possibility of providing gender-specific care within a service providing care to both women and men, the aim of this book is to help providers to do this within the inevitable limitations of the setting in which they work, using the skills, diagnostic and therapeutic, that they already possess. These settings and skills are largely derived from 'gender-blind' theories, policies, research and training. We begin with Cutting's critique of this situation and Busfield and Dally's chapter on the historical background to it in Part I. In Parts II, IV, V and VI the authors describe the settings, diagnoses and therapeutic methods involved in psychiatric treatment, and try to identify the implications for all women of having care provided on this basis. Further introduction to these sections can be found below. In Part III the authors address particular groups of women, based either on demographic features that may result in discrimination (ethnicity and age) and/or biological events that require special consideration (pregnancy, childbirth and aging).

Part II: treatment settings

The importance of the type of setting in which mental health care is provided has been recognised since the founding of Bethlem Royal Hospital in 1247. The role which this particular setting plays, as either therapeutic in itself or actively harmful, has attracted much interest from researchers, policymakers and the news media. In the nineteenth century, many of the non-medical superintendents of lunatic asylums and the psychiatrists who replaced them had firm beliefs about the importance of the physical environment of asylums. They were built set in quiet countryside far from polluted cities to provide clean fresh air, plenty of light and not too much sensory stimulation.

In post-war Britain the use of individual and group psychotherapy expanded along with the development of a new care setting, the day hospital. The need to provide access to more outpatient care meant that hospitals, whose countryside was in any case disappearing under expanding suburbs, were no longer the single best location for mental health treatment. In the 1960s, both the physical and social environment in mental hospitals came under increasingly critical scrutiny from government inquiry committees, the media and researchers. The Ward Atmosphere Scale and others were developed to try to measure and compare these environments, and a link was made between the poverty of the social environment and the large size and geographical isolation of asylums. The impact of long-term exposure to this environment became known as institutionalism.

Responses to try to prevent institutionalism and to provide greater rehabilitation included the creation of therapeutic communities, where the social environment was designed to help treat as opposed to worsen psychiatric disorders. To 'normalise' the social environment in other hospitals, wards were desegregated along gender lines and patients were allowed their own clothes and possessions. Finally, faced with the high overheads and refurbishment costs of large psychiatric hospitals along with increasingly expensive technologies in other areas of medicine, successive governments carried out a programme of asylum closure. Two-thirds are now closed, and the others are much reduced in size. Long-stay beds were re-provided in supported flats, group homes and hostels, while acute units were added to general hospital sites. However, some of the locked wards which were closed have effectively been replaced in the forensic sector, a setting which provides particular challenges in providing appropriate care for women (see Travers's chapter). Women form a tiny minority on medium secure units, often of one. In theory, the existence of female wards in the high security hospitals allows care that better meets their needs, but the extent to which this opportunity has been taken is debatable.

Community mental health teams are now mostly located in 'resource centres', to provide outpatient care closer to home than the nearest hospital and to provide a base from which staff can make domiciliary visits. For a discussion of the extent to which these arrangements benefit women, see Johnson's chapter. Meanwhile, epidemiological research has shown that the vast majority of people with common mental health problems (depressive and anxiety disorders) are seen only in primary care settings. This stimulated a drive to ensure their recognition and adequate treatment by general practitioners and other primary care professionals, as discussed in the chapter by Buszewicz and Burd.

The policy of 'Care in the Community' has thus had a greater impact on outpatient and long-term care than on acute care for severe episodes of illness, which is still almost entirely provided in hospitals. Acute wards are now the focus of much concern and complaint on the part of managers, professionals, user groups and voluntary sector bodies, particularly in London. Many wards suffer from a lack of permanent staff, occupancy rates often over 100 per cent, high levels of violence and illicit drug use, and there may be little available in the way of meaningful activity. The resulting environment is at best boring and at worst traumatic (see Beaumont's section of the chapter on inpatient treatment). Patients referred to private hospitals due to the lack of beds on NHS wards may experience more materially comfortable and quieter surroundings but are often sent long distances, a particular problem for women with children.

The response to these problems includes a national policy to re-segregate wards along gender lines; an example of a women-only ward is described by Kohen. Across the country, there are also many local innovations providing acute care in alternative settings to hospital (see McNicholas's section of the chapter on inpatient treatment as an example). The diversity of such innovations suggests that theoretically it should be possible to offer a range of care settings to someone experiencing an episode of severe illness. Examples other than hospital care are:

- free-standing community inpatient units catering for a particular group based on age, sex or ethnicity;
- home treatment teams;
- units linked to resource centres or general practices;
- self-catering accommodation for whole families, with mental health staff on the same site;
- crisis houses run by former service users or voluntary sector staff with backup from NHS professionals.

There are thus many opportunities for innovation of new treatment settings, particularly with respect to acute care. As the chapters in this part will show, one focus for any evaluation of such an innovation must be the extent to which women's particular needs are met. Further discussion of future research in this area can be found in Part VII.

Part III: treatment of particular groups

The rationale for this section is that for these groups, mental health professionals' ideas about the female role are complicated either by stereotypes related to ethnicity or aging or by attitudes towards motherhood. The profound impact of childbearing on biological, psychological and social functioning is described by Seneviratne *et al.* in the chapter on motherhood and mental illness. The importance of recognising the needs of an increasingly aged population, the majority of whom will be female, is described by Sheehan. Smith gives us an understanding of the institutional racist factors that can create a 'double whammy' situation for women from ethnic minority populations who encounter mental health problems.

Part IV: specific disorders

This section will serve as an *aide-mémoire* for the treatment of most psychiatric disorders the reader will encounter, with the added factor that the way in which these illnesses manifest in women is also discussed. The part not only deals with mental illness that occurs primarily in women, e.g. eating disorders, but also discusses major mental illness and more common disorders and how being female affects their presentation, outcome and treatment.

Howard and Smith give a very useful overview of the different psychotic illnesses, expanding not only on the different presentations in women, but also on the way in which the psychosis impacts on women's ability to parent. Palazidou discusses the pharmacological treatment of depression in women, emphasising the need for more gender-specific research, particularly as women are the most frequent sufferers of this illness. The social, psychological and complementary treatments of depression are dealt with elsewhere in the book (see chapters by Williams and Evans). Anxiety and somatoform disorders are explained by Wilson-Jones who gives an excellent overview on giving immediate practical help to those in difficulty. The majority of sufferers from eating disorders are women, and Todd gives an admirable overview of the latest ideas about managing these all-too-often intractable disorders. Bearn and Marshall talk about the problems of being a female substance or alcohol abuser in a very male environment and how more female-oriented services may improve outcome in these women.

Women are frequently subjected to traumatic experiences and the impact of these is discussed by Erskine, who gives a clear explanation of post-traumatic stress disorder, together with an outline of the latest treatments available. She uses vignettes to illustrate the condition in women and how it can best be managed. Finally, Mostyn turns our attention to a very overlooked, yet fundamental, aspect of being a woman: sexuality. She explains in detail the different sexual disorders that can affect women, the lack of information and research in many areas to do with women's sexuality and how we as clinicians can elucidate sexual problems and begin to help remedy them in women.

Part V: management of the sequelae of trauma

This part discusses the potential sequelae of severe trauma, experienced both in childhood and later life, and how the manifestations of this suffering may be detected and treated.

The section is presented in two chapters, each in a very different manner but each giving the reader a fascinating insight into the diagnosis and treatment of a group of patients who, traditionally, have been very difficult to manage with any degree of success.

The first chapter deals with the sequelae of trauma experienced in childhood, and focuses particularly on the development and subsequent management of borderline personality disorder (BPD). There is a comprehensive discussion of the treatment options currently available, with emphasis being placed on the practicalities of treating these individuals. In addition there is a comprehensive reading list for those who wish to explore the subject further.

The second chapter discusses issues pertaining to the management of patients who deliberately self-harm (DSH). It highlights the need for professionals to attempt to understand self-harming behaviour and illustrates them, again, by the use of clinical vignettes. There is also a helpful list of factors to aid the clinician in their assessment of suicide risk or intent, bearing in mind that in the year following an act of DSH, 1 per cent of these individuals will commit suicide.

Part VI: therapies

This part of the book is concerned with the different types of therapy available to women who suffer with mental health problems. These 'therapies' comprise a diverse group of treatments which includes pharmacological interventions aimed at specific symptoms, psychological interventions both short- and longer-term some of which aim to target specific symptoms and others which take a wider, more in-depth approach and the 'alternative treatments' which are based on alternative philosophies to that of conventional western medicine. The availability of these different treatments will vary widely across regions and may not all be available in each area.

It is an exciting time in both the pharmacological and psychological treatment fields as new research findings lead to more effective treatment regimes. In the psychological field there have been recent advances with Cognitive Behavioural Therapy (CBT) effectively expanding into the psychosis arena and the more dynamic psychological treatments being successfully adapted to treat a wider range of patients often over shorter time periods, notable examples being the relatively new introduction of Cognitive Analytical Therapy (CAT), interpersonal therapies, the brief psychodynamic approaches and the longer therapies being effectively applied to patient groups with difficult symptoms in both out-, day- and inpatient settings.

In the pharmacological field the relatively recent introduction of effective, safer and more tolerable drugs, together with an expanding understanding of their effects in women, will hopefully lead to better adherence and improved health.

The biological therapy chapter in this part looks at the individual classes of drugs available for the treatment of mental illness and the considerations that are pertinent when prescribing for women. It also looks at the historical, sociological and physiological factors that effect the prescription, utilisation and effectiveness of these medications. The controversial topics of ECT and psychosurgery are also covered.

The fundamental principles and features of the different psychological therapies are covered in the psychotherapy chapters. They give a comprehensive account of what the therapies entail and which women are likely to benefit from which approach.

Interest in complementary therapies continues to grow as people seek alternative solutions to their symptoms. These approaches, that comprise a fairly diverse group, can be used alone or together with more mainstream treatments. Increasingly they are being offered alongside conventional medicine in GP surgeries and psychiatric wards for women with mental health problems. The underlying philosophy, scientific principles and basics of application are well explained by Jo Evans in the complementary therapies chapter.

Part I
The background

1 The problem with psychiatry–a woman's perspective

Penny Cutting

Introduction

A few years ago whilst working for a now closed psychiatric hospital I witnessed an elderly female patient being forced to masturbate a young male patient. They were sitting in the grounds of the hospital in full view of the reception desk. The woman was crying and the young man was laughing as he gripped her hands around his penis. I intervened to stop what was happening, the young man ran off and the elderly woman sat sobbing. When I reported the matter it was apparently well-known that the same incident had happened before. A Police enquiry came to nothing because the woman who was chronically mentally ill was not seen as fit to give evidence. This distressing violation symbolised for me what I had already discovered about the way in which the institution of psychiatry has its own set of rules and norms that often silence and humiliate women service users.

This chapter will attempt to illuminate why so many women service users have a problem with psychiatry. This will be done by outlining what psychiatry's stated aims are; exploring gender as a construct and looking at how this effects the care and treatment that women receive. This will be followed by an example of patriarchy in psychiatry. There will be a brief overview of the sociology of women's mental health care and the chapter ends with a look at women-only mental health services.

Psychiatry and Diagnoses

Stein (1998) sees the job of the psychiatrist as the management of common disorders. In short, the job of the psychiatrist is the diagnosis and prescription of treatment, and he states that the field of psychiatry requires 'rigorous scientific evidence before any new information can be incorporated into the fabric of existing knowledge'.

In general, the 'diagnosis' of mental illness is based upon a person's (usually a 'professional') subjective view of the acceptability or not of another person's behaviour. Busfield (1996) notes, 'madness and mental disorder are concepts that set the boundaries of 'unreason'. Precisely what counts as unreason is socially variable: changing over time and differing between societies.'

In the Western world there has been an attempt to make explicit what can be called 'unreason' using two main classification systems: The Diagnostic and Statistical Manual of Mental Disorders (DSM-IV) (American Psychiatric Association, 1994) and the International Classification of Diseases (ICD-10) (World Health Organisation, 1992). Both are used by psychiatrists in the diagnosis of mental illness.

There is much controversy around the use of these classification systems and in particular recently there has been a focus on the dubious claims made by the creators of DSM of its reliability. Far from being a bastion of 'rigorous scientific evidence,' Kutchins and Kirk (1999) suggest that there is not one single major study showing that the DSM is used with reliability. They report the Williams et al (1992) study on reliability of DSM across sites, which they say showed that even experienced clinicians with extensive training in the use of the manual are as likely to agree as disagree about the diagnosis of a particular person.

How do women fare within these classification systems which are purported to be gender neutral? From a very basic level and all the way through the system there is clear evidence of attempts to suggest that women's known responses to particular sets of circumstances and life events are medicalised. This is demonstrated in Kutchins and Kirk's (1999) account of the debate on the proposed inclusion within the DSM of Masochistic Personality Disorder, which, it is argued, comprised stereotypical female traits and behaviours and could also be seen in women who were on the receiving end of violence from their partners.

The make-up of the group of people involved in deciding what goes in and what is kept out of the DSM is predominantly male (Kutchins and Kirk, 1999). In addition they note the lack of consultation with women about various diagnostic categories and the lack of time given to listening to the voices of women who challenge the decision-makers.

Worell and Remer (1992), writing about the DSM-111-R state:

> The location of pathology in the individual, the minimisation of effects of sexist environmental stressors, the use of category descriptions which parallel traditional sex-role stereotypes, the use of trait rather than behavioural descriptors, and the lack of empirical research evidence.. all contribute to the sex-biased structure of the DSM'.

What we have is a classification system which uses men's madness as the yardstick by which to measure women's madness. So women and men receive the same biochemical treatment, they are categorized by a system which purports to be gender neutral but which is in fact a male dominated system.

Imagine for a moment a world in which there were only women, a classification of women's distress or madness would be hugely different. What would schizophrenia look like in a world where there were only women? How many women present with 'atypical' versions of various mental illnesses? For example, when looking at what is known as cycloid psychosis, you will find that in this 'atypical' psychosis 90% of sufferers are women (Cutting, Clare and Mann, 1978). Perhaps this is how women's madness is expressed, and calling it atypical only emphasizes the male dominated system.

Women's expression of distress is very different from men's. Their presentation, patterns of onset of ill health, causal reasons for their distress, outcome/prognosis, response to treatment and the consequences of their mental distress are all specific to them and all are influenced by gender stereotyping.

Gender as a construct: how this affects women's treatment

The term gender is sometimes used interchangeably with the term sex. This creates a confusion that should be clarified, particularly within the context of this book, which is focusing specifically upon women. As psychiatry is currently dominated by the biological basis of mental distress, it is important to distinguish that which may be of biological origin from that which is created by cultural/societal norms.

The term 'sex' is really just referring to the biological make-up of a human: they are either male or female. (This does not take into account those babies who are born with indistinct genitalia). Gender, on the other hand, is determined by our culture. The way in which different cultures raise their boys and girls shapes the traits and behaviour each display. What emerges from this are the characteristics or qualities regarded by specific cultures as appropriate to men and women within that culture. This leads to the development of gender stereotypes within cultures and implicit understanding of what is reasonable behaviour for the men and women within that culture.

Broverman et al (1970) studied this phenomenon in relation to stereotypes and judgements about mental health. They found that attributes used to stereotypically define women were also those used to define madness. Women who conformed to the stereotype and women who deviated from the stereotype (or demonstrated 'male' characteristics) were both labelled mentally ill. Stereotypical men, on the other hand, were given attributes that were equated with adult mental health.

Once there is a stereotypical view of a group of people it is possible to develop a negative or positive view of that group as a whole. A negative view of women based upon stereotypical views is known as sexism. This is a form of prejudice or discrimination. Within the mental health system there is a vast history of basing judgements about the health and ill-health of women on stereotypical views and sexist attitudes (Ussher 1991).

In particular, as Ussher (1991) notes, *'a woman who neglects her children, has sexual relationships with men other than her husband, becomes angry and violent, or consumes large amounts of alcohol is at risk of being labelled mad.'* She suggests this comes about because she does not play her social role.

A man doing the same things would not necessarily be seen as mad because these behaviours are often associated with the stereotypical view of men.

Patriarchy and Psychiatry: the links and their effects on women.

It is easy to demonstrate that psychiatry is a patriarchal system by returning to Stein's (1998) phrase–'the management of common disorders'–not management of people with common disorders–the people seem to be superfluous! This may be pedantic, but as Basow (1986) suggests, 'language plays a major role in defining and maintaining male power over women'. It is language that can be used in this way to oppress women, to strip them of their humanity and to see them as a set of problems or conditions to which treatment is applied.

Language is a powerful tool and that which is used in everyday parlance is what undermines women and becomes the norm. It is so subtle that it creeps up on us and before we know it we are referring to fellow human beings as hysterics, schizophrenics, depressives and so on. All of a sudden people are no longer people, they are the label they are given. This is important; how can psychiatry offer a reasonable service to women when its fundamental way of viewing them is from a position of looking down at those 'under' their care?

This looking down upon has been a feature throughout history of women's and men's mental health care. For women it is most clearly demonstrated by the presence of patriarchy within psychiatry. Patriarchy is the hierarchical relationship between men and women in which men are dominant and women are subordinate.

Patriarchy in psychiatry is evidenced by the way in which the hierarchical system works, with a few men at the top in powerful positions. Since the inception of the National Health Service psychiatry has been and still is dominated by men. The Royal College of Psychiatrist annual census continues to show that women consultant psychiatrists are still very much in the minority for example of the 2679 consultant post in England only 736.8 were filled by women (Royal College of Psychiatrist 2004). Based on these figures it can be seen that women's mental health in the UK has been, and still is, defined by men as men are the dominant group.

This can be clearly seen in action in drug advertisements in journals such as the British Journal of Psychiatry. Repeatedly, women are portrayed in photos that only reveal their heads, as beautiful objects to be looked at, often engaging in leisure activities (having coffee/chatting, exercising etc.), Whereas men are portrayed as strong or as doing a worthwhile job. Measures of the success of a particular drug are often portrayed in very different ways for men and women too. One recent advertisement showed a woman putting on lipstick–this supposedly being a sign of improving mood–whilst all the advertisements involving male images showed men returning to work. You may say this is the responsibility of the advertisers not of psychiatry.

However, not challenging the advertisers or indeed the drug companies that place the adverts perpetuates the gender stereotyping that pervades the psychiatric system.

Sociology of women's mental health care

One cannot examine women's mental health care without thinking about the social and political context in which it has developed. In particular, it is important to acknowledge the way in which women have been defined by men. Historically women's role in society has been prescribed by men; what they should say, do, think, feel, and even own, has largely been very tightly controlled (Showalter, 1987). It is only as recently as 1990, when the divorce laws in the UK were changed, that women were at last not seen as the property of their husbands.

Surveys of mental distress in the UK (Meltzer et al, 1995) showed that women are a third more likely to have a generalised anxiety disorder and two thirds more likely to have a mixed anxiety and depressive disorder, whereas being female decreased the likelihood of drug and alcohol dependence. This has significance for the way in which women and men access mental health care. Stein (1998) notes that in the wake of community care legislation a series of filters are worked through by the client who first sees the GP, and that GPs are more likely to refer men to psychiatrists than they are women.

The gender roles of men and women throughout history demonstrate that the 'care' and treatment of distressed women were dependent upon the social norms at that particular point in history. The Victorian era epitomised the wholesale oppression of women who were seen as 'childlike, irrational and sexually unstable' (Showalter, 1987). In conjunction with women's lack of rights and political power a situation emerged where it was very easy to label a woman as deviant if she rebelled against what was deemed suitable behaviour for a woman. In this era of great expansion of psychiatric institutions women made up the majority of 'in-mates' and the treatment offered involved 'moral management'. This basically involved women being expected to engage in activities that were seen as suitably feminine, such as sewing or doing the laundry for the whole asylum; if they did not do this then they were subjected to solitary confinement and other treatments such as cold baths.

Over time, as women became more powerful, then the focus of the origins of mental illness in women shifted to their physical make-up. A woman's physical self has been the focus of medicine and psychiatry in its quest to find the cause and cure of her mental distress. In the Eighteenth Century the womb was deemed to wander around the body of the woman sucking life energy or intellect from her, thus causing the condition of hysteria (Ussher, 1991). In the Nineteenth Century the surgical treatment of women with mental distress was carried out–operations such as clitoridectomy. It was believed that madness in women was caused by masturbation, and that the removal of the clitoris would cure them.

Geller and Harris (1994) state it was thought that, *'unfeminine activities caused uterine derangement which in turn caused mental illness'*. They suggest that this came about as women were beginning to do jobs that were traditionally seen to be men's work and resulted in psychiatrists believing that madness in women was caused by a woman not fulfilling her role as wife and mother.

Removal of the ovaries and uterus was thought to cure insanity and a range of psychological disorders, too. Daly (1991) suggests that this bodily mutilation of women arose in direct response to the rise of feminism and out of men's fear of a change in the social order (their loss of power).

The treatment of women's distress within the psychiatric system has continued to focus on their bodies and biology. Much store is placed upon the connection of menstruation, pregnancy, and the menopause to mental distress in women. Ashurst and Hall (1989) suggest that this focus on biology misses the real message conveyed by many women's mental distress–that it is often brought about by the social, political, economic, psychological and physical environment in which she was raised and in which she currently exists.

It is paradoxical that the focus on a woman's body has nevertheless overlooked the fact that more women with severe mental health problems die of undetected physical illnesses than non-mentally ill women (Corten et al, 1991).

The desire of men to have control over women's bodies could be seen as being related to their enormous fear of women's creative potential. Irigaray (1993) suggests that women's ability to create and sustain life presents the continuing spectre of castration to men. Minsky (1996) states: ' To the extent that for men the castration complex is about fear of loss of identity, women threaten men with potential disintegration.' Men may equate women with death, and thus strive to control them bodily out of the unconscious quest to preserve male life, or from fear of them. It is also of interest to note that Frosh (1983) suggests that psychosis emerges from the fear of dissolution and disintegration of the self; and according to this analysis psychiatric control of women may be an unconscious attempt by men to prevent their own madness!

Johnson and Buszewicz (1996) established that among people with severe mental health problems such as schizophrenia, women are more likely than men to be married or cohabiting and to have children, and that they often experience difficulties in sustaining these roles. If so, then they clearly require services which recognise their unique needs and which can respond in a women-centred way. This also means that the response should be one which does not define their health in terms of whether they can perform the functions of the stereotypical female role given them.

Bebbington et al (1981) found that psychiatric disorder was highest in unemployed married women whereas it was lowest in employed, married men. This applies particularly if she were caring for children or other dependents. This type of unpaid work adds to women's social isolation. The under valuing of this work adds to women's sense of low self-esteem and keeps women in a position of poverty. The links between poverty and development of mental health problems has been established (Bruce et al, 1991). Andrews (1994) notes that domestic violence occurs to women in 1 in 4 households, and the links between violence and mental health problems are well established (Holmshaw and Hillier, 2000). They also note that women's social roles lead to them experiencing greater stress, 'greater burden of work and pressure of time, lack of uninterrupted time for rest and leisure activities, poverty, violence and abuse' (Holmshaw and Hillier, 2000). All of these issues are supported and again raised in the Department of Health's (2002) document 'Women's Mental Health: Into the Mainstream'. Where the particular difficulties and gender specific needs of women are noted to be inadequately addressed within the mental health system.

Goodman *et al*. (1997) also suggest that a majority of women with serious mental illness have experienced violent victimisation in their lives and that a large amount of these women suffer not just single episodes of abuse but many repeated acts throughout their lives. When they enter the psychiatric system they find that their experiences of abuse are often replicated by the coercive style of care and the levels of violence they are confronted with.

Because of the patriarchal psychiatric system's failure to prevent the replication of violence, abuse and neglect in the lives of women, there were widespread calls for women-only services (MIND, 1994), to not only specifically address these factors but also provide a safe haven away from predatory males at a time when women are most vulnerable. This was eventually taken up nationally by the government via the Department of Health (2002 & 2003) and there is now a strong national agenda aimed at ensuring gender sensitive services for women. There is much work to be done, women are still feeling unsafe, unheard, and there is enormous resistance to change as commentators in George's (2005) article note.

Women and men have been cared for separately or together over the history of psychiatry, but since the 1960's the trend has been for women and men to have been brought together, sharing the living facilities in the wards of psychiatric hospitals. The idea of mixing the sexes in this way came about primarily for the convenience of the consultant psychiatrist or psychiatrists in training who found it inconvenient to have to travel to different wards to see 'their patients'. It was also thought to be unnatural by these psychiatrists to separate men from women and desirable for a woman's recovery for women to learn how to behave in the company of men (Russell, 1997). Whether this is efficacious has never been proven (Batcup, 1995).

So far anecdotal evidence regarding mixing the sexes on psychiatric wards seems to show that the presence of women tends to reduce the incidence of male violence (Huges, 1992). However as history shows us, this is at a cost, as reducing male violence in this way clearly exposes women to intimidation and sexual assault Russell (1997).

Women are infantalised in institutions (psychiatric hospitals) where their civil liberties are removed. To earn comforts such as extra tea, sweets and cigarettes, they may be subjected to pressure from male patients, visitors and staff to provide sexual favours.

(McNamara and Radclyffe, 1998)

One might be forgiven for thinking that that date is wrong on the above quote and that it should read 1888. Sadly, this is not the case. The above quote reminds us that women in mental health services are still subject to bullying, sexual harassment, rape, molestation, and violent assault, and, in long term care, are frequently coerced into prostituting themselves for items such as cigarettes and tea bags. This is not psychiatry of times gone by; this is the current state of affairs as evidenced by MIND (2004) in their campaign 'Ward Watch'.

Women-Only Services

Providing women-only space within the mental health services although a first step, really only scratches the surface, and actually avoids confronting the real issue which is the continued oppression of women. It has been shown that women in the mental health services are subjected to high levels of violence, sexual assault and harassment (MIND, 1992). The services are not safe for them nor for their visiting children, their distress is misunderstood, and very little is done other than to offer physical treatments such as ECT or medication.

A focus on therapeutic relationships has been lost in current acute psychiatric facilities, where the emphasis is very much on the medical and behavioural management of psychiatric symptomology, e.g. Becker et al (1998), Mind (2004). Medication is given, its effects are monitored, and success of the treatment is judged upon the cessation of the troublesome or antisocial symptom. This is not to suggest that medication does not have a place. However, the reported dulling of the senses that ensues for some types of medication provides nothing more than a temporary alleviation of such symptoms (Burstow, 1992).

Given that many women patients feel powerless and out of control within the mental health system, there is a risk that telling them that medication will cure them may exacerbate this feeling of powerlessness, as it keeps them in the position of feeling as if they have no power over themselves or their mental distress. This also perpetuates psychiatry's fascination with them as bodily creatures rather than as multidimensional people.

If no attempt is made to understand the meaning of the symptom in the context of the woman's life, then the 'revolving door' syndrome continues, with women going in and out of hospital with regularity. When a woman who can no longer cope with her unbearable life situation displays 'anti-social' behaviour she then becomes prey to the psychiatric system again. Once she has been labelled, this label sticks for life (Goffman, 1963), a permanent record in her medical notes which often then obscures any further health problems she might have. The psychiatric diagnosis is more important to the 'professionals' than listening to her or exploring what also might be present.

It is not acceptable that in this new millennium women in contact with psychiatric services should basically be almost in the same conditions as their predecessors at the turn of the last millennium. During this time, women have changed how society views them, but this does not seem to have transferred into the institution of psychiatry, which as we see from the McNamara and Radclyffe (1998) quote above, treats women as less than human, overrides their rights, and perpetuates the abuse of them in many ways. It is not acceptable for women just to be surviving the service, or having to mask the severity of their distress, in a desperate attempt to extricate themselves from the mental health system, particularly the psychiatric hospital.

One concern for those involved in the creation of women-only services is the constant demands made, often by men in the system, but also by women, that these services should have men on the staff. Old arguments are used which have their basis in Victorian beliefs systems about women, e.g. 'surely women should be exposed to 'good' men'. This author has often been confronted with the statement that, 'good men can be role models for women who need to learn that not all men are harmful'. It could be argued that the point of acute mental breakdown which leads to the need for 24 hour care is not the best time for women to unlearn centuries of male oppression.

This resistance to change stems from the patriarchal psychiatric system which fails to acknowledge its oppressive practices. Williams (2005: 152-3) notes, 'members of dominant groups do not like to hear about or think about inequality in their social relations, and prefer the social world to be described in other ways. They prefer to believe that the status quo is right and good for all parties. Having power makes this easy.'

In general women may feel that another woman can understand their needs more readily than a man. However, there are no conclusive studies available that illuminate or explore the preference for either male or female mental health worker. Any studies that were to be developed would need to be carried out after the respondents had had the experience of male or female worker, otherwise they would not be in a position to assess the potential benefits of either. What can be said is that in those places where there are women only mental health services staffed by women there is a high degree of client satisfaction with the service (see for example quotes in the Department of Health's 2003 publication), women are protected from male violence and in the author's own workplace there are indications that there are also good clinical outcomes, (to be published in due course).

One area where women working with women is the topic of study is psychotherapy. In her study of women's experiences of feminist therapy and counselling, McLeod (1994) found that the women in her study preferred female therapists for a number of reasons: freedom from subordination, where they could freely express their emotions without being silenced; their emotional needs and capabilities were not treated as inferior; there was opportunity to concentrate on their own emotional needs; a real sense of being cared for; having the opportunity to challenge the negative stereotypical views of themselves that they had introjected over time; and finally, there was an opportunity to have therapy that was not limited in time but was based upon what the woman actually needed. It is not beyond the realms of possibility that these issues are pertinent to the experiences of women in the psychiatric system and their contact with mental health workers.

In relation to women seeing male therapists some studies have shown that women stay in therapy with a male therapist much longer than women with women therapists. Fabrikant (1974) suggests that this is a way of male therapists keeping female clients in a state of dependency for as long as possible. Barnes and Maple (1992) suggest that the male mental health worker's practice is informed by assumptions about women's subordination and is often therefore sexist in nature.

There is also some evidence to suggest that in mixed sex groups women say less than men, but in single sex groups they communicate more freely and feel more able to discuss their real difficulties (Cutting & Henderson 2002).

The choice of male or female mental health worker is also context-specific. Whilst in extreme distress, e.g. when women are detained under the Mental Health Act, there is a case for suggesting that women are not in a position to make an informed choice about the sex of the staff working with them. For their own protection, and to prevent history (as outlined in this chapter) repeating itself, it may be wise to have a women-only team caring for her. When a woman is in a position to choose, then her wishes need to be taken into account. In an ideal situation the decision is not just about the sex of the worker, but how qualified they are to help. But until services are truly safe for women the author believes that women on acute units should be cared for by skilled, humane, women who have had training in gender awareness and who have high quality women-centred supervision.

Conclusion

In this chapter I have tried to illuminate some of the difficulties that exist for women within the psychiatric system. For a book of this nature I found it necessary to speak of women as a whole group rather than perhaps focusing on women of differing social classes, lesbian women or women from diverse ethnic backgrounds. For some readers this may be a cause for concern. However, in any critique of psychiatry the fundamental issues seem to revolve around the way in which psychiatry continues to re-enact the past so that the treatment of all women within the system mirrors the way they were viewed in society throughout history. Even though there is greater equality between men and women within society at large now, there are still problems to do with the imbalance of power between men and women, poverty, violence and the pressures of women's multiple roles. We have seen from the evidence quoted above that psychiatry still holds an antiquated view of women and that the system is not really in tune with providing help that is beneficial to women's lives as they are now. There are, as always of course, a few exceptions as highlighted in the documents 'Secure futures for women: making a difference.' (Department of Health, 2000), 'Women's Mental Health: Into the Mainstream–Strategic Development of Health Care for Women.' (Department of Health 2002) and 'Mainstreaming Gender and Women's Mental Health: Implementation Guidance.' (Department of Health 2003).

We cannot expect psychiatry and mental health services to be responsible for sorting out the social precipitants of mental distress. However, we can expect that they address these as factors essential when thinking about how best to help women in distress. In particular psychiatry needs to tackle its inherent patriarchy.

The future of women's mental health care is currently on the national agenda however little or no money has been attached to the proposed changes needed. Issues to do with training, recruitment, and development of women working with women, need addressing alongside greater political pressure to ensure that changes in the care of women go further than just having separate sleeping and washing facilities.

The issues are numerous and are different for many differing groups of women. As stated previously, women-only services are a start but can only begin to touch the lives of a few of the women needing mental health care.

Real change will only take place when the social and psychological stressors that lead to women's mental health problems are tackled. This requires major political, educational, and social reform. As history has shown us the most helpful changes in women's lives are best achieved when women are listened to. Given the opportunity, resources, and support they are able to design and implement systems and services that they feel would be of most help to them.

References

American Psychiatric Association (1994) *Diagnostic and Statistical Manual of Mental Disorders, fourth edition* (DSM-IV), Washington: American Psychiatric Association.

Andrews, C., Nadirshaw, Z., Curtis, Z. and Ellis, J. (1994) *Women, Mental Health and Good Practice,* Brighton: Pavilion Publishing.

Ashurst, P. and Hall, Z. (1989) *Understanding Women in Distress.* London: Routledge.

Barnes, M. and Maple, N. (1992) *Women and Mental Health: Challenging the Stereotypes.* Birmingham: Venture Press.

Basow, S.A. (1986) *Gender Stereotypes: Traditions and Alternatives.* (2nd edition), Monterey: Brooks-Cole.

Batcup, D. (1995) 'Mixed Sex Wards: Evaluating their Safety and Effectiveness for Women'. London: Bethlem and Maudsley NHS Trust.

Bebbington, P., Hurry, J. Tennant et al (1981) Epidemiology of mental disorders in Camberwell. *Psychological medicine*, 11: 561–569.

Becker, T., Holloway, F., McCrone, P. and Thornicroft, G. (1998) Evolving Service Intervention in Nunhead and Norwood: Prism Psychosis Study 2. *British Journal of Psychiatry* 173, 371–375.

Broverman, I.K., Broverman, D.M., Clarkson, F.E., Rosenkrantz, P.S. and Vogel, S.R. (1970) Sex Role Stereotypes and Clinical Judgement of Mental Health, *Journal of Consulting and Clinical Psychology,* 34: 1–7.

Bruce, M.L., Takenchi, D.T. and Leaf, P.J. (1991) Poverty and Psychiatric status: longitudinal evidence from the New Haven Epidemiologic Catchment Area Study, *Archives of General Psychiatry* 48(5): 470–4.

Burstow, B. (1992) *Radical Feminist therapy: working in the context of violence*. London: Sage Publications.

Busfield, J. (1996) *Men Women and Madness: understanding gender and mental disorder*. London: Macmillan Press ltd.

Corten, P., Ribourdouille, M., Dramaix, M. (1991) Premature Deaths Among Outpatients at a Community Mental Health Centre. *Hospital and Community Psychiatry*, 42, 12: 1248–1251.

A reference has been deleted from here (Crimlisk et

Cutting, J. C. and Clare, A. W. and Mann, A. H. (1978) Cycloid Psychosis: an investigation of the diagnostic concept. *Psychological Medicine* 8: 637–648.

Cutting, P. and Henderson, C. (2002) Women's experiences of hospital admission. *Journal of Psychiatric and Mental Health Nursing*, 9 (6): 705–712.

Daly, M. (1991) *Gyn/Ecology: The Metaethics of Radical Feminism*. London: The Women's Press.

Department of Health (2000) *Secure futures for women: making a difference*. London: HMSO.

Department of Health (2002) *Women's Mental Health: Into the Mainstream–Strategic Development of Mental Health Care for Women.* London: Department of Health.

Department of Health (2003) *Mainstreaming Gender and Women's Mental Health: Implementation Guidance.* London: Department of Health.

Fabrikant, B. (1974) 'The Psychotherapist and the Female Patient: perceptions, misperceptions and change', in V. Franks, and V. Burtle, (eds.) (1974) *Women in Therapy*. New York: Brunner/Mazel.

Frosh, J. (1983) *The Psychotic Process*. New York: International Universities Press, Inc.

George, C (2005) Zero Tolerance. *Mental Health Today*, March, 14–15.

Goffman, E. (1963) *Stigma: notes on the management of spoiled identity*. New York: Simon and Schuster, Inc.

Goodman, L. A., Rosenberg, S. D., Mueser, K. T., and Drake, R. E. (1997) Physical and Sexual Assault History in Women with Serious Mental Illness: Prevalence, Correlates, Treatment, and Future Research Directions. *Schizophrenia Bulletin* 23, 4: 685–696.

Holmshaw, J. and Hillier, S. (2000) 'Gender and culture: a sociological perspective to mental health problems in women', in D. Kohen (ed.) *Women and Mental Health*. London: Routledge.

Huges, P. (1992) Therapeutic for Whom? *The Guardian Newspaper*. July 2, 36.

Irigaray, L. (1993) *An Ethics of Sexual Difference*. London: Athlone Press.

Johnson, S. and Buszewicz, M. (1996) 'Women's Mental Health in the UK', in. K. Abel, M. Buszewicz, S. Davidson, S. Johnson and E. Staples, (eds) *Planning Community Mental Health Services for Women: a Multiprofessional Handbook*, London: Routledge.

Kutchins, H. and Kirk, S.A. (1999) *Making Us Crazy: DSM–the Psychiatric Bible and The Creation of Mental Disorders*, London: Constable and Co Ltd.

McLeod, E. (1994) *Women's Experience of Feminist Therapy and Counselling*, Philadelphia: Open University Press.

McNamara, J. and Radclyffe, K. (1998) Women and Mental Health Forum: *Newsletter of the Women and Mental Health Network U.K.* (3), 8.

Meltzer, H., Gill, B., Petticrew, M. and Hinds, K. (1995) OPCS *Surveys of Psychiatric Morbidity in Great Britain Report 1: the prevalence of psychiatric morbidity among adults living in private households*, London: HMSO.

MIND (1992) *Stress on Women Campaign*, London: MIND

MIND (1994) *Eve Fights Back: MIND's Stress on Women Campaign*, London: MIND

MIND (2004) *Ward Watch: Mind's campaign to improve hospital conditions for mental health patients*. London: MIND.

Minsky, R. (1996) *Psychoanalysis and Gender*, London: Routledge.

Royal College of Psychiatrists (2004) *Annual Census of Psychiatric Staffing*. London: Royal College of Psychiatrists.

Russell, D. (1997) *Scenes from Bedlam: A History of Caring for the Mentally Disordered at Bethlem Royal Hospital and The Maudsley*, London: Bailliere Tindall.

Showalter, E. (1987) *The Female Malady: Women, Madness and English Culture 1830–1980*, London: Virago.

Stein, G. (1998) 'Preface', in G. Stein and G. Wilkinson, (eds) *Seminars in General Adult Psychiatry Volume 1*. London: Royal College of Psychiatrists.

Ussher, J. (1991) *Women's Madness: Misogyny or Mental Illness?* London: Harvester Wheatsheaf.

Williams, J. (2005) *Women's Mental Health: Taking Inequality into Account*. In Tew, J. (2005) *Social Perspectives in Mental Health: Developing Social Models to Understand and Work With Mental Distress*. London: Jessica Kingsley.

Williams, J.B. et al (1992) The Structured Clinical Interview for DSM- III R (SCID): II Multi-site Test-retest Reliability. *Archives of General Psychiatry* 49: 630–36.

Worell, J. and Remer, P. (1992) *Feminist Perspectives in Therapy: an empowerment model for women*. Chichester: John Wiley and Sons Ltd.

World Health Organisation (1992) *The ICD-10 Classification of Mental and Behavioural Disorders*, Geneva: World Health Organisation.

Part II
Treatment settings

2 Looking after patients with mental health problems in a primary care setting*

Marta Buszewicz and Mary Burd

Introduction: the primary care setting

Primary Health Care Teams (PHCTs) play a major role in the care of people with all types and severity of mental health problems, in that at least 30 per cent of all consultations in General Practice have some psychological component and 90 per cent of people with mental health problems are cared for in primary care settings (Goldberg and Huxley, 1992). The majority of these people will be suffering from anxiety and or depression and many will have self-limiting or short-lived problems, but the general practitioner (GP) will also be first point of contact for people with many other psychiatric or psychological disorders. A significant number of patients will have recurrent or chronic disorders, with accompanying medical and social difficulties. GPs are in a unique position, because of the knowledge they usually have of the patient's family or relationships and social circumstances. Contact with the same local GP or practice often extends over many years, with the opportunity to intervene periodically at times of crisis, as well as providing more regular contact.

Although GPs only refer 5–10 per cent of the patients they see with mental health problems to secondary care services as described by Goldberg and Huxley (1992), an increasing number of mental health professionals are now working in primary care settings. How these individuals work together in caring for patients, and how effectively there is liaison with secondary care services situated elsewhere, varies greatly between practices and areas and is likely to have a significant impact on both patient care and outcome. These and other themes will be explored in more detail below.

THE CURRENT POLITICAL CONTEXT

There has been a major political change in recent years, with the emphasis on the GP and the primary health care team (PHCT) as the centre of patient care, and an accompanying increase in the potential power of GPs in the distribution of resources through Primary Care Trusts (PCTs). Recent government thinking was put forward in a major Department of Health publication, the *National Service Framework for Mental Health* (1999). By locating commissioning in PCTs, primary care has been given a great deal of potential influence over the distribution of local resources for the treatment of their patients. They are, however, expected to be accountable, in that all services that are provided or commissioned need to fit into the local health improvement strategy and take account of evidence-based information as to which treatments are likely to be effective. There also needs to be good integration between not only primary and secondary care, but also social services and the voluntary sector.

REASONS WHY PATIENTS PREFER TO SEE GPS

There is a comprehensive literature about users' views and wishes regarding the nature and availability of mental health services, but relatively little looks specifically at whether patients prefer to receive care from GPs or psychiatrists. A study by Pilgrim and Rogers (1993), commissioned by MIND, found that patients with psychiatric problems who had had contact with both GPs and psychiatrists often rated the GPs higher as regards certain aspects of their care. In particular they were more likely to perceive the GP as helpful, having a positive attitude to their patients, giving more adequate treatment information and giving satisfactory explanations. These factors are as much to do with good communication skills as detailed psychiatric knowledge and may, to some extent, be associated with the increased emphasis on this in GP postgraduate training. This study did not distinguish between female and male respondents, but it is likely that women in particular appreciate other aspects of receiving care in the primary care environment such as accessibility, familiarity of the environment and lack of associated stigma (Strathdee *et al.*, 1990).

WOMEN WITH MENTAL HEALTH PROBLEMS:
DETECTION AND REFERRAL RATES

Although more women are found to have significant psychiatric symptoms on screening in the community (OPCS Surveys of Psychiatric Morbidity, 1995), and more women are detected by GPs as having psychological morbidity (OPCS GP Morbidity Statistics, 1995), fewer women than men are referred by their GPs to secondary care psychiatric services and there appears to be a bias towards the referral of men to secondary care (Goldberg and Huxley, 1992). Women are particularly over-represented in terms of common mental disorders in both primary and secondary care. The debate about the various possible reasons for this, social or physiological, and whether this is a real difference or primarily a social phenomenon, secondary to women's role in society, has been discussed in detail elsewhere (Johnson and Buszewicz, 1996).

WHAT IS AVAILABLE FOR PATIENTS IN PRIMARY CARE

Since women are more likely than men to have a mental health problem both detected and treated within primary care, what is available within primary care is of key concern to women. There are enormous differences nationally, both in levels of provision in general practice for patients presenting with mental health problems, and the ways in which this care is given. In some cases large general practices have a primary care mental health team located within them, comprising regular sessions from psychiatrists, practice-based psychologists and Community Psychiatric Nurses (CPNs). In others, the practice team does few interventions and refer patients with a range of symptoms on to secondary care mental health services. Some secondary care services are almost entirely community-based and may sometimes share premises with a primary care team, while others are based in hospitals with little work done out in the community. If communication is good, the location of services need not be a prime consideration for the professionals but, for the majority of patients and particularly women, there is a preference for consultations to take place near to home and in a familiar, unstigmatising environment.

COMMON MENTAL DISORDERS

These affect the majority of patients presenting to the GP with mental health problems and consist predominantly of depressive illnesses and anxiety-related disorders. However, of the one in ten people per year on an average GP list of two thousand patients, who present overtly in primary care with a psychological problem, a similar number will present 'covertly' with physical symptoms or social problems (Goldberg and Huxley, 1992). Women are more likely to present psychologically than men; hence they are more likely to have such problems detected and diagnosed by GPs. Diagnostic classification of these disorders in primary care is often difficult; it is increasingly clear that there is a spectrum of disorder, with anxiety and depression not being as clear cut and separate as once thought. From the patients' perspective, the most important reason for making a diagnosis is to initiate the correct treatment and there is much debate about the treatment of psychological disorders in primary care, particularly about whether pharmacological or psychological treatments are indicated and by whom they should be given.

Antidepressants

Patients with depression treated in general practice with the older tricyclic antidepressants have tended to receive lower doses of antidepressants than those in secondary care (Donoghue and Tylee, 1996) and the duration of treatment is often shorter. A study of GP attitudes to depression revealed a reluctance amongst many GPs to prescribe antidepressants and a preference for psychological therapies (Botega *et al.*, 1992). Patients also frequently have reservations about taking antidepressants and public campaigns such as the Defeat Depression Campaign have attempted to address this. Although many of those consulting their GPs have less severe disorders than patients looked after in secondary care, significant numbers of patients with major depression, for which antidepressants are known to have some benefit, are seen in primary care (Paykel and Priest, 1992). With the increased prescribing of the newer SSRIs with standard daily doses, dosage is likely to become less of an issue, but duration of treatment is still important. Currently, those who have chronic 'neurotic' symptoms appear to be relatively under-treated in primary care, as regards both antidepressants and referral to other mental health professionals (Lloyd *et al.*, 1996) and many are at risk of following a chronic course which is both psychologically and socially disabling.

Psychological treatments

Psychological treatments are often more popular with both GPs and patients in the treatment of depression and anxiety, but there is enormous variation in what is available in different general practices. Over a third of practices are now likely to have a counsellor working at least one session per week, but the type of counselling offered and the degree of training which the therapist has received will vary greatly between practices (Sibbald *et al.*, 1993). Counselling is often appreciated by patients, although results in terms of whether it reduces drug prescriptions or amount of contact with GPs and other agencies are equivocal (Friedli and King, 1996). Overall, despite its popularity, evidence for the clinical- or cost-effectiveness of counselling, particularly when not clearly focused on particular types of problems, is still lacking.

A clear advantage for patients is that the counsellor is likely to be based 'on site', whereas other psychological therapies such as cognitive behavioural therapy (CBT) or psychodynamic therapy may require them to travel elsewhere, although in some cases psychologists or other practitioners may have sessions in the practice. There is evidence that CBT, brief focal psychoanalytic psychotherapy and interpersonal therapy (IPP) can be beneficial for patients seen in primary care (Scott and Freeman, 1992; Roth and Fonagy, 1996), but these interventions require time and trained therapists, which has resource implications. Primary care teams can also take steps themselves to develop mental health skills within the team; activities such as structured problem-solving (Mynors-Wallis *et al.*, 2000), relaxation techniques or simple diary-keeping can be helpful in the first instance.

EATING DISORDERS

Eating disorders, such as bulimia and anorexia, are an increasingly common problem affecting mainly young women and GPs need training in both their detection and management, as those affected may initially be reluctant to disclose the problem. Those at the milder end of the spectrum can be effectively managed in primary care with monitoring of food intake and use of self-help literature (APA, 1996) but those with more severe disorders will need specialist referral.

ALCOHOL AND DRUG ABUSE

Alcohol and drug abuse, traditionally more prevalent amongst men than women, also affects increasing numbers of women and GPs need to consider this as a main diagnosis as well as the possibility of co-morbidity with other mental health problems. This is an area with great health promotion potential and one where joint working with specialised voluntary sector agencies in the community is often very important.

In summary, focused psychological therapies appear to be effective in primary care, but more research is required to establish which treatments are likely to be most effective for which patients, particularly those who would otherwise have a more prolonged or complicated disorder. For example, psychological therapies such as CBT may reduce the risk of relapse in depression (Paykel, 1989) and CBT should be considered for all patients presenting with severe depression, and those with moderate or severe depression not responding to other treatments (NICE guidelines 2004). Patients generally prefer treatment in primary care settings for mental health problems, but PHCT staff will need training to ensure appropriate assessment and referrals to other mental health professionals are carried out, and the potential role of mental health teams in this is discussed below. For patients who do not speak good English, or where cultural factors are likely to play a major role in their difficulties, referral to community agencies providing appropriate psychological treatments should be considered, and practices need to be well informed about the needs of their local population and the relevant facilities available.

LONG-TERM ENDURING MENTAL ILLNESS

This refers predominantly to patients with chronic psychotic illnesses such as schizophrenia or, less commonly, a paranoid psychosis or manic depressive disorder. These patients make up a relatively small number of patients on each GP's list (an average of 10–20 patients on a GP list of 2,000 patients according to Strathdee and Jenkins (1996). A significant minority of these patients (estimates range from 25 per cent to 40 per cent) will not be attending psychiatric services and will be getting all their care from their PHCT. Individual GPs vary in whether they wish to have the key role with such patients or to have a CPN as the key worker (Kendrick *et al.* 1991). In a survey by Bindman *et al.* (1997), most GPs looking after patients with severe mental illness perceived their role as providing physical care and prescribing for these patients. Relatively few were involved in monitoring their mental state, although they also tended to rate themselves as more involved in the care of female patients with such problems. Some patients on depot medication may have this administered by the practice nurse, most of whom have little formal training in psychiatry. In other cases a CPN will be involved who may be attached to the practice, or more often to the Community Mental Health Team (CMHT).

Unfortunately, if the key worker is not practice-based, communication with the practice may be poor, as in the above study where, if a key worker from the CMHT was involved, communication from key workers was much less regular than letters following outpatient appointments. Improving communication between primary care and CMHTs is clearly a high priority, as GPs have a role, not only in caring for patients with enduring mental illnesses, but also in the support and education of their family and close friends about the disease and its consequences. With adequate back-up they can also help to monitor for early signs of relapse and the implementation of appropriate treatment (Cohen and Singh, 2001). In addition, the National Service Framework highlights the importance of GPs being aware of the mental and physical health of the carers of the long-term mentally ill and ensuring that this is regularly reviewed. Closer collaboration between primary care and community mental health teams would be assisted by more liaison services based in GP surgeries and psychiatric catchment areas that are determined by general practice populations.

MENTAL HEALTH TEAMWORK IN PRIMARY CARE

Over the past ten to twenty years there has been a great increase in the number and variety of mental health professionals working alongside GPs in primary care. These were initially informal arrangements, largely dependent on secondary care staff choosing to spend a proportion of their time working in primary care but, with the new GP contract of 1990, GPs were allowed more flexibility in the reimbursement of attached staff. In 1992, a survey by Thomas and Corney of every general practice within six randomly selected health districts in England found that 50 per cent of the 261 practices had a specific link with a CPN, 21 per cent with a social worker, 17 per cent with a counsellor, 15 per cent with a clinical psychologist and 16 per cent with a psychiatrist. If a practice had links with one professional, they were more likely to have others, while some similarly sized practices had no links. The types of links that other mental health professionals have with general practices vary and may include liaison, attachment or employment models. The employment by practices of some, but not all, of their attached mental health workers may be important in terms of case management. There is currently great variability in how mental health professionals working in primary care operate, as some will have regular meetings to discuss potential referrals and feedback about clinical outcome, but many will have no face-to-face contact and decisions about referral will all pass through the GP.

Meetings between the various professionals involved can be helpful, not only to share background and management information about patients, but also to decide which team member may most appropriately take a new referral and to increase members' skills and knowledge about local resources. However, the team will probably have to go through a period of negotiation as to their various roles, since most mental health professionals have relatively little understanding of the professional background of other team members (Sainsbury Centre for Mental Health, 1997), and there may be other PHCT members involved who do not have a formal mental health training. Practice nurses, midwives and health visitors are all in a position to detect psychological problems in their patients and may well be able to intervene successfully given suitable training and adequate support (Holden *et al.*, 1989). In addition, medically trained GPs and psychiatrists will be more used to hierarchical structures, while evidence for effective teams indicates a flatter organisation is preferable (Pritchard and Pritchard, 1994). A recent systematic review by Bower and Sibbald (2000) indicated that attached mental health professionals in primary care have relatively little effect on behaviour within the whole practice, even if individual patients are affected. This may be different if several professionals meet together within the practice; the potential impact of mental health teamwork in primary care has been little researched.

Such procedures are time-consuming and will require additional resources. Not all GPs wish to spend so much time involved in the care of mental health problems in the practice. It may be appropriate for some GPs with a particular interest to become more specialised and spend more time seeing patients with mental health problems, while other less interested partners are less involved (MACA, 1999).

TRAINING PRIMARY CARE STAFF IN MENTAL HEATH WORK

Prior to the recent government initiatives to raise the profile of mental health care, there were few incentives for mental health training in primary care and health promotion funds were harder to access. With the political recognition that patients with mental health problems are often cared for solely in primary care, things are rapidly changing. However, GPs and other members of the team may feel unskilled and ill-equipped for the task and thus not effective in the care they give (MACA, 1999). It is important that members of the PHCT, although not expected to be mental health professionals in their own right, are equipped with the knowledge to detect common mental health problems, assess a person's mental health needs and have some under-standing of effective interventions, whether delivered by themselves or others. Achieving this can demand new ways of learning and working together.

Over the past ten years there have been many projects aimed at training primary care teams to work better with patients with mental health problems. The move is now towards multi-professional training and with the gradual coming together of GP continuing medical education and non-medical, interdisciplinary training, there will be opportunities to develop more creative approaches to this work. Examples of initiatives particularly relevant to women include the work of Elizabeth Armstrong in training practice and community nurses (Armstrong, 1994). Elliott (1989) has emphasised the important role of health visitors and midwives in recognising depression in women, both antenatally and in the postpartum period. She has helped to develop specialist training using the Edinburgh Postnatal Depression Scale and particular listening skills – of great importance when one considers that at least one woman in ten develops clinical depression in the months after childbirth.

More general training involving the whole PHCT can use packages developed at the RCGP Mental Health Education Unit (Armstrong, 1997). Initiating and running such programmes does, however, require considerable commitment, not only in extra training but in continuing support. Whatever the enhanced skills of a primary care team in providing mental health care, it cannot be done without appropriate back-up from accessible and sensitive psychological and psychiatric services. Primary care mental health should be seen as an integral part of all health care training – from medical students to GP registrars and for nurses, psychologists and other health care professionals.

An area of recent discussion relevant to training in primary health care is that of domestic violence. Most incidents of domestic violence are not reported to the police, but a much higher proportion of women visit their GP for treatment of injuries inflicted by male partners. General practice therefore represents a setting currently underused for the recognition and provision of help for domestic violence, including management for its psychological effects. These include: anxiety in anticipation of the next attack; symptoms of post-traumatic stress disorder; and after repeated experience of violence, depression, substance abuse and a state of helplessness where an alternative existence is impossible to visualise. Since domestic violence is common (Richardson *et al.*, 2002) and it is estimated that around 90 per cent of violent incidents between partners are perpetrated by men on women, it has been suggested that primary care professionals should be trained to ask screening questions of all women. However, there is no current evidence that screening results in any reduction in violence (Ramsay *et al.*, 2002); further, one study found that 20 per cent of women found such questioning objectionable (Richardson *et al.*, 2002). Nevertheless, primary health care professionals should ask about domestic violence when women present with unexplained psychological symptoms as described above, or with suggestive injuries.

Summary

The national recognition of the extent to which psychological morbidity is dealt with in primary care is associated with great potential opportunity in allowing Primary Care Trusts considerable control over the services they commission. However, there is also the danger that many different services will be set up and the current inequities perpetuated. Without adequate training and research into effective interventions and resources for their implementation, it will not be possible for primary care to fulfil its potential to take a lead on the treatment of mental health problems in the community and this requires clear central direction.

Recommendations for the future

- Needs assessment to be carried out within the local population;
- Interventions recommended should be evidence-based;
- Provision of relevant training for GPs and other members of the PHCT in recognition, assessment, relevant interventions and appropriate referral;
- Health promotion strategies for mental health problems in primary care and for the physical health of those with mental illnesses;
- Additional resources required if effective treatments to be given in primary care;
- Systems for good liaison with secondary care, social services and voluntary sector;
- Aim to get even distribution of good primary care mental health services.

Note

* We would like to acknowledge the contribution of Jo Paton in helping us to organise our thoughts about this chapter.

References

American Psychiatric Association (APA) (1996) *American Psychiatric Association Practice Guidelines*, Washington DC: APA.

Armstrong, E. (1994) A framework for depression. *Practice Nurse* 15–31 May 1994: 516–19.

Armstrong, E. (1997) *The Primary Mental Health Care Toolkit*. RCGP Mental Health Education Unit.

Bindman, J., Johnson, S., Wright, S., Szmukler, G., Bebbington, P., Kuipers, E. and Thornicroft, G. (1997) Integration between primary and secondary services in the care of the severely mentally ill: patients' and general practitioners' views, *British Journal of Psychiatry* 171: 169–74.

Botega, N., Mann, A., Blizard, R. and Wilkinson, G. (1992) General practitioners and depression: first use of the depression attitude questionnaire, *International Journal of Methods in Psychiatric Research* 2: 169–80.

Bower, P. and Sibbald, B. (2000) Systematic review of the effect of on-site mental health professionals on the clinical behaviour of general practitioners, *British Medical Journal* 320: 614–17.

Cohen, A. and Singh, S. (2001) *GP's Guide to Managing Severe Mental Illness*. London: Sainsbury Centre for Mental Health.

Department of Health (1999) *National Service Framework for Mental Health: Modern Standards and Service Models*. London: Department of Health.

Donoghue, J. and Tylee, A. (1996) The treatment of depression: prescribing patterns of antidepressants in primary care in the UK, *British Journal of Psychiatry* 168: 164–8.

Elliott, S. (1989) Psychological strategies in the prevention and treatment of post-natal depression. *Balliere's Clinical Obstetrics and Gynaecology* 3: 879–903.

Friedli, K. and King, M. (1996) Counselling in general practice: a review, *Primary Care Psychiatry* 2: 205–16.

Goldberg, D. and Huxley, P. (1992) *Common Mental Disorders*. London: Routledge.

Holden, J., Sagovsky, R. and Cox, J. (1989) Counselling in a general practice setting: controlled study of health visitor intervention in treatment of postnatal depression, *British Medical Journal* 298: 223–6.

Johnson, S. and Buszewicz, M. (1996) Women's mental health in the UK, in Abel, K., Buszewicz, M., Davison, S., Johnson, S. and Staples, E. (eds.), *Planning Community Mental Health Services for Women, a Multi-professional Handbook*. London: Routledge.

Kendrick, T., Sibbald, B., Burns, T. and Freeling, P. (1991) Role of general practitioners in care of long term mentally ill patients, *British Medical Journal* 302: 508–10.

Lloyd, K., Jenkins, R. and Mann, A. (1996) Long-term outcome of patients with neurotic illness in general practice. *British Medical Journal* 313: 26–8.

MACA Partners in Mental Health (1999) First national GP survey of mental health in primary care. MACA.

Mynors-Wallis, L., Gath, D., Day, A. and Baker, F. (2000) Randomised controlled trial of problem solving treatment, antidepressant medication, and combined treatment for major depression in primary care, *British Medical Journal* 320: 26–30.

NICE Guidelines for Depresssion (2004) National Institute for Health and Clinical Excellence.

OPCS Surveys of Psychiatric Morbidity in Great Britain (1995) *Report 1: The Prevalence of Psychiatric Morbidity among Adults Living in Private Households.* London: HMSO.

OPCS (1995) *Morbidity Statistics from General Practice: Fourth National Study 1991–1992.* London: HMSO.

Paykel, E. (1989) Treatment of depression: the relevance of research for clinical practice. *British Journal of Psychiatry* 155: 754–63.

Paykel, E. and Priest, R. (1992) Recognition and management of depression in general practice: consensus statement, *British Medical Journal* 305: 1198–202.

Pilgrim, D. and Rogers, A. (1993) Mental health service users' views of medical practitioners. *Journal of Interprofessional Care* 7(2): 167–76.

Pritchard, P. and Pritchard, J. (1994) *Teamwork for Primary and Shared care.* Oxford: Oxford University Press.

Ramsay, J., Richardson, J., Carter, Y.H., Davidson, L.L. and Feder, G. (2002) Should health professionals screen women for domestic violence? Systematic Review. *British Medical Journal* 325(7359): 314.

Richardson, J., Coid, J., Petruckevitch, A., Chung, W.S., Moorey, S. and Feder, G. (2002) Identifying domestic violence: cross-sectional study in primary care. *British Medical Journal* 324(7332): 274.

Roth, A. and Fonagy, P. (1996) *What Works for Whom?* New York: Guilford Press.

Sainsbury Centre for Mental Health (1997) *Pulling Together: The Future Roles and Training of Mental Health Staff.* London: Sainsbury Centre for Mental Health.

Scott, A. and Freeman, C. (1992) Edinburgh primary care depression study: treatment outcome, patient satisfaction and cost after 16 weeks. *British Medical Journal* 304: 883–7.

Sibbald, B., Addington-Hall, J., Brenneman, D. and Freeling, P. (1993) Counsellors in English and Welsh general practices: their nature and distribution. *British Medical Journal* 306: 29–33.

Strathdee, G., Brown, R. and Doig, R. (1990) A standardised assessment of patients referred to primary care and hospital psychiatric clinics. *Psychological Medicine* 20: 219–24.

Strathdee, G. and Jenkins, R. (1996) Purchasing mental health for primary care, in G. Thornicroft and G. Strathdee (eds.), *Commissioning Mental Health Services.* London: HMSO.

Thomas, R. and Corney, R. (1992) A survey of links between mental health professionals and general practice in six district health authorities. *British Journal of General Practice* 42: 358–61.

3 Community and outpatient services for women

Sonia Johnson

Introduction

In the UK, as in many other countries, the organisation and functioning of community mental health services continues to be the object of extensive scrutiny and sometimes heated debate among service users, carers, clinicians, managers, policy makers and the media. Several decades of extensive change have resulted in service delivery which is to a considerable extent based in community rather than hospital settings, involves multidisciplinary teams, and integrates health and social care provision. Innovative ways of organising and delivering mental health services have been introduced and, sometimes, evaluated. However, politicians, service users and carers, and journalists are among the groups who have been vocal in their criticisms of community mental health services, though with great variations in views about the nature of the malady and the appropriate remedy. A series of recent policy initiatives has now resulted in a further wave of reorganisation of community mental health services (Department of Health 1999, 2000 and 2001).

Throughout the service reorganisations of the 1980s and 1990s, the specific effects on women of changes in community service provision received little attention. A few individuals and organisations instigated debates, a notable example being the MIND campaigns regarding women (Sayce, 1996a). Ways of providing services which fit the particular needs of women have been explored in a range of local initiatives around the country, mostly in the voluntary sector (Department of Health, 2002a). However, discussions about women's needs and how to meet them have tended to remain on the sidelines in national debates about provision of effective community care, over-shadowed by issues such as the impact of community-based care on the risks associated with mental illness and on levels of homelessness. A shift to more community-based care promises in some ways to benefit women and to answer some of the vociferous criticisms levelled in the past against psychiatry's relationship with them. Accusations recurring in feminist critiques have been that psychiatrists' concepts of 'normal' female behaviour are based on outdated and oppressive gender role stereotypes, and that psychiatry reinforces women's powerlessness by formulating biological explanations for distress which actually results from women's oppressed and deprived social situations (Chesler, 1972; Showalter, 1987). Community-based mental health care has the potential to serve women better than traditional institutional care, as the social contexts of distress and the diversity of women's roles, experiences and mental health may be more visible to professionals working in community settings (Johnson and Buszewicz, 1996).

The appearance of the first major UK national policy document on women's mental health is a welcome indication that attention to their needs may be increasing (Department of Health, 2002a). Evidence as to whether the potential advantages for women of community-based mental health care have begun to be realised is still lacking, nor is there a clear basis for deciding which community service models meet their needs best. In this chapter, I will set out a framework for such an evaluation by discussing some questions which are relevant in considering whether current community and outpatient services meet the needs of women. I will focus on service provision for women whose mental health problems are so severe that their needs cannot be met by primary care level interventions. Primary care and inpatient services are dealt with elsewhere in this book.

ARE WOMEN'S NEEDS FOR WOMEN-ONLY SPACE AND WOMEN-ONLY SERVICES ADEQUATELY MET?

The case for women-only areas or facilities on inpatient units has been discussed elsewhere in this book, and has been a major focus for campaigning and policy in the last few years. Less attention has been paid to considering whether women-only services are needed in community settings. Some of the arguments for segregation in inpatient services also apply outside hospital. Women may be deterred from using community-based facilities such as day centres because they may feel harassed or intimidated by some male service users, a difficulty that may also arise in mixed supported housing. Particularly when women have problems which arise in part from current or past relationships with men, they may benefit from opportunities to discuss or gain respite from such difficulties in single-sex settings. Those who lack confidence and self-esteem, or who are intensely aware of stigma associated with their problems, may sometimes also find such settings helpful. As integrated living is usual in most parts of the community, there is probably also a role for day care with a mixed-sex client group. However, achieving the optimum balance between mixed and single-sex service provision needs further attention and investigation of service users' views and experiences. This applies especially for those women whose daily lives usually involve only limited contact with men, such as women from religious or ethnic minority backgrounds in which social contact between the sexes is limited, lesbian women and women who tend to avoid men following experiences of abuse or violence. In response to these needs, the NHS Plan (Department of Health, 2001) stipulated that there should be women-only day centres available in every catchment area in England by 2004. Availability of women-only day care, often in the form of women-only sessions within generic day centres, seems to be increasing (Department of Health, 2002a), though little evidence is available so far about the characteristics of the women who use such day care, the types of care provided and the extent to which they meet severely mentally ill women's needs.

As well as women-only areas in hospital, community-based alternatives to admission are a way of avoiding the distress and discomfort which may be associated with admission to a mixed ward. One such alternative to hospital admission is the community-based women's crisis house described by McNicholas in this volume. Crisis resolution teams, which work intensively with service users in their own homes, also avoid the problems associated with admission and may considerably improve the care available to some severely mentally ill women who find hospital admission unhelpful and distressing (Brimblecombe, 2001). However, home treatment may have disadvantages for women who experience abuse or excessive demands at home and might benefit from the respite provided by admission.

ARE THE SOCIAL CHARACTERISTICS OF SEVERELY MENTALLY ILL WOMEN FULLY TAKEN INTO ACCOUNT?

Recent research shows substantial gender differences in living situations and patterns of relationships among individuals with schizophrenia and other psychotic illnesses. Whether services for severely mentally ill women are tailored as much to the social characteristics prevalent among women as to those which are more typical for men is thus an issue of equity, though obviously a wide range of ways of living is found within each gender.

Gender differences between men and women with schizophrenia favour women in a number of respects, as is discussed in Howard's chapter in this volume, with better outcomes and quality of life in various domains (Angermeyer *et al.* 1989; Röder-Wanner and Priebe, 1995). However, differences in living situations make some needs more prominent for women. Test *et al.* (1990) have argued that service provision is inequitable in that it is often geared to a stereotyped expectation that people with schizophrenia are single, live alone, with parents or in supported accommodation, and do not have children. This expectation is unreliable if applied wholesale to either gender, but fits men with schizophrenia better than women.

Perhaps the most obvious gender difference is in parenthood. In a study of users of a community rehabilitation service, Test *et al.* (1990) found that 33 per cent of women, but only 5 per cent of men, had primary caretaking responsibility for at least one child. In the PriSM study, a large epidemiological study which aimed to identify all individuals with psychotic illnesses living in two inner South London catchment areas, 63 per cent of women but only 26 per cent of men had at least one child (Thornicroft *et al.*, 1998; Howard *et al.*, 2001). Custody loss is frequent among women with severe mental illnesses. In a small survey of a group of hospitalised women in the US, Joseph *et al.* (1999) reported that only about 20 per cent of mothers retained full custody of the children. Kumar *et al.* (1995) reported that 50 per cent of women with schizophrenia discharged from a mother and baby unit went home without their child, while Coverdale and Aruffo (1989) found that 60 per cent of children of long-term psychiatric patients were reared by others, most frequently the child's father or an adoptive family.

The impact of being a parent on women with severe mental illness is complex. It was explored by Nicholson and colleagues (1998a, 1998b) in a US qualitative study based on focus groups with mentally ill mothers who used community mental health services. They described often facing great stigma, with friends and professionals assuming that they would be unable to cope with bringing up their children. This is reflected in the reports of mentally ill women interviewed by Joseph *et al.* (1999) that their pregnancies tended to be generally regarded as a calamity, even though many had in fact wanted to have children. Despite this, Nicholson *et al.* identify some very positive aspects of parenting: many mothers regarded it as a very fulfilling role, which provided a motivation for getting better and a source of self-esteem. Significant difficulties were also reported, including reduced frustration tolerance, stress due to the competing demands of managing symptoms of illness and parenting, and lack of confidence in disciplining children. For some women, treatment of mental illness was disrupted as they were reluctant to leave their children and go to hospital or decided not to take medication in case it slowed them down and made it more difficult to cope with the children. Fear of losing custody was prominent. These difficulties are compounded by a greater likelihood of economic hardship and of being a single parent than among mothers with no mental illness (Ritsher *et al.*, 1997). In a UK qualitative study, mothers described fear of custody loss as dominating their interactions with professionals, and they reported that the stigma of mental illness affected people's views not only of them, but also of their children (Diaz-Caneja and Johnson, 2004).

In terms of service provision, mother and baby units have been an important development in the UK, but usually cater only for mothers of infants in the first few months of life. Outside a few centres with innovative programmes and some voluntary sector initiatives, specific provision for mentally ill mothers in the community has been very limited (Sayce, 1996b; Pounde and Abel, 1996). Availability of childcare to allow women to make use of mental health services is a basic need, which is infrequently catered for, so that facilities such as day centres are often unavailable to women with children. Given the high proportion of severely mentally ill women who have children, there is ample justification for a substantial programme of specific interventions to be available in every local catchment area. This could include help in improving parenting skills and coping with the competing demands of managing symptoms and caring for children, facilities for respite, work with relatives and professionals aimed at helping them to support mentally ill mothers, and an overall aim of minimising the numbers of children taken into care. Given the fear many women have of losing custody, it would be particularly valuable to have facilities for respite childcare which are clearly distinct from the mechanisms for taking children into local authority care. Such a range of interventions is not generally available, nor has there been a substantial programme of research on how to improve experiences and outcomes of severely mentally ill mothers and their children.

Maintenance and management of sexual relationships is a further area in which women with schizophrenia are more likely to have needs than men. Women with schizophrenia are more likely than men to be married, in relationships and/or sexually active. In the PriSM study (Thornicraft *et al.*, 1998), 73 per cent of men in the sample of people with a history of psychotic illness, but only 40 per cent of women, were single; 36 per cent of women and 14 per cent of men were currently married or cohabiting, whilst 24 per cent of women but only 14 per cent of men were divorced. The proportions of each sex living alone were similar, but men were more likely to live in supported accommodation and women with a partner. Test *et al.* (1990) investigated psychosexual history, and found that 74 per cent of the women with schizo- phrenia in their sample had been sexually active over the preceding two years, compared with 42 per cent of men. Whilst these differences may reasonably be regarded as aspects of a better social prognosis amongst women, particu- lar difficulties and needs are associated with them. Oyserman *et al.* (1994) and Test *et al.* (1990) argue that service providers tend to ignore the fact that people with severe mental illness, especially women, are often sexually active. Thus few attempts are made in services for the severely mentally ill to provide information about contraception and safe sexual behaviour, avoiding exploitation and unwanted sexual contact, and management of intimate relationships. Coverdale and Aruffo (1989) report that substantial numbers of women with severe mental illness are not succeeding in avoiding unwanted pregnancy: among 80 severely mentally ill women interviewed in their study, 31 per cent had had a termination of pregnancy. Of those who had had intercourse in the previous year and had not wanted to become pregnant, 33 per cent had had intercourse without using any contraception. Women with severe mental illnesses have been found to be at increased risk of sexual coercion, which may endanger both their physical and mental health (Weinhardt *et al.* 1999). High rates of relationship breakdown have been reported among severely mentally ill women, and their partners appear also to have relatively high rates of mental illness, which may increase difficulties in maintaining relationships (Ritsher *et al.*, 1997). Women who are conspicu- ously distressed or disinhibited because of illness may be particularly vul- nerable to sexual coercion. Severe mental illness may be associated with poor confidence and self-esteem, difficulties with social interactions, and symptoms which distract from coping with everyday life, and these impede formation and maintenance of relationships. Extra needs for help and support from partners and awareness of stigma may make it difficult for people with mental illness to feel that they are on an equal footing with their partners in relationships and entitled to respectful treatment. Risk of HIV infection makes it especially important for severely mentally ill women to be able to assert their own wishes and protect their health in sexual relationships. For these reasons, appropriate help with management of relationships and sexual behaviour is likely to be a particularly salient need for severely mentally ill women. To address this need, it may be useful for clinicians and researchers to collaborate with service users in exploring further their experiences of sex and relationships and developing training for mental health staff which increases their awareness of the difficulties service users may experience in this area. Staff need to be confident, but appropriately sensitive and respectful of privacy in discussing relationships and sexual behaviour with clients, and should be able to provide support and realistic guidance in areas such as safer sexual behaviour and resisting or escaping coercive and abusive relationships.

DO COMMUNITY SERVICES RESPOND TO THE FULL RANGE OF SEVERE MENTAL HEALTH PROBLEMS ENCOUNTERED AMONG WOMEN?

In order to ensure that those with the greatest needs are prioritised, policy makers and experts on service development have urged clinicians and managers in community mental health services to focus on the severely mentally ill. Severe mental illness is a vague term that has attracted a range of operational definitions (Slade *et al.*, 1997), but generally people with schizophrenia, manic depressive illness and other forms of psychotic illness have been regarded as the central group of severely mentally ill service users. A prominent focus has been on service provision for people who are difficult to engage, have committed or are at high risk of committing violence, and/or have psychotic illnesses complicated by substance misuse or major personality problems (e.g. Sainsbury Centre, 1998, Department of Health, 1999, 2001). This is probably at least in part a response to public and media preoccupations with the perceived threat of violence from the mentally ill and with street homelessness and public nuisance. Service models such as assertive outreach teams are intended to meet the needs of this group and reduce the risk they pose, and are currently advocated as cornerstones of community mental health service planning.

Whilst meeting the needs of these difficult to engage individuals with multiple needs is certainly an appropriate aim, there is a risk of overlooking those who are disabled by severe mental health problems, but are willing to engage with services and do not behave violently or in irritating or frightening ways in public places. Women are in a minority on caseloads of assertive outreach teams (Priebe *et al.*, 2003) and among mentally ill people who behave violently (Linaker, 2000), or who have a dual diagnosis of psychosis and substance misuse (Menezes *et al.*, 1996). However, they may well make up a rather higher proportion of the severely disabled but publicly inconspicuous.

Equity also needs to be assessed in terms of the diagnoses which are given highest priority. Women are at particular risk of eating disorders and of distress and difficulties in functioning following rape, domestic violence and childhood sexual abuse. Responding to the latter tends not to be seen as part of the central business of community mental health services, nor is there a well-established consensus about the responses that are most helpful. Women are also at greater risk than men of presenting to services with recurrent self-harm or of attracting a diagnosis of borderline personality disorder (Widiger and Weissman, 1991), and this group has often been regarded with considerable ambivalence by mental health professionals. Grounds for greater optimism about the outcomes of working with them are provided by new models such as the 'dialectical behaviour therapy' developed by Linehan and colleagues (1993): how far such models are disseminated and developed is particularly salient for women. Service provision for postnatal disorders is also obviously particularly relevant to women.

The emphasis on severe mental illness also raises questions about the care now available to the moderately mentally ill. Increased prioritisation is likely to mean that some less floridly and conspicuously unwell individuals are no longer eligible for the specialist psychiatric care they might once have received. People with depressive or anxiety disorders of moderate severity are likely to be highly represented in this group, and women are probably in the majority. Well-resourced primary care and voluntary sector services may be able to meet the needs of this group, but whether this is happening in practice needs to be investigated. A danger of removing this group from secondary mental health service caseloads is that they may have little access to alternatives to medication, such as cognitive behavioural therapy and other forms of psychotherapy.

Thus ensuring equity in community mental health service provision requires policy makers and service providers to consider the needs of individuals with a full range of mental health diagnoses, to examine whether effective treatments have been established and are available for each form of problem, and to assess whether, where more than one reasonably cost-effective treatment exists, a choice is available to service users. In particular, the possibility that women tend currently to be prioritised less because they are less likely to be violent or alarming to the public needs to be considered.

IS THE DIVERSITY OF WOMEN'S ROLES AND EXPERIENCES TAKEN INTO ACCOUNT IN CURRENT COMMUNITY SERVICE PROVISION?

Mental health services have often been criticised for assessing and treating women in relation to a definition of femininity which is narrow and stereotyped. For example, Perkins (1996) describes 'women's groups' in rehabilitation services which, in their encouragement of 'feminine' behaviours such as wearing of make-up, seem to be aiming to socialise women into narrowly traditional heterosexual roles, regardless of their actual values or sexual orientation. In 1991, Perkins and Rowland found that in a rehabilitation service for the severely mentally ill, expectations of women's performance in vocational rehabilitation settings appeared to be lower than for men, perhaps reflecting a view that work is more central to good mental health and social functioning for men than for women (Perkins and Rowland, 1991). The danger that professionals make judgements on the basis of stereotyped expectations and fail to understand individual women's values and experiences is all the greater for service users from ethnic minority backgrounds. For example, Kalhan (1996) describes a set of expectations which tends to be applied wholesale to Asian women with a very wide range of backgrounds, experiences and values. These include a representation of them as 'passive' or 'oppressed' and beliefs that they want treatment which is directive and lack a language in which to express emotional distress.

Where such stereotyped expectations persist, they are at odds with the great diversity in values, aspirations, experiences, living situations, patterns of relationships and working lives now found among women. Mental health professionals working in community settings have opportunities to gain a better understanding of women's social environments than in institutional settings and to provide flexible care which takes women's circumstances, values and preferences into account. Little evidence is available that this has resulted in community care which is adapted to women's individual needs, and there is ample scope here for further research. This should include studies of a qualitative form and should involve active participation by service users and careful investigation of their own and one another's practice by mental health professionals.

HOW DO CURRENT FORMS OF MENTAL HEALTH SERVICE PROVISION AFFECT CARERS?

A final key issue for women regarding community mental health services is their effect on carers, the majority of whom are women (Tausig *et al.*, 1992; Parker, 1996). Community services which fail adequately to meet a full range of clinical and social needs run the risk of placing a heavy burden on relatives, partners and friends trying to support people with mental health problems. Thus evaluating the effects of the move towards community-based models on carers is highly salient for women. The experiences of carers of mentally ill individuals under the care of ordinary community mental health services and not only of innovative model services need to be investigated. For example, despite very encouraging findings regarding carers' views of early innovative home treatment services, in Fulford and Farhall's (2001) survey of carers of patients of the crisis teams now well established throughout Victoria, Australia, around half the respondents said they would prefer their relative to receive inpatient rather than crisis team care during future relapses. Effective strategies need to be developed for supporting carers. Active collaboration between service planners and providers and the carers' groups and voluntary sector organisations already working in this area will be needed to do this effectively. Carers have become a significant focus in recent UK policy guidance: community services are now required to offer assessment of carers' needs and written support plans for them (Department of Health, 2002b), though it is uncertain how far and with what consequences this has so far been implemented.

Conclusion

Thus the effects on women of the move towards community-based mental health care and the service models which are best for them still need to be further examined. This will best be achieved in active collaboration with service users and carers. In this chapter, a set of questions relevant to such an investigation have been set out. These relate to women's needs for services that take into account each of the following:

- The social contexts of women's distress
- The diversity of their roles, attitudes and experiences
- The full range of severe mental health problems they may experience,
- The social characteristics and experiences particularly prevalent among women with psychotic illnesses
- The experiences of informal carers for the severely mentally ill
- Needs for single-sex areas and service provision.

References

Angermeyer, M., Goldstein, J. and Kuehn, L. (1989) Gender differences in schizophrenia: rehospitalisation and community survival. *Psychological Medicine* 19: 365–82.
Brimblecombe, N. (ed.) (2001) *Acute Mental Health Care in the Community: Intensive Home Treatment*. London: Whurr.
Brockington, I. (1996) *Motherhood and Mental Health*. Oxford: Oxford University Press.
Chesler, P. (1972) *Women and Madness*. New York: Doubleday.

Coverdale, J.H. and Aruffo, J.A. (1989) Family planning needs of female chronic psychiatric patients. *American Journal of Psychiatry* 146: 1489–91.

Department of Health (1999) *National Service Framework for Mental Health: Modern Standards and Service Models.* London: The Stationery Office,

Department of Health (2000) *The NHS Plan.* London: Department of Health Publications.

Department of Health (2001) *The Mental Health Policy Implementation Guide.* London: Department of Health Publications.

Department of Health (2002a) *Women's Mental Health: Into the Mainstream. Strategic Development in Women's Mental Health Care.* London: Department of Health Publications.

Department of Health (2002b) *Developing Services for Carers and Families of People with Mental Illness.* London: Department of Health Publications.

Diaz-Caneja, A. and Johnson, S. (2004) The views and experiences of severely mentally ill mothers – a qualitative study. *Social Psychiatry and Psychiatric Epidemiology* 39: 472–482.

Fulford, M. and Farhall, J. (2001) Hospital versus home care for the acutely mentally ill? Preferences of caregivers who have experienced both forms of service. *Australia and New Zealand Journal of Psychiatry* 35: 619–25.

Howard, L., Kumar, R. and Thornicroft, G. (2001) Psychosocial characteristics and needs of mothers with psychotic disorders. *British Journal of Psychiatry* 178: 427–32.

Johnson, S. and Buszewicz, M. (1996) Introduction, in K. Abel, M. Buszewicz, S. Davison, S. Johnson and E. Staples (eds), *Planning Community Mental Health Services for Women: A Multiprofessional Handbook.* London, Routledge.

Joseph, J., Joshi, S., Lewin, A. and Abrams, M. (1999) Characteristics and perceived needs of mothers with serious mental illness. *Psychiatric Services* 50: 1357–9.

Kalhan, S. (1996) Asian Women, in Perkins, R., Copperman, J., Andrews, C. and Nadirshaw, Z. (eds), *Women in Context: Good Practice in Mental Health Services for Women.* London: Good Practices in Mental Health.

Kumar, R., Marks, M., Platz, C. and Yoshida, K. (1995) Clinical survey of a psychiatric mother and baby unit: characteristics of 100 consecutive admissions. *Journal of Affective Disorders* 33: 11–22.

Linaker, O. (2000) Dangerous female psychiatric patients: prevalences and characteristics. *Acta Psychiatrica Scandinavica* 101: 67–72.

Linehan, M.M., Heard, H.L. and Armstrong, H.E. (1993) Naturalistic follow-up of a behavioural treatment or chronically parasuicidal borderline patients. *Archives of General Psychiatry* 50: 971–4.

Menezes, P., Johnson, S., Thornicroft, G., Marshall, J., Prosser, D., Bebbington, P. and Kuipers, E. (1996) Drug and alcohol problems among individuals with severe mental illness in South London. *British Journal of Psychiatry* 168: 612–19.

Nicholson, J., Sweeney, E. and Geller, J. (1998a) Mothers with mental illness: 1. The competing demands of parenting and living with mental illness. *Psychiatric Services* 49: 635–42.

Nicholson, J., Sweeney, E.M. and Geller, J.S. (1998b) Mothers with mental illness II. Family relationships and the context of parenting. *Psychiatric Services* 49: 643–9.

Oyserman, D., Mowbray, C.T. and Zemencuk, J.K. (1994) Resources and supports for mothers with a severe mental illness. *Health and Social Work* 19: 132–42.

Parker, G. (1996) Carers and the development of community mental health policy, in K. Abel, M. Buszewicz, S. Davison, S. Johnson and E. Staples (eds), *Planning Mental Health Services for Women: A Multiprofessional Approach*. London: Routledge.

Perkins, R. (1996) Women with serious long-term mental health problems, in R. Perkins, J. Copperman, C. Andrews and Z. Nadirshaw (eds.), *Women in Context: Good Practice in Mental Health Services for Women*. London: Good Practices in Mental Health.

Perkins, R.E. and Rowland, L.A. (1991) Sex differences in service usage in long-term psychiatric care: are women adequately served? *British Journal of Psychiatry* 158 (supp. 10): 75–9.

Pounde, A. and Abel, K. (1996) Motherhood and mental illness, in K. Abel, M. Buszewicz, S. Davison, S. Johnson and E. Staples (eds.), *Planning Community Mental Health Services for Women: A Multiprofessional Handbook*. London: Routledge.

Priebe, S., Fakhoury, W., Watts, J., Bebbington, P., Burns, T., Johnson, S., Muijen, M., Ryrie, I., White, I., Wright, C. (2003) Assertive outreach teams in London: patient characteristics and outcomes. Pan-London Assertive Outreach Study, part 3. *British Journal of Psychiatry* 183: 148–54.

Ritsher, J., Coursey, R. and Farrell, E. (1997) A survey on issues in the lives of women with severe mental illness. *Psychiatric Services* 48: 1273–82.

Röder-Wanner, U.-U. and Priebe, S. (1995) Schizophrenie und lebensqualität – geschlechtsspezifische aspekte. *Fortschritte in Neurologie und Psychiatrie* 61: 393–401.

Sainsbury Centre (1998) *Keys to Engagement*. London: Sainsbury Centre for Mental Health.

Sayce, L. (1996a) Campaigning for women, in K. Abel, M. Buszewicz, S. Davison, S. Johnson and E. Staples (eds.), *Planning Community Mental Health Services for Women: A Multiprofessional Handbook*. London, Routledge.

Sayce, L. (1996b) Women with children, in R. Perkins, J. Copperman, C. Andrews, and Z. Nadirshaw (eds.), *Women in Context: Good Practice in Mental Health Services for Women*. London: Good Practices in Mental Health.

Showalter, E. (1987) *The Female Malady: Women, Madness and English Culture, 1830–1980*. London, Virago.

Slade, M., Powell, R. and Strathdee, G. (1997) Current approaches to identifying the severely mentally ill. *Social Psychiatry and Psychiatric Epidemiology* 32: 177–84.

Tausig, M., Fisher, G. and Tessler, R. (1992) Informal systems of care for the chronically mentally ill. *Community Mental Health Journal* 28:413–25.

Test, M.A., Burke, S.S. and Wallisch, L.S. (1990) Gender differences of young adults with schizophrenic disorders in community care. *Schizophrenia Bulletin* 16: 331–44.

Thornicroft, G., Strathdee, G., Phelan, M., Holloway, F., Wykes, T., Dunn, G., McCrone, P., Leese, M., Johnson, S. and Szmukler, G. (1998) Rationale and design: PRiSM Psychosis Study 1. *British Journal of Psychiatry* 173: 363–70.

Weinhardt, L.S., Bichham, N.L. and Carey, M.P. (1999) Sexual coercion among women living with a severe and persistent mental illness: review of the literature and recommendations for mental health providers. *Aggression and Violent Behaviour* 4: 307–17.

Widiger, T. and Weissman, M. (1991) Epidemiology of borderline personality disorder. *Hospital and Community Psychiatry* 42: 1015–21.

4 Inpatient psychiatric services for women

Dora Kohen, Shirley McNicholas and Kay Beaumont

This chapter will review the research evidence and the clinical concerns that underpin the rationale for separate inpatient services for women. Three examples of responses to these concerns are then given. The establishment and running of two women-only services, both located in inner London are described: a hospital ward and a crisis house for women located separately from any hospital. Third, the setting up of a policy on sexual assault in a psychiatric hospital with mixed-sex wards is described.

WOMEN-ONLY ACUTE PSYCHIATRIC SERVICES

Dora Kohen

Introduction

Until the 1960s women and men were admitted to single-sex psychiatric wards in large mental hospitals. With the rise of the civil liberties movement and the closure of large institutions, this practice came to an end. Mixed-sex psychiatric wards allowing mentally ill men and women to be admitted to the same facility became an accepted practice. Acutely psychotic and behaviourally disturbed men who frequently had a substance misuse disorder as well were treated in the same wards with vulnerable, confused, disinhibited and sometimes subdued women. They were expected to share not only daytime recreational activities but also every other facility including wards, sleeping areas, showers and toilets. Psychiatric wards were therefore no longer places of asylum where people could recover in peace from frightening and distressing experiences.

In the mid 1990's this practice has raised concern in many professionals involved in the care of women admitted to mixed wards. Disenchanted professionals continued to pass information on females distressed in mixed-gender wards but these complaints did not receive the attention they deserved until recently. There are now in the UK many voluntary and statutory organisations involved in the care of mentally ill women who are able to draw attention to the vulnerability of Severely Mentally Ill (SMI) women and the unmet needs of female patients.

At the same time as these changes in policy and the concern they have caused have occurred, research data on the epidemiology and social and psychological aspects of psychiatric disorders has provided more insight into the specific needs of female patients. In North America, many psychiatric departments accepted women's mental health as a subspecialty. Research into perinatal psychiatry and the epidemiological studies of postpartum and prepartum depression and the results of lack of specific treatment are now widely accepted.

Gender differences in the prevalence of psychiatric disorders

Gender differences in the prevalence of psychiatric disorders are well established. Depression, dysthymia, deliberate self-harm, seasonal affective disorder, generalized anxiety disorder, panic attacks, social phobias, eating disorders including anorexia nervosa and bulimia are more common in women (Meltzer *et al.*, 1995).

Women are twice as likely to have complaints of somatic symptoms such as pain or gastrointestinal disturbances, phobias, obsessions, compulsions, poor concentration, forgetfulness and fatigue (Hagnell, 1966). In addition the periods around puberty, childbirth and the menopause are associated with higher risk of psychiatric diagnoses and mental health problems. (Brockington, 1996). These are scattered in a wide spectrum ranging from irritability and premenstrual distress to premenstrual dysphoric disorder, prenatal and postnatal depression, postpartum psychosis and depression before or following the perimenopausal period. (Burt, 1997; Palazidou, 2000).

The different symptomatology and outcome of severe mental illness in males in comparison to females is well documented (Seeman, 1986; Canuso *et al.*, 1998). Female patients also have different social and personal needs. These differences are greater at times of crisis and relapse and hence the need for admission to gender specific inpatient treatment.

Mixed psychiatric wards: do they offer a therapeutic environment?

The population of acute psychiatric wards has changed over the last ten years. As more people are being treated and cared for in the community, acute wards are likely to contain people who are very ill, many of whom will be detained under the Mental Health Act 1983, and therefore not in hospital by choice. Wards have men and women patients from a specific geographical area rather than patients with particular needs. This means that people with severe depression are alongside people who are acutely psychotic. Young male inpatients can be noisy, boisterous and demanding. Sedated female inpatients could be considerably distressed by men who may become physically and sexually disinhibited.

Drug and alcohol abuse and dual diagnoses are more common in males (Office for National Statistics, 1997). It is well known that, especially in inner-city districts, mixed psychiatric wards can became fertile areas for drug dealers. Drug problems and visitors who put patients at risk may use a lot of nursing time and attention. These facts may increase the marginalisation of women who tend to be less demanding.

Under difficult circumstances behaviourally disturbed male patients are likely to get all the attention while sedated and non-demanding females may be neglected. The need for structure to the day, occupational therapy, dance and movement therapy, inpatient groups and sensitivity meetings are sometimes sabotaged by disturbed male patients who may form the majority of the ward.

In such circumstances, the women with severe mental illness who need one-to- one attention to discuss their personal and social circumstances leading to the admission may not have a chance to express their concerns.

There have been many studies showing high levels of sexual assault and sexual harassment in inpatient services. In 1997 the Mental Health Commission (Sainsbury Centre for Mental Health, 1998) organised a one-day visit to 309 Acute Psychiatric Wards and reported that staff on 57 per cent of wards said there were problems in terms of the safety of women patients. A King's Fund Report (Goldberg, 1997) reported that in a survey of twelve inner London mental health trusts there were over 160 incidents of physical assault, sexual assault and sexual harassment during two weeks (one before and one after the census date) during each of 1994 and 1995. Mixed psychiatric wards attract a lot of negative feedback from female inpatients, their relatives and all involved in their care.

New Legislation and New Practices
How to establish a women-only acute psychiatric service

A women-only psychiatric service or a women and mental health unit consists of a women's ward,and a multidisciplinary community team and a new philosophy and outlook on the gender equality and sensitivity issues. In recent years women's wards have been the focus of many panels and discussions.

Although the support of the Department of Health and the recent Guidelines of National Service Framework (1999) have given great impetus in establishing women-only psychiatric wards, it is important to involve user groups and other local organisations in the initial discussions. Recognition of existing sensitivities around the issue has helped dialogue and realistic approach to these wards.

In establishing a women-only psychiatric service it is important to have a clear idea of the local population needs. The ethnic background of the community needs major consideration. The levels of single parenthood, drug and alcohol misuse, homelessness and documented domestic violence rates will help to clarify the number of beds. The locality mental health teams, assertive outreach teams, and the level of organisation of the community services will also help with getting a clearer picture of unmet needs.

The district general hospital, the obstetrics and gynaecology department and the antenatal clinics will give a realistic prediction of the numbers of women with perinatal mental health problems that will need input.

Women with borderline personality disorder who may require repeated admissions may lead to inappropriate use of the women's acute psychiatric ward. It is very clear that different voluntary and statutory organisations should collaborate in keeping such patients in the community and decreasing unnecessary admissions.

Primary care trusts and commissioners should be briefed on the regional needs and the benefits and gains of single sex wards.

Mermaid ward: an acute psychiatric ward for women in Hackney

Mermaid ward was established in March 1996 following several incidents that showed SMI women were not safe in mixed wards in City and Hackney.

Admission criteria (1996–2001)

This acute psychiatric ward only admits women who need inpatient psychiatric care and cannot be cared for in the community. Admission criteria have been set to give priority to SMI women with pregnancy who come from various ethnic backgrounds, women with first episode psychoses, women who have a history of domestic violence and any other women who request admission to a single-sex ward (Kohen, 1999, 2001).

In an area of great deprivation such as City and Hackney, it has been important to establish a referral system whereby the ward does not become a substitute for a respite care unit. It has also been important to ensure that the high rate of deliberate self-harm (DSH) in City and Hackney is not reflected in the admission rates of the ward. The liaison nurses who deal with the assessment of DSH have been instrumental in gatekeeping for the above.

The women with diagnosis of borderline personality disorder have been admitted only for short stays. Although this seemed to be a source of conflict to start with it has been resolved through firm commitment and resolution of the staff.

Vulnerable women, for example with hebephrenic schizophrenia or treatment-resistant schizophrenia, have been using the ward appropriately. It is our belief that they have gained the most of the ward atmosphere and our growing expertise in the treatment of women with such conditions.

The patients with SMI who needed repeated admission because of poor compliance with medication and other treatment, leading to breakdown of community care, have also made appropriate use of this resource.

Women with the diagnosis of severe depression have responded well to the ward environment. It has been rewarding to see an appropriate ward environment contributing to the treatment of depressed women, who found acute psychiatric wards, with young, boisterous and sometimes excessively demanding young males with SMI difficult to tolerate.

Staffing

The idea of having only female staff was abandoned following evaluations and discussions with all parties involved. Male and female ward staff who have shown care and understanding towards women's issues have been chosen. Many patients have been happy to have male-named nurses in the ward and male nurses have appreciated the experience of a women's ward. Nevertheless patients have been given a choice of their named nurses and there have been patients who have requested female-named nurses.

Ward atmospheres from 1996

The ward atmosphere has generally been quiet and non-demanding. The ward has been much cleaner than mixed wards in the same building. It has one smoking room and a dining area. Visitors are welcome in the general sitting area but not the dormitory. There are interview rooms that have been used by families when necessary. The ward sets clear rules and offers boundaries and structure that are appreciated by patients and families.

Activities

It is interesting to see that women in acute phases of their illnesses contribute more to occupational therapy and dance and movement therapy than they would in mixed wards. The privacy, the understanding and the lack of criticism would play a part in this.

Five years' experience (1996–2001)

Mermaid ward has been a major gain to City and Hackney. The patients and their families have expressed great satisfaction with the ward. Ethnic minorities such as Middle Eastern, Jewish orthodox and South East Asian women who refused to be admitted to mixed wards have used the ward successfully. Turkish and Kurdish women with SMI have been very appreciative of the environment.

General Practitioners have come to more Care Programme Approach (CPA) and ward meetings and have referred patients who previously would not accept admissions.

There has been a major gain of expertise in the non-medical professionals in the ward. Nursing staff have gained sensitivity in the assessment and management of women with SMI and especially pregnancy.

There has been great collaboration in multidisciplinary work. Regular involvement of child and adolescent psychiatrists, child and family social services, clinical psychology, family therapists and voluntary organisations has been very rewarding for the patients. They have brought a sense of value and support for the inpatient team. Social services in the district general hospital and working in the maternity wards have been fully involved in the planning meetings of pregnant women.

The problems of children born to and growing up with mothers with schizophrenia have become an important topic of discussion. Clinical psychologists now assess children living with a parent with schizophrenia and liaise with other professionals including schools to help those young people. The numbers and demographic variables of young people living with single parents with SMI have been a revelation for the authorities.

The psychiatric team has gained expertise in mental health issues for women including psychopharmacology and perinatal psychiatry, particularly pregnancy and the severely mentally ill, psychotropics and the treatment of pregnant women and sedation and hypotonia in the new born.

Psychopharmacological considerations in women and the topics of sex, gender and hormones have received attention (Jensvold *et al.*, 1996). The issue of amenorrhea and galactorrhoea in premenopausal women on antipsychotic treatment has been widely discussed by all involved. Serum prolactin levels in women treated with classical or atypical antipsychotic medication has been closely monitored.

The data on the large group of pregnant women with SMI who have been admitted and treated successfully contributed to discussions about the lack of teratogenesis with psychotropic treatment. The ward database now contributes to the National Teratology Information Service, which is a member of the European Network of Teratology Information Services (ENTIS) and a WHO Collaborating Centre for Drug Policy and Drug Safety Research.

On the other hand, the increased occurrence of adverse pregnancy outcomes expected among women with schizophrenia due to smoking, illicit substance misuse and socio-economic disadvantage is receiving close attention. Preterm birth and intrauterine growth retardation among children of women with schizophrenia has raised awareness among voluntary groups (Bennedsen *et al.*, 1999).

As from 1996, the ward has become a centre of information for perinatal psychiatry. There have been lectures, conferences and a steep learning curve on different topics of perinatal psychiatry. It is very clear that women's wards will provide the nucleus for future academic units of women and mental health studies.

Single sex Wards (2002–2006)

Women and Mental Health: Into the Mainstream (2002) Mainstreaming Gender and Women's mental Health: Implementation guidelines (2003), Women's Mental Health Strategy (2003) and the regional and local implementation guidelines have contributed to major changes in the way women and inpatient mental health issues have been viewed. Mixed inpatient wards have become a practice of the past. The Department of Health guidelines on gender specific inpatient facilities and the importance of gender sensitivity has led to reorganization of most of the psychiatric wards and services in England and Wales. Most wards have been redesigned to serve single sex population. Recent s reviews have shown that the great majority of mental health trusts have managed to make the change successfully and women now have separate sleeping and living facilities while they make be sharing day time inpatient activities.

The issue now remain to continue to train inpatient staff to recognize gender issues and to approach them with the necessary sensitivity, knowledge and respect.

Conclusions

1. Women should have access to well-integrated, tiered, specific and local inpatient services

Inpatient psychiatric services will provide better patient satisfaction if the need for privacy and safety is taken into account. Each service should be designed to respond to female needs and should be able to reflect the local needs of the women in the area. (Kohen, 1999, 2001). The ethnic mix and background of the local women should be part of consideration in staffing.

The services should have a clear referral, admission, treatment and management policy (Kohen, 1999; 2000). This policy should be updated yearly to reflect the progress and learning curve.

An inpatient service would not be complete without the community components attached to it. Community services should be integrated with inpatient facilities and community mental health teams should be part of the same philosophy and should endeavour to provide gender-specific services. Integrated community facilities should include services for alcohol and drug abuse, services for emotional or physical abuse and domestic violence, child and family services, pregnancy, antenatal and genito-urinary medicine clinics. It should also include perinatal psychiatric services, mother and baby units and maintain close links with social services, voluntary organisations and self-help groups.

2. Services for women should not be seen as yet another specialised but rather marginal service

It is correct to assume that gender-specific services may promote segregation or fragmentation of community and hospital services if they are not set up as an integral part of the whole mental health service.

Establishing a gender-specific service requires a change of philosophy from the old to the new. It requires a modern understanding of service, a progressive outlook and a positive attitude to management of change.

Gender-specific services should be viewed as a step forward in understanding mental disorder in women and meeting needs of the female population. They should not be seen as yet another specialised service but should become a necessary addition to a seamless psychiatric service. It is clear that more appropriate services may improve quality of life and patient satisfaction and eventually decrease the number of admissions.

3. The NHS should contribute to training in gender-sensitive mental health issues

Appropriate training offered at every professional level will lead to greater awareness of gender differences and service needs in psychiatry.

DRAYTON PARK: A RESIDENTIAL CRISIS PROJECT FOR WOMEN

Shirley McNicholas

Introduction

Drayton Park is the first women-only residential mental health crisis service in the UK. It opened in December 1995 and has been successful in offering women an alternative to hospital admission. It is committed to understanding the behaviour of women in crisis as a reaction to distressing life events, assisting them to have control of their current and future life circumstances. This chapter will offer information on the development and history of the project, more detail on the actual service and will discuss some of the challenging issues it has faced since its opening.

The project serves residents of Camden and Islington, both inner London areas with recognised complex needs. Islington ranks as the tenth most deprived local authority and Camden the seventeenth (Dept of Environment, Transport and the Regions (DETR) Index of Local Deprivation). Mental health problems are extremely high relative to other areas (hospital episode rates 50 per cent above the average for inner London) and the fourth highest suicide rate in England (Camden and Islington Health Action Zone, 1999).

History

It is difficult to pinpoint an exact date when the idea of the project began to grow as it had many influences. However, placing the project in context helps understand why different services are developed at certain times. The Community Care Act 1990 laid a major foundation, setting an agenda for a different way of working with mental health problems in society. Increasingly services have become more community-focused and influenced by service user experiences. Crisis services are a key part of the government's agenda for services in the twenty-first century.

Local context

Islington had already developed a crisis service over ten years ago, from a residential service, Sunnyside Road. This reflected Islington's reputation of leading the way as providers of a diverse range of services. Islington MIND was commissioned to complete a user consultation in August 1994, *User Consultation on Crisis Care*. This gave clear and detailed information directly from users about the services they wanted. At this stage I was appointed to the post of crisis project development worker for two projects. In the first instance Islington used Mental Illness Specific Grant funding to develop a residential mixed crisis service, now known as Highbury Grove. The second project, for women only, became Drayton Park, mental health crisis project for women.

Whilst groups such as MIND and Survivors Speak Out were campaigning for a greater range and choice of mental health services for all service users, there was an added concern about women. This focused on the difficulties women experienced in society that may lead to mental health problems and the further issues that arose when they came into contact with services. These concerns were not new and had been widely discussed previously by women such as Ussher (1991) and Chesler (1972). MIND's *Stress on Women* campaign (1994) made very clear demands for the needs of women who would use mental health services. The report *Purchasing Effective Mental Health Services for women: A framework for Action* clearly stated key areas that had to change, such as 'Acknowledge the hidden causes of women's mental health difficulties' (Williams *et al.*, 1993). This pressure demanded a response from commissioners, providers and politicians.

There was also concern about the over-occupancy of the inpatient wards, and Camden and Islington Community Health Services Trust was looking to develop new ways of responding to the increasing demands on acute services.

The Trust coordinated a planning group to develop a business case for a new service. Rabbi Julia Neuberger, former chair of the Trust and a keen advocate of women's services and different models of mental health care, was a key part of this initial plan. Other stakeholders within the organisation including senior nurse managers, psychiatrists and psychologists and in the local area, service user groups, the Community Health Council and voluntary sector groups, were supportive of the notion of a women-only service. A bid was presented to the London Implementation Group and the Trust was successful in attracting funding for three years. The project now has permanent funding from the Mental Health Challenge Fund.

As the crisis project development worker for the Islington project I was then required to develop these ideas into services.

The foundations of the service were already in place from the user consultation document and from the view of key players within Camden and Islington. However, it was important to consult with those who were already offering crisis services, successfully or otherwise, and to consult with other women-only services. A number of visits took place over the first six months of the development to places such as the Wokingham MIND User Led Crisis House, and liaison occurred with others such as the Barnet Crisis Intervention Service. They gave insights into what is possible with alternative ways of thinking and working and how, with creative interventions, people do manage in less restrictive environments.

It was also important to learn from other women's services such as domestic violence units to gain some insight and appreciate some of the challenges a women-only environment may hold. One aspect of this was that women have high expectations of each other, and in a women-only environment they expect and demand more of what they want. The project staff have felt these demands from women users. Support and supervision structures need to be firmly in place to manage the intensity of feelings that are transferred from the women onto the team.

A vital aspect of the planning was that of consulting the local community, holding open forums in local community centres. Camden and Islington are heavily populated inner-city areas, rich in diversity in terms of ethnicity, sexual orientation and class. For these services to respond to the needs of the local people respectfully and with flexibility, the different voices of the community needed to be accommodated. Both crisis services organised management advisory groups with representation from the Trust, social services, voluntary providers such as MIND and local users groups. Both groups aimed to reflect the diversity in the area in terms of ethnicity.

Members of the groups recognised that developing new ways of working might be experienced as threatening to other service providers and could attract hostility, both in the development stages and once operational. It was vital to recognise and appreciate the existing services, such as the local acute units, which struggled to provide the best, within the constraints of negative environments. It was accepted however that, at some level, conflict is part of the creation of something new and has to be managed. At all times the energy and passion that was offered to the project by those involved sustained it through initial difficulties.

The issue of the service being for women only attracted some hostility. Often conversations would lead to the phrase 'what about men?' This had to be responded to sensitively, recognising services need to improve and develop for all. However, it was important to be confident about the reasons why women's issues continue to be a priority to any health service provider. There is overwhelming evidence highlighting the risks and danger to women in mixed mental health settings. Goodman *et al.* (1997) suggest that a majority of women with serious mental illness have experienced violent victimisation in their lives. Evidence such as this underpins the service provided at Drayton Park and the countless stories told by the women users serve only to reinforce the evidence.

Service model

The service offers women a safe and contained residential environment, which is an alternative to hospital, for a time-limited period in which they can work through a crisis. The policies and procedures for the service were formed by a number of women who had experience of using or working in mental health services. The model of service is based on a systemic model (Burnham, 1986). This is evident within the policies, assessment tool and the language used by the team to understand the presenting crisis. It is also a model that looks for change and difference and works on opportunities for movement. It offers a flexible and energising way for the staff team to work with the women in crisis. Most importantly it pays attention to language. Sta. are mindful of the power of their position and use respectful communication, listening to how the individual describes her experience.

From the moment a woman has contact with the service it aims to respect and value her opinion and knowledge about herself. This is reflected in each stage of the process and in the relationship built with the staff and the project.

Referral

A referral can be made by anyone at any time and all duty staff are able to take the initial referral details. The focus is very much on the current crisis, what interventions have been tried already to manage and where possible clarifying that the experience of crisis would warrant the level of intervention offered by DP, i.e. alternative to hospital admission. If this is clarified an assessment is offered. Data collected shows that 78 per cent of referrals were seen within 48 hrs. Women referred are often contained (for a short time) by the very offer of an assessment; in this way an offer is part of the intervention process. This piece of work in itself would be valuable to evaluate in terms of understanding what helps in crisis. The value of a containing response does not have to mean immediate face-to-face intervention.

Women attend the project for an assessment meeting with the staff and a further exploration takes place of what the crisis is about, who is involved and what needs to happen to assist in the resolution. Staff aim for this to be a respectful sharing of information and recognise the need for some to tell their story and be heard. Women often come with stories of domestic violence, and current or past sexual and physical abuse. Anecdotal reports suggest this is not something they have felt able to voice in other environments. The issues are often linked to relationships or social problems which have affected their mental state to such a degree that they are no longer able to manage. Using diagnostic criteria for 100 admissions showed 53 with depression, 16 with schizophrenia, 15 with bipolar affective disorder, 8 with personality disorders, 3 with schizoaffective disorders, 2 with drug-induced psychosis and 3 with acute situational crisis. A high proportion use drugs and alcohol, compounding their feelings of inability to cope and low self-esteem.

At assessment a reflective discussion is held concerning whether admission to the project is appropriate. If so, the next available place is offered or the woman is placed on a waiting list. They will be offered a second appointment to contain whilst awaiting a place and to reassess the situation if the wait is longer than four days. However, if a place is not offered staff aim to frame this response constructively and assist the women in finding other resources.

A residential stay

Women are initially offered a week's placement. The therapeutic relationships between the staff and the women are built around the 'Agreement Plan'. It documents the expectations of staff and residents, detailing who is carrying out which tasks. The work for the team is focused on networking with community workers or making referrals if those relationships are not already established.

Apart from the above individual plan and the liaison work, the women will have daily one-to-one sessions as a minimum, an opportunity to attend groups and have access to a visiting GP. A keystone to the project is the house meeting. All residents and staff meet on a daily basis for half an hour. Residents are asked what their plans are for the day, reminding them they are responsible for their lives, even though the plan may be to stay in all day and meet with staff. It is also an opportunity to explore any tensions that are building up toward the staff or conflicts between residents. The aim is to make these issues a shared responsibility and that all have a vested interest in their resolution. The meeting succeeds in its aim to provide a regular forum for communication within the house. It is vital to create and maintain a therapeutic environment in a residential crisis setting. However, going outside the project is encouraged as much as possible to maintain confidence and connection with home and the rest of the community. Women are supported in keeping contact with community professionals throughout the stay as joint working is recognised as essential.

Support groups facilitated by staff occur twice a week. These groups are open to former residents for six weeks after leaving. This recognises that although the stay is very short, leaving can be experienced as a difficult time.

Thought and planning needs to go into this process in order to prevent a further crisis occurring at the end of a stay, or shortly afterwards. The groups give staff and current residents an experience of seeing those who have recently left surviving and regaining confidence. This proves very useful when staff and residents become overwhelmed by the panic and anxiety created around leaving.

Medical cover

A local General Practice has been contracted to work with the project by the Trust. The practice offers 24-hour cover as well as three dedicated sessions. These sessions are very well used. Most of the women who use the service are already on medication for treatment or containment of their symptoms. The role of the GP within the project is to alter dosages and ensure safe dosages are being taken, to provide repeat prescriptions and to try new medication. Any major change in medication is done where possible in consultation with the women's sector consultant psychiatrist. This provides continuity and involvement throughout the stay at the project. It is important to say that central to the decision-making is the resident and her worker within the project. The GP will also attend to physical complaints that women may have neglected due to their mental state. If staff have immediate concerns that they assess would benefit from a psychiatric opinion, they will liaise with duty psychiatrists at the local Accident and Emergency Department. Women will then be seen there and decisions made about return to the project or admission to hospital. This is usually due to issues of safety for the individual woman in terms of risk to herself or a need for higher doses of medication which require a more medical environment.

The staff team

The staff team members were employed based on their skills, experiences and attitude. The team is not required to come from a particular professional background; this allows for diversity and a variety of options and views to be offered to the service user. Senior staff have responsibility for assessments and coordinate the house in the absence of the manager. As mentioned above the senior staff are constantly assessing the safety of the household and ensuring women are continuing to feel secure within the project. It is their responsibility to negotiate admission to hospital if the containment the project offers is no longer sufficient. This occurs approximately once a month and women are offered the option of returning at a later date. The staff team have worked in areas such as social work, homelessness, voluntary mental health work and nursing. Many staff have experience of working in the voluntary sector and bring this different attitude into the health service setting. It is essential in a project such as this that all staff have training and supervision to enhance their skills and manage the stress created by the work.

Staff have individual supervision and access to an externally supervised group on a monthly basis. Issues of conflict are constantly created in-house which are projected onto the team. In order for a team to survive, supervision and training regarding the management of conflict and anger is vital.

Diversity

The project aim is to have a multicultural team reflecting the Black and Ethnic Minority community the project serves. This undoubtedly allows a more responsive service to the women. For many women the issue of racism and discrimination has played a part in the crisis and contributed to ongoing psychological issues. This complex issue is more safely explored within a multicultural context.

For some cultures, staying in a mixed mental health setting would be totally unacceptable. Drayton Park therefore becomes a more viable option for some members of ethnic minority communities. This is an important and undervalued factor in the experience of receiving mental health services.

Complementary therapy

Other sessional workers provide massage, art and T'ai Chi. The aim of these groups is to introduce other ways of relieving stress, relaxing and feeling and expressing emotion. Women report that these groups have greatly contributed to the overall benefit of staying at the project. Massage has reintroduced touch in a safe way to many women for whom touch has become synonymous with abuse or violence.

Environment

The environment contributes greatly to the feeling of containment and relaxation women experience. The service is located in a beautiful large Victorian house. It was renovated sensitively in order to create a space that was conducive to well-being. It offers individual bedrooms with bathrooms en suite. All the communal rooms are large and decorated with pictures and images which aim to ensure that women from diverse backgrounds feel comfortable and welcome. It seems clear from the experience at Drayton Park that offering a respectful environment inspires those using it to treat it well and share the responsibility of its maintenance. Meals are freshly prepared and attention is paid to presentation, offering a range of food. The project aims for eating to be a nurturing experience and recognises that food has had different meanings for women. Women can participate in cooking or other chores but are not encouraged to do so as this may increase the likelihood of attachment to the project. The project walks a fine line of creating a therapeutic atmosphere but not setting up a therapeutic community.

Children

Another challenge for the project was to accommodate children with their mothers if this was a safe and desired option. This has made an enormous difference to the experience of receiving help for many women. Often the guilt over and fear of what will happen to their children results in women delaying the request for intervention until it is too late, a crisis occurs with damaging results for all concerned. Accommodating children demands careful planning as the needs of all parties have to be considered. For women who have lost their children, it can raise painful issues. The safety of the child has to be considered, acknowledging women can be a danger to children. It may also be that the woman is not able to parent her child for a short time and the children need to be cared for elsewhere. The aim again is for the project to recognise the specific needs of women and respect their ability to parent their child despite having mental health problems. For the child this is often a less traumatic experience seeing their mother seeking help rather than seeing her in an acute psychiatric unit. If children cannot stay, visiting the project is made relaxed and child-friendly. The evaluation project mentioned later hopes to explore this aspect of the service further.

The future

The project has succeeded in attracting funds to begin the evaluation project. It is overdue as the project needs to demonstrate what difference, if any, it is making to the lives of the women who use it. The evaluation has been developed sensitively and will be carried out in a style that matches the philosophy of the project. It will have an interest in quantitative data but the major focus is on the qualitative experience and effect the project has had on the lives of those who have used it. At the outset the project aimed to demonstrate an ability to reduce the pressure on inpatient beds. This proved almost impossible to show as the service works alongside four different inpatient sites, all with over-occupancy issues. However 85 per cent of service users had used inpatient services with 49 per cent more than twice. This indicates that the population using the service is similar to those occupying hospital places. The evaluation will expand on this information to clarify whether the service is offering a true alternative to those it was designed to serve.

There are further changes coming within mental health, such as the development of 24-hour crisis response teams. Within Camden and Islington the first crisis team was started in May 1999 and was to have an impact on Drayton Park. The project responded to the new service by renegotiating its operational systems whilst maintaining its own style and philosophy. It may mean the project can cope with women with higher risk behaviour as it has the support of the crisis team.

An important factor to consider, and one that will always be present in any service, is concerned with maintaining a very high standard of care, responding to the expectations of the women who use the service. The service is now more confident about its own existence and the right to be different within a health service setting but this needs to be robust and well supported as the project continues to be challenged by the dominant discourse of conventional services.

For any new service, well-established support systems are needed to withstand the difficulties it will face. As an alternative women-only service, Drayton Park is winning a battle to be heard and recognised nationally and within its own community. It was given an award by the Sainsbury Centre in 1996 for imaginative solutions to out-of-hours care, and continues to welcome visitors from this country and abroad to come and learn from its unique style and approach. In 1999 it became a beacon service centre of excellence to formalise and develop its training and development programme.

MANAGING SEXUAL ASSAULTS ON PSYCHIATRIC WARDS

Kay Beaumont

Introduction

The Bethlem and Maudsley Hospitals were the first hospitals to agree a policy for dealing with sexual assaults in psychiatric hospitals in 1994 (updated in 1999). I shall describe the process of writing the policy, which was a learning process for those involved and a challenge to hospital culture. However, while policies to protect people who are mentally ill in hospital and often at their most vulnerable are necessary, they do not stand alone and need to link into other aspects of care. Safety on the wards will also be influenced by effective inter-agency working, ward management, agreed principles of good practice, effective policy monitoring and staff attitudes towards users.

The production of a sexual assault policy

The process of writing the Maudsley and Bethlem (now the South London and Maudsley NHS Trust) sexual assault policy (1999) and getting it agreed was very arduous, because women's issues are rarely high on any agenda. A small group of vigilant and determined users and mental health care professionals fought to get these issues addressed initially and then to get the policy accepted and implemented.

As long ago as 1989 the Southwark Women and Mental Health Forum was set up. It was made up of users and professionals committed to 'raising the debate on good practice in mental health services for women, campaigning for more consumer involvement and appropriate services for women'. Users, social workers and nurses spoke about the extent of sexual assault and harassment in psychiatric hospitals, and set about trying to change the culture that allowed this to happen. In February 1990 the Forum raised this in a letter to all members of the then Regional Health Authority. It was a serious attempt to set up a constructive dialogue with services to increase the safety of women in hospital.

The response was mixed, ranging from support to an angry letter from one senior manager, who said the Forum was 'making extremely serious allegations without providing any evidence to substantiate them'. The fact that it was difficult to produce evidence in the absence of a formal reporting system was ignored.

The response of the Bethlem and Maudsley hospitals was to set up a working party of users, social workers and nurses to write a policy, of which I was a member. During the writing of the policy, advice was sought from other mental health staff, police, lawyers and the voluntary sector. However, many entrenched ideas had to be addressed as follows:

- Sexual assaults do not take place in hospitals
- Mentally ill women make up stories about sexual assaults
- Allegations are solely a symptom of mental illness
- Admission that an assault had taken place would reflect badly on a ward.

Early on in the writing of the policy, the working party agreed that the police should be notified following an allegation. There was a reluctance to involve any outside agency, especially the police, because hospital staff wanted to be able to carry out their own investigations. However, the working party was of the view that the hospitals should not police themselves. Hospitals have a duty of care towards their patients and therefore a responsibility to report allegations of sexual assault. It was also our view that abuse and exploitation is less likely to occur in an organisation with a culture of openness. Rather than reflecting badly on staff, the reporting of an allegation suggests that staff are taking user safety seriously.

There were other important reasons for police involvement. Early reporting means more chance of obtaining forensic evidence. If a crime has been committed, action has to be taken to prevent further criminal offences, protect the victim or any future victims. Hospital staff are not police officers and may need to consult with the police to find out if a crime has been committed.

A concern of hospital staff was that by informing the police the victim would be forced into cooperating fully with a criminal investigation against her wishes. However, it was clear from police procedures that while the hospital policy states that an incident should be reported, it is the victim's right to decide whether to be interviewed by the police and continue with the investigation. This goes to the heart of the philosophy underpinning the policy, which recognises that a hospital has a duty of care towards a patient, yet must also work with a patient who is the victim of an assault in a way that ensures she feels in control of the situation.

Writing the policy was difficult, but getting it accepted and implemented was at times disheartening. It seemed as if the hospitals hoped the working party would be satisfied to remain a permanent working party! We began to feel increasingly marginalised. However, with support from people outside the hospital including members of parliament, the Community Health Council and the health authority, along with a growing awareness within the hospital, the policy was eventually accepted in 1994.

Other components of ward safety

While the policy and the training that accompanied its implementation is important, it is only part of a process leading towards a safer ward environment.

Inter-agency working

The police have a statutory role in terms of Section 136 of the Mental Health Act. They are increasingly involved in community mental health assessments and ever since the publication of the Clunis Report (Ritchie, 1994) specific police officers have been designated mental health liaison officers. They are therefore very much part of the mental health system, even though their training is usually quite limited. Most hospitals now have police liaison committees where Section 136 policies can be agreed and operational matters discussed. These meetings provide an opportunity to address any interagency problems and also to improve practice. The Maudsley police liaison committee has representatives from health, social services, the voluntary sector, police and users.

The meetings are an effective way of setting up inter-agency training programmes. Generally, police officers want to increase their knowledge about mental illness. However, an equally important training area concerns an understanding of different agency roles and the limitation of those roles. The following are some misunderstandings:

1 *Police can enter the ward and search patients at the request of staff* – The police are bound by the Police and Criminal Evidence Act 1984 and can search patients, who are in a hospital which is a private establishment, in only very specific circumstances without a warrant.

2 *Police can restrain a person in order to enable staff to medicate them* – The police would not be able to restrain a person in such circumstances.

3 *Relatives can consent on behalf of a detained patient* – Police officers sometimes believe that a relative or staff member can act on behalf of a person who appears to lack capacity, either temporarily because of mental illness, or permanently because of old age or a learning disability. However, currently this country does not have a legal process that will enable any other person to consent on behalf of someone who lacks capacity.

4 *Police will always prosecute if an offence has been committed* – This is not the case. The police will want to proceed only if the victim is able or prepared to cooperate with an investigation.

5 *Detained patients cannot report a criminal offence to the police* – Users asked for this to be clarified at the Maudsley police liaison committee. It appears that some users were of the view that because they were detained under the Mental Health Act 1983 in hospital they could not speak to the police or report a criminal offence.

6 *Psychiatric patients are unreliable witnesses* – The police and the Crown Prosecution Service are often reluctant to proceed with a prosecution if the victim is considered 'unreliable'. Women with a mental illness frequently fall into this category, denying them access to the criminal justice system. Through training aimed at greater understanding of the nature of mental illness these attitudes can be challenged.

When a sexual assault allegation is reported it is vital that police and mental health staff cooperate. The policy describes the process that needs to be followed, for example ensuring the victim is safe and separated from the suspect and that an Appropriate Adult (Police and Criminal Evidence Act 1984) is obtained for both victim and suspect if the suspect is also a patient. However, there are important practical matters that are sometimes overlooked:

• When the police are called to the ward a member of staff must act as a coordinating person and provide relevant information to the police.
• If there have been difficulties, a meeting to address the problems should be set up as soon as possible after the incident.

Working with users

Policies and procedures should not be set up without the involvement of users. Prevention is also important. Users need to be informed as to what is and what is not acceptable behaviour on the wards. However, I am not aware of any specific information available for users concerning inappropriate sexual behaviour. I am also not aware of information on the wards which describes what will happen if an incident occurs. Information and a dialogue with users demonstrates a transparent, open approach which will be an important way of empowering users and enabling them to feel confident in reporting incidents. A more open approach will also be a preventive measure.

Another important initiative is inviting the police to the wards to give talks about crime prevention. It provides a health and criminal justice link but, perhaps most importantly, it will also encourage mentally ill women to believe that they have as much right to protection through the law as anyone else.

Conclusion

The messages for the planners and providers of mental health care is that sexual assaults do happen, and that it is the duty of hospitals to acknowledge that if assaults occur they are dealt with in an appropriate way. Users need to have more information about policies and appropriate behaviour on the wards as part of a preventive strategy. Policies should be monitored and reviewed and statistics kept of incidents. All agencies, including health, social services, police and the voluntary sector should be encouraged to work together. No one agency has all the knowledge about this area of work, but by working together understanding and knowledge will be improved. This is a difficult area and getting an inter-agency consensus is not always easy. However, the overriding principles are for those involved to respect each other, continue the dialogue and ensure that the needs of the patient are at the centre of the debate.

References

Bennedsen, B.E., Mortensen, P.B., Olesen, A.V. *et al.* (1999) Preterm birth and intra-uterine growth retardation among children of women with schizophrenia. *British Journal of Psychiatry* 175: 239–45.

Brockington, I. (1996) *Motherhood and Mental Health*. Oxford: Oxford Medical Publications.

Burnham, J.B. (1986) *Family Therapy: First Steps towards a Systemic Approach*. London: Tavistock Publications.

Burt V.K. and Hendrick, V.C. (1997) *Women's Mental Health*. Washington, DC: American Psychiatric Press.

Canuso, C.M., Goldstein J.M. and Green, A.I. (1998) The evaluation of women with schizophrenia. *Psychopharmacology Bulletin* 34(3): 271–7.

Camden and Islington Health Action Zone (1999) *Draft Plan*.

Chesler, P. (1972) *Women and Madness*. New York: Doubleday.

Department of Health, Women Mental Health: Into the Mainstream (October 2002) Strategic Development of mental Health care for Women. Department of Health, HMSO, London.

Department of Health Mainstreaming Gender and women's Mental Health: Implementation Guidelines (September 2003) Department of Health, HMSO, London.

Department of Health: Women's mental Health Strategy (October 2003) Department of Health, HMSO, London.

Goldberg, D. (ed.) (1997) *London's Mental Health*. London: King's Fund.

Goodman, L.A., Rosenberg, S.D., Mueser, K.T., and Drake, R.E. (1997) Physical and sexual assault history in women with serious mental illness: prevalence, correlates, treatment, and future research directions. *Schizophrenia Bulletin* 23, 685–96.

Hagnell O. (1966) Incidence and duration of episodes of mental illness in a total population, in E.M. Hare and J.K. Wing (eds.), *Psychiatric Epidemiology*. Oxford: Oxford University Press.

Islington MIND (1994) *User Consultation on Crisis Care*, commissioned by London Borough of Islington.

Jensvold M.F., Halbreich, U. and Hamilton, J.A. (1996) Gender sensitive psycho-pharmacology: an overview, in M.F. Jensvold, U. Halbreich and J.A. Hamilton (eds.), *Psychopharmacology and Women*. Washington DC: American Psychiatric Press Inc.

Kohen, D. (1999) Specialised inpatient psychiatric services for women. *Psychiatric Bulletin* 23: 31–3.

Kohen, D. (2000) Psychiatric services for women, in D. Kohen (ed.), *Women and Mental Health*. London: Routledge, pp.218–32.

Kohen D (2001) Psychiatric Services for Women, Advances in Psychiatric Treatment 7:328–334

Meltzer, H., Gill, B., Petticrew, M. and Hinds, K. (1995) *The Prevalence of Psychiatric Morbidity among Adults Living in Private Households*. OPCS (Office of Population Censuses and Surveys) Psychiatric Morbidity in Great Britain, Report 1. London: HMSO.

Sainsbury Centre for Mental Health (1998) *Acute Problems: A Survey of Quality of Care in Acute Psychiatric Wards*. London: Sainsbury Centre for Mental Health.

MIND (1994) *Stress on Women*. London: National MIND.

Office for National Statistics (1997) *Living in Britain: Preliminary Results from the 1996 General Household Survey*. London: Office for National Statistics.

Palazidou, E. (2000) Depression in Women, in D. Kohen (ed.), *Women and Mental Health*. London: Routledge, pp.106–32.

Ritchie (1994) *The Report of the Inquiry into the Care and Treatment of Christopher Clunis*. London: HMSO.

Seeman, M.V. (1986) Current outcome in schizophrenia: women versus men. *Acta Psychiatrica Scandinavia* 73: 609–17.

South London and Maudsley NHS Trust (1999) *Policy for Dealing with Allegations of Sexual Assault, Sexual Abuse and Rape in the South London and Maudsley NHS Trust*.

Ussher, J. (1991) *Women's Madness: Misogyny or Mental Illness*. London: Harvester Wheatsheaf.

Williams, J., Watson, G., Smith, H., Copperman, J., and Wood, D. (1993) *Purchasing Effective Mental Health Services for Women: A Framework for Action*. Canterbury: University of Kent/MIND Publications.

Further interest

Highbury Grove, mixed residential service with a night-time drop in. Contact 020 7288 1051.

5 Treatment of women in forensic settings

Ray Travers

Introduction

Women in secure psychiatric services have multiple and complex needs. However, in the absence of a national strategy and a dearth of local initiatives, two key challenges need to be confronted: first, addressing the barriers to improving psychiatric care for women; and second, removing traditional boundaries to ensure effective, responsive, integrated mental health services. For women who fall into the category of mentally disordered offenders, multiple disadvantage is experienced and this is compounded by reliance on a forensic mental health system which struggles to accommodate for their needs at any level. There has been increasing concern over recent years at the number of mentally disordered women offenders accumulating in the penal system. By their own admission, forensic psychiatrists are failing their women patients – indeed, have done so for decades – and are only just beginning to accept that fundamental changes are vital.

There are significant cultural implications for forensic facilities integrating gender-sensitive perspectives to service planning and delivery and thus adapt in a way that ensures women receive an appropriate response. An obvious one is the need for a shift from the prevailing male-orientated and medico-legal world views towards models which ensure an understanding and ability to meet the needs of women. Whether or not integration is actually possible remains a hotly debated topic. To do so requires professional women to receive appropriate support and supervision as well as equal opportunities. This in turn requires professional men to face potentially painful realities about their power and privilege and the way women are forced to struggle as a result.

GENDER ISSUES

Women are the minority gender in forensic settings which, historically, have been organised in response to the way male mentally disordered offender populations typically present. Though perhaps not immediately obvious, gender influences a number of important factors which require consideration in both the design of services and the delivery of care provision. Broadly speaking these include the following key points:

- The nature of women's criminality is different from that of men; women patients are less likely to have committed serious criminal offences in comparison with men, and this difference is rooted in social influences.
- Admission of women to forensic psychiatric settings is more likely to be determined by enduring behavioural disturbance in other residential environments rather than violent index offences against the person in community settings, as is the case for men.
- Behavioural stability more often determines movement out of the forensic setting for women compared to men by virtue of their typically less serious offending behaviour, amongst other criteria.
- Women present a significantly greater threat of violence to carers than do men. In this context, women staff appear to be most vulnerable.
- Women generally present a lower risk of absconding than do males. This may reflect a greater general level of dependency, in line with socially determined roles whereby autonomy features more highly in the socialisation of males.
- Women present with more extensive histories of trauma. Although mentally disordered offenders of both genders typically present with extensive histories of childhood victimisation, women's experiences are more likely to have continued into adult life. A violent trauma re-enactment as victim or victimiser is a central aspect of women's presentations in forensic settings.
- The psychodynamic interplay between women patients, clinical staff, the ward milieu, the wider hospital and the external world includes the use of primitive defence mechanisms to a much more powerful extent than between male patients and services. A consequence of this is a dysfunctional way of relating, which has coercive potential and diminishes all parties.
- Very serious self-harming behaviour is commonplace and unremitting among women patients; this is not the case for men.
- A wide range of related physical health problems occur in conjunction with mental health problems. The response by the institution to a patient's physical health needs seems less adequate for women than for men.
- Women patients experience a more concentrated and wider range of health and social needs than do men. Different service delivery, staff skills mix, training needs and organisational systems are indicated when compared to those for men within the hospital or prison setting. Therapies require adaptation to suit women.
- Due to the way all women are socialised, mentally disordered women are less likely to have adaptive strategies for managing their anger and rage

when compared with men. Opportunities within forensic settings are also narrow and impoverished, therefore reinforcing maladaptive coping strategies. The nature of traumatic backgrounds predicts that any therapeutic environment must safely contain expressions of this intense anger and rage to enable progress.

- The traditional institutional emphasis on reactive policies and procedures may be contra-indicated for women. For example, incidents of aggression are responded to by staff based on other wards. For women patients this necessarily involves being physically restrained by male staff. Either way, the clear trauma re-enactment here is likely to reinforce aggressive and antisocial behaviour rather than manage the potential for it.

  Further, reactive interventions to violence rely upon demonstrated violence. In forensic settings, the risk of violence is so great that failure to prevent it in the first instance leads to a highly dangerous environment where opportunities for positive work become greatly constricted. Risk assessment research (Aiyegbusi, 1996) shows that nurses in the services for women in Ashworth Hospital can fairly accurately predict physical aggression by patients but cannot prevent it.

- Forensic psychiatric services have a long-term history whereby professional women have an abnormally high casualty rate in terms of experiencing significant health problems, being victims of minor and also very serious assaults and of generally not progressing in career terms as male colleagues seem able to do. Failure to acknowledge that these circumstances are a result of poor service management is felt as abusive.

- Women in forensic settings are a less researched group than are men in the same situation. The absence of integrated clinical and managerial theory in regard to this population serves to increase the vulnerability of both mentally disordered women and staff caring for them. A theoretical framework for working with grossly traumatised women ought to be central to service design and delivery. In its absence, trauma re-enactment is highly predictable.

- From a societal perspective, all women are more likely to be victimised by men than the other way round. This basic forensic fact is important and necessarily influences the culture of forensic settings, which are primarily male-dominated environments. Strangely, it is barely referred to as part of the Home Office and Department of Health *Review of Mental Health and Social Services for Mentally Disordered Offenders* (Reed, 1993) which looked at services for women. This Report stated:

  In male-dominated environments, women's needs, including their more personal female needs, are liable to be overlooked. They are sometimes subjected to sexual harassment and other demeaning behaviour.

The Reed Report concluded that for women to receive equality of treatment they would need services that respond to their own particular needs. This will require different services to those tailored to meet the needs of men. A report by the charitable organisation, Women in Secure Hospitals (WISH), concluded that future strategies should be informed not only by clinical needs assessments of women patients, but also by gender issues, by the social and economic context of women's offending, and by listening to women patients and taking their views into account (Stafford, 1999). Other work has also highlighted problems associated with existing models and alternative models for the delivery of secure psychiatric services to women, in the UK and abroad (Lart *et al.*, 1998).

Clinical presentation

Case example

An 18-year-old woman was admitted as an emergency from prison where she had been remanded for an offence of wounding with intent. She had been assessed by local forensic services who had rejected her on the grounds that she had a personality disorder and did not meet the 'treatability' clause for the legal category of Psychopathic Disorder within the meaning of the 1983 Mental Health Act. She was assessed as not suffering from Mental Illness within the meaning of the Act. High secure services had assessed her and had concluded that she could be helped but did not require their level of security.

Because of her deteriorating mental state on remand, prison medical staff advocated for her transfer to conditions of high security and ultimately the woman was 'directed' by the Home Office into one of England's three High Secure Hospitals. Whilst on remand, Ms A had been sullen and hostile, had neither eaten nor drunk for a dangerous period of time, self-harmed repeatedly and had been very difficult to interview. Prison-based assessments have been brief, little collateral information about Ms A's background had been available and during her final interview she had kicked and spat at the interviewing doctor.

On admission Ms A has pieces of tin secreted under her skin and in her rectum. She makes several serious attempts to kill herself. She complains of hearing a sound like 'an out-of-tune radio'. Ms A presents as impulsively assaultative towards her carers, becomes quickly aroused for no apparent reason and has a very distressing and disruptive influence on the 'ward milieu'. Her diagnosis on admission is Borderline Personality Disorder.

It emerges that Ms A is frightened of vampires and had been blood-letting to stop them gaining access to her blood. Furthermore, she discloses that the blood-letting 'might get some of the evil out of me'. She is frightened of sleeping in case they get into her room at night.

Ms A's care team complete a comprehensive multidisciplinary assessment. The consultant psychiatrist commences her on a therapeutic trial of an antipsychotic licensed for treatment-resistant schizophrenia. The psychology assessment highlights Ms A's impulsivity, suicidality and her tendency to dissociate.

Various assessment reports underline Ms A's horrendous childhood antecedents, school failure, reception into care at an early age, multiple moves within the care system, sexual abuse by a male carer resulting in a termination of pregnancy at age 14, drug abuse, promiscuity bordering on prostitution, and escalating deliberate self-harm from the age of 15. Input from the probation services confirms a history of cautions for public disorder offences, a previous conviction for possession of an offensive weapon and assault.

Medical records indicate that Ms A had been repeatedly admitted for assessment following numerous overdoses and self-harming episodes. Most of her admissions have been informal and she has taken her own discharge. On one occasion she was detained under the Mental Health Act for four weeks, regularly left the ward without permission, returning drunk and behaving in either a hostile or sexualised way towards carers. On one occasion she alleged that she had been sexually assaulted by a male nurse. Following a protracted period of suspension, a hospital management review had concluded that Ms A's allegations could not be upheld.

Ms A's father was serving a life sentence for the murder of a man with whom Ms A's mother had had an affair. Ms A had apparently been found hiding in the kitchen cupboard by neighbours who discovered the body of her father's victim in the kitchen of the family home when she was 6. Over the years Ms A had maintained a tempestuous relationship with her mother and her elder brother. Medical records confirmed that her mother was alcohol-dependent and intermittently suffered from severe depression. Her brother was serving a three-year sentence for aggravated burglary.

During the assessment period the care team are caught up in heated discussions about the nature of Ms A's difficulties, the choice of treatments and the degree of risk she presents to others. The security liaison nurse suggests that the team's dynamics reflect the patient's psychopathology and organises for an independent review of Ms A's case to be undertaken by a consultant psychotherapist. The dynamic formulation confirms Ms A's emotional immaturity and underlines the toxic effects of primitive defence mechanisms such as projection, splitting and projective identification. These findings are integrated with the observations of the clinical nurse specialist in trauma who emphasises the traumatic roots of Ms A's destructiveness.

Ms A's psychiatrist liaises with her solicitor and she is returned to court where she is converted from transferred prisoner status to remanded patient for treatment. Over the next three months the frequency of Ms A's self-harming reduces. She requires consistent encouragement and supervision at meal times to ensure life-sustaining caloric intake. She begins menstruating for the first time in two years, and worries that the vampires now have a new source of blood.

In regular sessions with her primary nurse she details the reasons why she stabbed her 44-year-old boyfriend in their flat after spending the day with him in the pub. She didn't enjoy sex with him but felt that it was something that she had to do to keep him. She says that she can't remember much about what happened at the time of the stabbing. The couple had had an argument about her boyfriend's alleged interest in one of Ms A's friends. It wasn't unusual for them to push each other around. Ms A can remember pulling out the knife that she always carries when her boyfriend had said to her, 'you are just a mother hen'. Ms A is not sure why she stabbed her boyfriend. She is adamant that she loves him and is annoyed that her boyfriend's attempts to visit her whilst in hospital have been denied by the care team.

A variety of assessment tools have confirmed the presence of paranoid, borderline and dependent personality traits. These exist alongside depressive, psychosomatic and anxiety symptoms. During periods of acute disturbance, clinical observations support a hypomanic presentation characterised by hostility, extreme paranoid ideation directed towards carers, illogical thinking and acts of extreme violence directed towards others.

Ms A evokes a great deal of empathy from her carers outside her 'hypomanic' episodes. She comes across as emotionally vulnerable and needy. Her perception that she is being ignored seems to lead to increasing arousal. Usually immediate and exclusive attention to her needs by nursing staff can reduce her arousal and avoid escalation towards violence. Not all staff can succeed in doing this as Ms A has already decided which staff she likes and dislikes. As the ward has twelve other women patients, staff cannot consistently respond in the exclusive way that Ms A demands. Following such incidents Ms A behaves as if they had never happened and apparently has no appreciation of why her care plans have been altered accordingly.

Ms A's care team invite the local forensic services to review her. The local team will not accept that Ms A is suffering from a mental illness though it does acknowledge that there has been an overall improvement in her presentations since admission and commencement on antipsychotic medication. They are not convinced by the care team's arguments that she does not require long-term care in conditions of high security and openly admit that 'they could not cope with her in any case'. At the pre-trial case conference Ms A indicates that she does not wish to be returned to hospital as she believes that she 'would get out quicker' by getting a prison sentence. She cannot understand why her local services have turned her down; when the reasons are explained she becomes acutely distressed, attempts to assault her consultant psychiatrist and has to be secluded.

The care team decide to recommend a hospital disposal, which is accepted by the courts. Ms A returns to the ward tearful, angry and determined to fight the system. She becomes non-compliant with her oral medication, attempts to hang herself in the toilets, assaults the female staff nurse who cuts the ligature, and is again secluded.

Ms A's treatment in conditions of high security has commenced!

Comment

Ms A's case is fictional. She is less disturbed than many women who are admitted to high secure women's services in England. Important themes arising from her case include:

- her complex presentation and the consequent lack of diagnostic clarity;
- the way in which her psychopathology manifests itself within the ward environment;
- the dilemmas inherent in managing the risk to self and others;
- the paucity of resources outside prisons/high secure hospitals to begin to address these needs.

Would Ms A be better off in a prison environment? She certainly feels that she would be. Is it acceptable that forensic services are so configured that Ms A can only choose between prison and a high secure hospital placement? How should one approach her habilitation? Facilitating her empowerment implies ensuring that she is held accountable for her actions. I have no doubts about the necessity of treating Ms A but I remain uncomfortable that her care will be very distressing for her and will undoubtedly include ongoing assaults against those tasked with caring for her, particularly female nursing staff. How should one develop a long-term treatment strategy for her?

Therapeutic interventions

More than half a century ago, a Boston physician, Francis Peabody, counselled that the secret of care of the patient is caring for the patient (Lown, 1996). A clinician thereby gains courage to deal with the pervasive uncertainties for which technical skill alone is inadequate. Patient and clinician then enter into a partnership of equals. As the patient is empowered, the clinician's curing power is enhanced.

Assessment

It is recognised that the tendency to regard women as a distinct group with 'special needs' may have led to insufficient attention being paid to the diversity of this population. However, 'Listening to women' (Humphreys and Eaton, 1996) provided knowledge of common issues for many of the women currently in secure care, including: a background of social and economic deprivation, histories of abuse and impoverished parenting experiences, previous rejection by caring services, the presence of multiple-diagnoses, ambivalence about help, non-compliance with treatment and specific problems such as severe self-harm, eating disorders and complex physical health needs. Offence-related themes usually include arson and violence to others, often to their own children.

As a group, offending women will have general difficulties in social communication, assertiveness, accepting direction, working cooperatively, negotiating, accepting boundaries, controlling impulsive behaviour, establishing self-reliance and accepting responsibility for self. They struggle to find solutions to personal and practical living problems. Often a patient's history will show a lot of rigidity in problem behaviours without enough possibilities for safe and trusting experimentation. They find it very difficult to delineate areas of personal responsibility, from areas of shared group responsibility on the ward and from areas of staff responsibility.

KEY ISSUES

Nature of abuse

The vast majority of women in forensic services have been chronically and repeatedly abused, physically, sexually and/or emotionally. Over time the patient will usually disclose her past experiences or information becomes available from collateral sources. Common findings include early onset, severe sexual abuse, sadistic abuse and torture, gross neglect, familial secrecy, fear caused by repeated threats, high levels of inflicted physical and emotional pain, multiple perpetrators including women, and having experienced or witnessed significant violence as a child or adolescent.

Developmental influences

One explanation for why the women described in this chapter develop grossly dysfunctional 'internalised working models' is the extreme nature of their traumatic antecedents. All human beings need to be protected and provided for in order to develop normal mental health. As a rule these women were perversely protected and perversely provided for (Hardy, 1999).

Many clinicians understand such women as suffering from either a Borderline Personality Disorder, or an antisocial personality disorder. Mealey (1995), who summarises the controversial literature on the subject of sociopathy, describes two categories of sociopaths: those congenitally incapable of experiencing social emotions that give rise to conscience and empathy, whom she terms 'primary' sociopaths; and 'secondary sociopaths' who develop a response to adverse rearing and environmental conditions. The women described in this chapter are drawn mainly from the 'secondary sociopaths' group.

Dissociative processes

Dissociation is the disruption of the normal integration of experience and is a common experience under stressful conditions. In response to severely traumatic events, dissociative symptoms serve an important defensive function. Dissociative experiences often do not remain dormant and the severity and complexity of dissociative symptoms appears generally consistent with the severity of early traumatisation. The available literature on dissociation is extensive and beyond the scope of this chapter.

The women found in forensic settings present complex dissociative syndromes. These are best understood as being on a continuum comprising four components: behaviour, affect, sensations and knowledge; fragmentations occur within each component or between combinations of components. It becomes very confusing when dissociative processes occur within a group of women rather than within an individual. This group dynamic contributes to the well-established and accepted view that working with women in forensic settings is emotionally more challenging than working with a group of men in a similar setting.

Traumatic events are often experienced with an intense sense of *aloneness*. It is only with the support and sense of connection with another person that the events and all those attendant feelings can be tolerated, retained and integrated into memory as past experience, rather than remaining a dissociated psychological time bomb waiting to explode into consciousness. The sense of interpersonal connection is crucial because reliving trauma without appropriate interpersonal support will cause the patient to be overwhelmed again and retraumatised by the experience (Chu, 1998).

Meaning

When compiling the patient's life history from her own self-report and from collateral sources, it is vital to consider links between the woman's antisocial behaviours, especially the index offence and past traumas. When an element of re-enactment of previous traumatic experiences is considered relevant to understanding offending behaviour, then this needs to be integrated into the case formulation. This clinical approach is time-consuming and essentially involves a series of hypotheses being formed and continually refined according to the patient's disclosures, additional information from collateral sources and the patient's behaviour in relationships with her carers and other patients. Given the variety of complex ways that previously dissociated traumatic events can be re-experienced, this process of hypothesis formation is essential if the woman's risk is to inform treatment interventions and long-term management strategies. The care team needs to achieve a sense of coherence about the patients' past and present lives in order that this can ultimately be nurtured in the patients themselves.

Chronic disempowerment syndrome

The assessment process for women in forensic settings is protracted. Notwithstanding any controversy surrounding medical diagnoses, these patients are chronically psychiatrically disabled. The literature refers to the evolution of a single chronic disempowerment syndrome (Pearlman and Saakvitne, 1995) which results in an ingrained sense of self that is defective, helpless and powerless and which both perpetuates the effects of the traumatic antecedents these women have experienced and interferes with their later ability to take control of their lives. Moreover, profound difficulty in negotiating supportive relationships results in chronic isolation for the women and promotes a tendency towards re-enactment and revictimisation. Their negative thoughts and beliefs perpetuate feelings of shame, misery and torment. Rather than being able to engage with others in a mutually empowering fashion, they repeatedly relate to others in ways that recapitulate abusive or exploitative past relationships or flee into dysfunctional isolation. Indeed, these women often cling to their sense of disempowerment as the only reality they have known.

This chronic disempowerment is not always fully acknowledged by the women's care team, particularly the nursing team, by the hospital management and especially by external agencies such as advocacy services, charitable organisations and the Mental Health Act Commissioners. These groups may assume that patients understand empowerment and are inclined to move forward. In reality they do not have such an understanding and react by becoming more resistant, distant, or angry, and the care team, under pressure from external groups or from within itself, becomes overwhelmed, frustrated and blaming.

Case example

Ms A is very unhappy at being back in hospital. She has assumptions about herself as chronically victimised and powerless and is intensely angry. Whereas the care team's inclination might be to embark on treatment which would allow Ms A to gain a greater sense of mastery over her life, through social learning, gaining control over her feelings and impulses and understanding how her life experiences have contributed to her offending, Ms A has other ideas. She assumes that there must be some external locus of control in her life. She feels that the care team has trapped her. Ms A is not able to conceive of developing a sense of mastery over her life.

Patience and the passage of time will be necessary before any sense of shared goals of the treatment plan can be realistically agreed with Ms A. Repeated explanations interspersed with management of behavioural crises will characterise the initial treatment phase. It is difficult to anticipate how long this phase will last. Prior to her court appearance Ms A had begun to engage with staff but, in the absence of alternative placements, this therapeutic opportunity has suffered a setback. The necessary support to help Ms A through her angry period as quickly as possible depends on many factors beyond the control of the care team.

Just as assessment is intermingled with treatment processes, the delivery of treatment interventions in forensic settings is influenced by a host of factors internal and external to the ward milieu. It is unlikely that women's issues are central to the forensic institution's corporate agenda and hence organising and delivering therapeutic services to meet its identified needs will be compromised. In the absence of appropriate less secure provision, developing long-term treatment strategies will be haphazard and, certainly in Ms A's case, concrete plans to move her on will not be possible to establish until much later in her treatment when she is behaviourally settled.

Ms A is unlikely to engage with her carers in a collaborative way; she will probably rely on control and manipulation as ways of meeting her needs. This style is familiar and adaptive for her: because it feels impossible to trust enough to do things *with* others, the only alternative is to do things *to* others. Though Ms A's anticipated future behaviour is understandable, it will often be painful for her caregivers. Her anger will challenge the development of consistent relationships with ward-based staff and with non-ward-based therapists. Ms A is likely to react by feeling victimised whenever she does not receive a response that gratifies her.

Should this pattern become obvious then it will be difficult for staff either to resist avoiding necessary interventions or refrain from retreating from crucial therapeutic stances. The scale of therapeutic challenge is best appreciated when one considers the fact that the ward environment will have approximately twelve Ms As living together. The ingrained responses of those patients who feel repetitively victimised are infectious; this probably explains the phrases used by staff such as 'the ward is bubbling' or 'it is toxic'.

BARRIERS TO DELIVERING EFFECTIVE SERVICES

Political challenges

Until the early 1990s women were overshadowed by the much larger population of detained men. The facts that there have been no intellectual framework for gender differences and no adequate facilities to treat their complex psychopathology (Gorsuch, 1999) probably reflect a chronic flaw in the system of provision which has proven detrimental to many women patients. It is now recognised amongst the majority of clinicians working with women in forensic settings that women, though a minority in secure environments (16–20 per cent), require care that is not masculinised and steeped in the medical model traditions of present psychiatric practice. Great enthusiasm followed the publication of a governmental strategy for action on women's issues which included the areas of poverty, domestic violence and health. Unfortunately, such governmental initiatives have not resulted in clearly articulated policies for women who require forensic psychiatric care.

Policy makers and the therapeutic context

Just as chronically disempowered patients adapt to the culture of the institution's treatment, chronically disempowered policy makers also adapt to the prevailing political culture in similar ways. Policy makers become facile in the language of therapeutic settings, citing 'the need for focused treatment for women', 'the need to reconfigure service provision' and 'the need to promote gender awareness'. Policy makers thus go through the motions of being committed to translating strategy into action and serve only to obscure their underlying agenda of seeking attention from the electorate. To truly make progress in improving services for women, policy makers must learn a new kind of authenticity, acknowledging their sense of helplessness. Without such a shift, forensic services for women will change little.

Endless patience

Staff in women's units in forensic institutions often report a kind of professional trauma re-enactment. They are constantly encouraged to develop strategies and operational plans for reconfiguring and redeveloping services, only to have their aspirations dashed by the inability of senior managers and governmental leaders to implement change. Clinicians working with women in forensic settings require endless patience, not only for treating their patients but also for dealing with policy makers. Lapses by policy makers with regression to old behaviours (de-prioritising women's issues or reinforcing patriarchal views of how women's needs should be met) are best understood as minor violations of the therapeutic contract. These should be tolerated only if there is progress over time towards the agreed goals of service development.

Financial haemorrhage

The development of forensic services for women outside special hospitals has been painfully slow. The development of dedicated women's forensic units has primarily occurred outside the NHS in the 'private sector'. In England by the end of 2002 it was anticipated that there would be approximately 200 'beds' in the private sector offering dedicated medium secure provision for women. At a conservative estimate of £130,000 per year per bed, this implies a future haemorrhage of £26 million per year. In the absence of a dedicated National Strategy for Forensic Services for women, with the delegation of strategic responsibility to regions, and the dearth of local provision, the pressure will be on health authorities to fund placements for women in the private (for profit) sector. The concern for clinicians in existing NHS forensic women's services is that the most challenging patients will be the least attractive to the 'private sector' and will continue to be admitted to constricting, perpetually underfunded NHS provision that will have lost its best staff to the private sector through market forces.

Supportive pathways

As in the therapy of all severely traumatised patients, the essential interpersonal process for chronically disempowered patients such as the women in forensic settings is to help them establish mutual and collaborative relationships. Forensic services for women are themselves chronically disempowered and the essential strategic process is to genuinely assist them in establishing real pathways between different levels of secure care within the NHS, where the private sector has only a minor influence. I would argue that it is crucial for the development of chronically disempowered services that senior managers and politicians understand that corrective emotional experiences (for the women patients and for their carers) involve services being facilitated in learning to care for themselves, in the context of supportive networks with the wider NHS forensic provision, rather than allowing existing services to be taken over by 'for profit' health care systems.

Recent progress

In recent years the dedicated women's services in the three special hospitals in England and Wales and some regional secure psychiatric hospitals have undertaken major reviews of their existing models of service delivery. To varying extents these units have implemented more appropriate systems to meet the needs of the women patients and their carers. A medical model persists but a greater awareness of its limitations is emphasised. A recurring theme has been the ongoing disappointment for clinicians when their enthusiastic and ambitious demands for change have been frustrated. There seems to be an unending series of obstacles which impede integration of gender aspects into provision. Without such gender awareness, the care and treatment of the patients remains more problematic than it might otherwise be.

The emerging models of care include aspects of the following components.

Assessment facilities

The emphasis here is on completion of pre-admission assessments and development of outreach teams to liaise with referring agencies. Much effort has gone into reviewing existing assessment procedures and tools in an effort to standardise an assessment 'package'.

Experience shows patients should not be 'overloaded' following their initial admission for treatment. Applying a battery of assessments has implications for resources on two levels: (a) the availability of clinicians working on the admission ward; and (b) specialised training and development needs for the staff. The advantage of delivering a standardised assessment programme is the provision of a baseline for the evaluation of treatment. This minimises repetition of work by different disciplines and is a way of engaging patients, most of whom actively engage in the assessment process and appreciate the feedback that it allows for.

However, it is important that the use of standardised assessment tools is also supported with more enriched information gathered through self-report semi- and unstructured interviews. These interviews tend to address topics such as experience of anger, rationales for self-injurious behaviour and history of fire-setting.

Treatment facilities

Accurate needs assessment ensures that patients can be moved from the assessment environment to alternative environments that reflect their treatment needs. Ideally, these treatment areas ought to be small, e.g. six-bedded units, so that the environments can more precisely respond to the needs of the patients placed in them. In reality the number of patients in any given ward environment remains unacceptably high. Despite this, hospitals with dedicated forensic services for women have attempted to define core philosophies for different 'therapeutic streams', such as high-dependency areas, areas primarily focused on mental illness or primarily focused on personality disorder, 'quality of life' areas, active psychological treatment areas and 'moving on' pre-discharge areas, so that therapeutic interventions can be more accurately targeted.

Therapeutic objectives

Dedicated forensic services for women must primarily provide a safe environment in which a woman can experiment and try out new behaviours that may be frightening for her but accepted in society. This contrasts with her previous offending and problem behaviours which were frightening or dangerous in society, though possibly acceptable to the woman herself. The aspiration is to provide care, support and treatment appropriate to the woman's developmental abilities. The aim is to shape the woman's maturational processes, so that she can proceed through successive therapeutic environments that maximise the empowerment process whilst allowing her to acknowledge and accept her own responsibility and accountability for both her behaviours and their consequences.

Although extreme levels of disturbance or fragility may preclude psychotherapy, it has been suggested that if much of the behavioural and psychological disturbance is the result of cumulative experiences of trauma, abuse and deprivation, psychotherapy may be crucial in terms of allowing the woman to make some meaningful connection between the past events and her current distress and dysfunction (Bland, Mezey and Dolan, 1999). Helping women to make sense of their 'disorder' as an understandable response and adaptation to intolerable events in the past may help to integrate these experiences, reassure them that they are not 'mad', challenge the pejorative label of personality disorder and restore to their lives some sense of self-respect and self-control.

In their endeavours to defy description and avoid the gender contract, mentally disordered women in secure forensic settings employ mechanisms that could be interpreted by their carers as elusiveness, manipulativeness, deviousness and refusal to engage in treatment plans. These self-defeating modes of behaviour often lead carers to experience feelings of frustration and powerlessness. Similar feelings are engendered in carers by the sparseness of the evidence-base for interventions aimed at addressing such mechanisms. Available treatment interventions fail to appreciate the restricted range of legitimate responses that mentally disordered women actually have. Despite these frustrations, it is possible for carers to experience a sense of achievement when the contradictions of the gender contract are exploited to the benefit of the women patients, or when some of the women patients are empowered to find non-self-destructive solutions to the gender contract for themselves.

Poverty, isolation and lack of self-esteem do not create conditions conducive to the negotiation of the rational, fair and acceptable contract implied by traditional psychotherapy approaches. Visible, concrete boundaries, staged, developmentally appropriate reward schemes, clear procedures promoting consistency in how staff relate to such women, robust policies to minimise care team dysfunction and sophisticated approaches to staff support constitute the 'therapeutic currency'.

Although it has been a slow and painful realisation, it is to the credit of existing dedicated women's forensic services that clinical, managerial, training and developmental approaches have been adapted so that these dynamics can be positively confronted.

References

Aiyegbusi, A. (1996) Chapter 8, in N. Jeffcote and T. Watson (eds.). *Working Therapeutically with Women in Secure Mental Health Settings*. London: Jessica Kingsley.

Bland, J., Mezey, G. and Dolan, B. (1999) Special women, special needs: a descriptive study of female special hospital patients. *The Journal of Forensic Psychiatry* 10(1): 34–45.

Chu, K.A. (1998) *Rebuilding Shattered Lives: The Responsible Treatment of Complex Post-Traumatic and Dissociative Disorders*. New York: John Wiley and Sons.

Department of Health/ Home Office (1994) *Report of the Finance Advisory Group*. London: DoH/Home Office (Reed Report).

Gorsuch, N. (1999) Disturbed female offenders: helping the 'untreatable'. *The Journal of Forensic Psychiatry* 10(1): 98–118.

Hardy, S.B. (1999) *Mother Nature: Natural Selection and the Female of the Species*. London: Chatto and Windus.

Humphreys, J. and Eaton, M. (1996) *Listening to Women in Special Hospitals*. Twickenham: St Mary's University College.

Lart, R., Payne, S., Beaumont, B., *et al.* (1998) Women and secure psychiatric services: Literature Review. *Report to the NHS Centre for Reviews and Dissemination*. Bristol University School for Policy Studies.

Lown, B. (1996) *The Lost Art of Healing*. New York: Valentine Books.

Mealey, L. (1995) The sociobiology of sociopathy: an integrated evolutionary model. *Behavioral and Brain Sciences* 18: 523–99.

Pearlman, L.A. and Saakvitne, K.W. (1995) *Trauma and the Therapist: Counter-Transference and Vicarious Traumatisation in Psychotherapy with Incest Survivors*. New York: W.W. Norton and Co.

Reed Report (1993) *Review of Mental Health and Social Services for Mentally Disordered Offenders and Others Requiring Similar Services*, Vol. 5: *Special Issues and Differing Needs*. London: HMSO.

Stafford, P. (1999) *Defining Gender Issues: Redefining Women's Services*. London: WISH.

Useful address

Women in Secure Hospitals (WISH)

Address: 15 Great St Thomas Apostle, London, EC4V 2BJ

Phone: 0207 329 2415

Fax: 0207 329 2416

Description: support service for women detained in secure psychiatric hospitals, both NHS and private. Provide information and advice on all issues concerning women's detention, access to advocacy services, visits by arrangements, etc.

Special interest activities: campaign for changes in mental health law on women's issues, can provide resource materials, etc.

Opening hours: phone during office hours

Referral: self or any other source

Criteria/catchment: women held in secure hospitals

Part III

Treatment of particular groups

6 Motherhood and mental illness

Trudi Seneviratne and Sue Conroy

Introduction

Pregnancy and childbirth have an enormous combined psychological and physiological effect on a woman's life. Historically, physicians have postulated a link between childbirth and mental illness, since BC 5, when Hippocrates hypothesised that puerperal psychosis was a result of milk diverted from breast to brain. In the nineteenth century, the French psychiatrists Marce and Esquirol documented a series of clinical observations of women during this period (Cox, 1993). More recently, studies have shown that childbearing is associated with a marked increase in the incidence and prevalence of psychiatric disorder but exact causal mechanisms (such as hormonal changes) remain unclear. Postnatal depression is extremely common, being consistently found in 10–15 per cent of mothers (O'Hara and Swain, 1996). Postpartum affective or schizoaffective psychosis is less common, afflicting about two in every thousand deliveries, usually requiring hospitalisation. In addition, passing through obstetric services there will also be about 2 per cent of pregnant women who have chronic mental health problems (Kumar and O'Dowd, 2000).

This chapter will first, explore how childbirth contributes to the onset of these psychiatric disorders and secondly, the extent to which childbirth affects women with a history of a chronic mental illness. Such disorders highlight the need for specialist perinatal psychiatric services, which deploy a multidisciplinary team and individualised treatment plans, as described in the final section of this chapter.

POSTPARTUM PSYCHIATRIC ILLNESS

Psychiatric disorders associated with childbirth are traditionally divided into three categories, reflecting severity: postpartum blues, postpartum depression and postpartum psychosis. 'Maternity blues' is not a disorder, but is included to distinguish it from the more important and clinically significant disorders of postnatal depression and postpartum psychosis. Current classification systems, such as DSM – IV (APA, 1994) and ICD 10 (WHO, 1993) contain no clear definitions of the disorders (such as onset post-delivery) which reflect the overall lack of consensus on whether they are etiologically related to childbirth.

The 'maternity blues' (minor transitory mood disturbance)

The 'blues' is considered to be a normal phenomenon in terms of both its mildness and transience. It is very common with a prevalence of 50 per cent to 75 per cent of women experiencing a dysphoric reaction in the first week following delivery. As women in the immediate postpartum period may experience mild 'highs' as well as depressive episodes (Glover *et al.*, 1994; Hannah *et al.*, 1993), the term is somewhat deceptive and 'minor transitory mood disturbance' is therefore preferable. The cause of the 'blues' remains unknown; literature has been inconsistent on associated aetiological factors such as hormonal changes. O'Hara *et al.* (1991) for example, found an association between a greater fall in pre- to postnatal oestriol concentration and the blues but no such association with oestradiol or progesterone. Harris *et al.* (1994) found a similar link in the fall in progesterone concentration; another study suggested an association between high blues scores and concurrent cortisol concentrations (Okano and Nomura, 1992).

The condition may cause considerable distress to the mother and relatives, but usually does not require any specific treatment other than reassurance and explanation. It is important, however, that if the clinical symptoms (episodes of crying, irritability, depression, emotional lability) are extreme or prolonged, they be differentiated from the prodromal features of a puerperal psychosis, which often commences in the same time period. Similarly, if the symptoms persist for over two weeks, then a diagnosis of depression should be considered.

POSTNATAL DEPRESSION (NON-PSYCHOTIC DEPRESSIVE DISORDERS)

Depression following childbirth is not only the most common, but also one of the most important conditions affecting a mother and infant during this period. Recent studies have demonstrated adverse effects of postnatal depression on: the mother–infant relationship (Martins and Gaffan, 2000) and children's (particularly boys) later cognitive and social development, attachments and emotional regulation (Murray and Cooper, 1996; Sharpe *et al.*, 1995; Essex *et al.*, 2001), which may persist till the age of 11 (Hay *et al.*, 2001). These effects highlight the need for early detection and effective interventions. A prevalence of 10 per cent was placed by Pitt's (1968) study, which was the first to describe the onset of depression occurring in the first six weeks following delivery, in women who were not depressed antenatally. A recent meta-analysis of nearly sixty studies (O'Hara and Swain, 1996) placed the prevalence at 13 per cent.

The concept of postnatal depression as a specific clinical entity, however, has been challenged. Cox, Connor and Kendell (1982), for example, said that there were no pathognomonic symptoms in postnatal depression, but subsequently showed that the relative risk of depression is about three times greater in childbearing women in comparison to approximately matched controls, but only in the first month postpartum (Cox *et al.*, 1993). Whilst some studies have reported that the rates of depression in childbearing women were not greater than the rates in non-childbearing control women or in the general population (Cooper *et al.*, 1988; O'Hara *et al.*, 1990), others have reported that a history of depressive illness heightens the risk of postnatal depression (O'Hara and Zekoski, 1988; Marks *et al.*, 1992). Thus the question of whether there are depressions specific to the postnatal period remains to be clarified.

Aetiology occur in two main areas: psychosocial factors and biological, more specifically neuroendocrine (Kumar and O'Dowd, 2000). A further question is whether there are aetiological differences between earlier (first month) versus later onset depressions and therefore their treatment options. There have been suggestions that earlier onset depression may in part have an endocrine cause. Childbirth is a time of massive endocrine changes in circulating concentrations of the sex steroids, thus the hypothalamic pituitary axis must adjust to the sudden loss of the placenta and re-establish its regulatory functions in relation to ovarian activity as well as starting lactation (Wieck *et al.*, 1996). Claims that the disorder was a result of progesterone insufficiency (Dalton, 1980) were undermined by subsequent studies (Harris *et al.*, 1994). There has been some evidence that oestrogen has mood-elevating properties. For example, in one study it was superior to placebo in treating postnatal depression (Henderson *et al.*, 1991) and another (Gregoire *et al.*, 1996) showed its antidepressant efficacy in childbearing women. There has also been some evidence that it has mood-elevating properties in the menopause (Sherwin, 1994). The mechanism of action and the role of oestrogen in postnatal depression, however, remain unclear.

Other biological investigations (which have also been inconsistent) have looked at the role of thyroid hormone dysfunction. For example, Harris (1992) described an overall increase in depressive symptoms in thyroid antibody-positive women followed for up to eight months postpartum. Finally, there are data that implicate cortisol dysregulation (Checkley, 1992).

Depressions that occur later may have an aetiological profile resembling depression that occurs at other times (Brown and Harris 1978; Paykel *et al.*, 1980), i.e. a combination of social adversity, life stress and vulnerability factors. Postnatal depression is linked with early stressful life experiences in the mother's own childhood, lack of supportive current relationships, marital difficulties and other life events. Sociological studies suggest first-time mothers in particular may become exhausted and demoralised in the first few weeks after birth (Boulton, 1983). Further, a significant minority do not find caring for children naturally rewarding and many report high levels of stress, for example due to conflicts between childcare, housework and employment (ibid.). These views are expressed by both depressed and non-depressed women (Romito, 1993). Thus, neither the experience of motherhood nor the symptoms of depression are qualitatively different from other women's experience of motherhood or depression respectively. Later occurring post-natal depression should not therefore be taken out of the context of either women's social experience or what is already known about depression in women.

Such distinctions allow the possibility that treatments may be tailored to each mother depending on causal mechanisms. For example, early-onset depression may respond better to certain therapeutic interventions than to others, e.g. hormones (Henderson *et al.*, 1991; Harris *et al.*, 1994; Gregoire *et al.*, 1996) versus psychological treatments (Holden *et al.*, 1989).

Diagnosis and management of postnatal depression occurs mainly in primary care, with the midwife, health visitor and GP in an ideal position to assess and diagnose, but up to 50 per cent of cases may be undetected (Sharpe, 1992). Only small percentages (2–3 per cent) of severe or treatment-resistant cases are referred to psychiatrists. The clinical picture is similar to other types of depression, but there are some features that should alert to the possibility of a depression. The woman may experience difficulty with practical parenting, such as handling or feeding, feel guilty that she is not coping, or express excessive concern about the baby's health. Despite the increases in psychiatric morbidity in the puerperium, the suicide rate in the first year postpartum is one-sixth that of an age- and sex-matched non-pregnant population (Appleby, 1991).

Treatment options retain a similar framework to other times. Reassurance and supportive counselling is usually all that is required and may be provided by a trained non-medical member of staff (Holden *et al.*, 1989). Self-help and support groups encourage mutual support and advice concerning mothering and childcare, as well as more specific issues related to depression. If the depression is due to social circumstances, such as marital or housing difficulties, then these should be tackled. Antidepressant medication may be indicated, and the criteria for prescribing are the same as for non-puerperal depression. Adequate doses should be used, and treatment continued for the appropriate length of time. Breastfeeding may usually be continued (Buist *et al.*, 1990; Yoshida *et al.*, 1999) with caution and whilst monitoring the baby. For severe, psychotic depression, neuroleptics or electroconvulsive therapy (ECT) may be indicated (Reed *et al.*, 1999).

POSTPARTUM PSYCHOSIS

There is much evidence to suggest that childbirth precipitates a bipolar affective or schizoaffective psychosis. Epidemiological studies (Kendell *et al.*, 1987; Paffenbarger 1964) have shown that there is a greatly increased risk of admission to psychiatric hospital in the first few months after delivery. For all mothers, the risk is increased seven-fold in the month after delivery. However, when the analysis is restricted to primiparae and to admissions for a psychotic illness, this relative risk rises even further to 35 months (Kendell *et al.*, 1987). This link is strengthened by the observation that the peak time of onset of psychosis is within two weeks of delivery (Brockington *et al.*, 1982) although there is a small but significantly elevated risk of illness for at least two years postpartum (Kendell *et al.*, 1987). Comparisons of rates across cultures and over time (150 years) have shown a remarkable consistency at about 1 per 1,000 births (Kumar, 1994). This figure has remained constant in England and Wales in the last fifty years, even though improvements in medical care have resulted in a reduction in maternal mortality rates by a factor of 35. Thus the mechanism by which childbirth triggers the psychosis does not seem to have been affected by societal changes or advances in medicine, obstetrics and midwifery (Kumar, 1994).

There have been speculations that the mechanism by which childbirth precipitates a psychosis is related to the abrupt fall in levels of sex steroids following labour but studies remain inconclusive. One suggestion is that dopaminergic functioning is effected by postpartum oestrogen withdrawal (Cookson, 1985; Wieck, 1996). This led some workers to examine the utility of both oestrogen and progesterone in the prevention of the condition (Wieck, 1996). One study (Hamilton and Sichel, 1992) reported no case of relapse in a series of 50 women described as being at high risk, who were administered a combination of oestrone and conjugated oestrogens for 14 days post-delivery. Administration of sex steroids is not part of routine clinical practice but clearly merits further investigation.

Symptoms may vary, but there is typically an initial 'lucid interval' lasting a few days following delivery and the prodromal features of the illness may coincide with the onset of the 'blues'. As mothers are now discharged early from maternity wards, initial symptoms may be observed by family members who notice sleeping difficulty, confusion and odd behaviour. 'Patchy perplexity' is common and the clinical picture may be that of a manic illness, characterised by irritability, overactivity, disinhibition, euphoria and grandiose ideas, which may be delusional, e.g. conviction that she is 'chosen' or that the baby has special powers. Disorders of perceptions may be complex and take the form of visions. An alternative picture is that of an agitated depression, with convictions of hopelessness and uselessness to the baby, sometimes reaching suicidal intensity. The mother may be preoccupied by rigid feeding routines or overwhelmed by minor health problems. Sometimes, the picture is of a labile kind with mixed depressive and manic symptoms. In other cases, there may be delusions of a paranoid nature or ideas of reference, such as special messages or hallucinations.

A mother suffering from a postpartum psychosis will generally require admission to hospital, preferably to a mother and baby unit, where they may be cared for together. However, there are few of these, and she may be admitted to a general psychiatric ward with a provision for the baby and failing that, on her own. A community-based service to manage severe postnatal illness in the home has been described in Nottingham (Oates, 1988). On a mother/baby unit, all contact between the mother and baby is initially constantly supervised by the nursing and nursery nurse staff, and gradually decreased as the mother's mental state improves. Pharmacological treatment is dictated by the clinical picture and conventional treatments including antidepressants, neuroleptics and mood stabilisers such as lithium, carbamezepine or valproate may be used. Some medications will affect breast-feeding (Yoshida *et al.*, 1999). ECT has been reported to be particularly useful in extreme cases, especially if there are symptoms of confusion and perplexity, but is usually reserved until other treatments have failed.

The short- to medium-term prognosis is good with most patients responding well to treatment and making complete recoveries and being able to resume usual activities. Illness relapse however is well recognised and risk of relapse following a subsequent pregnancy remains high, ranging from 20 per cent to 50 per cent (Marks *et al.*, 1992). This has prompted the suggestion of prophylaxis and one report suggested starting lithium immediately after delivery to protect against a relapse (Steward *et al.*, 1991).

At present, there are no good reasons for separating affective psychoses into subgroups on the basis that their first episode was or was not related to childbirth. There are no reliable differences in the symptomatology between puerperal and non-puerperal psychoses (Dean and Kendell, 1981); when such differences are found, e.g. the presence of patchy non-organic confusion in puerperal subjects, they may reflect acuteness of onset of the psychosis or selection bias in sampling. Family studies and follow-up investigations (Platz and Kendell, 1988) lead to the conclusions that puerperal psychoses are the same as affective psychoses at other times, but perhaps with a genetic predisposition to occur and recur after childbirth. The main challenge therefore is to discover how childbirth provokes an acute affective psychosis in some women but not in others, and thus develop specific pharmacological therapies.

CHRONIC MENTAL ILLNESS

Psychosis

Psychosis during pregnancy

Overall, there is a slight but significant reduction in rates of contact with psychiatric services and admissions during pregnancy compared with periods before and after childbirth studies (Paffenberger and McCabe, 1966; Pugh *et al.*, 1963; Kendell *et al.*, 1981, 1987). For bipolar (manic-depressive) illness, pregnancy is usually a time of remission (Marks *et al.*, 1992). Pregnancy does not seem to result in a flare-up of pre-existing schizophrenia (Yarden *et al.*, 1966; McNeil, 1986; Davies *et al.*, 1995).

Psychosis following childbirth

A history of bipolar affective disorder, irrespective of whether the previous episode was puerperal or not, confers an extremely high risk of relapse following childbirth. The rate rises from the general population prevalence of 0.1–0.2 per cent to between 25 per cent and 50 per cent, i.e. up to a 500-fold increase in risk (Marks *et al.*, 1992). It is therefore essential to enquire systematically about previous psychiatric history at antenatal clinic. There is no other medical complication of childbearing with a comparable relative risk of recurrence. The potential risk to both mother and baby of relapse and untreated illness requires proactive management and liaison.

A recent study of childbearing women with schizophrenia (Davies *et al.*, 1995) showed that women with chronic illnesses of the disorganised type or with residual symptoms (DSM IV 1994) showed little variation in their symptomatology, whereas those with a paranoid psychosis with shorter illnesses or periods of remission following treatment were at a high risk (40 per cent) of recurrence or exacerbation of their illnesses. Postnatal management of their illness will depend on type of illness, with a better outcome for women with 'positive' symptoms of schizophrenia both in terms of response to treatment and in their ability to be primary carers for their babies. For mothers with marked negative symptoms, it is advisable to take a proactive approach in planning during pregnancy. If it is considered that a mother is unlikely to be able to care for the baby and there is no alternative carer, then the process of identifying alternative carers should start sooner rather than later.

Non-psychotic disorder

Non-psychotic disorder during pregnancy

Studies have been inconclusive about the exacerbation of pre-existing affective disturbance during pregnancy – some suggesting an increase in rates especially in the early stages of pregnancy (Kumar and Robson, 1984; Kitamura *et al.*, 1993), but in a comparison study with non-pregnant women, no such association was found (O'Hara *et al.*, 1990).

Pregnancy may trigger the onset of Obsessive Compulsive Disorder (Buttolph and Holland, 1990; Neziroglu *et al.*, 1992) or may cause it to worsen (Shear and Mammen, 1995) possibly through effects of steroids on the serotonergic system (Stein *et al.*, 1993). There are limited data on the effects on other anxiety disorders.

Pregnancy only rarely precipitates the onset of an eating disorder, but it remains a difficult time for sufferers, particularly those with anorexia nervosa (Fahy and O'Donoghue, 1991). In severe cases of anorexia, there may be cessation of ovulation and menstruation (Brinch *et al.*, 1988) with fertility impaired initially but normalised on recovering. Fertility is less likely to be affected in bulimia nervosa, as the women are more likely to be of normal weight and to be more sexually active (McNicholas, 1996).

Non-psychotic disorder following childbirth

The likelihood of occurrence of depression after childbirth is raised about two-fold in women with histories of depression, and anticipatory support or preventive pharmacotherapy (Wisner and Wheeler, 1994) are possible options. Other conditions such as obsessive-compulsive disorders, anxiety and phobic states, and eating disorders may continue unchanged following delivery or they may worsen. In general, childbirth does not improve psychiatric outcome in women with histories of mental illness.

Management of chronic mental illness

It is advisable to manage all kinds of non-psychotic illness during pregnancy by psychotherapeutic and supportive measures. Psychotropic drugs should be prescribed only when absolutely necessary, using the lowest possible dose and following consultation with a psychiatrist. However, management of psychotic disorders such as schizophrenia may involve the continuation of maintenance neuroleptic medication and the decision is based on the knowledge of the illness and the likelihood of relapse on the cessation of pharmacotherapy. Fortunately most bipolar, manic depressive illnesses remain in remission during pregnancy and the time of maximum risk of relapse is the first few weeks after delivery. Thus medication with mood-stabilising or antipsychotic drugs is likely to be an issue only for the most vulnerable, who relapse rapidly if their drugs are discontinued. In such cases it is often necessary to maintain the medication and to monitor the foetus for possible malformations. In all cases, close collaboration between professionals is essential.

Specialised clinical services for mentally ill mothers and their babies

A report of services for mentally ill mothers and their infants in the UK (Royal College of Psychiatrists, 1992) was recently revised (Oates, 2001), taking into account developments in national health policy during the last decade, including the National Service Framework for Mental Health (DoH, 1999) and findings from key reports, including the *Confidential Enquiries into Maternal Deaths* (DoH, 1998), and *Fatal Child Abuse and*

Parental Psychiatric Disorder (Falkov, 1996). A key recommendation in the report was that 'Every health authority should have a perinatal mental health strategy that aims to ensure that the knowledge, skills and resources necessary for detection and prompt and effective treatment are in place at all levels of health care provision.'

Women are in contact with a range of health professionals throughout pregnancy, delivery and the postpartum period, therefore providing opportunities for screening, detection and early intervention where problems are identified. For example, at the antenatal booking clinic women may be asked about previous history of mental health problems. Unfortunately, opportunities for identifying women in pregnancy are rarely taken (Oates, 2001). In Britain, newly delivered mothers spend relatively short periods of time as inpatients; thus routine screening in hospital is less practical. However, all women are cared for by community midwives for the first ten days postpartum and a simple screen to detect an episode of severe 'blues', possibly leading to depression, or an early onset depression itself would be feasible at, for example, the tenth day. Health visitors routinely visit between ten and fourteen days postpartum, responsible for monitoring the health and well-being of both infant and mother, and in addition women are routinely examined by their doctor (the postnatal check) at around six weeks post-partum. Health visitors in many health authorities now routinely screen new mothers for postnatal depression using the Edinburgh Postnatal Depression Scale, a simple and validated screening instrument. However, some concern has been expressed that the instrument is not always administered in the recommended manner, for example used as a diagnostic rather than a screen-ing instrument, and that its widespread use has led to some women disguising their symptoms (Elliott and Leverton, 2000).

Where mental health problems are identified, women need to be treated and supported at a level appropriate to their needs – those at high risk are usually managed by specialist mental health services, while those with less severe mental health problems will be managed in primary care. As most detection and treatment will occur in the community, the greatest need is to organise care at a primary care level, although specialist liaison services are also required. In the UK, the relevant tiers of health care will include primary care (GPs and health visitors); secondary mental health care (community mental health teams; psychiatric outpatients, including specialist consultant sessions and perinatal psychotherapy); secondary obstetric care (midwives; medical teams); specialist mental health care (inpatient mother and baby units; specialist nurses in the community perinatal psychiatry service); and a range of voluntary sector services for parents and children.

The three main components of a perinatal psychiatric service include a consultation clinic, a psychiatric liaison service for obstetrics and an inpatient facility for the management of severe maternal mental illnesses.

Consultation clinic

The functions of a consultation clinic include giving advice to non-mental health professionals, including social workers, liaising with community mental teams and seeing pregnant women who either have a history of mental illness or have developed difficulties in the current pregnancy.

For women with a past history, preconception counselling may address concerns about the risks of recurrence of mental illness after a future pregnancy, including what can be done to prevent recurrence and how long a mother should wait before trying to conceive. Advice may be sought about contraception or possible infertility as a consequence of psychotropic medication. Continuing medication during a pregnancy will involve balancing the risk of possible *in utero* effects of medication versus that of a mother relapsing. There may also be concerns about illness being genetically transmitted to the baby.

Professionals need to coordinate services and plan effectively to support the most vulnerable patients. For example, in the case of a single, unsupported, chronically ill woman with schizophrenia or a bipolar affective disorder, intermittently maintained on depot neuroleptics, potential concerns include:

a   aspects of maternal psychopathology or behaviour during pregnancy that poses a threat to the pregnancy or to the foetus, for example suicidal ideation, self-neglect, malnutrition, ingestion of non-prescribed drugs, failure to attend for antenatal care;

b   hazard to the foetus from prescribed medication, such as teratogenicity, perinatal syndromes or longer-term neurobehavioural problems (Asthuler *et al.*, 1996);

c   risks of exacerbation or relapse postpartum and consideration of the need to plan for a prophylactic admission of the mother, including whether this should be with or without the baby; if only the mother is to be admitted, alternative care for the baby needs to be arranged;

d   risks to the new-born infant of poor parenting, neglect or impulsive acts; appropriate plans need to be made to commence child protection procedures, with close liaison with social services.

Such concerns indicate the need for joint working between mental health and children's services but there are a number of barriers that can impede effective joint working. Organisational barriers include the separate legal frameworks and service delivery structures for adults and children and the separate statutory service-planning frameworks. Specialisation in training, knowledge and practice can lead to mental health and children's services professionals holding differing perspectives and priorities (Falkov, 1996). Structures which encourage good communication and liaison between the different services are clearly beneficial.

Psychiatric liaison service for obstetrics

The main tasks of a liaison perinatal mental health team in obstetrics overlap considerably with those of the consultation clinic. Additional tasks may include:

a   Developing a reliable screening procedure to detect women attending antenatal clinics who have a history of psychiatric illness. A perinatal mental health team has a major role in advising on the importance of mental illness as a risk not only for the mother but also for the baby;
b   Good liaison with the obstetrician, GP, midwife and social worker to encourage notification of mothers so identified as well as appropriate supervision and monitoring;
c   Postnatally, the team should be available to deal rapidly with acute crises, to follow through 'cases' referred antenatally or postnatally and to alert other relevant professionals to possible impending problems.

Inpatient mother and baby services

The tradition of joint admission of an acutely and severely mentally ill mother and her baby into a special psychiatric facility is largely unknown outside the UK, Australia, Canada and New Zealand (and to a limited extent, countries such as France, Belgium and the Netherlands). The aim is to try to preserve and facilitate the relationship between mother and baby, often despite the presence of severe maternal psychopathology. In the UK, babies are usually admitted with their mothers into general adult psychiatric wards in which one or more rooms may flexibly be used as nurseries or bedrooms. There exist, in addition, a few specialised mother and baby units with facilities and staff entirely devoted to the care of severely mentally ill mothers together with their babies. Such units serve an important role in taking on difficult secondary or tertiary referrals and in carrying out research, and in education. Units can offer specialist therapeutic activities such as mother–infant interaction guidance and baby massage. Other thera-peutic activities may include family therapy, couple therapy, encouraging parenting skills (in the context of the baby's developmental progress). There is a strong emphasis on engaging fathers or partners. Men may also experience mental health problems in relation to childbirth and there have been reports of mild depressive episodes and anxiety (Ballard *et al.*, 1994) as well as relapse of a bipolar illness (Davenport and Adland, 1982). One study showed that around 50 per cent of partners of women admitted with severe postpartum mental illness suffered psychiatric illness themselves (Lovestone and Kumar, 1993). Their role within the context of maternal postnatal illness is important and warrants greater consideration in service development.

Finally, in addition to specialist services there are a number of other resources and voluntary organisations that may be useful in providing support in the community. Examples of these in Britain include 'Newpin', a national organisation that aims to support parents with mental health problems and their children, including the prevention of child abuse, and 'Sure Start' a recent government incentive, the aim being to improve the well-being of young children aged 0–3 years through better health, childcare, and educational opportunities and help for parents. A range of services are being developed, for example: baby clinics, nurseries, help with parenting skills, fathers' groups, midwives running extra antenatal clinics. Young parents are especially targeted in order to help them with housing, health care, parenting skills, education and childcare.

References

American Psychiatric Association (1994) *Diagnostic and Statistical Manual of Mental Disorders*, 4th edn. New York: American Psychiatric Association.

Appleby, L. (1991) Suicide in pregnancy and in the first postnatal year. *British Medical Journal* 302: 137–40.

Asthuler, L.L., Cohen, L., Szuba, M., Burt, V., Gitlin, M. and Mintz, J. (1996) Pharmacological management of psychiatric illness during pregnancy: dilemmas and guidelines. *American Journal of Psychiatry* 153: 592–606.

Ballard, C.G., Davis, R., Cullen, P.C., Mohan, R.N. and Dean, C. (1994) Prevalence of postnatal psychiatric morbidity in mothers and fathers. *British Journal of Psychiatry* 164: 782–8.

Boulton, M. (1983) *On Being a Mother*. London: Tavistock.

Brinch, M., Isager, T. and Tolstrup, K. (1988) Anorexia nervosa and motherhood: reproductional pattern and mothering behaviour of 50 women. *Acta Psychiatrica Scandinavica* 77: 98–104.

Brockington, I.F., Winokur, G. and Dean, C. (1982) Puerperal psychosis, in I.F. Brockington and R. Kumar (eds.), *Motherhood and Mental Illness*. London: Academic Press, pp. 37–69.

Brown, G.W. and Harris, T. (1978) *Social Origins of Depression*. London: Tavistock.

Buist, A., Norman, T.R. and Dennerstein, L. (1990) Breast feeding and the use of psychotropic medication: a review. *Journal of Affective Disorders* 19:197–206.

Buttolph, M.L. and Holland, D.A. (1990) Obsessive compulsive disorders in pregnancy and childbirth, in M.A. Jenike, L. Baier, and W.E. Minichiello, (eds.), *Obsessive Compulsive Disorders: Theory and Management*. Chicago: Year Book Medical.

Checkley, S. (1992) Neuroendocrine mechanisms and the precipitation of depression by life events. *British Journal of Psychiatry* 160 (suppl. 15): 7–17.

Cookson, J.C. (1985) The neuroendocrinology of mania. *Journal Affective Disorders* 8: 233–41.

Cooper, P.J., Campbell, E.A. and Day, A. *et al.* (1988) Non-psychotic disorder after childbirth: a prospective study of prevalence, incidence, course and nature. *British Journal of Psychiatry* 152: 799–806.

Cox, J.L., Connor, Y. and Kendell, R.E. (1982) Prospective study of the psychiatric Disorders of Childbirth. *British Journal of Psychiatry* 140: 111–17.

Cox, J. (1993) Psychiatric disorders of childbirth, in R. Kendell and A. Zeally (eds.), *Companion to Psychiatric Studies*, 5th edn. Edinburgh: Churchill Livingston, pp. 577–87.

Cox, J.L., Murray, D. and Chapman, G. (1993) A controlled study of the onset, duration and prevalence of postnatal depression. *British Journal of Psychiatry* 163: 27–31.

Dalton, K. (1980) *Depression after Childbirth*. Oxford: Oxford University Press.

Davenport, Y.B. and Adland, M.L. (1982) Postpartum psychoses in female and male bipolar manic depressive patients. *American Journal of Orthopsychiatry* 52: 288–97.

Davies, R.A., McIvor, R.J. and Kumar, R. (1995) Impact of childbirth on a series of schizophrenic mothers: a comment on possible influence of oestrogen on schizophrenia. *Schizophrenia Research* 16: 25–31.

Dean, C. and Kendell, R.E. (1981) The symptomatology of puerperal illness. *British Journal of Psychiatry* 139: 128–33.

Department of Health (1998) Deaths from psychiatric causes, suicide and substance abuse, in *Why Mothers Die: Report on Confidential Enquiries into Maternal Deaths in the United Kingdom 1994–1996*. London: Stationery Office.

Department of Health (1999) *A National Service Framework – Mental Health*. London: Stationery Office.

Elliott, S.A. and Leverton, T.J. (2000) Is the EPDS a magic wand? 2 'myths' and the evidence base. *Journal of Reproductive and Infant Psychology* 18(4): 297–309.

Essex, M.J., Klein, M.H., Miech, R. and Smider, N.A. (2001) Timing of initial exposure to maternal major depression and children's mental health symptoms in kindergarten. *British Journal of Psychiatry* 179: 151–6.

Fahy, T.A. and O'Donoghue, G. (1991) Eating disorders in pregnancy [editorial]. *Psychological Medicine* 21: 577–80.

Falkov, A. (1996) *Fatal Child Abuse and Parental Psychiatric Disorder: Study of Working Together, Part 8 Reports*. Department of Health ACPC Series, no. 1. London: HMSO.

Glover, V., Liddle, P., Taylor, A. *et al.* (1994) Mild hypomania (the highs) can be a feature of the first postpartum week: association with later depression. *British Journal of Psychiatry* 164: 517–21.

Gregoire, A.J.P., Kumar, R., Everritt, B. *et al.* (1996) Transdermal oestrogen for severe postnatal depression. *The Lancet* 347: 930–3.

Hamilton, J.A. and Sichel, D.A. (1992) Prophylactic measures, in J.A. Hamilton and P.N. Harberger (eds.), *Postpartum Psychiatric Illness*. Philadelphia: University of Pennsylvania Press, pp. 219–34.

Hannah, P., Cody, D., Glover, V. *et al.* (1993) The tyramine test is not a marker for postnatal depression: early postpartum euphoria may be. *Journal of Psychosomatic Obstetrics and Gynaecology* 14: 295–304.

Harris, B. (1993) A hormonal component to postnatal depression. *British Journal of Psychiatry* 163: 403–5.

Harris, B., Othman, S., Davies, J.A., Weppner, G.J., Richards, C.J., Newcombe, R.G., Lazarus, J.H., Parkes, A.B., Hall, R. and Phillips, D.I. (1992) Association between postpartum thyroid dysfunction and thyroid antibodies and depression. *British Medical Journal* 305(6846): 152–6.

Harris, B., Lovett, L., Newcombe, R. *et al.* (1994) Cardiff mood and hormone study, Paper 2: Maternity blues and major endocrine changes: the progesterone factor. *British Medical Journal* 308: 949–53.

Hay, D.F., Pawlby, S., Sharp, D., Asten, P., Mills, A. and Kumar, R. (2001) Intellectual problems shown by 11-year-old children whose mothers had postnatal depression. *Journal of Child Psychology and Psychiatry* 42: 871–90.

Henderson, A.F., Gregoire, A.J.P., Kumar, R.C. and Studd, J.W.W. (1991) Treatment of severe postnatal depression with oestradiol skin patches. *Lancet* 338: 816–17.

Holden, J.M., Sagovsky, R. and Cox, J.L. (1989) Counselling in the general practice setting: Control of health visitor intervention in treatment of postnatal depression. *British Medical Journal* 298: 223–6.

Kendell, R.E., Rennie, D., Clarke, J. A. and Dean, C. (1981) The social and obstetric correlates of psychiatric admission in the puerperium. *Psychological Medicine* 11: 341–50.

Kendell, R.E., Chalmers, J.C. and Platz, C. (1987) Epidemiology of puerperal psychosis. *British Journal of Psychiatry* 150: 662–73.

Kitamura, T., Shima, S., Sugawara, M. and Toda, M.A. (1993) Psychological and social correlates of the onset of affective disorders among pregnant women. *Psychological Medicine* 23: 967–75.

Kumar, R. and Robson, K.M. (1984) A prospective study of emotional disorders in childbearing women. *British Journal of Psychiatry* 144: 35–47.

Kumar, R. (1994) Postnatal mental illness: a transcultural perspective. *Social Psychiatry and Psychiatric Epidemiology* 29: 250–64.

Kumar, R. and O'Dowd, L. (2000) Psychiatric problems in pregnancy and purperium, in M.D. Lindheimer, J. Davison and W.M. Barrow (eds.), *Medical Disorders during Pregnancy*, 3rd edn. St Louis, Miss.: Mosby Inc.

Lovestone, S. and Kumar, R. (1993) Postnatal mental illness: the impact on spouses. *British Journal of Psychiatry* 163: 210–16.

McNeil, T.F. (1986) A prospective study of postpartum psychosis in a high risk group. *Acta Psychiatrica Scandinavica* 74: 204–16.

McNicholas, F. (1996) Eating psychopathology and its effect on pregnancy, infant growth and development. *Irish Journal of Psychological Medicine* 13(2): 67–9.

Marks, M.N., Wieck, A., Checkley, S.A. and Kumar, R. (1992) Contribution of psychological and social factors to psychiatric and non psychiatric relapse after childbirth in women with previous histories of affective disorder. *Journal of Affective Disorders* 29: 253–64.

Martins, C. and Gaffan, E.A. (2000) Effects of early maternal depression on patterns of infant–mother attachment: a meta-analytic investigation. *Journal of Child Psychology and Psychiatry*, 41(6): 737–46.

Murray, L. and Cooper, P.J. (1996) Impact of postpartum depression on child development. *International Review of Psychiatry* 8: 55–63.

Neziroglu, F., Anemone, R. and Yaryura-Tobias, J.A. (1992) Onset of obsessive-compulsive disorder in pregnancy. *American Journal of Psychiatry* 149: 947–50.

Oates, M. (1988) The development of an integrated community-oriented community service for severe postnatal mental illness, in R. Kumar and I.F. Brockington (eds.), *Motherhood and Mental Illness: Causes and Consequences*. London: Wright, pp. 133–58.

Oates, M. (2001) Perinatal mental health services: recommendations for provision of services for childbearing women. *Council Report Royal College of Pychiatrists*. London: Gaskell.

O'Hara, M. and Zekoski, E.M. (1988) Postpartum depression: a comprehensive review, in R. Kumar and I.F. Brockington (eds.), *Motherhood and Mental Illness 2: Cause and Consequences*. London: Wright, pp. 17–63.

O'Hara, M., Zekoski, E.M., Phillips, L.H. and Wright, E.J. (1990) Controlled prospective study of mood disorders: comparison of childbearing and non child-bearing women. *Journal of Abnormal Psychology* 99: 3–15.

O'Hara, M.W., Schlechte, J.A., Lewis, D.A. and Wright, E.J. (1991) Prospective study of postpartum blues biological and psychosocial factors. *Archives of General Psychiatry* 48: 801–6.

O'Hara, M. and Swain, A. (1996) Rates and risk of postpartum depression: a meta-analysis. *International Review of Psychiatry* 8(1): 37–54.

Okano, T. and Nomura, J. (1992) Endocrine study of the maternity blues. *Progress in Neuropsychopharmacology and Biological Psychiatry* 16: 921–32.

Paffenbarger, R.S. (1964) Epidemiological aspects of parapartum mental illness. *British Journal of Preventive and Social Medicine* 18: 189–95.

Paffenbarger, R.S. and McCabe, L.J. (1966) The effect of obstetric and perinatal events on risk of mental illness in women of childbearing age. *American Journal Public Health*, 56: 400–7.

Paykel, E.S., Emms, E.M., Fletcher, J. and Rassaby, E.S. (1980) Life events and social support in puerperal depression. *British Journal of Psychiatry*, 136: 339–46.

Pitt, B. (1968) Atypical depression following childbirth. *British Journal of Psychiatry* 136: 339–46.

Pitt, B. (1973) Maternity blues. *British Journal of Psychiatry* 128: 431–5.

Platz, C. and Kendell, R.E. (1988) A matched control study and family study of puerperal psychosis. *British Journal Psychiatry* 153: 90–4.

Pugh, T.F., Jerath, B.K., Schmidt, W.M. and Reed, R.B. (1963) Rates of mental disease related to childbearing. *New England Journal of Medicine* 268: 1224–8.

Reed, P., Sermin, N., Appleby, L. and Faragher, B. (1999) A comparison of clinical response to electroconvulsive therapy in puerperal and non-puerperal psychoses. *Journal of Affective Disorders* 54(3): 255–60.

Romito, P. (1993) Work and health in mothers of young children: who cares? *Proceedings of Conference on Women, Health and Work*. Barcelona: CAPS, 11–12 November.

Royal College of Psychiatrists (1992) Working party report on postnatal mental illness. *Council Report CR 28*. London: Gaskell.

Sharpe, D. (1992) A prospective longitudinal study of childbirth related emotional disorders in primary care. Ph.D thesis, University of London.

Sharpe, D., Hay, D., Pawlby, S. *et al.* (1995) The impact of postnatal depression on boys' intellectual development. *Journal of Child Psychology and Psychiatry* 36: 1315–36.

Shear, M.K. and Mammen, O. (1995) Anxiety disorders in pregnancy and postpartum women. *Psychopharmacology Bulletin* 31(4): 693–703.

Sherwin, B.B. (1994) Impact of the changing hormonal milieu on psychological functioning, in: Lobo (ed.), *Treatment of Postmenopausal Women: Basic and Clinical Aspects*. New York: Raven Press.

Stein, D.J., Hollander, E., Simeon, D., Cohen, L. and Hwany, M. (1993) Pregnancy and obsessive compulsive disorder. *American Journal of Psychiatry* 150: 1131–2.

Steward, D.E., Klompenhower, J.L., Kendell, R.E. and Van Hulst, A.M. (1991)

Prophylactic lithium in puerperal psychosis: the experience of three centres. *British Journal of Psychiatry* 158: 393–7.

Wieck, A. (1996) Ovarian hormones, mood and neurotransmitters. *International Review of Psychiatry* 8:17–25.

Wieck, A., Kumar, R., Hirst, A.D., Marks, M.N., Campbell, I.C., Checkley, S.A. (1991) Increased sensitivity of dopamine receptors and recurrence of affective psychosis after childbirth. *British Medical Journal* 303(6803): 613–16.

Wisner, K.L. and Wheeler, S.D. (1994) Prevention of recurrent postpartum major depression. *Hospital and Community Psychiatry* 45(11): 1191–6.

World Health Organisation (1993) *The ICD-10 Classification of Mental and Behavioural Disorders: Diagnostic Criteria for Research*. Geneva: WHO.

Yarden, P.E., Max, D.M. and Eisenbach, Z. (1966) The effect of childbirth on the prognosis of married schizophrenic women. *British Journal of Psychiatry* 112: 491–9.

Yoshida, K., Smith, B. and Kumar, R. (1999) Psychotropic drugs in mothers' milk: a comprehensive review of assay methods, pharmakokinetics and safety of breast-feeding. *Journal of Psychopharmacology* 139(1): 64–80.

Useful addresses

Association for Post-Natal Illness

145 Dawes Road, London SW6 7EB
Phone: 020 7386 0868
Fax: 020 7386 8885
Email: info@apni.org
Website: www.apni.org
Description: provides information and advice, network of local contacts, also post and email correspondence. Information service for partners and families as well as sufferers. Send SAE for info pack or call for further details.
Opening hours: telephone service: Mon and Fri 10am–2pm; Tue–Thurs 10am–5pm. Answerphone at other times
Referral: open access
Criteria/catchment: national catchment

Meet a Mum Association

Waterside Centre, 26 Avenue Road, London SE25 4DX
Phone: Office: 020 8771 5595   Helpline: 020 8768 0123
Fax: 020 8239 1153
Email: meet-a-mum.assoc@cableinet.co.uk
Website: www.mama.org.uk
Description: support for mothers who are or have been suffering from isolation or postnatal depression. Local self-help groups, networking, telephone advice line, etc.
Special interest activities: local groups have lots of family activities

Opening hours: helpline: Mon–Fri 7–10pm
Referral: open access
Criteria/catchment: parents and health professionals

Miscarriage Association

C/o Clayton Hospital, Northgate, Wakefield, WF1 3JS
Phone 01924 200799   Helpline: 01924 200799
Fax: 01924 298834
Website: www.miscarriageassociation.org.uk
Description: national network which provides information and support
on the subject of pregnancy loss. Phone for details of local groups/contact
numbers, etc.
Opening hours: telephone helpline Mon–Fri 9am–4pm
Referral: open access

Newpin: Head Office

Sutherland House, 35 Sutherland Square, London SE17 3EE
Phone 020 7358 5900
Fax: 020 7701 2660
Email: newpin@nationalnewpin.freeserve.co.uk
Description: head office of national organisation that runs a variety of
projects in London offering help and support to parents and carers of
children and young families. The overall aim of Newpin is to help change
destructive patterns of behaviour within families.
Opening hours: office: Mon–Fri 9am–5pm
Referral: self or other agencies
Criteria/catchment: phone for details of catchment for different projects

Parentline Plus

520 Highgate Studios, 53/79 Highgate Road, London NW5 1TL
Phone 020 8800 2222 Textline 0800 783 6783
Email: centraloffice@parentlineplus.org.uk
Website: www.parentlineplus.org.uk
Description: a free confidential helpline for parents. Also offer parenting
courses and publish information leaflets available by post or on their
website.
Opening hours: helpline: Mon–Fri 9am–9pm, Sat 9.30am–5pm, Sun 10am–
3pm
Referral: self or any other source
Criteria/catchment: open to all parents

Stillbirth and Neonatal Death Society (SANDS)

28 Portland Place, London W1B 1LY
Phone: 020 7436 5881   Admin: 020 7436 7940
Fax: 020 7436 3715
Email: support@uk-sands.org
Website: www.uk-sands.org
Opening hours: office hours, helpline Mon–Wed 10am–3pm
Criteria/catchment: bereaved parents and families only

7   Treatment of elderly women

Bart Sheehan and Angela Stevens

Introduction

The treatment of mental health problems in the elderly is assuming an ever-increasing importance as the proportion of the over 65s in the western population continues to rise. The mental health problems of the elderly are distinct from those of the young, and psychiatric services in the United Kingdom have already been configured to reflect this difference. As the elderly population expands, the proportion that is female expands also. Data from the Office of Population Censuses and Surveys (Coleman *et al.*, 1993) show startling historical changes in Britain's population structure. In 1851, one million people in Britain were aged 65 years or older. By 1991, that figure rose to 8.7 million. Amongst these, there were 123 women aged 65–74 for every 100 men, a ratio of 1.2:1.0. For those aged 85 and over, the ratio rose to 2.9:1.0. Life expectancy for women is typically 4–10 years in excess of that for men in western countries (Sen, 1996). Surveying referrals to the author's most recent old-age psychiatry sector showed that there were three female referrals for every male referral, so the imbalance clearly filters through to services.

The use of health care facilities differs between genders. Although women live longer than men, they report more ill health. Reviews in this area (Mechanic, 1978) indicate that women may be no more ill than men but that they are more likely than men to bring forward symptoms and seek treatment.

Thus for those treating mental health problems in the elderly, their patients will be predominantly women and so a clear understanding of their problems and needs is essential if they are to be treated effectively.

NORMAL AGING

There are a number of theories as to the cause of the normal aging process. One is of 'programmed aging' in which it is postulated that human cells have a genetically predetermined life span and that once this life span is reached the cells die. This cell death is said to be caused by progressive damage to the cell's DNA so that the ability of the DNA to replicate is compromised. Others postulate that aging is more related to the observation that mito-chondrial (the powerhouses of living cells) function tails off as cells age. They become enlarged and their numbers decline, possibly in response to damage caused by free radicals. Yet another school of thought says that the aging process is not caused by the mitochondrial decline *per se* but by the free radicals themselves, which are well known to damage cell membranes, with fatal consequences for the cells.

Neuropsychology of aging

It is the general perception amongst younger generations that their elderly relatives have poor memory and are 'intellectually dimmed', but is there any substance to this perception?

As an individual ages, their intellectual function does decline, starting at around the age of 60–70 years, with verbal IQ being relatively better pre-served than performance IQ. Aspects of intellectual function that are most affected by the aging process are the speed of information processing and flexibility of problem-solving.

With respect to the decline in memory in the elderly, one needs to examine separately the different types of memory. Short-term memory appears to be relatively well preserved; however, working memory, particularly involving more complex strategic decision-making procedures, is not so well preserved and shows a significant decline into old age.

Uncued recall of information from the long-term memory store is poor in the elderly; however, it can be significantly improved if cues are provided, a strategy used to excellent effect in reminiscence therapy groups.

SOCIAL CHANGES THAT OLD AGE BRINGS

Significant alterations in life circumstances are the norm for older women. Women live longer and are therefore more likely to experience the death of their spouse. Of households in the UK that include a person over the age of 75, 38 per cent are of single women (Bond, 1993) and many of these are widows. Major life events such as bereavement were initially thought to explain the incidence of depression in the elderly female population (Murphy, 1982). However, subsequent work has shown that the elderly are less affected, emotionally, by these events than was previously thought. It would appear that the most important factor in predicting an elderly individual's response to a negative life event is their prior reaction to previous such events (Davies, 1994). Despite losses, informal support networks for older women are main-tained over time and are often very satisfying for the individual concerned (Davies, 1994, Wenger, 1994), with much of that support being provided by other older women.

Economic hardship in old age caused by the loss of paid employment following retirement is accompanied by the loss of social status that employment confers. Retirement may also result in the loss of the social support network that the individual has previously relied upon. However, many elderly women live fulfilling, outward-looking lives and it would be inaccurate to stereotype all elderly women as living a socially isolated and financially impoverished existence.

Assessment

Ideally, the assessment of an elderly female patient by the psychiatric team should take place in the person's home, with appropriate informants being readily available to corroborate and supplement information if necessary. A standard psychiatric assessment is carried out with the interviewer being vigilant also for the presence of physical illness masquerading as mental illness. The interviewer should pay particular attention to the patient's hygiene and nutrition as this may be indicative of the patient's capacity to care adequately for themselves. Other key points of the assessment include the person's cognitive function, in particular their memory which may be an early indicator of a dementing illness. Physical examination is essential in the elderly and due attention should be paid to the presence of any sensory impairments, e.g. hearing loss or failing visual acuity.

Investigations

An elderly woman admitted to a psychiatric ward should have the following investigations as a minimum standard: full blood count, urea and electrolytes, creatinine, liver function tests with calcium and proteins, glucose, thyroid function tests, electrocardiogram, chest X-ray and a mid-stream urinalysis.

In addition, if dementia is suspected then a CT or MRI scan of the brain may be helpful.

Psychological assessment

This is generally performed by a clinical psychologist and can be extremely helpful to clarify diagnosis, predict outcome, predict need and to monitor progress (or lack of it). The list of tests employed by psychologists is extensive and the reader is referred to a clinical psychology text but, whatever test is used, care should be taken that it has been validated for use in the elderly. Tests commonly used include the Geriatric Depression Scale, The National Adult Reading Test, The Wechsler Adult Intelligence Scale, The Folstein Mini-Mental State Examination and the Cambridge Cognitive Assessment.

Social assessment

It is essential to carry out a detailed assessment of the person's living conditions and social network, particularly if they live alone. The degree of family support, their financial status and level of independence are also key issues to elucidate.

Closely linked to their social assessment is an assessment of the patient's activities of daily living (ADL) which will give an idea of their ability to care for themselves in the home, e.g. cooking, shopping, cleaning, self-care.

CLINICAL ISSUES

The psychiatric disorders likely to affect elderly women are broadly similar to those that affect the elderly male population. The most common disorders seen in the elderly by mental health services are dementia and depression. However, other affective disorders and the psychoses also cause a significant degree of morbidity in the older population. Addiction problems, such as alcohol addiction, are not so commonly seen and are more likely to be addiction to prescribed medication such as benzodiazepines. Personality disorders are less commonly seen in the elderly as is panic disorder. On the other hand, psychosexual disorders are probably more prevalent than was once thought. Sleep disorders in the ageing population are also very common, for a variety of reasons, both psychological and physical.

Dementia

Dementia refers to an acquired condition of later life in which a disease of the brain leads to global cognitive impairment, personality change (e.g. irritability, apathy) and behavioural problems (e.g. aggression, wandering, sleep disruption) with no clouding of consciousness.

The most common cause of dementia is Alzheimer's disease in which neuronal loss is accompanied by the laying down of characteristic amyloid plaques and neurofibrillary tangles in the cerebral cortex. Progression from onset of symptoms to death takes on average around ten years but earlier onset of Alzheimer's disease tends to have a more rapidly progressive course. The disease is slightly more common in women, typically affecting 4 per cent of women over the age of 70 years (Spagnoli, 1996). Most cases are of late onset and unknown aetiology but in a minority of early-onset cases abnormal genes on chromosomes 1, 14 and 21 have been implicated.

The next most common causes of dementia are cerebrovascular disease and Cortical Lewy body disease. A stepwise deterioration in cognitive function is suggestive of the former, accompanied by CT evidence of cerebral infarction and possibly focal neurological deficits. Lewy body disease is suggested by the early onset of psychotic symptoms and Parkinsonism, although an accurate diagnosis can be made only at post-mortem.

A mixed bag of rarer causes of dementia include inherited conditions such as Huntingdon's disease and Pick's disease, metabolic disorders (e.g. hypothyroidism), head injuries, hydrocephalus and intracranial infections or haemorrhage. Depressive illness may cause a temporary impairment in cognitive function, leading to the so-called depressive pseudodementia.

The treatment of dementia is best approached in a holistic manner using a multidisciplinary team that also includes support for the carer. This will usually involve social services (e.g. home help, laundry services), daycare facilities and later on residential care when the burden of caring for the patient at home becomes too daunting. The psychiatric team are involved in monitoring the decline in cognitive function and the emergence of behavioural problems, and should be alert to the occurrence of superimposed confusional states (delirium) and depression. The use of medication to treat behavioural problems is often necessary (e.g. neuroleptic medication, sedatives or antidepressants) but should be used with caution as the elderly are often exquisitely sensitive to toxic effects of drugs and those with dementia even more so. It should be borne in mind also that the evidence for the efficacy of these drugs in the dementing population is poor (McGrath and Jackson, 1996).

Recent advances in the pharmacological treatment of dementia include the drug Donepezil, licensed for use in the NHS in the UK in April 1997. It is a cholinesterase inhibitor and prevents the profound loss of the neurotransmitter acetylcholine which is seen in the brains of those with Alzheimer's disease. Donepezil has shown moderate efficacy in at least delaying the progress of Alzheimer's disease in some patients (Rogers *et al.*, 1996) and may herald the gateway to a new era in the treatment of dementia. Since 1997 a number of new antidementia drugs that act in a similar way have started to come on to the market.

Depression

Depressive illness is common in elderly women, with clinically significant depression found in over 10 per cent of the aging population (Blazer *et al.*, 1991) and serious depressive illness in perhaps 2 per cent (Blazer and Williams, 1980). Although many of the symptoms of depression are the same as in younger individuals, among the depressed elderly, retardation, paranoid ideation, agitation and nihilistic thinking are common.

Causes of depression in elderly women are manifold and include the presence of debilitating physical illness, severe life events and iatrogenic causes such as steroids, beta-blockers, digitalis and nifedipine, to name but a few. The influence of genetic factors appears to have a lesser impact in older individuals.

The treatment of depression in the elderly is essentially the same as that in the younger population. However, older people are often intolerant of standard doses of medication and the principle of 'starting low and going slow' is a prudent one. This is particularly pertinent if the patient has a history of cardiovascular, renal or hepatic disease.

Particular points to heed when prescribing for the elderly are to avoid polypharmacy wherever possible and keep drug regimes simple. Try to avoid drugs that have sedation in their side-effect profile as this may predispose the patient to falls. Always ask if they are taking 'over-the-counter' medication that may interact with prescribed drugs. Before prescribing, assess for potential causes of non-compliance, e.g. poor sight, arthritis, memory impairment, social isolation. Where possible non-drug treatments should be considered, e.g. psychotherapy, cognitive behavioural therapy (CBT).

If antidepressants are to be used then the specific serotonin reuptake inhibitors (SSRIs) or moclobemide have a better cardiac side-effect profile and are better tolerated by the elderly. Trazodone and nefazodone are also of use in the elderly but may precipitate orthostatic hypotension. Of the tricyclic antidepressants, nortriptyline is preferable to its more commonly used relatives.

In the treatment of severe depression, depression resistant to medication, or when the side-effects of medication preclude its use, then the use of electroconvulsive therapy (ECT) should be considered. It is still the most acutely effective antidepressant treatment available (McCall, 2001) and is better tolerated by some elderly people than are pharmacological treatments (see also biological therapies chapter).

Psychological treatment should always be considered and can often be helpful as an alternative to drug therapy in mild to moderate depression. Both individual and group treatments have been shown to be effective (Scogin and McElreath, 1994) and where a partner is involved then couple therapy should also be considered. The use of CBT in the elderly is also increasingly being used to good effect.

Mania

In the elderly population, mania is not a common occurrence, but when it does occur it can be so devastating that the clinician should always be alert to the possibility of its presence. Most cases of mania in the elderly begin in younger adult life with the peak age of onset in the mid-thirties. However, there is a second smaller peak of onset in the early seventies.

The clinical features of mania in the elderly are generally the same as those seen in younger patients but cognitive impairment, irritability and rapid swings in mood are often seen more frequently.

The choice of treatment for mania in elderly women is lithium but if an antipsychotic is required as well then olanzapine is better tolerated than the traditional antipsychotics. If a mood stabiliser is needed then sodium valproate is less cardiotoxic than carbamazepine. Whatever drug regime is adopted, the doses required are likely to be much lower than in younger patients and this is especially true of lithium, which should be started at least 50 per cent lower than the standard starting dose. ECT is also effective in the treatment of mania.

Anxiety disorders

The most commonly seen anxiety disorders in the elderly female population are phobias, with a prevalence rate of approximately 10 per cent, followed by generalised anxiety disorder which has a prevalence rate of around 4 per cent. Clinical symptoms are broadly similar to those seen in younger individuals but may show greater comorbidity with depression.

Treatment of anxiety disorders in elderly women involves the use of CBT, behavioural treatment or anxiety management training. Drug regimes involving SSRIs may be useful, particularly when there is a comorbid depressive illness. The use of benzodiazepines should be avoided due to their propensity to cause confusion, dependence and to precipitate falls.

Suicide in the elderly

As a proportion of the population the elderly account for more of the completed suicides recorded, with the figure being quoted as 25 per cent. This is an alarming statistic as the elderly comprise only 15 per cent of the total population in the UK. What is more, the elderly are more likely to be successful than younger people when they attempt suicide. The vast majority of the elderly committing suicide are depressed at the time and it is vitally important that the clinician is alert to the presence of suicidal ideations when assessing a depressed elderly woman. Having said that, elderly men are more likely to kill themselves than are their female counterparts. Other factors that are known to influence an older person's decision to take their own life include the presence of physical illness, chronic pain, loneliness, bereavement and alcohol abuse.

Psychoses

Late life psychotic illness is relatively uncommon in the elderly, although the so-called late paraphrenia is more prevalent in older women than in men. Factors that may predispose women to paranoid illness include sensory impairment, particularly deafness, social isolation and organic brain disease. The role of genetic factors is unclear in late life psychoses.

Treatment involves the use of antipsychotics, with the newer atypical antipsychotics being the drugs of choice. They are much less likely to cause the Parkinsonian side-effects that are so prevalent with the traditional antipsychotics. Very small doses may be effective and well tolerated. However, care should be taken when using risperidone and olanzapine, as both drugs have recently been associated with cerebrovascular accidents in those at increased risk of strokes.

Alcohol and drug abuse

Alcohol abuse in elderly women is considerably less prevalent than that in younger people. This is due to a number of factors, in particular lower disposable income and reduced tolerance to the effects of alcohol. Treatment of cases of alcohol dependence is along similar lines to that in the younger population.

The abuse of illegal drugs among the elderly is also uncommon and they are more likely to be dependent upon prescribed medication. Benzodiazepines, opiates and analgesics are the major culprits. Withdrawal from drugs on which the person is dependent should be considered in most elderly patients, although there is an argument for maintenance treatment in the very elderly, particularly if they have very strong objections to stopping the drug.

LEGAL ISSUES

Testamentary capacity

Difficult issues likely to be faced by those caring for elderly mentally ill patients include the legal matters surrounding the judgement of an elderly person. The issue usually arises in a patient with dementia and bitter legal disputes may ensue. The capacity to make a will is known as Testamentary Capacity and is present if: (a) the patient understands that she is giving her property to one or more particular people; (b) she understands the extent of her property; and (c) she understands the reasonable claims on her property of those she chooses to include in, or exclude from, the will. It is important to note that a degree of memory loss or even definite early dementia does not necessarily imply loss of testamentary capacity. Medical opinions on this matter are often sought from general practitioners and old age psychiatrists.

Power of attorney

The legal system has rules to allow a person, usually a relative, to take responsibility for an infirm person's affairs. In England this is controlled by the Court of Protection. Mechanisms exist for both the aging person, if not yet mentally impaired, and for the Court of Protection to bestow powers on an individual to manage the affected person's affairs. The person may convey Power of Attorney, which lapses if the person becomes mentally ill, or Enduring Power of Attorney, which does not lapse. The Court of Protection can appoint a receiver for a person already impaired. It is also important to note that once an aging person becomes mentally impaired, Power of Attorney cannot be given by that person.

It is also of note that in recent years it has become common practice for social services to require a person with significant assets to pay for their own care. Clinical experience has shown that this practice often causes distress for those who expected to have assets to pass on to their relatives. It has been sufficiently controversial to provoke a national media debate as to the appropriateness of this practice.

The Mental Health Act

The Mental Health Act is used frequently in old age psychiatry. Compulsory admission, usually under sections of the Act requiring three professional opinions to concur, is available with criteria identical to those used with younger people. In the last two years, problems have arisen whereby demented patients have been detained under the Mental Health Act on the grounds that they could not consent to admission: this practice is no longer necessary but the issue may be revisited in a proposed new Mental Health Act for England and Wales.

Elder abuse

Abuse of elderly women has received increased attention in the last two decades in the wake of scandals in residential care, though it is more commonly encountered outside institutions, simply because the number of elderly women living in the community far exceeds those living in residential care. This complex and often hidden problem may involve sexual or financial exploitation, emotional abuse, neglect or direct violence. The prevalence is unclear but a fair estimate is 4 per cent of older people suffering per year (Fisk, 1991). Clues include women who are fearful, malnourished or have many bruises or burns, or carers who abuse alcohol or give implausible accounts of injuries. The law can protect older people. While reporting is important, rehabilitative approaches to a stressed and exhausted carer should be considered.

Carers

There are millions of carers of the elderly infirm in the UK; themselves often older women (Levin, 1991). Half of these receive no help but as many as 15 per cent of carers of people with dementia themselves suffer from depression (Burns *et al.*, 1997). Caring for a person with dementia is especially stressful. The most telling problems include behavioural problems such as incontinence, aggression and sleep disturbance with nocturnal wandering. It is perhaps curious that despite the nurturing role often entered as mothers by this generation of women, female carers appear to fare worse than male carers in terms of depression. The previous relationship of the carer with the cared for person may be crucial.

Services

Most elderly female patients in the UK with mental disorders are cared for by their general practitioners (GP). GPs have access both to social services and to specialist old age psychiatry services and the latter are now available throughout most of the UK. Old age psychiatry services are usually based on the community mental health team model. Teams offer a comprehensive assessment and treatment service, typically receiving referrals from GPs, social services and general hospital teams. They differ from most other services in that they offer a seamless 'all in' plan.

The multidisciplinary team consists of:

- Consultant old age psychiatrist: covering an area including 15–20,000 elderly people
- Community psychiatric nurse (CPN): typical case load of forty patients
- Ward-based psychiatric nurses for inpatient care
- Day hospital psychiatric nurses
- Occupational therapist: may be hospital, day unit or community-based
- Social worker: often based at the community headquarters.

The key to the system is good communication between team members and rapid response to referrals. The social worker is often crucial in the purchasing of an integrated aftercare package that may involve the patient living at home or in residential care.

For elderly depressed people, day hospitals are often available and can offer group treatments for depression and anxiety as well as specific treatments such as reminiscence groups or women's groups. Huge gains in personal attention and social contact often accrue and conventional notions of admission and treatment followed by discharge may founder on a degree of dependency. Many elderly sufferers of depression will also respond to conventional community treatment with monitoring of progress at outpatient clinics, the GP surgery or by their designated CPN.

Old age services in the UK have expanded greatly in the last two decades. Workload is bound to increase with demographic change, but services are generally well organised and provide an environment and service both acceptable to, and tailored to, the needs of elderly women. Those working in the field can look forward to this challenge.

References

Blazer, D.G. and Williams, C.D. (1980) The epidemiology of dysphonia and depression in the elderly population. *American Journal of Psychiatry* 137: 439–44.

Blazer, D.G., Burchet, B., Services, C. and George, L.K. (1991) The association of age and depression among the elderly: an epidemiologic exploration. *Journal of Gerontology* 46: 210–15.

Bond, J. (1993) Living arrangements of elderly people, in J. Bond, P. Coleman and S. Peace (eds.), *Ageing in Society*. London: Sage.

Burns, A., Howard, R. and Pettit, W. (1997) Carers and services, in A. Burns, R. Howard and W. Pettit (eds.), *Alzheimer's Disease*. Oxford, Blackwell, pp.107–24.

Coleman, P., Bond, J. and Peace, S. (1993) Ageing in the twentieth century, in J. Bond, P. Coleman and S. Peace (eds.), *Ageing in Society*. London: SAGE, pp.1–18.

Davies, A.D.M. (1994) Life events in the normal elderly, in J.R.M. Copeland, M.T. Abou-Saleh and D.G. Blazer (eds.), *Principles and Practice of Geriatric Psychiatry*. Chichester: Wiley and Sons, pp.106–14.

Fisk, J. (1991) Abuse of the Elderly, in R. Jacoby and C. Oppenheimer (ed.), *Psychiatry in the Elderly*. Oxford: Oxford University Press, pp. 901–15.

Levin, E. (1991) Carers: problems, strains and services, in R. Jacoby and C. Oppenheimer (eds.), *Psychiatry in the Elderly*. Oxford: Oxford University Press, pp. 301–12.

McCall, W.V. (2001) Electroconvulsive therapy in the era of modern psychopharmacology. *International Journal of Neuropsychopharmacology* 4: 315–24.

McGrath, A.M. and Jackson, G.A. (1996) Survey of neuroleptic prescribing in residents of nursing homes in Glasgow. *British Medical Journal* 312: 611–12.

Mechanic, D. (1978) Sex, illness, illness behaviour, and the use of health services. *Social Science and Medicine* 1212: 207–14.

Murphy, E. (1982) Social origins of depression in old age. *British Journal of Psychiatry* 141: 135–42.

Rogers, S.L., Friedhoff, L.T. and The Donepezil Study Group (1996) The efficacy and safety of Donepezil in patients with Alzheimer's disease: results of a US multicenter, randomized, double blind placebo controlled trial. *Dementia* 7: 293–303.

Scogin, F. and McElreath, L. (1994) Efficacy of psychosocial treatments for geriatric depression: a quantitative review. *Journal of Consulting and Clinical Psychology* 62(1): 69–74.

Sen, K. (1996) Gender, in H. Ebrahim and A. Kalache (eds.), *Epidemiology in Old Age*. London: BMJ publishing group, pp. 210–20.

Spagnoli, A. (1996) Alzheimer's disease, in H. Ebrahim (ed.), *Epidemiology in Old Age*. London: BMJ, pp. 270–8.

Wenger, G.C. (1994). Support networks, in J.R.M. Copeland, M.T. Abou-Saleh and D.G. Blazer (eds.), *Principles and Practice of Geriatric Psychiatry*. Chichester: John Wiley and Sons, pp.123–5.

Useful telephone numbers

The Alzheimer's Disease Society   020 7306 0606
CRUSE (Bereavement Counselling)   0870 167 1677
Help the Aged: SeniorLine   0800 800 6565

8 Treatment of women from other cultures

Shubulade Smith

Introduction

This short chapter will try to give an overview of those factors that are most likely to influence care delivery to women from cultural minorities, and describe ways in which changes in clinical practice can facilitate and improve the care that these women receive.

THE CONTEXT

Understanding the factors that influence the ways in which women from cultural minorities receive and access care for their mental health problems cannot be understood without a primary understanding of the context within which they live. There is evidence that disparities exist in the care that women from different cultures receive. This reflects the societal inequalities that exist within the United Kingdom. Psychiatry is a discipline based on western cultural norms, mainly practised by males of Northern European descent and catering to a mainstream white western majority. This clearly has an influence on psychiatric practice.

Historical beliefs about women from ethnic minority populations

When white Europeans first arrived in Africa, they described the people variously as 'barbaric, primitive, childlike, simple, unpredictable'. There then followed many 'scientific' anthropological studies which served to prove that these societies were more primitive, less 'human' than white western societies. This facilitated the enslavement of African people. 'It is not possible to enslave men without logically making them inferior, through and through' (Fanon, 1956, Racism and Culture, speech given to first congress of Negro Writers and Artists).

European colonialists were shocked at the polygamous culture which existed in certain of the African tribes they met. They believed that this was an indication that the women were more subservient to their men than white women were to theirs and that they had little understanding of true family values (Bush, 1990). Black women were felt to lack modesty and be overly sexualised (because unlike white women, they appeared naked in public). Slavers would advertise African women as 'hot constitution'd ladies' in an effort to attract white male buyers (Jordan, 1968). African women were also described as strong and muscular ('less like women, more like men') and this was felt to be an indication that they were designed to toil in the fields. The only other stereotype commonly associated with being a black female was that of a domineering mother. Thus there were no positive stereotypes of black females. They were over-sexualised, morally degenerate, poor mothers who contributed little to the betterment of society. In the pecking order of society, black women came firmly at the end of the list. Thus black women could be raped yet this was not seen as an offence in the way it might have been against a white woman (Bush, 1990).

Although women from the Indian subcontinent were not formally enslaved, the British colonial power also considered the Indian population as inferior to white Europeans, eventually consigning them to the role of bonded labourers. As in Africa, Indian culture and religious practice was denigrated and specific policies were put in place to eradicate Indian ways of thinking and replace them with Western European philosophies. Indian women, already of low status, were marginalised even further. They were generally discounted as citizens, described as 'simple, primitive and unable to be educated'. Many of the white European males would decide that the Indian women were nautch girls (professional dancers or even prostitutes). This would be seen as an excuse to have sex with the women, even against their will. Many Indian women were felt to carry disease, such that the Communicable Diseases Act of 1858 was passed, allowing women to be taken off the streets and forced into labour camps if they were thought to have any kind of infection. Indian women had no rights and despite outlawing *Sati* (the practice of widows being compelled, forced or praised to throw themselves onto their dead husband's funeral pyre), British colonial rule did little to change this.

These negative ideas about non-white women under colonial rule were disseminated back to the homelands and used to inform political policy and religious ideas. This led to social policies being instituted which made it legal to discriminate against non-white Europeans, e.g. apartheid. Some ideas from colonial times have prevailed, such that even now people from Africa or the Asian subcontinent are required to undergo health checks at the border before they can enter certain territories.

Individual and institutional racism

An individual may not hold racist views, but may be part of an organisation that unwittingly treats people from minority cultures differently. A recent damning report (Inquiry into the death of David Bennett) has found that institutional racism is rife within psychiatry and that black patients in particular receive poor-quality care as a result (Blofeld, 2003). This is despite the fact that the mental health system has a significant proportion of ethnic minority staff. Ethnic minority staff are less likely to hold senior positions and may therefore lack the power or confidence to influence institutional racist attitudes. These staff are often at the frontline of clinical services, but because of this, they are also directly implicated in delivering, at times, low-quality care to ethnic minority patients. Britain is a multicultural country and there are many different ethnic groups that are represented. The largest groups are Irish, Asian and black Caribbean, and black African. There are also large numbers of European immigrants from Greece and Italy and Arabic immigrants from Turkey and Cyprus. More recently, immigration of Eastern Europeans from Bosnia, Romania and Albania has further diversified the cultural groups represented in this country. Non-western European immigrants seem to suffer more inequality than other groups. Most of these people are not white and are thus 'visible' minorities. This chapter will focus primarily on these populations.

Ethnic minority populations tend to live in or around inner-city areas. They are less likely to be employed than the majority white population, have less gross income and more likely to be living in substandard or overcrowded accommodation. Five per cent of the total female population are from an ethnic minority; 47 per cent of ethnic women aged between 14 and 24 years are in full-time education compared to 32 per cent of white women; 55 per cent of ethnic minority women are economically active compared to 73 per cent of white women. A Runnymede Report (Sanglin-Grant and Schneider, 2000) found that 21 per cent of black and Asian workers have degrees, compared with 16 per cent of their white counterparts, yet they are far less likely to make it to a senior position in the workplace.

It is in this context that women from ethnic minorities enter psychiatric services. Without recognition of the fact of institutional racism, it is difficult to begin to understand the problems and potential stresses faced by any individual from a cultural minority. This is not to say that every patient from a cultural minority is suffering under the burden of racism on an everyday palpable level. Like other victims of abuse, some people are more likely to be affected than others. The point is that women from cultural minorities might be less likely to approach services for help or to believe that psychiatric services may have their best interests at heart. This is particularly so if they themselves or those they know have been treated in a discriminatory way either directly or indirectly by other institutional systems, e.g., educational systems, criminal justice systems, etc.

It is important to note that all health professionals, working in mainstream psychiatry, regardless of cultural background, may be perceived by individual patients as being part of the cultural majority.

EPIDEMIOLOGY

See Table 9.1

- Black women (both African and African-Caribbean) are more likely to be admitted compulsorily (Davies *et al.*, 1996).
- Asian and especially black patients experience more complex pathways into hospital and have higher levels of involvement with the police than their white counterparts. They are also less likely to perceive themselves as having a psychiatric problem or as needing to go into hospital and express less satisfaction with the admission process (Commander *et al.*, 1999).
- Black women are less likely to have their depression diagnosed and treated by their GP than white women are (Nazroo, 1997).
- Research into depression in ethnic minority patients has been criticised because of inadequate conceptual models, diagnostic tools and treatment approaches.
- Dementias – Parkinson's disease and Alzheimer's disease are seen in lower rates in black compared with white women. Multi-infarct dementia is found in higher rates in blacks and Asians compared with whites.
- Asian women (particularly 15–34 years) are more likely to attempt and complete suicide than white or black women (Raleigh, 1996; Bhugra *et al.*, 1999).

Table 9.1 Rates of psychiatric disorder by ethnic background

	African	*African-Caribbean*	*South Asian*	*Chinese*	*White*
Depression[1,2]	?	6%	3%	1.6%	3%
Anxiety disorder[2]	?	12%	10%	8%	16%
Obsessional compulsive disorder[3]	?	?	?	?	1.5%
Alcohol dependence[3]	?	?	?	?	2%
Substance misuse[3]	?	?	?	?	1.5%
Psychosis[2] (rates per 1000)	?	14	6	2	8
Suicide[4] (rates per 100,000)	?	~7–8	~30	?	10–12

Notes: ? = insufficient data
[1] Shaw *et al.*, 1999
[2] Nazroo, 1997
[3] Jenkins *et al.*, 1998
[4] Raleigh, 1996

MANAGEMENT

The Royal College of Psychiatrists has stated that services have to be accessible, acceptable, user-friendly and culturally sensitive. In order to improve the care given to women from cultural minorities, the following need to be addressed.

At an institutional level

• Social policy – this should reflect the needs of the population at a local and countrywide level. Resources should be directed towards improving the social factors (frequently negative), which influence the health of ethnic minority women.

• Health promotion – mental illness is taboo in many cultures. Because of social inequality, minority women are perhaps more at risk of mental illness yet are probably unaware of the symptoms and signs of illness and, moreover, what to do if this interferes with their normal functioning. Health promotion campaigns may help these women understand that they might have a problem for which they can receive help.

• Information sharing and communication – many ethnic minority women do not consider English as their main spoken language and a significant proportion cannot read English. Thus language is a barrier to obtaining adequate services. As well as translating services, information on mental ill-health, staffing, medications, psychological treatments and the Mental Health Act should be readily available in user-friendly formats. This might include pamphlets in different languages, but also visual and audio media can be used to increase accessibility.

• Commissioning of services – this is one of the main ways to improve psychiatric services for minority women. Health Authorities should involve ethnic minority groups (community groups, religious groups) at an early stage in the planning of services in order to ensure the commissioning of appropriate services for their local area (Grant-Pearce and Deane, 1999). Needs assessments undertaken with effective consultation with ethnic minority groups will probably highlight the need for different models of psychiatric service delivery in different areas (Rawaf and Bahl, 1998).

• Recruitment and retention of ethnic minority staff in the NHS – there is under-representation of ethnic minority staff particularly in senior positions within the NHS. This means that ethnic minority staff are unlikely to be involved in decision-making processes with regard to service provision. However, just adding 'visible' minorities to the psychiatric workforce will not improve the service delivery to ethnic minority women. In fact, this approach increases the risk of *tokenism*. Employing one or two minority staff and assuming that they possess the necessary cultural competence (see below) to meet the needs of ethnic minority women will result in a false sense of accomplishment without any real change in service. Government policy should encompass incentives for NHS Trusts to recruit new and train existing minority staff to take up senior managerial positions. Frequently ethnic minority staff complain that they are not given access to more senior positions because they are not involved in the 'old boy network' and that applicants had already been identified long before the post had been advertised, giving them no real chance of getting the job.

• Staff training – all mental health professionals, regardless of seniority or cultural background, should be trained to be culturally competent (see Chandra, 1999). This includes race awareness training, i.e. awareness of racism and its implications; cultural awareness training to provide information on the habits, belief systems and life-style of black and minority people in Britain; and anti-discriminatory training: acknowledgement and understanding of the individual's own beliefs, actions and clinical practice which may be discriminatory and the encouragement of more appropriate behaviours.

> Culturally competent agencies are characterised by acceptance and respect of difference, continuing self-assessment regarding culture, careful attention to the dynamics of difference, continuous expansion of cultural knowledge and resources and a variety of adaptations to service models in order to meet the needs of minority populations better. (Juss, 1999)

• Research – there is a considerable body of research looking at the relationship between ethnic status and mental health. However, this research tends to have been focused in the area of psychosis, particularly in African-Caribbean males. Most of these studies have looked at rates of illness in treated populations and have failed to look at community rates of mental ill-health and very few studies have looked at the mental health of women. The government has become aware of the inequalities in mental health provision for ethnic minority groups and therefore more research is being funded in this area. Unfortunately there is a risk that the work may continue to focus on highly publicised problems to the exclusion of other types of mental disorder. In addition to resourcing specific areas, e.g. suicide in Asian females, research and funding should be directed towards looking at pathways into care, untreated populations, types of treatment and community surveys to assess other psychiatric problems in cultural minority women.

FACTORS IN THE INDIVIDUAL

For each individual woman, there will be various factors which interplay to influence the onset of mental ill-health, its presentation and the way in which the woman might best be treated. It should be emphasised that this is not an exhaustive list but rather an aid to direct the practitioner towards those areas that might assist them to optimise the treatment of minority women in an holistic manner.

1 Biological factors

• *Drug handling* – most research into new drugs is carried out on young white males. Data on the effects of psychiatric medications in different ethnic minority populations is rarely available, and until recently, women have been excluded from drug trials as pharmaceutical companies fear the consequences of potential teratogenicity in women of reproductive age. This means that drugs are tested in white males and the data from these tests is extrapolated to minority women. The very few studies (mainly American) that have addressed this issue have found important differences in the way in which drugs are handled by different ethnic groups. For example, lithium levels remain higher for longer in black patients compared with white and Asian (Far East) patients. This means that black patients may be at an increased risk of lithium toxicity compared with other ethnic groups (Okpaku *et al.*, 1980). Chinese patients achieve higher plasma haloperidol levels for the same dose of medication compared with black and caucasian patients. Also, black patients achieve higher reduced haloperidol (rHpl, a metabolite of haloperidol which may act as a pro-drug) than other ethnic groups. RHpl may act as a reservoir for haloperidol and thus increase the exposure of black patients to the active drug beyond that usually expected from studies in caucasians (Jann *et al.*, 1993). Black patients appear to respond better and more rapidly to tricyclic antidepressants (TCA) than caucasians; this may be due to higher TCA concentrations being achieved in black compared with white patients (Silver *et al.*, 1993). Clearly, there is a very small data pool regarding ethnic differences in drug handling and the data specific to women is almost non-existent. This is a greatly under-researched area and this needs to be addressed.

• *Genetic susceptibility* – there is more and more evidence that certain mental illnesses are genetically loaded. This indicates that there may also be ethnic differences in susceptibility to mental illness.

2 Social factors

• *Economic* – as stated earlier, minority women are particularly at risk of economic deprivation. Poverty is associated with unemployment, inadequate housing, overcrowding and low educational achievement. These are all factors which increase the risk of mental ill-health, independent of ethnicity.

• *Religion* – there are many different sub-cultural groups within the main ethnic groups represented in this country. There are thus many different religious beliefs (including Islam, Hinduism, Christianity, Buddhism) and these may affect the way in which a woman understands any emotional problem she has. Involvement in a religious community is often a protective factor against mental ill-health, but occasionally, women may find themselves castigated if they become mentally unwell. Religious beliefs may result in late presentation of mental illness, as the woman suffering may see this as 'God's will'. It is important to explore the woman's religious beliefs as this may have an impact on her ability to adhere to certain types of treatment regimes, e.g. some medicines come in gelatine capsules. Gelatine is often made from the bones, skin and tendons of dead cows. Hindus regard all living things, particularly cows, as sacred and therefore may be reluctant to take such medications. Although not always the case, religious leaders can often be helpful in communicating ideas and understanding of illness within the context of the woman's religion and if the woman is willing it may be useful to involve them.

• *Spirituality* – although this may be linked to a woman's religious beliefs, many minority women who would not count themselves as religious, feel themselves to be deeply spiritual and this spirituality is intimately involved with beliefs about their mental well-being. Again exploration of the woman's philosophical and spiritual beliefs may assist in finding an optimum treatment package for that individual.

• *Marital relationships* – some women from the Asian subcontinent have arranged marriages. For westerners this is an alien concept but it is clear that many people choose to have arranged marriages and that these marriages work well. However, some women may feel coerced into a marriage by their family and this can have a negative influence on their mental health. The impact of the woman's marital relationship on her illness should be explored with the woman, independent of her husband. The presence of her spouse may inhibit a woman's ability to speak, thus it is important to ensure that there is an independent translator, rather than relying on family members to translate particularly as the family dynamics may be implicated in the woman's illness. For many South Asian women, marital difficulties are something they feel unable to share with outsiders, for fear of bringing shame on their family. This means that domestic violence or marital rape may not be reported. If the practitioner discovers abuse within the marriage it is important not to accept this behaviour as cultural. If it is possible to involve the woman's own family, then they may be able to evoke a change in the spouse, or even persuade and encourage the woman to leave. At times though, women brought from South Asian countries to be married to British-born South Asian males find themselves extremely isolated. They may present with their problem, but be reluctant to take any steps to remove themselves from an abusive relationship. If the woman is unwilling to take such an approach, it does not mean that she is happy with her situation. It is important to reaffirm that the situation is wrong and always keep the door open by offering regular appointments or discussion through health visitors or baby clinics.

A significant proportion of African-Caribbean women raise their children with little support from their partners. Although the lack of an emotionally supportive partner has been shown to be associated with an increased risk of mental illness, Nazroo (1997) found the converse, that marriage or co-habitation increased the risk of mental illness for Caribbean women, although it reduced the risk for whites and South Asians (Nazroo, 1997). The presence of an emotionally confiding relationship and good social network, e.g. parents and sisters, may mitigate against illness.

3 Psychological factors

• Racial identity, individual reaction to racism, individual response to living in a country where you are perceived as different regardless of how Anglicised your personal culture may all influence mental well-being. Main-stream psychotherapies rarely deal with the interrelated themes of race and powerlessness and thus increasingly there is a need for culturally centred therapy such as that delivered by organisations such as NAFSIYAT in North London.

• Parental separation – some African-Caribbean and African women suffered parental separation at an early age. For African-Caribbean women this was often when their parents left them behind in the West Indies to be cared for by the extended family. In the case of African women this may have been when their parents returned home to Africa, leaving them behind in England, often with English foster parents, in order that they might continue their schooling. We now know that these types of separations may be associated with attachment problems which may be associated with psycho-pathology in later life.

References

Bhugra, D., Desai, M. and Baldwin, D.S. (1999) Attempted suicide in west London: I. Rates across ethnic communities. *Psychological Medicine* 29 (5):1125–30.

Blofeld, J. *et al.* (2003) *Independent Inquiry into the death of David Bennett.* Norfolk, Suffolk and Cambridgeshire Strategic Health Authority.

Bush, B. (1990) Slave women in Caribbean society 1650–1838. Oxford: James Currey.

Chandra, J. (1999) Managing for cultural competence in K. Bhui and D. Olajide (eds.), *Mental Health Service Provision for a Multi-cultural Society.* London/ Edinburgh: W.B. Saunders.

Commander, M.J., Cochrane, R., Sashidharan, S.P., Akilu, F. and Wildsmith, E. (1999) Mental health care for Asian, black and white patients with non-affective psychoses: pathways to the psychiatric hospital, in-patient and after-care. *Social Psychiatry and Psychiatric Epidemiology* (Sept)34(9): 484–91.

Davies, S., Thornicroft, G., Leese, M., Higgingbotham, A. and Phelan, M. (1996) Ethnic differences in risk of compulsory psychiatric admission among representa-tive cases of psychosis in London. *British Medical Journal* 312: 533–7

Fanon (1956) Racism and culture. Speech given to first congress of Negro Writers and Artists.

Grant-Pearce, C. and Deane, J. (1999) Joint working between the public and purchasing authorities to determine mental health information needs, in D.Bhugra and V. Bhal (eds.), *Ethnicity: An Agenda for Mental Health.* London: Gaskell.

Jann, M., Lam, Y. and Chang, W. (1993) Haloperidol and reduced haloperidol plasma concentrations in different ethnic populations and interindividual variabilities in haloperidol metabolism, in K. Lin, R. Poland and G. Nakasaki (eds.), *Psychopharmacology and Psychobiology of Ethnicity: Progress in Psychiatry.* Washington DC London, England: American Psychiatric Press.

Jenkins, R., Bebbington, P., Brugha, T.S., Farrell, M., Lewis, G. and Meltzer, H. (1998) British psychiatric morbidity survey. *British Journal of Psychiatry* 173: 4–7.

Jordan, W.D. (1968) White over Black: American attitudes toward the Negro 1550–1812. Chapel Hill, N.C.: University of North Carolina Press.

Juss, S. (1999) Cultural competence and the law of mental health, in K. Bhui and D. Olajide (eds.), *Mental Health Service Provision for a Multi-cultural Society.* London/Edinburgh: W.B. Saunders.

Nazroo, J. (1997) *Ethnicity and Mental Health: Fourth National Survey of Ethnic Minorities.* London: Policy Studies Institute.

Raleigh, V.S. (1996) Suicide patterns and trends in people of Indian subcontinent and Caribbean origin in England and Wales. *Ethnicity and Health* 1:55–63.

Rawaf, S. and Bahl, V. (eds.) (1998) *Assessing the Health Needs of People from Minority Ethnic Groups.* London: Royal College of Physicians and Faculty of Public Health Medicine.

Sanglin-Grant, S. and Schneider, R. (2000) *Moving On Up? Racial Equality and the Corporate Agenda: A Study of FTSE 100 Companies.* London: Runnymede Trust.

Shaw, C.M., Creed, F., Tomenson, B., Riste, L. and Cruickshank, J.K. (1999) Prevalence of anxiety and depressive illness and help seeking behaviour in African Caribbeans and white Europeans: two phase general population survey. *British Medical Journal* 318: 302–5.

Silver, B., Poland, R. and Lin, K. (1993) Ethnicity and the pharmacology of tricyclic antidepressants, in K. Lin, R. Poland and G. Nakasaki (eds.), *Psychopharmacology and Psychobiology of Ethnicity: Progress in Psychiatry.* Washington DC London, England: American Psychiatric Press.

Useful addresses

African-Caribbean Mental Health Advocacy

49 Effra Road, Brixton, London SW2 1BZ
Phone: Office: 020 7737 3603
Description: offers advice, counselling and advocacy for African and Caribbean people with mental health problems.

Black Women's Mental Health Project

12 Donovan Court, Exton Crescent, Stonebridge, London NW10 8DA
Phone: 020 8691 6324
Description: drop-in, advice and information helpline

Chinese Mental Health Association

2nd Floor
Zenith House
155 Curtain Road
London
EC2A 3QY
Tel: 020 7613 1008
Fax: 020 7739 6577
Web: www.cmha.org.uk
Best time to telephone: Mon–Fri, 9.30am–5.30pm
Description: range of services for Chinese people with mental health problems including translation/interpreting services, befriending, counselling, clinical assessment, etc. Limited access to supported housing. Phone for details.
Opening hours: Office: Mon–Fri 9.30am–5pm
Referral: self or other agencies
Criteria/ catchment: Chinese people with a mental health problem

Muslim Women's Helpline

11 Main Drive, East Lane Business Park, Wembley, London, HA9 7PX
Phone: Office: 0208 908 3205
Other numbers: Helpline: 0208 904 8193
Email: mwhl@amrnet.demon.co.uk
Website: www.amrnet.demon.co.uk/related/mwhl.html
Description: telephone helpline for Muslim women, offering advice and support on a range of issues. One-to-one counselling by phone or in person where appropriate. Culturally sensitive service for Muslim/Islamic women.
Opening hours: Office: Mon–Fri 10am–4pm Helpline: anytime, leave number on answerphone if nobody available
Referral: open access
Criteria/ catchment: Muslim women only

Nafsiyat

278 Seven Sisters Road, Finsbury Park, London N4 2HY
Phone: 020 7263 4130
Description: offers culturally sensitive therapy to black and ethnic minority groups.

Vietnamese Mental Health Services

Thomas Calton Centre, Alpha Street, London, SE15 4NX
Phone: 0207 639 2288
Fax: 0207 639 0008
Email: vietnamesemhs@cix.co.uk

Description: information, advice and support for Vietnamese people with mental health problems. Housing and benefits advice, interpretation services, outreach service, counselling, access to education opportunities, representation at tribunals, etc.

Additional info: limited supported accommodation may be available. Phone for details.

Opening hours: Office: Mon–Fri 9am–5pm

Referral: self or other agencies

Criteria/catchment: anyone from Vietnam living in the UK with mental health problems.

Cares of Life Project
Peckham Settlement
Goldsmith Road
Peckham
London SE15 5TF
Tel: 020 7732 4504
Fax: 020 7732 2698
Email: info@caresoflife.org
Mon–Fri, 9am–5pm

Part IV
Specific disorders

9   The Psychoses

Louise Howard

The term 'psychotic' is used as a descriptive term for disorders with hallucinations, delusions or severe abnormalities of behaviour (e.g. psychomotor retardation, catatonic behaviour). In this chapter this term is retained and disorders are discussed in turn as classified in the International Classification of Diseases (ICD 10) (WHO, 1992). The research literature on the main categories of disorder is reviewed here, focusing on the epidemiology, outcome, aetiology and treatment for women with psychotic disorders and does not attempt to cover the wider research literature in these areas.

SCHIZOPHRENIA AND SCHIZO-AFFECTIVE PSYCHOSIS

Epidemiology

The schizophrenic disorders are characterised by fundamental and characteristic distortions of thinking (delusions) and perception (hallucinations), and by inappropriate and blunted affect. Schizophrenia and schizophreniform disorders have an equal prevalence in men and women (lifetime morbidity risk of 1 per cent) but men have a younger age at onset. Conversely, studies of late-onset schizophrenia (after age 45) have consistently shown increased rates in women (see Piccinelli and Gomez-Homen, 1997). Women also have a higher risk of familial morbidity (Goldstein et al., 1990).

Outcome

Schizophrenia in women appears to be a different disorder to that in men. There is considerable evidence that women with schizophrenia have a better outcome compared with men. Women have less evidence of negative symptoms (Roy et al 2001), are less socially impaired (Usall et al, 2002), are more likely to live independently and spend more time in remission than men (e.g. Angermeyer et al., 1990; Gur et al., 1996; Navarro et al., 1996). Women also have a better treatment response, though in neuroleptic-refractory schizophrenia women may do worse than men (Szymanski et al., 1995). Women are more likely to have affective symptoms such as dysphoria, depression and hostility (Castle et al, 1994) and more positive symptoms especially persecutory hallucinations (Golstein et al, 1990) and auditory hallucinations (Rector and Seeman, 1992).

Although measures of objective life situation are generally better for female than for male patients with schizophrenia, no differences have been found between men and women in subjective quality of life, in a first admission sample or in a prevalence sample (Röder-Wanner and Priebe, 1997; Röder-Wanner and Priebe, 1998; Solomon and Draine, 1993). However, this may be because the instruments used to measure quality of life in psychotic patients are not designed to detect gender-specific differences.

There also appear to be no gender differences in satisfaction with services (Lebow, 1983; Like and Zyzansky, 1987) despite a trend for women to receive less inpatient care compared with men (Piccinelli and Gomez-Homen, 1997). In general though, there are no gender differences in readmission to hospital (Piccinelli and Gomez-Homen, 1997) or treatment in outpatient mental health settings (Leaf and Livingstone, 1987).

Aetiology of gender differences

The gender differences described above have been postulated to be due to biologically different forms of psychotic disorder (hypothesised to be due to differential hemispheric organisation, e.g. Flor-Henry, 1990), genetic differences, normal sex-related maturational changes with differential timing in males and females (Spauwen et al, 2003), greater exposure to birth injury in males (Kirov et al, 1996), increased emotional reactivity to daily life stress in females (Myin–Germeys et al 2004) and the protective effect of oestrogen on brain receptors (Seeman et al 1997). Sex hormones are postulated to influence gender differences in utero when brain development is differentiated by gender depending on the type of hormonal exposure ('organisational effects'), and after puberty when sex hormones rise and differentially affect neuronal function ('activational effects'). There is some clinical data to suggest that women with schizophrenia have fewer psychotic symptoms at times of high oestrogen levels (e.g. in the pre-menopausal period), though the epidemiology of gender differences in psychosis cannot readily be accounted for in terms of differing oestrogen levels. For example, the preponderance of women in late-onset schizophrenia cannot be explained by further declines in oestrogen levels as they remain relatively unchanged in late postmenopause (Molnar et al., 1988).

Nevertheless, some women have periodic psychoses which recur solely in association with specific phases of the menstrual cycle (Gerada and Reveley, 1988; Lovestone, 1992). This may be due to oestrogen's effects on D2 receptors, though effects on the serotonergic system are also likely to be involved as oestrogen treatment enhances 5-HT responsivity (Halbreich et al., 1995).

Women with schizophrenia may be initially misdiagnosed. Narrow diagnostic criteria exclude episodes that are brief and that consist predominantly of affective symptoms (Castle, 2000) and these individuals are mainly women. Social factors will also play a part in the gender differences reported. Lower expectations of women, less stigma being attached to illness in women, less concern about social deviance in women and different attitudes to services could all be relevant.

Treatment

Women are more likely to develop tardive dyskinesia (Yassa and Jeste, 1992) and human studies have shown that the pharmacokinetics and pharmacodynamics of drugs differ between men and women (Seeman 2004); women should therefore usually be on lower dosages of neuroleptics when used (or preferably atypical antipsychotic drugs, see Part VI, Chapter 20). In a chronically ill population men were found to need two times as high a dose as women for effective maintenance (Melkersson et al, 2001). Traditional neuroleptics are also associated with anovulatory menstrual cycles and amenorrhoea (Smith et al., 2002). Women are also more likely to need mood stabilisers in addition to antipsychotic medication due to the affective nature of their clinical picture. Some women find their symptoms worsen around the time of their menstrual cycle and temporary increases in antipsychotic dose should be considered for the perimenstrual period in these cases. While care programmes are intended to be individually tailored to patients' needs, researchers have found no explicit consideration of gender-specific needs in a day hospital setting (Perkins and Rowland, 1991) – these include access to contraception and physical screening programmes (e.g. cervical and breast screening) and help with parenting (see below).

AFFECTIVE PSYCHOSES: BIPOLAR DISORDER (BPD) AND DEPRESSIVE PSYCHOSIS

Epidemiology

Bipolar disorder is defined as a disorder with at least two episodes in which the patient's mood and activity levels are significantly disturbed, which on some occasions consists of elevation of mood and increased activity (mania) and on others of lowering of mood with decreased energy and activity depression). Severe episodes may have psychotic symptoms (delusions, hallucinations or stupor). Women are more likely (approximately two-fold) to have major depression than men but there is no gender difference in the rate of bipolar disorder. There are also no differences in the age at onset of mood disorders.

Outcome

Women with bipolar disorder are more likely to have rapid cycling manic depression and more episodes of depression than men with the same diagnosis (Blehar, 1995). There is also evidence that women have longer index episodes of major depression and lower rates of spontaneous remission than men (Sargeant et al., 1990).

Aetiology of gender differences

Some studies have found the heritability of major depression to be higher in women than in men (McGuffin et al, 1996, Kendler et al, 2001)–in the largest sample to date the heritability of liability to depression in women was 42% compared with 29% in men (Kendler et al, 2006). While the other biological factors mentioned above for schizophrenia may also be relevant in affective psychoses, different gender roles and cultural norms are also likely to be relevant. Brown and Harris's work on life events and social support highlighted the importance of environmental factors in the development of depressive disorders. No gender differences in the risk of depression have been found in communities where social roles are protective against depression in women and men are not able to mask depression by using alcohol or adopting violent behaviour, e.g. in the Amish community (Egeland and Hostetter, 1983) and in the Orthodox Jewish community (Loewenthal et al., 1995). In bipolar disorder these social factors may play a part in explaining the increased risk of depressive episodes in women compared with men.

Treatment

It has been claimed that women appear to be less responsive to tricyclic antidepressants, take longer to respond and need longer courses of treatment (Weissman and Olfson, 1995; Kornstein, 1997). This may be due to gender differences in drug absorption, distribution and metabolism. However a recent meta – analysis examining gender differences in response to tricyclic antidepressants in a dataset that included published and unpublished RCTs found few significant differences, which were probably chance results (Wohlfarth et al, 2004). The authors also pointed out that other factors such as age, concomitant medication and smoking status may also differentially influence efficacy. It has also been suggested, e.g. from data from 15 RCTs, that women are more likely to respond to lower doses of Selective Serotonin Reuptake Inhibitors compared with men (Khan et al, 2005).

Women and men appear to have similar outcomes after cognitive behavioural therapy. Women with a history of bipolar disorder have a high risk (1 in 2 to 5) of relapse postpartum (Marks et al., 1992). It is therefore important to discuss this increased risk in women of childbearing age who may decide to avoid or delay conception (relapse of depression is more likely if conception occurs less than two years after a previous postpartum epi-sode). If conception is planned women should be advised on the advantages and disadvantages of medication through pregnancy. Lithium in particular is known to cause an approximately ten-fold increase in the risk of teratogenic effects. If lithium is prescribed through the first trimester of pregnancy ultra-sound scans should be considered during the second trimester to look for major abnormalities so that foetal or neonatal treatment can be planned (where possible) or termination of pregnancy can be considered (see also Part VI, Chapter 20 on biological treatments).

SUBSTANCE MISUSE AND PSYCHOSIS

In some patients who have a psychotic disorder co-existing substance misuse can be associated with an exacerbation of symptoms or may be the main cause of the psychotic symptoms (e.g. in amphetamine psychosis). Patients who have substance misuse disorders and a psychotic disorder have been categorised as having a 'dual diagnosis'. Patients with a dual diagnosis are at increased risk of poor outcome, including relapses and rehospitalisation, homelessness and higher use of services.

Dual diagnosis is associated with younger age and male gender across many studies (e.g. Menezes et al., 1996; Mueser et al., 2000), though women have been reported to be more likely than male patients to use stimulants (Mueser et al., 2000). A study of patients with first episode psychosis found that women are less likely than men to have substance-related psychosis (Cantwell et al., 1999). Female patients are nevertheless at risk of dual diagnosis – a recent study of hospitalised patients with severe mental illness found alcohol use disorders in 50 per cent women (66 per cent in men), cannabis use disorder in 22 per cent women (39 per cent in men) and cocaine use disorders in 15 per cent women (14 per cent men) (Mueser et al., 2000). These women are more socially connected than men with dual diagnosis but are also likely to have greater problems with violent victimisation. They are also more likely to have children, yet have little contact with their extended families (Brunette and Drake, 1997; Brunette and Drake, 1998). It is signifi-cant that women with schizophrenia and comorbid substance abuse disorders are less likely to receive substance abuse treatment than men (Alexander, 1996; Comtois and Ries, 1995).

PARENTING AND PSYCHOSIS

Women with chronic mental illness are more likely to be heterosexually active than men but birth control information and contraception are relatively inaccessible to these women (Test and Berlin, 1981). Psychiatric professionals appear to be unlikely to discuss birth control with women with psychiatric disorders (Rudolph et al., 1990). Of female inpatients 33 per cent report having intercourse without using contraception, despite not wanting to get pregnant, with a similar proportion having a history of induced abortions (Coverdale and Aruffo, 1989). Antenatal and perinatal care may be particularly important in women with psychotic disorders as they appear to be more likely than normal controls to experience obstetric complications (Goodman and Emory, 1992; Sacker et al., 1996).

Women with severe mental illness are more likely than men to be involved in childcare – of 551 Mental Health Act assessments involving parents living with dependent children, 72 per cent involved women (Hatfield et al., 1997). It is increasingly recognised that a significant proportion of women with psychotic disorders have parental responsibilities (e.g. White et al., 1995; Hearle et al., 1999) which needs to be remembered when planning care. The impact of the parental illness on the child and associations between parental mental illness and subsequent disturbances in the child are well documented (e.g. Rutter, 1966; Rutter and Quinton, 1984). Genetic transmission, as well as correlates of mental illness such as parental discord, aggressive behaviour or neglect determine such difficulties.

Parenting difficulties appear to be common in women with psychosis though it is not clear how to assess parenting in these families (Appleby and Dickens, 1993). Studies have reported that a significant proportion of mothers with psychotic disorders do not maintain full custody of their children (Mowbray et al., 1995; Wang and Goldschmidt, 1996; Joseph et al., 1999; Kumar et al., 1995; Hearle et al., 1999). This means that in addition to coping with a severe mental illness, women with psychotic disorders have to cope with the stress of caring for a child or cope with the loss or potential loss of their parenting role (Apfel and Handel, 1993).

Services

Women and men are cared for alongside each other in most modern services, whether as outpatients or inpatients. However, women with psychotic disorders can be very vulnerable in these environments as they are at risk of sexual exploitation, assaults and harassment (Mental Health Act Commission, 1999).Single sex units are not necessarily seen as a safe option by female patients though–a recent qualitative study of women on medium secure units found that women in single units reported intimidation, threats and abuse by women, though they were less vulnerable to sexual abuse and exploitation and serious physical assault (Mezey et el, 2005).

They may also be reluctant to be admitted to hospital if they are mothers as this will involve separation from their children. There are several mother and baby units in the UK for mothers who are ill in the perinatal period, though some areas (e.g. Wales) have no inpatient service at all. There are almost no similar units for women with older children though some services are currently being developed which offer completely separate services for women where they can be admitted with their children in crisis (Killaspy et al., 2000). In the UK the National Service Framework for Mental Health (Department of Health, 1999) stresses the government's aim of achieving fully segregated sleeping, washing and toilet facilities and single-sex day space when women are in hospital.

Conclusion

Women have the same lifetime prevalence of psychotic disorders as men but tend to have a better outcome. It is unclear why women are to some extent protected from the severity of psychotic disorders. However, this can mean that women's particular needs are neglected by psychiatric services which tend to focus resources on the most severely ill patients and those who are at risk of violence. Substance misuse may be under-detected and under-treated in women with psychosis. Increasing recognition of these issues should lead to the development of services which offer gender-specific assessments and care programmes; treatments that take into account the relevant gender differences, and support in the areas detailed above including parenting, gynaecological screening, family planning and domestic violence. This may only be possible in a psychiatric service set up specifically for women with psychotic disorders.

References

Alexander, M.J. (1996) Women with co-occurring addictive and mental disorders: an emerging profile of vulnerability. American Journal of Orthopsychiatry 66: 61–70.

Angermeyer, M.C., Kuhn, L. and Goldstein, J.M. (1990) Sex and the course of schizophrenia: differences in treated outcomes. Schizophrenia Bulletin 16: 293–307.

Apfel, R.J. and Handel, M.H. (1993) Madness and Loss of Motherhood: Sexuality, Reproduction and Long-Term Mental Illness. Washington, DC: American Psychiatric Press.

Appleby, L. and Dickens, C. (1993) Mothering skills of women with mental illness. British Medical Journal 306: 348–9.

Blehar, M.C. (1995) Gender differences in risk factors for mood and anxiety disorders: implications for clinical treatment research. Psychopharmacology Bulletin 31(4): 687–91.

Brunette, M.F. and Drake, R.E. (1997) Gender differences in patients with schizophrenia and substance abuse. Comprehensive Psychiatry 38(2): 109–16.

Brunette, M.F. and Drake, R.E. (1998) Gender differences in homeless persons with schizoprehnia and substance abuse. Community Mental Health Journal 34(6): 627–42.

Cantwell, R., Brewin, J., Glazerbrook, C. et al. (1999) Prevalence of substance misuse in first-episode psychosis. British Journal of Psychiatry 174: 150–3.

Castle D.J., Sham P.C., Wessely S. et al. (1994) The subtyping of schizophrenia in men and women: a latent class analysis. Psychological Medicine 24:41-51

Castle, D.J., (2000) Epidemiology of women and schizophrenia. In Women and Schizophrenia. Eds Castle D.J., McGrath J., Kulkarni J. Cambridge University Press

Comtois, K.A. and Ries, R. (1995) Sex differences in dually diagnosed severely mentally ill clients in dual diagnosis outpatient treatment. American Journal of Addiction 4: 245–53.

Coverdale, J.H. and Aruffo, J.A. (1989) Family planning needs of female chronic psychiatric patients. American Journal of Psychiatry 146: 1489–91.

Department of Health National Service Framework for Mental Health (1999) Modern Standards and Service Models. London: The Stationary Office.

Egeland, J.A. and Hostetter, A.M. (1983) Amish study, I: affective disorders among the Amish, 1976–1980. American Journal of Psychiatry 140(1): 56–61.

Flor-Henry, P. (1990) Influence of gender in schizophrenia as related to other psycho-pathological syndromes. Schizophrenia Bulletin 16: 211–27.

Gerada, C. and Reveley, A. (1988) Schizophreniform psychosis associated with the menstrual cycle. British Journal of Psychiatry 152: 700–2.

Goldstein, J.M., Faraone, S.V., Chen, W.J. et al. (1990) Sex differences in the familial transmission of schizophrenia. British Journal of Psychiatry 156: 819–26.

Goodman, S.H. and Emory, E.K. (1992) Perinatal complications in births to low socio-economic status schizophrenic and depressed women. Journal of Abnormal Psychology 101: 225–9.

Gur, R.G., Petty, R.G., Turetsky, B.I. and Gur, R.C. (1996) Schizophrenia throughout life: sex differences in severity and profile of symptoms. Schizophrenia Research 21: 1–12.

Halbreich U., Rojansky, N., Palter, S., Tworek, H., Hissin, P. and Wang, K. (1995) Estrogen augments serotonergic activity in postmenopausal women. Biological Psychiatry 37: 434–41.

Hatfield, B., Webster, J. and Mohamad, H. (1997) Psychiatric emergencies: assessing parents of dependent children. Psychiatric Bulletin 21: 19–22.

Hearle, J., Plant, K., Jenner, L. et al. (1999) A survey of contact with offspring and assistance with child care among parents with psychotic disorders. Psychiatric Services 50(10): 1354–6.

Joseph, J.G., Joshi, S.V., Lewin, A. and Abrams, M. (1999) Characteristics and Perceived needs of mothers with serious mental illness. Psychiatric Services 50(10): 1357–9.

Kendler K.S., Gardner C.O., Neale M.C., Prescott C.A. (2001) Genetic risk factors for major depression in men and women: similar or different heritabilities and same or partly distinct genes? Psychological Medicine 31:605-616

Kendler K.S., Gatz M., Gardner C.O., Pedersen N.L. (2006) A Swedish National Twin Study of Lifetime Major Depression. American Journal of Psychiatry 163: 109-114.

Khan A., Brodhead A.E., Schwartz K.A., Kolts R.L., Brown W.A. (2005) Sex Differences in Antidepressant Response in Recent Antidepressant Clinical Trials. Journal of Clinical Psychiatry 25 (4): 318-324.

Killaspy, H., Dalton, J., McNicholas, J. and Johnson, S. (2000) Drayton Park, an alternative to hospital admission for women in acute mental health crisis. Psychiatric Bulletin 24(3): 101–4.

Kirov G., Jones P.B., Harvey I., Lewis S.W., Toone B.K., Rifkin L., Sham P., Murray R.M. (!996) Do obstetric complications cause the earlier age at onset in male than female schizophrenics? Schizophrenia Research 20:117-124.

Kornstein, S.G. (1997) Gender differences in depression: implications for treatment. Journal of Clinical Psychiatry 58 Suppl. 15: 12–18.

Kumar, R., Marks, M., Platz, C. and Yoshida, K. (1995) Clinical survey of a psychiatric mother and baby unit: characteristics of 100 consecutive admissions. Journal of Affective Disorders 33: 11–22.

Leaf, P.J. and Livingstone, B.M. (1987) Gender differences in the use of mental health-related services: a re-examination. Journal of Health and Social Behaviour 28: 171–83.

Lebow, J.L. (1983) Client satisfaction with mental health treatment: methodological considerations in assessment. Evaluation Reviews 7: 729–52.

Like, R. and Zyzansky, J. (1987) Patient satisfaction with the clinical encounter: social psychological determinants. Social Science and Medicine 24: 351–7.

Loewenthal, K., Goldblatt, V., Gorton, T., Lubitsch, G., Bicknell, H., Fellowes, D. and Sowden, A. (1995) Gender and depression in Anglo-Jewry. Psychological Medicine 25(5): 1051–63.

Lovestone, S. (1992) Periodic psychosis associated with the menstrual cycle and increased blink rate. British Journal of Psychiatry 161: 402–4.

Marks, M.N., Wieck, A., Checkley, S.A. et al. (1992) Contribution of psychological and social factors to psychotic and non-psychotic relapse after childbirth in women with previous histories of affective disorder. Journal of Affective Disorders 29: 253–64.

McGuffin P., Katz R., Watkins S., Rutherford J. (1996) A hospital-based twin register of the heritabilities of DSM-IV unipolar depression. Archives of General Psychiatry 53:129-136

Melkersson K.I., Hulting A.L., Rane A.J. (2001) Dose requirement and prolactin elevation of antipsychotics in male and female patients with schizophrenia or related psychoses. British Journal of Clinical Pharmacology 51:317-324

Menezes, P.R., Johnson, S., Thornicroft, G., Marshall, J., Prosser, D., Bebbington, P. and Kuipers, E. (1996) Drug and alcohol problems among individuals with severe mental illness in south London. British Journal of Psychiatry 168(5): 612–19.

Mental Health Act Commission (1999) Eighth Biennial Report. London: The Stationery Office.

Mezey G., Hassell Y., Bartlett A. (2005) Safety of women in mixed-sex and single-sex medium secure units: staff and patient perceptions. British Journal of Psychiatry 187: 579-582

Molnar, G., Takacs, I. and Bazsane, Z. (1988) Endocrine changes in endogenous psychoses of climacteric and involution. European Journal of Psychiatry 2: 147–58.

Mowbray, C.T., Oyserman, D., Zemencuk, J.K. and Ross, S.R. (1995) Motherhood for women with serious mental illness. American Journal of Orthopsychiatry (1995) 65: 21–38.

Mueser, K.T., Yarnold, P.R., Rosenberg, S.D. et al. (2000) Substance use disorder in hospitalised severely mentally ill psychiatric patients: prevalence, correlates and subgroups. Schizophrenia Bulletin 26(1): 179–92.

Murray, R.M., O'Callaghan, E., Castle, D.J., et al. (1992) A neurodevelopmental approach to the classification of schizophrenia. Schizophrenia Bulletin (1992) 18: 319–32.

Myin-Germeys I., Krabbendam L., Delespaul P.A.E.G., van Os J. (2004) Sex Differences in Emotional Reactivity to Daily Life Stress in Psychosis. Journal of Clinical Psychiatry 65:805-809.

Navarro, F., van Os J., Jones P. and Murray, R. (1996) Explaining sex differences in course and outcome in the functional psychoses. Schizophrenia Research 21: 161–70.

Perkins, R.E. and Rowland, L.A. (1991) Sex differences in service usage in long-term psychiatric care: are women adequately served? British Journal of Psychiatry 158(suppl. 10): 75–9.

Piccinelli, M. and Gomez-Homen, F. (1997) Gender Differences in the Epidemiology of Affective Disorders and Schizophrenia. Geneva: World Health Organisation.

Rector N.A., Seeman M.V., (1992) Auditory hallucinations in women and men. Schizophrenia Research 7:233-236

Röder-Wanner, U.U. and Priebe, S. (1997) Does quality of life differ in schizophrenic women and men? An empirical study. International Journal of Social Psychiatry 43: 129–43.

Röder-Wanner, U.U. and Priebe, S. (1998) Objective and subjective quality of life of first-admitted women and men with schizophrenia. European Archives of Psychiatry and Clinical Neuroscience 248: 250–8.

Roy M.A., Maziade M., Labbe A., et al. (2001) Male gender is associated with deficit schizophrenia: a meta-analysis. Schizophrenia Research 47:141-147.

Rudolph, B., Larson, G., Sweeney, S., Hough, E.E. and Arorian, K. (1990) Hospitalized pregnant women: characteristics and treatment issues. Hospital and Community Psychiatry 41: 159–63, 1990.

Rutter, M. (1966) Children of Sick Parents: An Environmental and Psychiatric Study. Institute of Psychiatry Maudsely Monographs 16. London: Oxford University Press.

Rutter, M. and Quinton, D. (1984) Parental psychiatric disorder: effects on children, Psychological Medicine 14: 853–80.

Sacker, A., Done, D.J. and Crow, T.J. (1996) Obstetric complications in children born to parents with schizophrenia: a meta-analysis of case-control studies. Psychological Medicine 26(2): 279–87.

Sargeant, J.K., Bruce, M.L., Florio, L.P. and Weissman, M.M. (1990) Factors associated with 1-year outcome of major depression in the community. Archives of General Psychiatry 47(6): 519–26.

Seeman M.V. (1997) Psychopathology in women and men; focus on female hormones. American Journal of Psychiatry. 154:1641-1647.

Seeman, M.V. (2004) Gender Differences in the Prescribing of Antipsychotic Drugs. American Journal of Psychiatry 161:1324-1333.

Smith, S., Wheeler, M.J., Murray, R. and O'Keane, V. (2002) The effects of antipsychotic-induced hyperprolactinaemia on the hypothalamic–pituitary–gonadal axis. Journal of Clinical Psychopharmacology 22: 109–14.

Solomon, P. and Draine, J. (1993) An assessment of gender as a factor among severely mentally disabled case management clients. Social Work in Health Care 19(1): 39–60.

Spauwen J., Krabbendam L., Lieb R., Wittchen H., van Os J. (2003) Sex differences in psychosis: normal or pathological? Schizophrenia Research 62 (1-2): 45-49

Szymanski, S., Lieberman, J., Pollack, S. et al. (1996) Gender differences in neuroleptic nonresponsive clozapine-treated schizophrenics. Biological Psychiatry 39(4): 249–54.

Test, M.A. and Berlin, S.B. (1981) Issues of special concern to chronically mentally ill women. Professional Psychology 12(1): 136–45.

Usall J., Haro J.M., Ochoa S., Marquez M., Araya S., Needs of Patients with Schizo-phrenia group. (2002) Influence of gender on social outcome in schizophrenia. Acta Psychiatrica Scandinavica. 106(5): 337-342

Wang, A. and Goldschmidt, V. (1993) Interviews with psychiatric inpatients about professional intervention with regard to their children. Acta Psychiatrica Scandinavica 93: 57–61.

Weissman, M. and Klerman, G.L. (1977) Sex differences and the epidemiology of depression. Archives of General Psychiatry 34: 98–111.

Weissman, M.M. and Olfson, M. (1995) Depression in women: implications for health care research. Science 269(5225): 799–801.

White, C.L., Nicholson, J., Fisher, W.H. and Geller, J.L. (1995) Mothers with severe mental illness caring for children. Journal of Nervous and Mental Disease 183: 398–403.

Wohlfarth T., Storosum J.G., Elferink A.J.A., van Zweiten B.J., Fouwels A., van den Brink W. (2004) Response to Tricyclic Antidepressants: Independent of Gender? American Journal of Psychiatry 161:370-372.

World Health Organisation (WHO) (1992) Tenth Revision of the International Classification of Diseases and Related Health Problems: Clinical Descriptions and Diagnostic Guidelines. Geneva: WHO.

Yassa, R. and Jeste, D.V. (1992) Gender differences in tardive dyskinesia: a critical review of the literature. Schizophrenia Bulletin 18(4): 701–15.

Useful addresses

Rethink

National advice service
Tel: 020 8974 6814 (open Mon–Fri 10am – 3pm) or e-mail
advice@rethink.org

10 Depressive illness

Eleni Palazidou

Introduction

Irrespective of the nature of the population studied major depressive disorder is the most common psychiatric diagnosis. This is a consistent finding in community and primary care surveys as well as in specialist psychiatric inpatient or outpatient population studies.

It has been estimated that by the year 2020 major depressive disorder will be the second most common cause of disability after heart disease (Davidson and Meltzer-Brody, 1999). This is a worrying prospect, particularly for women, who appear to be more vulnerable to this condition.

The need to treat depressive illness, effectively, cannot be underestimated. Despite the availability of effective treatments and a wide choice of anti-depressant drugs a substantial number of sufferers do not receive medical treatment. The reasons for this, unfortunately, include not only 'negative' public attitudes but also poor recognition of the disorder and failure to treat or insufficient treatment, particularly in primary care settings.

'Negative' public attitude

Major efforts have been made to 'educate' the public and reduce the stigma of depression. The five-year 'Defeat Depression' campaign (1991–1996), launched by the Royal College of Psychiatrists and the Royal College of General Practitioners, claimed to have achieved statistically significant changes in public attitudes to depression, reported experience of depression and attitudes to antidepressant drugs. These changes, however, were only in the magnitude of 5 per cent to 10 per cent.

The 'stigma' of mental illness remains one major factor that discourages sufferers from seeking professional help. This is particularly the case if they have to attend a specialist psychiatric hospital. Furthermore there appears to be a misconception by the lay public that antidepressant drug treatment is addictive. It should be noted, however, that women are more likely than men to seek professional help. In the Zurich Study (Ernst *et al.*, 1992), two-thirds of women compared to one-third of men with major depressive disorder sought health care.

Another important factor, which discourages the seeking of professional help, is the perceived 'understandability' of the depressive state. The difference between the symptoms of depressive illness and the feelings experienced in existential unhappiness may seem obvious to the professional but are not so clear to the lay sufferer who considers her mood state understandable.

Under-recognition of depression

The recognition of depression remains relatively poor in primary care settings. A common reason is the masking of depressive symptomatology by physical symptom presentation.

Undertreatment of depression

A survey of the prescription database and suicides between 1970 and 1984 in Jamtland County (Isacsson *et al.*, 1992) showed an association between *low antidepressant use and high suicide rates*. Only a tenth of the patients who had sought medical attention in the three months prior to suicide were prescribed antidepressants, often in low doses. Although the likelihood of prescribing antidepressant drug treatment increased in the 1990s, the findings of more recent studies are not encouraging (Tylee *et al.*, 1999).

In a second phase of the DEPRES study (DEPRES II), patients who had been previously identified as suffering with depression and who had consulted a health care professional about their symptoms during the previous six months, were interviewed. Only one-third (30 per cent) had received antidepressant drug treatment during this latest period of depression while 17 per cent were prescribed benzodiazepines (Tylee *et al.*, 1999).

EPIDEMIOLOGY OF DEPRESSIVE DISORDER

Gender differences in prevalence

In most epidemiological surveys, depressed females outnumber depressed males with an average ratio of 2:1. Lifetime prevalence of major depressive disorder as reported by the National Co-morbidity Survey (Kessler *et al.*, 1994), including a total of over 8,000 individuals, aged 15–54 years, from a number of states in the USA, was 17.1 per cent (females 21.3 per cent and males 12.7 per cent). DEPRES (Depression Research in European Society, Lepine *et al.*, 1997), the first pan-European study of the epidemiology of depression found a six-month prevalence of 17 per cent for depression in general and 6.9 per cent for major depressive disorder (8.7 per cent females; 5.0 per cent males).

The female preponderance in depression rates persists in incidence data, which rely on statistically more robust, prospective studies. The ECA (Epidemiologic Catchment Area) Study which collected data from 1 year follow-up across all age groups found an incidence rate of 1.56 per 100 person years and provided strong evidence in favour of females being at higher risk for depression (males 1.1: females 1.98) (Eaton *et al.*, 1989).

The prevalence of minor depressive disorder and dysthymia is also thought to be higher in women although the reliability of these data can be questioned considering the methodological difficulties in carrying out such studies (differences in definition and reliability of diagnosis and in the case of dysthymia, the reliance of memory).

It has been argued that the gender differences in the prevalence of depression are not 'real' but accounted for by methodological factors, for example unequal reporting of symptoms and differential forgetting between males and females (Wilhelm and Parker, 1994), or an artefact of definition (criteria for diagnosis too broad). (Angst and Dobler-Mikola, 1984). However, the large majority of studies show women to be more likely than men to suffer with major depressive disorder, at least during their reproductive period of life (Hankin *et al.*, 1998; Bebbington *et al.*, 1998). Although there does not appear to be a real increase in the overall prevalence of depression over time there is redistribution by sex and age with a more recent increase in the rates of depression in younger women (Murphy *et al.*, 2000).

CLINICAL PRESENTATION AND COURSE OF ILLNESS

Gender differences

Depressive disorder is a long-term, recurring disorder. Earlier in the course of illness the risk of recurrence may be higher in women. The overall risk of recurrence increases with each new episode irrespective of sex, age or type of disorder (Kessing, 1998). There do not appear to be any gender differences in the duration and severity of recurrences (Simpson *et al.*, 1987).

Bipolar disorder (manic depression)

Although the prevalence of bipolar disorder is equally distributed between the sexes, the presentation of the clinical picture shows some differences. Bipolar women may have more depressive and fewer manic episodes and be more likely to suffer from mixed affective states, as opposed to pure mania, than bipolar men. In bipolar-II disorder women outnumber the men (67.3% females) particularly in those of younger onset (Benazzi, 2006). It should be noted, also, that bipolar women are at higher risk for postpartum episodes; the effects of other reproductive system events (menstrual cycle, menopause, use of oral contraception or hormone replacement therapy) have not been fully studied.

Rapid cycling is more common in bipolar women than bipolar men. Higher rates of hypothyroidism, greater use of antidepressants and gonadal steroid effects are possible explanations for the higher prevalence of rapid cycling in women.

Clinical presentation

Women have higher severity of symptoms as measured by the standard depression scales such as HAM-D (Hamilton Rating Scale for Depression), BDI (Beck Depression Inventory) and CGI (Clinical Global Impression) in chronic (at least two years' duration) major depression. They experience more psychomotor retardation and report more significant impairment in marital and family adjustment (SAS-SR) while men have more alcohol and drug abuse problems (Kornstein *et al.*, 1995).

Suicide

It is generally recognized that men are at higher risk of completed suicide than women. However, the rates of attempted suicide increased by as much as 47 per cent in men in the 1980s compared to the 1970s while they decreased by 9 per cent in women, reducing the female to male ratio from 2.3 to 1.4. Similarly, although there was an overall increase in suicide attempts between the 1980 and 1990 surveys (USA), the sex ratio has again decreased. In most countries, females compared with males have only marginally higher rates of suicidal ideation but more consistently higher rates for suicide attempts. Suicidal ideation and attempts in most countries are associated with being currently divorced/separated as compared to currently married (Weissman *et al.*, 1999).

Deliberate self-poisoning rates increased in the late 1980s and early 1990s in both sexes, the greatest rise being in women aged 15–24 and men aged 15–39.

Co-morbidity

About half of patients with major depressive disorder suffer concomitantly with other physical or psychiatric disorders and this adversely influences both the course and outcome of illness. Women are more likely to suffer with thyroid disease, rheumatological conditions, such as rheumatoid arthritis, fibrositis and polymyalgia rheumatica, and migraine.

Co-morbidity of lifetime major depressive disorder and at least one DSM-III anxiety disorder is as high as 44.4 per cent in epidemiological samples and even higher in clinical samples (67.8 per cent). The most common anxiety disorder co-morbid with depression is panic disorder (70 per cent). It should be noted that co-existent anxiety and depression worsens the short- and long-term outcomes of both conditions and that the presence of severe anxiety and agitation in depression increases suicidal risk.

AETIOLOGICAL FACTORS

The pathogenesis of depressive illness both in unipolar and bipolar disorder is dependent on the interaction between sexual and environmental factors with sexual vulnerability being higher in bipolar disorder compared to unipolar, the concordance rate in monozygotic twins being about 65 per cent–70 per cent and 40 per cent–45 per cent respectively.

Genetic

The heritability of lifetime major depressive disorder is around 70 per cent and family history of mental illness in first-degree relatives is a vulnerability factor predicting poor long-term outcome.

Sex differences in the genetics of depression have not been studied widely. In Kendler and Prescott's (1999) twin study there were no differences in the heritability of major depressive disorder between men and women while a community-based Australian twin study (Bierut *et al.*, 1999) estimated the heritability of depression in women to be at around 40 per cent; in men depression was only modestly familial and thus individual environmental factors seemed to play a more significant role in the development of male depression in this study.

It is reasonable to consider depressive disorder to be aetiologically dependent on an interaction between sexual vulnerability and environmental influences in both males and females, although there may be differences in the types of environmental factors being instrumental in females compared to males. In particular the female physiology and cyclic hormonal changes or those related to the onset of puberty or menopause and the postpartum period have major influences on brain neurotransmitter system function and may explain the sex differences in the prevalence of depression.

Psychosocial

Women's social role has been considered as one of the factors involved in the increased prevalence of depression in women, although the 'role strain' hypothesis was recently challenged (Weich *et al.*, 1998). Perugi *et al.* (1990) found no gender differences in stressors precipitating an episode.

There is a link between depressive symptoms in women and marital status. Marriage is significantly less advantageous for women than for men, highest rates of depression being found in unemployed divorced women, lowest in employed married men (Gutierrez-Lobos *et al.*, 2000). Of note is that women with 1 or 2 children are 30 per cent less likely than nulliparous women to have a history of mood disorder (Harlow *et al.*, 1999). Women with lower levels of social support are at greater risk of depression (Kendler et al., 2005).

Women are more likely than men to be sexually abused in childhood (Cutler and Nolen-Hoeksema, 1991). This is associated with an increased risk of psychopathology in later life (see Part V Chapter 18).

Biochemical

Until recently, despite the major progress made during the last forty years, the original 'Monoamine Hypothesis' of depression formulated in the 1960s has remained central to any new theories. These seem to simply build on to it, refining and adding detail to the main concept of reduced activity within two major central neurotransmitter systems (noradrenergic and serotonergic). These notions have underpinned the development of pharmacological treatments and existing antidepressant drugs work by increasing the activity of one or both of the above neurotransmitter systems. However the rapid growth of molecular biology, neuroimaging and other modern technologies hold a promise for better understanding of the biochemistry of depression and hence the development of more effective treatments.

PRACTICAL CONSIDERATIONS IN ANTIDEPRESSANT DRUG TREATMENT

Treatment aims

Antidepressant treatment should aim to ultimately achieve complete resolution of symptoms and return to premorbid levels of functioning and prevention of return of symptoms. Compliance with drug treatment is often a problem. This can be improved significantly by spending some extra time with the patient prior to initiation of treatment explaining the treatment plan. Informing the depressed woman that the improvement will be relatively slow, that treatment should continue for several months (certainly >4–6 months after full symptom control), what the side-effects may be and that antidepressants are not addictive drugs will gain her cooperation. Monitoring progress over time helps sustain treatment and facilitates monitoring of mood state and suicidal risk with prompt intervention as necessary.

Choice of antidepressant

The choice of antidepressant should be tailored to the individual. The following factors should be taken into consideration:

1   Severity of illness
2   Clinical presentation
3   Suicidal risk
4   Previous response to treatment
5   Tolerability of potential side effects
6   The potential benefit of certain side-effects such as sedation
7   Pregnancy or breastfeeding
8   Concomitant drug treatment for physical illness or other psychiatric disorders with the potential of pharmacokinetic/pharmacodynamic interaction

9   The presence of relevant physical illness (for example cardiovascular disease).

PHARMACOKINETICS

When considering the prescribing of antidepressants or discontinuing treatment it is essential to bear in mind the pharmacokinetics of the drug in use. There are three major considerations:

1   the antidepressant's half-life
2   whether it has active metabolites and their half-life, and
3   the involvement of the cytochrome P450 (CYP) in their metabolism.

The antidepressants vary in terms of their half-life, the length of which determines the frequency of dosing, the speed of achieving steady-state levels and the potential for a withdrawal syndrome. For example, paroxetine or venlafaxine both have short half-lives and have been associated with withdrawal symptoms. Tricyclic antidepressants (TCAs) also can have withdrawal effects and a 'cholinergic crisis' can be induced on abrupt discontinuation. Care should be taken in the case of most of the antidepressants to taper off the dose over a reasonable period of time. In contrast, fluoxetine and its active metabolite have a long half-life of several weeks which allows abrupt discontinuation but requires a longer drug-free period prior to initiating other treatments with the potential for interaction (e.g. MAOIs).

Cytochrome P450 2D6 is the subtype involved in the metabolism of most psychotropic drugs. Some SSRIs, in particular fluoxetine and paroxetine, are potent inhibitors of this enzyme while sertraline, fluvoxamine and citalopram are weaker 2D6 inhibitors. Inhibition of CYP 2D6 may cause an elevation in the concentrations of secondary amine TCAs, some antipsychotics and antiarrhythmics. Fluvoxamine powerfully inhibits CYP 1A2 (can increase clozapine plasma concentrations; fluvoxamine concentrations are reduced by cigarette smoking) and moderately inhibits CYP 3A4 (increases the concentrations of some benzodiazepines, warfarin and propranolol).

ANTIDEPRESSANT DRUG TREATMENT IN WOMEN

Despite the higher prevalence of depressive disorder in women (making them the highest consumers of antidepressant drugs) and the major leaps made in our understanding of the effects of these drugs on the brain, relatively little research has focused on possible pharmacodynamic or pharmacokinetic differences between the sexes or indeed differences in clinical efficacy and tolerability. Until a few years ago the Food and Drugs Administration (FDA), the organisation responsible for the licensing of drugs in the USA, did not allow women of reproductive potential to be included in clinical trials of new pharmacological agents.

The large numbers of subjects currently taking part in multicentre clinical trials, in order to conform with the requirements of the licensing bodies (such as the FDA in the USA or the MHRA in the UK), offer ample opportunity to study possible sex differences in clinical response, tolerability and possible hormonal effects (such as physiological fluctuations of gonadal hormones during menstrual cycle, oral contraception or hormone replacement therapy) on the pharmacokinetics and pharmacodynamics of the drug under investigation. However, unless the relevant licensing bodies impose such investigations, it is unlikely that the pharmaceutical companies will consider the extra effort and expense worthwhile.

Drug prescribing for women of childbearing potential

Following the experience with thalidomide and the realisation that any drug ingested during gestation may have teratogenic effects, strict regulations have been introduced to protect the unborn child. The lack of teratogenic effects of a drug in animals does not preclude the possibility of such effects in humans. Women of reproductive potential are required to use adequate contraception prior to taking part in any clinical trial of new drugs. This means that none of the licensed antidepressants have been subjected to controlled clinical trials in pregnancy. Information on the safety (or lack of safety) of drugs is gathered over time via case reports or retrospective surveys. It is essential for the prescriber to be conversant with the pharmacology of the antidepressants and their potential not only for teratogenicity but also for adverse effects on the new born including the possibility of withdrawal symptoms. If needed, information can be obtained from the National Drug Information Service which is part of the European Network of Teratology Information Services.

Antidepressant drug treatment during pregnancy and breastfeeding

The British National Formulary (BNF) warns 'no drug is safe beyond all doubt in early pregnancy'. This places a major responsibility on the prescriber. It is important therefore for both ethical as well as medico-legal reasons that the decision to treat and the choice of treatment is made with the active participation of a fully informed patient. With the cooperation of the patient and time to plan ahead it is possible to achieve optimum care plans. Unfortunately, in the UK almost 50 per cent of pregnancies are unplanned. Often by the time the pregnancy is recognised organogenesis has started or been already completed (embryonic phase: 6–8 weeks post-conception; foetal phase: up to 13–14 weeks).

In the event of unexpected pregnancy serious consideration should be given to the drug treatment being discontinued as soon as possible. The mother's condition should be assessed, taking into account the severity of illness and suicidal risk. A decision should be made only after very careful assessment of risks and benefits both for the mother and the foetus. Sudden discontinuation of antidepressants such as the TCAs and some SSRIs with short half-life should be avoided as it may cause potentially harmful withdrawal symptoms in the foetus.

It is advised that MAOIs are avoided during pregnancy because of their known side-effect profile and lack of long-term studies on children exposed to these agents during gestation.

Breastfeeding

Several studies have examined ratios between concentrations of antidepressants in the maternal plasma and the breast milk. The data suggest that all antidepressants are excreted in the breast milk, although there are very limited reports of adverse effects on the baby (Llewellyn and Stowe, 1998).

It is advisable that antidepressants are avoided during breastfeeding and if treatment is needed a careful risk/benefit assessment should be carried out.

Efficacy

There appear to be gender differences in clinical responses to treatment with some TCAs. In particular there is preferential response to imipramine in males compared to females (Dawkins and Potter, 1991). The impaired response to imipramine in women may be related to oestrogen levels and this may fluctuate during the menstrual cycle. Oestrogens enhance serotonergic activity and this may explain the recent finding that SSRIs are less effective in menopausal compared to non-menopausal women (Pinto-Meza et al., 2006).

Gender differences in pharmacokinetics

There is some evidence that absorption, distribution and metabolism of drugs may be different in women. Gastric acid secretion is lower and gastro-intestinal transit time slower in women and both fluctuate during the menstrual cycle. Women have a higher body fat/muscle ratio, which increases with age and can affect drug distribution. The female gonadal hormones may affect the activity of some isoenzymes of the cytochrome P450 system and monoamine oxidase (MAO) (Dawkins and Potter, 1991). Such pharmacokinetic effects may potentially cause fluctuations in antidepressant drug concentrations and their half-lives in relation to hormonal changes. These may influence the occurrence of side-effects and efficacy.

During pregnancy various physiological changes occur such as increased protein binding capacity, decreased absorption, decreased gastrointestinal motility and increased hepatic metabolism with variable effects on drug metabolism. It may be necessary for the doses of antidepressants to be changed particularly during the last trimester of the pregnancy.

PREMENSTRUAL DYSPHORIC DISORDER (PMDD)

PMDD as defined by the DSM IV affects about 3–5 per cent of women. Although the precise pathophysiology of PMDD is not as yet fully understood it is believed that there is a dysregulation of the central serotonergic neurotransmitter system influenced by the fluctuation in gonadal hormones. The blunted prolactin responses to dl-fenfluramine, a serotonin-releasing agent, during the luteal phase of women suffering with PMDD (Fitzgerald *et al.*, 1997) suggest impaired serotonergic neurotransmission in this condition. The preferential response of PMDD sufferers to serotonergic as compared to selective noradrenergic or dopaminergic agents (Eriksson *et al.*, 1995; Steiner, 1997), lends further support to this hypothesis. SSRIs are the antidepressants of choice in the treatment of PMDD.

In summary, there are significant sex differences in depression which have significant implications. Women are more likely to suffer depression than men particularly during their reproductive period. Physiological, hormonal, and psychosocial factors have major influence on the clinical presentation and response to treatment in women. The clinician needs to be aware of these differences in order to achieve optimum results.

References

Benazzi, F. (2006) Gender differences in Bipolar-II disorder. *Eur Arch Psychiat & Clin Neurosc* 256: 67–71.

Bierut, L.J., Heath, A.C., Bucholtz, K.K., Dinwiddie, S.H., Madden, P.A., Statham, D.J., Dunne, M.P. and Martin, N.G. (1999) Major depressive disorder in a community-based twin sample: are there different genetic and environmental contributions for men and women? *Archives of General Psychiatry* 56(6): 557–63.

Cutler, S.E. and Nolen-Hoeksema, S. (1991) Accounting for sex differences in depression through female victimization: childhood sexual abuse. *Sex Roles* 24: 425–38.

Davidson, J.R., and Meltzer-Brody, S.E. (1999) The underrecognition and under-treatment of depression: what is the breadth and depth of the problem? *Journal of Clinical Psychiatry* 60(7): 4–9; discussion 10-1.

Dawkins, K. and Potter, W.Z. (1991) Gender differences in pharmacokinetics and pharmacodynamics of psychotropics: focus on women. *Psychopharmacology Bulletin* 27(4): 417–26.

Eaton, W.W., Kramer, M., Anthony, J.C., *et al.* (1989) The incidence of specificDIS/DSM-III mental disorders: data from the NIMH Epidemiologic Catchment Area Programme. *Acta Psychiatrica Scandinavica* 79: 163–78.

Eriksson, E., Hedberg, M.A., Andersch, B. and Sundblad, C. (1995) The serotonin reuptake inhibitor, paroxetine is superior to the noradrenaline reuptake inhibitor maprotiline in the treatment of premenstrual syndrome. *Neuropsychopharmacology* 12(2): 167–76.

Ernst, C., Schmid, G., and Angst, J. (1992) The Zurich Study XVI. Early antecedents of depression: a longitudinal prospective study on incidence in young adults. *European Archives of Psychiatric Clinics and Neuroscience* 242(2–3): 142–51.

Fitzgerald, M., Malone, K.M., Li, S., *et al.* (1997) Blunted serotonin responses to fenfluramine challenge in premenstrual dysphoric disorder. *American Journal of Psychiatry* 1544: 556–8.

Gutierrez-Lobos, K., Wolfl, G., Scherer, M., Anderer, P. and Schmidl-Mohl, B. (2000) The gender gap in depression reconsidered: the influence of marital and employment status on the female/male ratio of treated incidence rates. *Social Psychiatry and Psychiatric Epidemiology* 35(5): 202–10.

Harlow, B.L., Cohen, L.S., Otto, M.W., Spiegelman, D. and Cramer, D.W. (1999) Prevalence and predictors of depressive symptoms in older premenopausal women: the Harvard study of moods and cycles. *Archives of General Psychiatry* 56(5): 418–24.

Isacsson, G., Boethius, G. and Bergman, U. (1992) Low level of an antidepressant prescription for people who later commit suicide: 15 years of experience from a population-based drug database in Sweden. *Acta Psychiatrica Scandinavica* 85, 6: 444–8.

Kendler, K. and Prescott, C. (1999) A population-based twin study of lifetime major depression in men and women. *Archives of General Psychiatry* 56(1): 39–44.

Kessing, L.V. (1998) Recurrence in affective disorder II: effect of age and gender. *British Journal of Psychiatry* 172: 29–34.

Kessler, R.C., McGonagle, K.A., Zhao, S., Nelson, C.B., Hughes, M., Eshleman, S., Wittchen, H.U. and Kendler, K.S. (1994) Lifetime and 12 month prevalence of DSM IIIR psychiatric disorder in the United States: results from the National Co-morbidity Survey. *Archives of General Psychiatry* 51(1): 8–19.

Kornstein, S.G., Schatzberg, A.F., Yonkers, K.A., Thase, M.E., Keitner, G.I., Ryan, C.E. and Schlager, D. (1995) Gender differences in the presentation of chronic major depression. *Psychopharmacology Bulletin* 31(4): 711–18.

Lepine, J.P., Gastpar, M., Mendlewicz, J. and Tylee, A. (1997) Depression in the community: the first pan-European study, DEPRES (Depression research in European society). *International Clinical Psychopharmacology* 12(1):19–29.

Llewellyn, A. and Stowe, Z.N. (1998) Psychotropic medications during lactation. *Journal of Clinical Psychiatry* 59(suppl. 2): 41–52.

Perugi, G., Musetti, L., Simonini, E. *et al.* (1990) Gender mediated clinical features of depressive illness: the importance of temperamental differences. *British Journal of Psychiatry* 157: 835–41.

Pinto-Meza, A. (2006) SSRIs may be less effective in menopausal women. *J Affect Disord* 93: 53–60.

Simpson, H.B., Nee, J.C. and Endicott, J. (1987) First episode major depression: few sex differences in course. *Archives of General Psychiatry* 54(7): 633–9.

Steiner, M. (1997) Premenstrual syndromes. *Annual Review of Medicine* 48: 447–55.

Tylee, A., Gastpar, M., Lepine, J.P. and Mendlewitz, J. (1999) DEPRES II (Depression research in European society II): a patient survey of the symptoms, disability and current management of depression in the community. DEPRES Steering Committee. *International Clinical Psychopharmacological* 14(3): 139–51.

Weich, S., Sloggett, A. and Glynn, L. (1998) Social roles and gender difference in the prevalence of common mental disorders. *British Journal of Psychiatry* 173: 489–93.

Weissman, M.M., Bland, R.C., Canino, G.J., Greenwald, S., Hwu, H-G., Joyce, P.R., Karam, E.G., Lee, C-K., Lellouch, J., Lepine, J-P., Newman, S.C., Rubio-Stipec, M., Wells, J.E., Wickramaratne, P.J., Wittchen, H-U. and Yeh, E.K. (1999) Prevalence of suicide ideation and suicide attempts in nine countries. *Psychological Medicine* 29(1): 9–17.

Wilhelm, K. and Parker, G. (1994) Sex differences in lifetime depression rates: fact or artefact? *Psychological Medicine* 34: 97–111.

Useful addresses

Depression Alliance

Address: 35 Westminster Bridge Road, London SE1 7JB

Phone: 0207 633 0557

Fax: 0207 633 0559

Email: information@depressionalliance.org

Website: www.depressionalliance.org

Description: head office of a national organisation coordinating a network of self-help groups for people with depression, their friends and family. Services include information and advice, confidential support services, pen-friend scheme, etc. Phone for details.

Special interest activities: phone for details of your local group

Additional info: head office provides information and advice by phone only

Opening hours: Mon–Fri 10am–5pm

Referral: self or any other source

Criteria/catchment: national organisation

Fellowship of Depressives Anonymous

Address: PO Box FDA, Orminston House, 32/36 Pelham Street, Nottingham NG1 2EG

Phone: 01702 433838

Fax: 01702 433843

Email: fdainfo@aol.com

Description: this service provides a helpline and up-to-date information on depression self-help groups running nationwide. A newsletter is published every two months which is available to members, regular meetings on self-management issues, etc. Phone for further details.

Opening hours: no set times for the helpline but it is usually staffed for 4 to 6 hours every day. Answerphone if nobody immediately available.

Referral: open access

Criteria/catchment: for people suffering from depression and their carers

11 Anxiety and somatoform disorders

Charlotte Wilson-Jones

Introduction

Anxiety and depressive disorders are the main psychiatric problems presenting to general practitioners and, although common, these and the somatoform disorders are often unrecognised and therefore untreated. Somatic complaints are often the presenting complaint in the disorders considered in this chapter (although less so in OCD). These symptoms treated in isolation may therefore fail to reveal the true diagnosis and, even when recognised, these disorders are often anxiety-provoking for medical staff. The overlap between the symptoms of the anxiety disorders and somatoform disorders and their co-morbidity with other psychiatric disorders can lead to diagnostic and management concerns.

About 60 per cent of people in the UK visit their GP in a year. Having a neurotic disorder increases the likelihood of consulting a GP, with estimates of 90 per cent of people with a neurotic disorder consulting a GP per year (Goldberg and Huxley, 1992).

The UK National Psychiatric Morbidity Survey (Meltzer *et al.*, 1995) showed an association between neurotic disorder and social class, with 18.2 per cent of social class five and 10.0 per cent of social class one suffering from a neurotic condition.

WOMEN

One of the most striking features of the disorders described in this chapter are that, with the exception of OCD and social phobia, all are more common in women and some markedly so. The reasons for this are still debated but theories include:

*   Social roles: more women are in low status jobs and are stretched by expectations to fulfil numerous other roles, e.g. mother, homemaker, etc.
*   Help seeking: women are more likely to seek help and disclose psychological problems.

- Developmental factors: women may be more vulnerable to adverse events, such as childhood sexual abuse.
- Biological factors: differences may be due to genetic differences, particularly affecting endocrine systems.

ANXIETY DISORDERS

A study of psychiatric morbidity in general practice found complaints of anxiety or worry in 82 per cent of subjects (Goldberg *et al.*, 1976). Indeed we all at some time feel the stresses of life and have felt anxious. Whilst anxiety is a natural and often appropriate response which can be productive, for example in enhancing performance and productivity, it is important to distinguish this from pathological states which can lead to marked morbidity for individual sufferers and their families. Anxiety disorders as separate entities were first described in DSM-III. Classification can sometimes appear confusing, particularly due to the considerable overlap between the disorders and their association with depression. Of those diagnosed with anxiety disorder about 50 per cent also fulfil the criteria for depression and of those with a primary diagnosis of depression more than a third have symptoms diagnostic of an anxiety disorder. However, there is a subjective difference in symptoms for the patient. The previous chapter has concentrated on the diagnosis and management of affective disorders.

Generalised anxiety disorder

The distinguishing feature of this disorder is that the anxiety is 'free-floating' in that it is not restricted to specific circumstances. The symptoms of anxiety should have been present for several weeks or months.

Making the diagnosis

It is important to be aware that patients with generalised anxiety disorder often present with one or more physical symptoms from any system of the body. The somatic symptoms result from autonomic arousal, hyper-ventilation and muscular tension; therefore a full systems review is invaluable and is likely to reveal at least a few of the symptoms below:

Somatic symptoms

- Cardiovascular Palpitations, chest pain, complaints of throbbing in head or neck, complaints of missed heartbeats
- Respiratory Difficulty breathing, shortness of breath, tight chest, overbreathing

- Gastrointestinal   Swallowing problems, abdominal discomfort, diarrhoea, flatulence, dry mouth
- Genitourinary   Micturition frequency, poor libido, menorrhagia, erectile problems
- Neurological   Headaches, parasthesiae and numbness, tinnitus, dizziness, faint, tremor, blurred vision
- Musculoskeletal   Aches, stiffness, perspiration.

Psychological symptoms

Apprehension/fearfulness/excessive worry
Feeling tense or nervous
Irritable/short-tempered
Insomnia, nightmares
Poor concentration
Sensitivity to noise
Complaints of poor memory

Although screening for the above symptoms usually provides enough information to make the diagnosis, it is important to rule out physical conditions which very occasionally mimic some of the symptoms. Disorders that may present with anxiety symptoms include withdrawal states from alcohol or drugs (including benzodiazepines), some endocrine disorders (hypoglycaemia, hyperthyroidism, hyperparathyroidism, phaeochromocytoma) and some cardiac disorders (mitral valve disease, arrhythmias).

Management of generalised anxiety disorder

The management can be divided into general measures, more specific psychological interventions and pharmacotherapy. The initial approach in mild to moderate forms should aim to be non-biological.

General measures

- *Reassurance and education:* it is useful to name the disorder to the patient, explaining in particular that the physical symptoms are a well-known part of the disorder and reassure her they are not life-threatening. Such patients often do not take in all the information provided in a consultation and written educational material is useful. Although seemingly time-consuming, it is often worth offering to see close family/friends in order to explain the nature of the condition to them.
- *Normalisation:* in order to prevent secondary avoidance, it is beneficial to encourage the patient that she should continue or resume her normal activities, including socialisation, family and occupational life and the

activities of daily living. A review of life-style may reveal a need to encourage leisure time or reorganisation of responsibilities.

• *Psychosocial issues:* a detailed psychosocial history may reveal specific stressors that may need addressing such as relationship difficulties, financial worries or childcare issues. These may require other more specific help from other agencies such as Citizens Advice, welfare, couple counselling.

• *Caffeine:* check for excess intake of caffeine. It is estimated that 10 per cent of Americans suffer symptoms from excess caffeine intake and it can exacerbate and mimic symptoms of anxiety.

• *Exercise:* regular exercise and techniques such as yoga and the Alexander technique can be used to dissipate nervous energy.

• *Meditation:* meditation has been shown to be beneficial in anxiety, insomnia and other stress-related disorders.

• *Relaxation tapes:* these are now widely available. Patients are often instructed to use them twice a day for about 20 minutes and at times when they are feeling particularly anxious.

• *Self-help/advisory organisations:* there are a number of organisations offering helplines, workshops, support groups, etc. Patients can be informed of these.

More specific relaxation and psychological techniques

• *Progressive muscular relaxation*: this technique was originally developed by Jacobsen in the 1930s (Jacobsen, 1983) and is used to combat the somatic symptoms of anxiety. The basic principle is that each muscle group, usually starting in the feet, is tensed then relaxed sequentially. The patient learns to be aware of muscle tension and therefore to overcome it. It is a relatively simple technique to explain and a useful initial step. Mental tranquillity as well as physical relaxation can be promoted by such methods (Benson, 1975). Biofeedback machines, which give physiological feedback, can be used to increase learning speed and muscular relaxation.

• *Breathing techniques*: these are used to address the hyperventilation associated with anxiety and panic disorder. The patient can be educated about the following cycle and taught how to manage it by controlling their breathing.

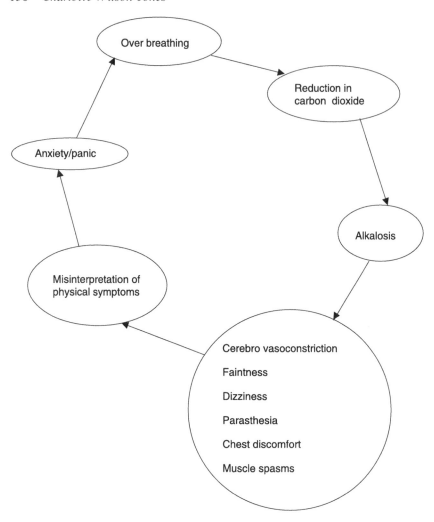

- *Cognitive Behaviour Therapy*: research to date regarding CBT looks
  promising. Clark *et al.* (1994) compared waiting list controls with applied
  relaxation, imipramine and cognitive therapy and found cognitive
  therapy to be the most effective both post treatment and at follow-up.
  Unfortunately the availability of CBT is very variable and trained
  therapists are required. The overall aim is to learn coping techniques
  targeted at somatic symptoms, maladaptive behaviours and cognitive
  responses.

Pharmacological treatment

Benzodiazepines

Placebo-controlled trials support the efficacy of benzodiazepines in GAD (Greenblatt, 1993) where the response is a rapid improvement occurring in the first week (Downing and Rickels, 1985). Studies suggest that benzodiazepines give relief to symptoms but do not provide a 'cure' for the disorder. If a patient is unresponsive to one benzodiazepine at adequate dose, then trial of another benzodiazepine is not indicated.

However, the side-effects and the risk of potential dependence need to be taken into consideration when prescribing benzodiazepines. Generally the advice is, use for acute, short-term symptomatic relief only. If they are used patients should be warned of potential side-effects and that they should not be stopped abruptly. Between 25 per cent and 45 per cent of people taking benzodiazepines for over a year report withdrawal symptoms, although research in this area is poor. Many of the symptoms are similar to symptoms of anxiety and can therefore be hard to distinguish from re-emergence of symptoms of the primary disorder. Serious symptoms such as seizures, psychosis and distorted perceptions have been reported (Tyrer, 1990). Dependence is particularly associated with shorter-acting drugs, e.g. lorazepam. It is more common in those using the drugs for longer than four months and in those with dependent and other pre-morbid personality disorders. Dependence on alcohol or other drugs is a risk factor.

Beta-blockers

Beta-blockers such as propanolol can be used to reduce autonomic symptoms such as tremor and palpitations but do not affect psychological symptoms. They can be used before a particularly stressful situation to reduce physical symptoms and should be given two hours beforehand.

Buspirone

Buspirone is an azapirone demonstrated to have some efficacy in GAD, with particular benefit to psychological symptoms such as irritability and worry. Some studies suggest greater efficacy on these symptoms than benzodiazepines; however, further research needs to be done to establish its role. The onset of action is slow and can take two to four weeks. An adequate trial appears to be at least four weeks at 20–45mg/day. It is not suitable for treating benzodiazepine withdrawal. There is also some evidence for decreased efficacy in those who previously responded to treatment with benzodiazepines. It has minimal withdrawal or tolerance and its abuse potential is low. It is licensed for short-term use only.

Antidepressant use and anxiety

Tricyclic antidepressants have been shown to be effective even when depression has been excluded (Rickels *et al.*, 1993). There is most evidence for the efficacy of imipramine but it may take four weeks before a useful response is seen. Currently none of the serotonin specific reuptake inhibitors (SSRIs) are licensed in the UK for treatment of generalised anxiety disorder although some (fluoxetine, paroxetine, sertraline) are indicated for symptoms of anxiety accompanying depression. There is ongoing research into their efficacy in GAD alone, with some data suggesting effectiveness. Although not licensed for GAD, Trazodone has been shown to have anxiolytic properties but it should be borne in mind that Trazodone is relatively sedative compared with other antidepressants used for anxiety. Venlafaxine has been shown to be effective for anxiety associated with depression and evidence is emerging for its effectiveness in anxiety alone. It has been licensed in the USA for use in GAD. The monoamine oxidase inhibitors (MAOIs) have been shown to be useful in treating GAD, but their use has been limited by the hypertensive 'cheese reaction' when taken with certain foodstuffs.

In severe anxiety antipsychotics, in low doses, are sometimes used for their sedative action but due to the risk of tardive dyskinesia, long-term use should be avoided.

PANIC DISORDER (EPISODIC PAROXYSMAL ANXIETY)

Panic disorder is characterised by severe, sudden and unpredictable and recurrent attacks of anxiety that are not related to a specific phobic situation. Secondary fear of losing control, going mad or dying is almost invariable. Approximately 3 per cent of the population have at least one panic attack in a six-month period. In most studies the prevalence of panic disorder in women is approximately twice that seen in men. Many who experience panic attacks do not fulfil criteria for the disorder, the ICD-10 criteria requiring several severe attacks within one month.

There is some dispute about its place as a discrete diagnostic category. There is marked overlap with depression, with up to three-quarters of those diagnosed with panic disorder having depression at some time and 30 per cent of those with major depression experiencing panic attacks. The association with agoraphobia is well known; however, the nature of the co-morbidity and their aetiology is unclear. This is reflected in the differences between ICD-10 and the American DSM-IV. In DSM-IV agoraphobia is not codable and mainly comes under panic disorder, reflecting the view that agoraphobia occurs as a response to panic attacks, whereas in ICD-10 panic disorder is only diagnosed in the absence of a phobia.

Management

The general measures as described in the section on GAD may be helpful.
People may present during an acute attack. Basic management includes:

- Sit patient in a quiet environment, with as little external stimulation as possible and reassure.
- Get the patient to exhale into a paper bag and re-breathe from the bag.
- Quick acting benzodiazepines can be used if the above measures are not working; however, most panic attacks are over within a few minutes.

Psychological methods

The general relaxation and breathing methods described above may be helpful. The most promising results have been shown by controlled studies of cognitive behavioural therapy. Cognitive behavioural therapy has been shown to be at least as effective as imipramine and probably have a longer-lasting effect, the theory behind the treatment being that patients misinterpret bodily sensations, develop secondary cognitive distortions, become vigilant for bodily sensations, further misinterpretation then leading to fear and eventually a panic attack.

Pharmacological treatments

Imipramine should be started at a low dose and can be used as a prophylactic for panic attacks. The relapse rate is quite high even after being stable following six months of treatment and the optimum length of treatment is unclear. Many of the American studies have been done on those with agoraphobia and panic attacks rather than panic disorder alone. There is also evidence of clomipramine being effective (Gentil *et al.*, 1993). High doses of benzo-diazepines can be used for short periods but there is little research evidence to show any added benefits after 4–6 weeks of use. The SSRIs citalopram and paroxetine are now licensed for panic disorder but their use is for prevention not for acute attacks. The starting dose should be half that used for the initial treatment of depression. Beta-blockers will not prevent attacks, but may relieve some of the somatic, anticipatory anxiety symptoms.

OBSESSIVE COMPULSIVE DISORDER (OCD)

This disorder is characterised by:

- Obsessional thoughts, images and doubts that are recurrent, intrusive, unwanted and usually unpleasant.
- Competitive acts/rituals that are repetitive, stereotyped, unwanted and unproductive. They are often viewed by the patient as preventing an

unpleasant, unlikely event and cleaning, checking and counting are the most commonly encountered phenomena.

Both the thoughts and rituals are recognised by the individual as coming from themselves and are usually recognised as senseless. Resisting at least one thought or action is part of the diagnostic criteria for ICD-10, although about half make little attempt at resistance, particularly in chronic cases.

Patients may suffer from either obsessions or compulsions alone. Obsessions alone are more common, especially in community samples. In psychiatric settings, most women have both. It is useful to distinguish which predominates for treatment purposes. OCD tends to run a chronic, fluctuating course.

Co-morbidity

• of patients with OCD 30 per cent fulfil criteria for major depressive disorder (Coryell, 1981), the lifetime prevalence of depression being about 50 per cent (Piggott *et al.*, 1990).
• of those with major depression 30 per cent have obsessional symptoms (Kendell and DiScipio, 1970).
• of patients with OCD 40 per cent have a pre-morbid personality disorder and 25 per cent have pre-morbid obsessional traits.
• of patients with OCD 40–60 per cent will reach the criteria for another anxiety disorder at sometime in their life (Austin *et al.*, 1990).

Epidemiology

It is generally accepted that OCD occurs equally in both sexes, and in clinic populations the sex ratio is usually equal. However, in studies of lifetime prevalence, the results vary from a female to male ratio of 1.2 to 3.8. The lifetime prevalence in the population is between 1.9 and 2.5 per cent (Weissman *et al.*, 1994).

Treatment

Co-morbid depression should be treated and the diagnosis explained. The patient's families are often affected and including them in discussion and sometimes treatment plans may be useful.

Psychological methods

Behaviour therapy is an effective treatment with a 60–70 per cent response rate. It is based on learning theory and involves exposure to a stimulus that provokes a compulsive act which is then prevented. This leads to anxiety, which is maintained until habituation occurs. A graded programme is usually worked out collaboratively with the patient and treatment programmes which combine response prevention with exposure have been shown to be superior to either used alone. It is more effective for compulsions, although associated obsessional thoughts generally diminish as the compulsions diminish. Obessional thoughts alone are more difficult to treat. Habituation of thoughts can occur by holding the obsessive thought in mind or listening to a tape recording of it, until habituation of anxiety occurs. Thought stopping uses distraction techniques such as snapping an elastic band on one's wrist when an obsessional thought occurs; however, its effectiveness has not been proven (Emmelkamp, 1987).

Pharmacological therapies

These treatments are based on the theory that OCD is associated with dysfunction of the serotonergic (5-hydroxytriptamine) function. Tricyclics which inhibit serotonin reuptake have been found to be beneficial. Clomipramine has been most extensively studied and used and the Clomipramine Collaborative study (1991) showed a 35 per cent reduction of symptoms in up to 60 per cent of patients, compared with about 7 per cent in placebo control. About 50 per cent of patients show marked improvement with SSRIs. The few studies that exist show a high level of relapse when medication is stopped (Thoren *et al.*, 1980; Pato *et al.*, 1988) but more research is required into the optimum length of treatment and there is a suggestion that long-term treatment may be required in chronic cases. A combination of behaviour and drug treatment can be used, with some evidence for an increased response (Balkom *et al.*, 1994).

SOMATOFORM DISORDERS

This group of disorders by their very nature of presenting with physical complaints are often difficult to diagnose. There is often a long medical history of contact with numerous different doctors, involving an excess of investigations. Numerous tests and in some cases needless operations are detrimental to the patient and costly and time-consuming to the health service. Contrary to the opinion of many doctors such tests do not serve to diminish the patient's anxiety but in fact often make it worse and can be positive re-enhancers of the sick role.

Making the diagnosis is complicated by the fact that such disorders may co-exist with organic physical conditions. A common example being the co-existence of non-epileptic seizures (pseudoseizures) and epilepsy. There is also a large overlap between this group of disorders and other psychiatric diagnoses, particularly anxiety and depression. It can also be difficult to separate these disorders into their specific ICD-10 classifications due to over-lap between the disorders, especially somatization disorder and dissociative disorder. This part of the chapter aims to clarify the key features of the individual disorders and consider treatment options.

Somatisation disorder

Somatisation disorder is about twenty times more common in women (Escobar *et al.*, 1987). It tends to start in early adulthood and runs a chronic, fluctuating course.

Characteristically females present with repeated complaints of physical symptoms in any body system. Gastrointestinal, skin and menstrual problems are particularly common. Symptoms have often resulted in numerous investigations and referrals for specialist opinions and there may also be a history of operations, particularly hysterectomy and cholecystectomy. Regardless of reassurance and advice the patient refuses to accept that there is no underlying physical complaint. Symptoms frequently change and may be exacerbated at times of particular stress. To make the diagnosis there should be some impairment of interpersonal or social functioning attributable to the symptoms.

The community prevalence of somatisation disorder is 0.1 per cent; however, 8–12 per cent of medical outpatients fulfil criteria for such a diagnosis (Van Hemert *et al.*, 1993). The magnitude of the problem is only fully appreciated when one considers the numerous women who present with somatic, medically unexplained symptoms but who do not fulfil the full criteria of somatisation disorder. Twenty per cent of new attendees to general practice present with such somatic symptoms compared with 5 per cent who present with primary psychological symptoms (Goldberg and Bridges, 1988).

Treatment

- Early recognition is important to prevent a chronic course which is more resistant to treatment and doctors should be alerted to patients with frequent attendance, thick sets of notes and fruitless investigations. It is also important to be alert to those asking for repeated prescriptions; particularly of analgesics or sedatives as dependence on such drugs is not uncommon.
- A thorough review of the patient's medical notes can be invaluable. This can help to check that the symptoms do not suggest a medical diagnosis which may require further investigation. It may also help confirm a pattern of repeated attendance with variable symptoms which do not conform to a specific medical diagnosis.
- Screen for other psychiatric disorders, especially anxiety and depression and if present treat the underlying disorder.
- History should be taken to reveal underlying psychosocial problems.
- Engaging the patient in psychological explanations is difficult and requires a sympathetic and consistent approach. Negative results should

be explained to the patient. The psychological aetiology of the symptoms should be explained, but it should be explained that this does not mean the symptoms are not real or imply that they are put on.

- Where possible care should be coordinated through one doctor, usually the general practitioner and specialist referrals and investigations should be limited.
- Symptoms are often worse at stressful times. This should be explained to the patient and stressors should be asked about at times when the patient represents.
- Reinforcement of symptoms from friends and relatives can be reduced by explaining the nature of the condition to them.
- Psychological therapies, in particular cognitive behavioural therapy by trained therapists, has been shown to be helpful (Sharpe *et al.*, 1992b). Dynamic psychotherapy may also be effective (Guthrie *et al.*, 1993).
- A specialist opinion from a psychiatrist or psychologist may be useful in complicated cases and for opinion as to suitability for psychological therapy.

DISSOCIATIVE (CONVERSION) DISORDERS

The terms dissociative or conversion disorder replace the use of 'hysteria', which now has numerous connotations in society and is often used pejoratively, particularly towards women. Dissociation refers to the impairment of conscious control that is presumed to occur. Conversion refers to the transformation of emotional conflict into symptoms.

Patients present with symptoms, usually of the neurological system, including paralysis, gait disturbance, sensory loss, non-epileptic seizures, movement disorders, amnesias and fugue states. Such symptoms cannot be explained by organic disease. The aetiology is presumed to be psychological and usually associated with trauma or internal psychological conflict.

The onset of symptoms is often described as sudden by the patient. A calm acceptance of the physical problem is classically described ('belle indifference') but actually is often absent (Lader and Satorius, 1968). Recent studies have shown a high co-morbidity with anxiety and affective disorder and personality disorder, 45 per cent having a personality disorder in a recent study (Crimlisk *et al.*, 1998).

The degree of the problem can be appreciated by the fact that British neurologists report that 20 per cent–40 per cent of their patients have medically unexplained symptoms (Mace and Trimble, 1996; Ewald *et al.* 1994). In contrast with the influential work of Slater at the National Hospital of Neurology and Neurosurgery (Slater, 1965), a more recent study at the same hospital (Crimlisk *et al.*, 1998) found that emergence of an organic explanation for such symptoms at a later date is rare. Slater had previously found that over half went on to develop a clear-cut neurological or psychiatric condition (Slater and Glithero, 1965).

Good prognostic factors include a short history and acute onset with a clear and resolvable problem precipitating the onset. Those with co-existent depression or anxiety also do better.

Treatment

This can be considered to be as for somatisation disorder. However, there may be secondary physical problems, due to lack of muscle use for example. Such problems may require physiotherapy. Such patients have often been seen by medical specialists, especially neurologists, prior to the diagnosis being suspected. Referrals for psychiatric help are then often made. It is important that all those involved in the patient's care are in close liaison. In order to enhance engagement with the patient it can be helpful for the psychiatrist to see her with the neurologist on occasions. Further investigations should be limited. Those with chronic problems often require a multidisciplinary approach involving doctors, psychologists, physiotherapists and occupational therapists.

HYPOCHONDRIACAL DISORDER

This is fear of having a serious medical condition, which preoccupies the individual and is persistent regardless of reassurance by doctors. It usually presents before the age of 50 and runs a fluctuating, chronic course.

Treatment

- Screen for other psychiatric illness as hypochondriasis often occurs as part of other disorders, especially anxiety.
- As for all the disorders in this section, engagement and explanation are important.
- Unnecessary investigations perpetuate anxiety and should be limited as much as possible.
- Cognitive Behavioural Therapy to challenge the beliefs about physical illness and change illness behaviour.

CHRONIC FATIGUE SYNDROME

Chronic fatigue syndrome remains a controversial problem of uncertain nosological status. It is recognised worldwide (Sinclair, 1988) and currently attracts a lot of media attention. It is arguably not a new condition; its similarity to neurasthenia, which was commonly diagnosed in the nineteenth century, has been well described (Wessely, 1990; 1994).

The syndrome is one of severe physical and mental fatigue after minimal effort, present for at least six months and unexplained by a primary physical or psychiatric cause. The fatigue is often accompanied by other associated problems, particularly muscular aches and pains, poor concentration and sleep problems. The effect on functioning is very variable but in chronic cases can be very severe and lead to inability to work, socialise or even carry out basic activities of daily living.

There is a high co-morbidity (71 per cent) with other psychiatric disorders (Ormel *et al.*, 1994) particularly depression and anxiety. Other medically unexplained symptoms such as irritable bowel and non-cardiac chest pain often co-exist with chronic fatigue syndrome.

The syndrome is more common in females. There is a tendency for sufferers to negate psychosocial factors which seem relevant to an observer and a strong belief in a purely physical aetiology is associated with a poor prognosis (Sharpe, 1992b; Wilson *et al.*, 1994).

Management

- Early detection is important to prevent further deterioration.
- Depression and anxiety disorders should be carefully screened for and treated appropriately.
- Engaging patients can be difficult and although the nature of the illness should be explained, arguments about the physical versus psychological aetiology are best avoided.
- There should be close collaboration between all medical staff involved in an individual's care.
- Contrary to some popular opinion rest should not be advocated. Inactivity sustains symptoms and increases sensitivity to them.
- There is a tendency for sufferers to have sudden bursts of activity after periods of rest. This leads to increased tiredness and perpetuates the belief that activity is detrimental. This should be explained and a graded approach to activity encouraged.
- Unhelpful illness beliefs, e.g. that exercise can do permanent damage, should be challenged.
- Avoid further unnecessary investigations.
- Cognitive Behavioural Therapy: there are good self-help books available using the principles of Cognitive Behavioural Therapy. Trained therapists conducting Cognitive Behavioural Therapy have been shown to be beneficial (Surawy *et al.*, 1995). This uses some of the principles outlined above and aims to identify perpetuating factors in the individual and work with them to break the vicious circle of fatigue, beliefs, behaviour and subsequent disability (Wessely *et al.*, 1989). The therapist works with the patient using a graded schedule of activity and identifying and modifying illness beliefs (Butler *et al.*, 1991).

References

Austin, L.S., Lydiard, R.M., Fossey, M.D. *et al.* (1990) Panic and phobic disorders in patients with obsessive compulsive disorder. *Journal of Clinical Psychiatry* 51: 456–8.

Balkom, A., van Oppen, P., Vermeulen, A. *et al.* (1994) A meta-analysis on the treatment of obsessive-compulsive disorder: a comparison of antidepressants, behaviour therapy and cognitive treatment. *Clinical Psychological Review* 14: 359–81.

Benson, H. (1975) *The Relaxation Response.* Glasgow: Collins Fount Publications.

Butler, A. T., Rush, A. J., Shaw, B.F. and Emery, G. (1991) Cognitive behaviour therapy in the chronic fatigue syndrome. *Journal of Neurology, Neurosurgery and Psychiatry* 54: 153–8.

Clark, D. M., Salkovskis, P., Hackmann, A. *et al.* (1994) A comparison of cognitive therapy, applied relaxation and imipramine in the treatment of panic disorder. *British Journal of Psychiatry* 164: 759–69.

Clomipramine Collaborative Study Group (1991) Clomipramine in the treatment of patients with obsessive-compulsive disorder. *Archives of General Psychiatry* 48: 730–8.

Coryell, W. (1981) Obsessive compulsive disorder and primary unipolar depression. *Journal of Nervous and Mental Disease* 169: 220–4.

Crimlisk, H., Bhatia, K., Cope, H., David, A. *et al.* (1998) Slater revisited: 6-year follow-up of patients with medically unexplained motor symptoms. *British Medical Journal* 316: 582–6.

Downing, R. W. and Rickels, K. (1985) Early treatment response in anxious outpatients treated with diazepam. *Acta Psychiatrica Scandinavica* 72: 522–8.

Emmelkamp, P.M.G. (1987) Obsessive-compulsive disorder. *Anxiety and Stress.* New York: Guilford Press.

Escobar, J. I., Burnam, M. A., Karno, M. *et al.* (1987) Somatization in the community. *Archives of General Psychiatry* 44: 713.

Ewald, H., Rogne, T., Ewald, K. and Fink, P. (1994) Somatisation in patients newly admitted to a neurology department. *Acta Psychiatrica Scandinavica* 89: 174–9.

Gentil, V., Lotufo-Neto, F., Andrade, L. *et al.* (1993) Clomipramine, a better reference drug for panic/agoraphobia: 1. Effectiveness comparison with imipramine. *Journal of Psychopharmacology* 7: 316–24.

Goldberg, D. and Bridges, K. (1988) Somatic presentation of psychiatric illness in primary care settings. *Journal of Psychosomatic Research* 32: 137–44.

Goldberg, D., Kay, C. and Thompson, L. (1976) Psychiatric morbidity in general practice and the community. *Psychological Medicine* 6: 565–9.

Goldberg, D. and Huxley, P. (1992) *Common Mental Disorders: A Bio-Social Model.* London: Routledge.

Greenblatt, D. J. (1993) Basic pharmacokinetic principles and their application to psychotropic drugs. *Journal of Clinical Psychiatry* 54 (supplement): 8–14.

Guthrie, E., Creed, F., Dawson, D. and Tomenson, B. (1993) A randomised controlled trail of psychotherapy in patients with refractory irritable bowel syndrome. *British Journal of Psychiatry* 163: 315–21.

Jacobsen, E. (1983) *Progressive Relaxation.* Chicago: University of Chicago Press.

Kendell, R. and DiScipio, W. (1970) Obsessional symptoms and personality traits in depressive illness. *Psychological Medicine* 1: 65–72.

Lader, M. and Sartorius, N. (1968) Anxiety in patients with hysterical conversion symptoms. *Journal of Neurology, Neurosurgery and Psychiatry* 31: 490–5.

Mace, C. J. and Trimble, M. R. (1996) Ten year prognosis of conversion disorder. *British Journal of Psychiatry* 169: 282–8.

Meltzer, H., Gill, B. and Petticrew, M. (1995) Report No.1: The prevalence of psychiatric morbidity among adults aged 16–64 living in private households in Great Britain. *OPCS Surveys of Psychiatric Morbidity in Great Britain.* London: HMSO.

Ormel, J., Von Korff, M., Ustun, B. *et al.* (1994) Common mental disorders and disability across cultures: results from the WHO collaborative study on psychological problems in general health care. *Journal of the American Medical Association* 272: 1741–8.

Pato, M. T., Zohar-Kadouch, R., Zohar, J., *et al.* (1988) Return of symptoms after discontinuation of clomipramine in patients with obsessive-compulsive disorder. *American Journal of Psychiatry* 145: 1521–5.

Piggot, T.A., Pato, M. T., Bernstein, S. E., Grover, G. N., Hill, J. L., Tolliver, T. J. and Murphy, D. I. (1990) Controlled comparisons of clomipramine and fluoxetine in the treatment of obsessive-compulsive disorder. *Archives of General Psychiatry* 47: 926–32.

Rickels, K., Downing, R., Schweizer, E. *et al.* (1993) Antidepressants for the treatment of generalised anxiety disorder. *Archives of General Psychiatry* 50: 51–60.

Sharpe, M., Hawton, K., Seagroatt, V. and Pasvol, G. (1992a) Follow up of patients with fatigue presentation to an infectious diseases clinic. *British Medical Journal* 305: 347–52.

Sharpe, M., Peveler, R. and Mayou, R. (1992b) The psychological treatment of patients with functional somatic symptoms: a practical guide. *Journal of Psychosomatic Research* 36: 515–29.

Sinclair, A. (1988) ME misery and the new stress syndrome. *South China Morning Post.*

Slater, E. (1965) Diagnosis of hysteria. *British Medical Journal* i: 1395–9.

Slater, E. and Glithero, E. (1965) A follow up of patients diagnosed as suffering from 'hysteria'. *Journal of Psychosomatic Research* 9: 9–13.

Surawy, C., Hackman, A., Hawton, K. and Sharpe, M. (1995) Chronic fatigue syndrome: a cognitive approach. *Behaviour Research and Therapy* 33 (5): 535–44.

Thoren, P., Asberg, M., Cronholm, B. *et al.* (1980) Clomipramine treatment of obsessive-compulsive disorder, 1: a controlled clinical trial. *Archives of General Psychiatry* 37: 1281–5.

Tyrer, P. (1990) *Current Problems with Benzodiazepines. The Anxiolytic Jungle: Where Next.* Chichester: John Wiley.

Van Hemert, A., Hengeveld, M., Bolk, J. *et al.* (1993) Psychiatric disorders in relation to medical illness among patients of a general medical outpatient clinic. *Psychological Medicine* 23: 379–90.

Weissman, M. M., Bland, R. C., Canino, G. J. *et al.* (1994) The cross national epidemiology of OCD. *Journal of Clinical Psychiatry* 55: 5–10.

Wessely, S., David, A., Butler, S. and Chalder, T. (1989) The management of chronic 'post viral' fatigue syndrome. *Journal of Royal College of General Practitioners* 39: 26–9.

Wessely, S. (1990) Old wine in new bottles: neurasthenia and 'ME'. *Psychological Medicine* 20: 35–53.

Wessely, S. (1994) Neurasthenia and chronic fatigue syndrome: theory and practice. *Transcultural Psychiatric Review* 31: 73–209.

Wilson, A., Hickie, I., Lloyd, A. *et al.* (1994) Longitudinal study of the outcome of chronic fatigue syndrome. *British Medical Journal* 308: 756–60.

Useful addresses

National Phobics Society

Zion Centre, Royce Road, Hulme, Manchester M15 5FQ

Phone: 0161 227 9898

Fax: 0161 227 9862

Email: natphob.soc@good.co.uk

Website: www.phobics-society.org.uk

Description: national network of self-help groups for people affected by anxiety disorders. Access to a range of services including helpline, local groups, book list, contact lists, counselling, clinical hypnotherapy, reflexology, relaxation techniques, etc.

Special interest activities: members' newsletter, local groups covering a wide range of anxiety disorders and tranquilliser issues. Phone for details.

Additional info: for free info booklet phone or write enclosing SEA. Membership forms can be printed directly from website. Interesting recommended book list.

Opening hours: helpline: Mon–Fri 10.30–4pm 0161 227 9898

Referral: open access

Criteria/catchment: national catchment

No Panic

Address: 93 Brands Farm Way, Randlay, Telford, TF3 2JQ

Phone: Helpline: 10am–10pm 01952 590545 Admin: 01592 590005

Fax: 01592 270962

Email: colin.hammond@euphony.net

Website: www.no-panic.co.uk

Description: service for people with anxiety disorders, phobias, panic attacks, OCD and tranquiliser withdrawal. Confidential helpline staffed by trained volunteers with crisis line overnight.

Opening hours: office: Mon–Fri 9am–5pm

Referral: self or any other source

Criteria/catchment: for people suffering from anxiety/phobias, their carers and families

Obsessive Action

Address: Aberdeen Centre, 22/24 Highbury Grove, London N5 2EA

Phone: 020 7226 4000/4545

Email: admin@obsessive-action.demon.co.uk

Website: www.obsessive-action.demon.co.uk

Description: help and advice for people suffering from obsessive-compulsive disorders and related conditions. There is a helpline, literature can be sent to you, quarterly newsletter, annual conference, etc. Phone for further details.

Special interest activities: Various fundraising events throughout the year.

Opening hours: helpline: Tues, Wed 9am–5pm and Thurs 9am–12pm

Referral: self or any other source

Criteria/catchment: for people suffering from obsessive-compulsive disorders and related conditions

12 Treating women with eating disorders

Lynda Todd

Introduction

The eating disorders of anorexia nervosa and bulimia nervosa are overwhelmingly women's disorders. Constituting the vast majority of sufferers, approximately 90 per cent of all reported cases are female.

Credit for the first medical descriptions of anorexia nervosa are attributed to the physicians Lasegue (1873) and Gull (1874), although earlier descriptions of Saints suffering from anorexia are to be found dating back to the thirteenth century. Anorexia typically involves a marked loss of body weight, cessation of menstruation in females and fear of fatness. Recently, however, there has been some concern about the inclusion of weight and shape concerns in diagnostic criteria for anorexia because there are many anorexics, particularly in non-western cultures, who do not fulfil this criteria (Lee, Ho and Hsu, 1993; Katzman and Lee, 1997).

It was the French physician Janet in the early 1900s who reported the first cases of bulimia nervosa, identifying individuals who alternated between food avoidance and overeating. Russell in 1979 termed the disorder bulimia nervosa, describing sufferers who would typically restrict their food intake, binge and then compensate by making themselves vomit or by abusing laxatives. In contrast to the case of anorexia, weight and shape concerns do appear to be valid criteria for diagnosis in bulimia nervosa.

Despite more than a century of documentation it has not been until recent decades that eating disorders have entered the centre stage of clinical efforts. The assessment and identification of appropriate and effective treatments for eating disorders is therefore in its infancy. Ussher (1991) suggests that eating disorders have remained in this clinical wilderness because of their gendered nature. Early theorists such as Freud (1895) posited that eating disorders were a result of female physiology and anatomy and therefore not open to psychological intervention, which may in part have contributed to the slow progression in the development of treatments. Also, there clearly has existed a male dominance within mental health professions and, as Wolf (1991) suggests, it is unlikely that eating disorders would have received such scant attention had they existed in such prevalence amongst the male population.

Despite the apparent lack of professional focus upon eating disorders and their treatment initially, the following attempts to describe how far we have travelled in our treatment provision. In addressing this issue, pharmacological, psychological and family treatments will be presented briefly and evidence relating to the effectiveness and acceptability of these treatments will be considered. It is not enough simply to consider which treatments work, but to think about when and under which circumstances treatments are effective. Does a combination of treatments provide greater benefits? Is the treatment acceptable to the patient? Although a treatment may be highly effective when utilised, if unacceptable it will not be made use of by the patient and therefore becomes a pointless provision.

In discussing treatment, this overview will focus upon anorexia and bulimia nervosa and I have not included binge eating disorder as it would not be possible to cover all sufficiently in this chapter. I would therefore refer you to Marcus (1998) for a review of treatment for binge eating disorder.

PHARMACOLOGICAL TREATMENTS

A variety of drugs, generally in addition to inpatient treatment, have been tried in an attempt to find a pharmacological treatment for anorexia nervosa. Although a number of trials have been conducted, findings have shown drug treatments to be limited in their effectiveness in anorexia. The opioid antagonist naloxone, an appetite stimulant, has been assessed in anorexia. Requiring continuous intravenous infusions, naloxone was found to enhance weight gain; however, this benefit decreased following cessation of the medication. Administration by intravenous infusion also severely restricted the ease of use.

Depressive symptoms are common in individuals suffering from anorexia nervosa and so antidepressants have been applied in the treatment process. Studies have compared clomipramine and amitriptyline with placebo but there is no evidence of any significant benefits in weight gain (Lacey and Crisp, 1980; Biederman, Herzog, Rivinus *et al.*, 1985; Halmi, Eckert, La Du and Cohen, 1986; Crisp, Lacey and Crutchfield, 1987). Selective serotonin reuptake inhibitors (SSRIs) have also been evaluated in trials for anorexia. This is based on the assumption that a vulnerability to anorexia is related to abnormal 5HT function (Collier, *et al.*, 1997). Fluoxetine, an SSRI, was tested in one study and it was found that if given after weight restoration, fluoxetine leads to maintenance of the weight gain and a reduced relapse rate (Kaye, Weltzin, Hsu and Bulik, 1991).

Again a range of pharmacological treatments have been tested in the treatment of bulimia nervosa. As in anorexia nervosa, investigations have examined opioid antagonists and in conjunction with weekly psychotherapy have been found to reduce binge–purge symptoms (Marrazzi *et al.*, 1995). It is antidepressant treatments for bulimia that appear to show the most consistent results. A number of double-blind, placebo-controlled trials have been conducted and findings show that imipramine (Pope, Hudson, Jonas and Yurgelun-Todd, 1983; Agras, Dorian, Kirkley *et al.*, 1987), desipramine (Blouin, Blouin, Perez *et al.*, 1988; McCann and Agras, 1990) and trazadone (Pope, Keck, McElroy and Hudson, 1989) are more effective than placebo in the short-term treatment of bulimia. SSRIs have also been used in bulimia treatment. Fluoxetine has been evaluated in two studies (Fluoxetine Bulimia Nervosa Collaborative Study Group, 1992; Goldstein, Wilson, Thompson *et al.* 1995) and it has been found to reduce bulimic and depressive symptoms, with 25 per cent and 18 per cent (respectively) of patients symptom free at the end of treatment. Investigation has also addressed the effect of combining both psychotherapy and medication. In a study comparing four different treatments it was found that imipramine alone, group Cognitive Behavioural Therapy (CBT) combined with imipramine and group CBT combined with placebo significantly reduced binge eating and purging symptoms compared to placebo alone (Mitchell, Pyle, Eckert *et al.*, 1990). Similarly it was found that CBT plus an antidepressant (fluoxetine or desipramine) significantly reduced binge eating and improved mood, compared to CBT alone or medication alone (Walsh, Wilson, Loeb *et al.*, 1997).

From the catalogue of studies conducted it would appear that medication alone and in combination with psychotherapy can produce beneficial outcomes for sufferers of eating disorders. It should, however, be noted that many of those drug studies are of a short duration and relapse rates are high if patients are followed up at six months (Walsh, Hadigan, Devlin *et al.*, 1991). It is also worth bearing in mind that there may be difficulties in prescribing medication because due to the weight-gaining side-effects, many patients may be unwilling to agree to antidepressant treatment.

PSYCHOLOGICAL TREATMENTS

Traditional treatment for anorexia nervosa has involved admission to an inpatient unit in which the central aims generally are re-feeding and weight gain. At the time of Gull (1874) it was believed that the most appropriate treatment involved removing the patient from her family, friends and home surroundings and implementing coercive, behavioural modification regimes involving forced re-feeding and complete bed-rest. Such approaches often simply compounded sufferers self-hatred and poor self-esteem and in some cases led to the development of symptoms consistent with post-traumatic stress disorder (Treasure and Ramsay, 1997).

There has now been a move away from treatment which proffers that 'The inclination of the patient must in no way be consulted' (Gull, 1874) to an approach which advocates a therapeutic alliance as a means of assisting the individual in change. This therefore requires that wherever possible the patient should be involved in the decision-making process. This means that the patient should be given a choice, with inpatient treatment as an option. The patient should be consulted with regard to her nutritional rehabilitation. An explanation and discussion should take place regarding the target weight to be set, with the patient gradually increasing the responsibility for her daily food intake.

Those suffering from anorexia nervosa will feel great anxiety and panic at the thought of eating and weight gain and the therapist should empathise with this and work in a supportive and collaborative manner. This is important because the strength of the therapeutic alliance, as perceived by the patient, is predictive of whether the patient will remain in treatment (Gallop, Kennedy and Stern, 1994). There may nevertheless be times when a patient becomes unable to view clearly the seriousness of her condition. At these points it may become necessary for staff to implement treatment under the Mental Health Act, to preserve her health, if not her life.

For patients suffering from bulimia nervosa outpatient treatment is the most common option, although at a point of crisis, when bulimic symptoms are particularly severe or when there exists a co-morbidity with alcohol or self-harm, admission may be warranted. A central aim of admission would be to begin on a more regular eating plan and so break the cycle of starvation which leads to an increased desire to binge, which in turn may trigger vomiting.

Studies investigating the efficacy of inpatient treatments for anorexia nervosa are somewhat limited. It has, however, been found that lenient treatment programmes are as effective as the more strict programmes (Touyz, Beaumont and Dunn, 1987) but the more flexible approach leads to improved compliance and is more acceptable to patients (Touyz *et al.*, 1987). It should be remembered that anorexia is often a chronic illness and relapse is common and so inpatient treatment, although intensive, should in no way be considered 'a cure'. For example, one study in New Zealand found that of 112 patients admitted for anorexia nervosa, 48 per cent were readmitted on more than one occasion (McKenzie and Joyce, 1990).

While inpatient treatment is certainly a very essential service for those who are in the grip of severe anorexia, and for whom their life may be dependent upon receiving such intensive care, many anorexics may be treated adequately as outpatients. One important benefit of outpatient treatment for sufferers of both anorexia and bulimia is that it allows the individual to maintain their social contacts, be it through family, friends, work or education.

Cognitive Behavioural therapy (CBT)

This is the most common treatment for bulimia nervosa and has often been termed 'the treatment of choice' (Freeman, 1995). It is regularly implemented as a time-limited, collaborative outpatient therapy, usually consisting of 16–20 sessions, with an agenda for each session set jointly between therapist and patient. CBT has also been applied as a group treatment.

CBT is based on the theory that bulimia is the result of poor self-esteem relating to weight and shape concerns. It is this focus on weight and shape which leads the individual into dieting and restricting food intake, which then results in the individual becoming increasingly preoccupied with food and in turn increases their desire to binge. Bingeing then leads to compensatory behaviours such as vomiting or laxative abuse. Behavioural techniques are applied with the aim of breaking these vicious cycles and reinstating some semblance of normal healthy eating. The focal point of treatment will then move towards cognitive restructuring. This involves the identification by the patient of her automatic thoughts. These are thoughts that just enter her head, and are based upon beliefs she holds about herself that are generally not based upon reality, although may appear to be believable. One example would be: 'I can't control my diet, I am a complete failure.' Once identified, the patient is required to record her automatic thoughts in a diary and the aim of therapy then becomes the challenging of these thoughts. Challenging involves considering evidence for and against these thoughts and evaluating what alternative interpretations of the evidence may exist. Treatment then progresses to focus upon the underlying assumptions (e.g. unless I am perfect no one will like me) and the schemas (e.g. I am unlovable) held by the individual.

Generally CBT appears to be at least as effective, if not more effective than any comparison treatment for bulimia nervosa. Fairburn and colleagues (1995) suggest that between 40 per cent and 60 per cent of those with bulimia nervosa become symptom free following a course of CBT treatment.

CBT has also been manualised and can be used in a self-help format. Self-help manuals aim to promote skills to assist sufferers in better managing their own illness. An investigation found 20 per cent of patients symptom free following eight weeks' use of a self-care manual (Treasure, Schmidt, Troop *et al.*, 1994). A further study also compared guided self-care, involving a limited amount of therapist intervention, to CBT treatment and found that both were equally effective in reducing bulimic symptoms (Thiels, Schmidt, Garthe *et al.*, 1998). It would therefore appear possible for effective treatment to be provided given minimum staffing provision.

In contrast to this, evidence for CBT in the treatment of anorexia is far more limited. One study compared traditional inpatient treatment to day-patient treatment involving CBT. A follow-up at three years indicated that those who had been randomised to the day-patient treatment had experienced fewer relapses, fewer readmissions and maintained a more stable weight. Clearly the day-patient programme consisted of more than simply the CBT component and therefore improvement cannot be attributed simply to the CBT.

It is important to consider the large proportion of bulimic patients who do not engage well in CBT. Certain factors appear to be predictive in this, including higher levels of co-morbidity with borderline personality disorder, self-harm and abuse of psychoactive substances (Coker, Vize, Wade and Cooper 1993; Waller, 1997). For this group we may need to look beyond CBT.

Interpersonal therapy (IPT)

In a number of randomised controlled trials CBT has been compared to Interpersonal therapy (IPT) as a treatment for bulimia nervosa. Initially IPT was designed as a treatment for depression for the New Haven–Boston Collaborative Depression Project but was adapted by Fairburn and associates (1991) in the treatment of bulimia. In contrast to CBT, IPT focuses upon the patient's current circumstances and relationships rather than concentrating upon the patient's eating behaviours or beliefs about shape and weight. IPT was found to be equally as effective as CBT in ending bingeing and purging behaviour by the one year follow-up (Fairburn, Jones, Peveler *et al.*, 1993) and this was maintained six years later (Fairburn, Norman, Welch *et al.*, 1995). It would appear therefore that IPT is a reasonable alternative to the more traditional CBT treatment for bulimia.

Cognitive Analytical therapy (CAT)

The integration of cognitive-behavioural and interpersonal aspects of treatment is operationalised within Cognitive Analytical therapy (CAT), which as the name suggests combines cognitive and psychoanalytic approaches to treatment (Ryle, 1990). CAT is a brief time-limited form of psychotherapy, usually involving 16–20 individual sessions with a therapist, and is collaborative in nature. Initially in CAT, therapist and patient will gather information and produce a written reformulation of the patient's history and presenting problems. The patient will also receive a sequential diagrammatic reformulation (SDR) which details her target problem procedures that underlie her target problems. The SDR also identifies the patient's reciprocal roles which have been learnt through early experiences and form the basis of later relationships.

In a pilot study 30 outpatients suffering from anorexia nervosa were randomised to either CAT or Supportive Educational Therapy (SET) (Treasure, Todd, Brolley *et al.*, 1995). During the SET treatment, information about nutrition, metabolism, anorexia and bulimia were given; issues around food and weight were also discussed and goals set. Results found no differences between the groups in weight gain after one year; meanwhile those in the CAT group reported a significantly greater improvement in global functioning. These findings relating to IPT and CAT suggest therefore that treatments that focus upon non-food- and non-weight-related issues can be effective in both anorexia and bulimia.

Even with the application of CAT drop-out rates remain a problem, with one-third dropping out of treatment in the above pilot study. Treasure and Ward (1997) therefore suggest a modification to CAT in the treatment of eating disorders. The application of motivational interviewing (Miller, Benefield and Tonigan, 1993) is proposed, based on the idea that change in eating-disordered behaviour can be represented by the transtheoretical model of change (Prochaska and DiClemente 1983, 1986). This model addresses 'how ready' people are to change their problem behaviour and identifies five stages through which individuals will pass in order to permanently change a behaviour: (1) precontemplation (neither interested nor considering change); (2) contemplation (considering change); (3) preparation (being ready to change); (4) action (engaging in change); and (5) maintenance (sustaining the change). This model further suggests that therapist strategies should reflect the patient's stage of change and, while the therapist may expect the patient to want to modify problematic procedural sequences, the therapist must instead accept that in fact the patient may be highly ambivalent about any shift in behaviour. Pushing too strongly for change or emphasising too greatly the problems inherent in the patient's status quo may lead to minimisation or denial of the problem and ultimately resistance on the part of the patient. Treasure and Ward therefore suggest that motivational enhancement techniques be applied along with CAT for those who are unmotivated or highly ambivalent.

Denman (1995), from her experiences of working with severely eating-disordered patients using CAT, suggests CAT may be suitable, not only for those suffering from anorexia nervosa, but also for 'patients who have bulimic symptoms and also suffer from marked personality disorganisation . . . (or) . . . patients with severe self-harming behaviour'; the very group which appear to respond less well to CBT.

Dialectical Behaviour therapy (DBT)

Developed originally for individuals with borderline personality disorder, and those displaying self-harming behaviour, Dialectical Behaviour therapy (Linehan, 1993) has now been modified and applied within the context of eating disorders. DBT is cognitive-behavioural in nature, although based upon the synthesis of Behaviourism and Zen practice. These may at first appear very opposing approaches; however, the essence of DBT is in the use of the dialectic, with therapy focusing upon both the need for change, and an acceptance of the individual as they are. There are two main components to DBT: individual therapy sessions and skills training groups. Within individual therapy, examples of problem behaviours will be targeted (e.g. bingeing) and behavioural chain analysis will be conducted. This requires that vulnerability factors and precipitating events to the problem behaviour are established, the outcome of the behaviour is ascertained and future alternative solutions and prevention strategies are discussed. Within the skills training groups focus is upon four core skills: mindfulness (the controlling of attention); interpersonal effectiveness (social skills development); emotion regulation (identifying and modulating emotions); and distress tolerance (short-term skills for coping in crises). Marcus, McCabe and Levine (1999) consider DBT to be a potentially effective treatment for individuals with eating disorders. This would appear probable because DBT is an already empirically supported treatment for borderline personality disorder and certain similarities exist between BPD and eating disorders. A high degree of emotion disregulation is displayed in sufferers of BPD, which is also a clear feature of eating-disordered patients and there is also a high co-morbidity between personality disorder and eating disorders. Although a promising path forward in treatment provision, further research is still required to empirically test the efficacy of DBT for sufferers of anorexia and bulimia.

Family treatments

Minuchin (Minuchin, Rosman and Baker, 1978) identified what he considered to be the typical structure of the anorexic's family, which he described as enmeshed, over-involved, lacking privacy and avoidant of conflict. These comments do not necessarily reflect the cause of the child's eating disorder but instead may be an understandable response to the experience of a severely ill individual within the family. This is supported by the fact that the degree of enmeshment and over-involvement is no greater than that seen in families with a child with cystic fibrosis (Blair, Freeman and Cull, 1995). If not causal factors, these patterns within the families may nevertheless act inadvertently to maintain the illness. Family approaches to treatment have therefore been tested, involving therapy with the family rather than just the individual suffering from the eating disorder.

The outcome of family therapy appears to be dependent upon the patient's age and their diagnosis. For those patients with a diagnosis of anorexia nervosa, and who are adolescent, or when the onset of their illness is in adolescence regardless of their present age, family therapy is a beneficial treatment (Russell, Szmukler, Dare and Eisler, 1987). Family counselling, an alternative to family therapy, has also been studied. This involves the parents being seen on their own for education and support and the child being seen individually (Le Grange, Eisler, Dare and Russell, 1992). Findings show that family counselling was as effective as family therapy, but was more acceptable to family members than traditional family therapy, which involves all family members. It would therefore appear that an intervention that incorporates the family system, while the individual remains embedded in that system, is effectual in change for sufferers of anorexia. In comparison, family therapies have not displayed much success in the treatment of bulimia.

Conclusion

How then do we bring together these findings into one overarching approach to the treatment of anorexia and bulimia nervosa? It seems that one of two approaches might be adopted.

The first and ideal approach would be to match the needs of the patient and the severity of their problems to the appropriate treatment at the point of presentation. A lack of information means that this cannot be achieved with a great degree of confidence, but all is not lost. From the research that has been reviewed certain factors do provide potential indicators of the most suitable treatment for enhancing outcome. In terms of individuals suffering from anorexia nervosa, age is an important factor. Certainly a first-line treatment for adolescents would involve either family therapy or family counselling with individual therapy for the adolescent. For adults it appears more difficult. The severe cases of anorexia nervosa, where there is a serious risk to life, clearly require inpatient treatment. There will, however, be many borderline cases that undoubtedly provoke great anxiety on the part of the therapist and family members, but who may successfully be able to maintain themselves as outpatients. If outpatient therapy is sufficient, which form of therapy should then be applied? From a preliminary study, cognitive analytical therapy currently appears to be beneficial as a psychological treatment, although additional motivational work may assist in shifting the ambivalence on the part of the patient. Once restoration of weight has been achieved, then prescription of fluoxetine could be an option.

In considering individuals with bulimia nervosa, for a relatively small number inpatient treatment may be required; otherwise it is necessary to look towards the most appropriate outpatient package, of which there are many options. For the bulimic group who also experience a co-morbidity with borderline personality disorder or self-harm then cognitive analytical therapy or dialectical behaviour therapy may be the therapies of choice. If the patient presents with more typical bulimia nervosa then treatment may combine a number of approaches, including CBT, IPT and medication. These may be used consecutively: if the patient seems not to respond, for example to CBT, then treatment may move on to adopt a more interpersonal approach. Medications, particularly fluoxetine or other antidepressants, may be usefully prescribed alongside psychotherapeutic interventions. Finally, if the individual is highly motivated, then a manual-based self-help approach may be sufficient.

While it is possible to attempt to match patient need and symptom severity to treatment, this is problematic because the exact factors which predict outcome under different treatment approaches is unclear. An alternative model, as recommended by the Royal College of Psychiatrists Report in 1992, is to develop a sequential model. This involves arranging the various treatments in a series of steps, graded from the least to the most intensive. This would then reduce the possibility of a patient being over-treated. On the negative side, it does lead to the possibility of increasing a patient's sense of failure, having completed one form of therapy only to have to move on to another, with the potential of damaging an already often injured sense of self-esteem.

Eating disorders are undoubtedly gendered in nature and this, some argue, has led to obstacles being placed in the path of development towards treatments for anorexia and bulimia. It seems clear that there exists a selection of treatment options available, particularly for bulimia, but the question remains of when and under which circumstances a treatment should be implemented. In order to answer this question, it seems necessary to consider sufferers of anorexia or bulimia, not simply as a homogenous group, but instead as individuals, with individual characteristics, problems and needs. In doing so, future research needs to focus not only upon the outcome of specific treatments, but should consider more specifically, individual factors and the interaction between the patient and the treatment.

References

Agras, W.S., Dorian, B., Kirkley, B.G., Arnow, B. and Bachman, J.A. (1987) Imipramine in the treatment of bulimia: a double-blind controlled study. *International Journal of Eating Disorders* 6: 29–38.

Biederman, J., Herzog, D.B., Rivinus, T.M., Harper, G.P., Rosenbaum, J.F., Hormatz, J.S., Tondorf, R., Orsulak, P.J. and Schildkraut, J.J. (1985) Amitriptyline in the treatment of anorexia nervosa: a double-blind, placebo-controlled study. *Journal of Clinical Psychopharmacology* 5: 10–16.

Blair, C., Freeman, C. and Cull, A. (1995) The families of anorexia nervosa and cystic fibrosis patients. *Psychological Bulletin* 25: 985–93.

Blouin, A.G., Blouin, J.H., Perez, E.L., Bushmik, T., Zuor, C. and Mulder, E. (1988) Treatment of bulimia with fenfluramine and desipramine. *Journal of Clinical Psychopharmacology* 8: 261–9.

Coker, S., Vize, C., Wade, T. and Cooper, P.J. (1993) Patients with bulimia nervosa who fail to engage in cognitive behavioural therapy. *International Journal of Eating Disorders* 13: 35–40.

Collier, D.A., Arranz, M.J., Li, T., Mupita, D., Brown, N. and Treasure, J. (1997) Association between 5HT2A gene promoter polymorphism and anorexia nervosa. *Lancet* 350: 350–412.

Crisp, A.H., Lacey, J.H. and Crutchfield. (1987) Clomipramine and 'drive' in people with anorexia nervosa: an inpatient study. *British Journal of Psychiatry* 150: 355–8.

Denman, F. (1995) Treating eating disorders using CAT: two case examples, in A. Ryle (ed.), *Cognitive Analytical Therapy: Developments in Theory and Practice.* Chichester: Wiley.

Fairburn, C.G., Jones, R., Peveler, R.C., Corr, S.C., Solomon, R.A., O'Connor, M.E., Burton, J. and Hope, R.A. (1991) Three psychological treatments for bulimia nervosa. *Archives of General Psychiatry* 48: 463–9.

Fairburn, C.G., Jones, R., Peveler, R.C., Hope, R.A. and O'Connor, M. (1993) Psychotherapy and bulimia nervosa: longer-term effects of interpersonal psychotherapy, behaviour therapy and cognitive behaviour therapy. *Archives of General Psychiatry* 50: 419–28.

Fairburn, C.G., Norman, P.A., Welch, S.L., O'Connor, M.E., Doll, H.A. and Peveler, R.C. (1995) A prospective study of outcome in bulimia nervosa and the long-term effects of three psychological treatments. *Archives of General Psychiatry* 52: 304–12.

Fluoxetine Bulimia Nervosa Collaborative Study Group (1992) Fluoxetine in the treatment of bulimia nervosa: a multi-center, placebo-controlled, double-blind trial. *Archives of General Psychiatry* 49: 139–47.

Freeman, C. (1995) Cognitive Therapy, in G. Szmukler, C. Dare and J. Treasure (eds.), *Handbook of Eating Disorders*. London: John Wiley & Sons.

Freud, S. (1895) *The Standard Edition of the Complete Works of Sigmund Freud. Volume 1: Pre-psychoanalytic Publications and Unpublished Drafts*. London: Hogarth Press (1966 reprint).

Gallop, R., Kennedy, S.H. and Stern, D. (1994) Therapeutic alliance on an inpatient unit for eating disorders. *International Journal of Eating Disorders* 16: 405–10.

Goldstein, D.J., Wilson, M.G., Thompson, V.L., Potvin, J.H., Rampey, A.H.Jr. and the Fluoxetine Bulimia Nervosa Research Group (1995) Long-term fluoxetine treatment of bulimia nervosa. *British Journal of Psychiatry* 134: 67–70.

Gull, W.W. (1874) Anorexia nervosa (apepsia hysterica, anorexia hysterica). *Transactions of the Clinical Society of London* 7: 22–8.

Halmi, K.A., Eckert, E., La Du, T. and Cohen, J. (1986) Anorexia nervosa: treatment efficacy of cyproheptidine and amitryptiline. *Archives of General Psychiatry* 43: 177–81.

Katzman, M. and Lee, S. (1997) Beyond body image: the integration of feminist and transcultural theories in the understanding of self starvation. *International Journal of Eating Disorders* 22: 385–94.

Kaye, W.H., Weltzin, T.E., Hsu, L.K. and Bulik, C.M. (1991) An open trial of fluoxetine in patients with anorexia nervosa. *Journal of Clinical Psychiatry* 52: 464–71.

Lacey, J.H. and Crisp, A.H. (1980) Hunger, food intake and weight: the impact of clomipramine on a refeeding anorexia nervosa population. *Postgraduate Medical Journal* 56: 79–85.

Lasegue, C. (1873) De l'anorexie hysterique. *Archives Générale de Médicine* 21 (April). 385–403.

Lee, S., Ho, T.P. and Hsu, L.K.G. (1993) Fat phobic and non-fat phobic anorexia nervosa: a comparative study of 70 Chinese patients in Hong Kong. *Psychological Medicine* 23: 99–1017.

Le Grange, D., Eisler, I., Dare, C. and Russell, G.F.M. (1992) Evaluation of family treatments in adolescent anorexia nervosa: a pilot study. *International Journal of Eating Disorders* 12: 347–57.

Linehan, M.M. (1993) *Cognitive-Behavioural Treatment of Borderline Personality Disorder*. New York: Guilford Press.

McCann, U.D. and Agras, W.S. (1990) Successful treatment of non-purging bulimia nervosa with desipramine: a double-blind, placebo-controlled study. *American Journal of Psychiatry* 147: 1509–13.

McKenzie, M.A. and Joyce, P.R. (1990) Hospitalization for anorexia nervosa. *International Journal of Eating Disorders* 11: 235–41.

Marcus, M. (1998) Binge eating disorder, in H.W. Hoek, J. Treasure and M. Katzman (eds.), *The Integration of Neurobiology in the Treatment of Eating Disorders*. Chichester: John Wiley.

Marcus, M.D., McCabe, E.B. and Levine, M.D. (1999) Dialectical Behaviour Therapy in the Treatment of Eating Disorders. The Fourth London International Conference on Eating Disorders, concurrent session 1h.

Marrazzi, M.A., Bacon, J.P., Kinzie, J. and Luby, E.D. (1995) Naltrexone use in the treatment of anorexia nervosa and bulimia nervosa. *International Clinical Psychopharmacology* 10: 163–72.

Miller, W.R., Benefield, G. and Tonigan, J.S. (1993) Enhancing motivation for change in problem drinking: a controlled comparison of two therapist styles. *Journal of Consulting and Clinical Psychology* 61: 455–61.

Minuchin, S., Rosman, B.L. and Baker, L. (1978) *Psychosomatic Families: Anorexia Nervosa in Context.* Cambridge, MA: Harvard University Press.

Mitchell, J.E., Pyle, R.L., Eckert, E.D., Hatsukami, D., Pomeroy, C. and Zimmerman, R. (1990) A comparison study of antidepressants and structured intensive group psychotherapy in the treatment of bulimia nervosa. *Archives of General Psychiatry* 47: 149–57.

Pope, H.G.Jr., Hudson, J.I., Jonas, J.M. and Yurgelun-Todd, D. (1983) Bulimia treated with imipramine: a placebo-controlled, double-blind study. *American Journal of Psychiatry* 140: 554–8.

Pope, H.G.Jr., Keck, P.E.Jr., McElroy, S.L. and Hudson, J.I. (1989) A placebo-controlled study of trazadone in bulimia nervosa. *Journal of Clinical Psychopharmacology* 9: 254–9.

Prochaska, J.O. and DiClemente, C.C. (1983) Stages and process of self change of smoking: toward an integrative model of change. *Journal of Consulting and Clinical Psychology* 51: 390–5.

Prochaska, J.O. and DiClemente, C.C. (1986) Toward a comprehensive model of change, in W.R. Miller and N. Heather (eds.), *Treating Addictive Behaviours: Processes of Change.* New York: Plenum.

Russell, G.F.M., Szmuckler, G., Dare, C. and Eisler, I. (1987) An evaluation of family therapy in anorexia nervosa and bulimia nervosa. *Archives of General Psychiatry* 44: 1047–56.

Ryle, A. (1990) *Cognitive Analytical Therapy: Active Participation in Change. A New Integration of Brief Psychotherapy.* Chichester: Wiley.

Thiels, C., Schmidt, U., Garthe, R., Treasure, J. and Troop, N. (1998) Guided self change for bulimia nervosa incorporating use of a self-care manual. *American Journal of Psychiatry* 155: 947–53.

Touyz, S.W., Beaumont, P.J. and Dunn, S.M. (1987) Behaviour therapy in the management of patients with anorexia nervosa: a lenient, flexible approach. *Psychotherapy and Psychosomatics* 48: 151–6.

Treasure, J. and Ramsay, R. (1997) *Hard to Swallow: Compulsory Treatment in Eating Disorders.* Maudsley Discussion Paper No.3.

Treasure, J. and Ward, A. (1997) Cognitive analytical therapy in the treatment of anorexia nervosa. *Clinical Psychology and Psychotherapy* 4: 62–71.

Treasure, J., Schmidt, U., Troop, N., Todd, G., Keilen, M. and Dodge, E. (1994) First step in managing bulimia nervosa: a controlled trial of a therapeutic manual. *British Medical Journal* 308: 686–9.

Treasure, J., Todd, G., Brolley, M., Tiller, J., Nehmed, A. and Denman, F. (1995) A Pilot Study of a Randomised Trial of Cognitive Analytic Therapy versus Educational Behavioural Therapy for Adult Anorexia Nervosa. *Behaviour Research and Therapy* 33: 363–7.

Ussher, J. (1991) *Women's Madness: Misogyny or Mental Illness?* London: Harvester Wheatsheaf.

Waller, G. (1997) Drop-out and failure to engage in individual outpatient cognitive behaviour therapy for bulimic disorders. *International Journal of Eating Disorders* 22: 35–41.

Walsh, B.T., Hadigan, C.M., Devlin, M.J., Gladis, M., and Roose, S.P. (1991) Long-term outcome of antidepressant treatment for bulimia nervosa. *American Journal of Psychiatry* 148: 1206–12.

Walsh, B.T., Wilson, G.T., Loeb, K.L., Devlin, M.J., Pike, K.M., Roose, S.P., Fleiss, J. and Waternaux, C. (1997) Medication and psychotherapy in the treatment of bulimia nervosa. *American Journal of Psychiatry* 154: 523–31.

Wolf, N. (1991) *The Beauty Myth.* New York: William Morrow.

Useful addresses

Eating Disorders Association

Address: 1st floor, Wensum House, 103 Prince of Wales Road, Norwich, NR1 1DW Phone: Helpline 01603 621414 Admin: 01603 619090 Youthline: 01603 765050

Fax: 01603 664915

Email: info@edauk.com

Website: www.edauk.com

Description: national network of self-help groups offering information and advice on a range of eating disorders. Telephone helpline, Youthline for people up to 18 years old, treatment options, quarterly newsletter, etc. Also offer training to professionals and other organisations. Phone for further details.

Opening hours: helpline: Mon–Fri 9am–6.30pm

Referral: open access

Criteria/catchment: national catchment

Overeaters Anonymous

Address: PO Box 19, Stretford, Manchester, M32 9EB

Phone: Helpline: 07000 784 985

Description: this is a fellowship of men and women recovering from compulsive overeating. The recovery is helped by attending their local meetings and completing a 12-step programme similar to that of Alcoholics Anonymous. Phone for details of local groups.

Additional info: support for all forms of eating disorders such as obesity, overeating, anorexia and bulimia, etc.

Opening hours: 24-hour Answerphone service

Referral: open access

Criteria/catchment: the only requirement is a desire to stop eating compulsively

13 Treating women with alcohol problems

E. Jane Marshall

Introduction

In most cultures, women are less likely to drink and to drink heavily compared with men. Women with alcohol problems are often viewed as deviant personalities by health professionals, who are not immune to the negative stereotype of the drinking woman.

Women are under-represented in treatment services. When they do enter treatment they are more likely than men to receive outpatient or non-residential care. They are also more likely to leave treatment prematurely, because services do not adequately meet their needs.

Failure to seek help may reflect barriers, either real or perceived. There is still a very powerful stigma surrounding women with alcohol problems and this stigma, in itself, can be a significant barrier to treatment.

This chapter opens with a review of the epidemiology of alcohol problems in women. Risk factors (genetic, psychological and socio-cultural) will be discussed and this will be followed by a summary of physical, psychological and social complications. Treatment issues will then be addressed. This section will include barriers to treatment, treatment outcomes, women-specific components of treatment programmes, and women-only treatment programmes.

EPIDEMIOLOGY OF ALCOHOL PROBLEMS IN WOMEN

In Great Britain, the proportion of women drinking above the recommended weekly benchmark of 14 units per week rose from 10 per cent in 1988 to 17 per cent in 2002 (Office for National Statistics, 2004). The increase was greatest in the 16–24 age group, more than doubling from 15 per cent in 1988 to 33 per cent in 2002. Average weekly consumption for women in this age group increased from 7.3 to 14.1 units over the same period.

Older women are also drinking more. The proportion of women aged 65 and over drinking above sensible levels increased from 3 per cent to 7 per cent between 1984 and 2002. Alcohol consumption amongst men remained fairly steady over the same time period, with 27 per cent of men drinking over 21 units per week in 1996 (Office for National Statistics, 2004).

The second National Survey of Psychiatric Morbidity, carried out in Great Britain between March and September 2000, found that prevalence rates of alcohol dependence were 3 per cent for women and 12 per cent for men (Coulthard *et al.*, 2002). In the United States the lifetime prevalence rate for the alcohol dependence syndrome in women has been reported to be in the order of 8.2 per cent (Anthony *et al.*, 1994).

WOMEN AT RISK

Women with alcohol problems are a heterogeneous population. Drinking behaviour is influenced by a range of demographic factors including age, marital status, employment and ethnicity (Plant, 1997; Edwards *et al.*, 2003). These factors interact with other risk factors such as genetic predisposition (Kendler *et al.*, 1992; Prescott *et al.*, 1997) and socio-cultural factors to determine the onset and course of drinking.

Genetic factors

In the United States population-based studies of female twins have shown that 40–60 per cent of the variance in 'alcoholism' amongst women can be attributed to genetically mediated factors (Kendler *et al.*, 1992).

Psychological factors

Women with alcohol problems have higher rates of anxiety disorder, psycho-sexual dysfunction, bulimia (Ross *et al.*, 1988), depressive symptoms (Walitzer and Sher, 1996), lower self-esteem and borderline personality disorder (Beckman, 1978; Walitzer and Sher, 1996), whereas their male counterparts have higher rates of antisocial personality disorder (Ross *et al.*, 1988). In women presenting for treatment, it is often very difficult to ascertain whether such psychological problems preceded the alcohol dependence or arose as a consequence of it. Longitudinal studies have gone some way to answering this, by showing that women who reported feelings of low self-esteem and impaired ability to cope at junior high and high school, later became problem drinkers (Jones, 1971). Likewise, women college students who developed drinking problems in later life were more likely to use alcohol to relieve anxiety and elevate mood in social situations, compared with men (Fillmore *et al.*, 1979).

Depression appears to pre-date alcohol problems in women, but seldom does so in men. In a general population study, Helzer and Pryzbeck (1998) found that depression was the primary problem in 66 per cent of women but in only 22 per cent of men.

Retrospective studies have explored the long-term effects of traumatic events in childhood. Childhood sexual abuse (CSA), loss of a parent in childhood through death or separation (Kendler *et al.*, 1996) and an unstable family of origin are all risk factors. A history of CSA increases the lifetime risk of alcohol problems by a factor of 3 (Winfield *et al.*, 1990).

Socio-cultural factors

Women are influenced by the drinking habits of their partners (Wilsnack and Wilsnack, 1995). Being single, divorced, separated or co-habitating is associated with heavy drinking (Wilsnack *et al.*, 1994). Divorce puts women without a problem at risk. However, many women with established heavy drinking reduce their consumption following divorce. Thus divorce can be seen as a 'risk or remedy' (Wilsnack *et al.*, 1994). Being in a violent relationship is another risk factor (Edwards *et al.*, 2003).

Women often date the onset of their heavy drinking to a stressful life event, explaining that they used alcohol in order to forget their problems and to increase their social confidence (Copeland *et al.*, 1993).

Although the addictive process itself is similar in men and women, the pattern and course in women is determined by the above factors.

PHYSICAL COMPLICATIONS OF ALCOHOL MISUSE DEPENDENCE IN WOMEN

Although women start to drink heavily at a later age than men, they seem to develop alcohol-related physical problems and alcohol dependence at an earlier stage in their drinking career. This so-called 'telescoping' process (Blume, 1992; Randall *et al.*, 1999) is thought to be due, at least in part, to the way in which women metabolise alcohol. First, women have more fatty tissue and less body water than men. Alcohol is more soluble in water than in fat; thus a standard drink gives rise to higher alcohol concentrations in blood and tissue in women, compared with men of the same weight. This in turn means a longer elimination time. Second, alcohol undergoes a 'first pass' metabolism in the stomach where it is oxidised by the enzyme gastric alcohol dehydrogenase (ADH). This process is important because it limits the amount of ingested alcohol that reaches the liver. Women have been reported to have lower levels of gastric ADH activity than men (Frezza *et al.*, 1990). Women with drinking problems appear to have extremely low levels of gastric ADH and no first pass metabolism. This means that a higher proportion of ingested alcohol reaches the liver than it does in men, probably predisposing these women to an earlier onset of alcoholic liver disease (Maher, 1997). Third, women who drink heavily may also be prone to fatty acid toxicity, another cause of liver damage (Maher, 1997). Finally, women show greater blood alcohol concentration (BAC) variability, have faster alcohol metabolism and less acute alcohol tolerance compared with men (Blume, 1992).

The way in which women metabolise alcohol therefore seems to put them at higher risk of developing physical complications than men, and of developing these complications earlier in their drinking careers. Such complications include alcoholic liver disease, cardiomyopathy and brain damage. Alcoholic hepatitis in women nearly always progresses to cirrhosis, even following abstinence (Edwards *et al.*, 2003). Studies carried out in Spain indicate that women are at greater risk of alcoholic cardiomyopathy than men (Urbano-Marquez *et al.*, 1995). Women appear to experience more sedation at similar BACs to men, suggesting that their brains are more vulnerable to the effects of alcohol (Aamon *et al.*, 1996).

Alcohol-dependent women have a much shorter life expectancy and a higher risk of premature death than their male counterparts (Lindberg and Agren, 1988). The causes of premature death include alcohol intoxication and delirium tremens, cirrhosis of the liver, suicide, violent death, stroke and breast cancer (Lindberg and Agren, 1988; Lewis *et al.*, 1995).

Other physical complications include inhibition of ovulation, infertility and a wide range of gynaecological and obstetric problems. Heavy alcohol consumption during pregnancy is associated with spontaneous abortion, intrauterine growth retardation and foetal alcohol syndrome (FAS). Excessive drinking also leads to diminished libido and inhibition within relationships, and has been linked to an early menopause.

Psychological complications

Both men and women with drinking problems have high rates of associated psychiatric disturbance. Women with alcohol problems are more likely than men to have secondary diagnoses of mania, somatisation, major depression, phobic disorder, panic disorder and drug abuse/dependence (Helzer *et al.*, 1991). Women also have higher rates of psychosexual dysfunction and bulimia (Ross *et al.*, 1988). A Canadian study found that psychiatric co-morbidity was associated with greater severity of problem drinking in a community sample (Ross and Shirley, 1997). Even socially intact women early in their drinking careers have been shown to have high levels of mood and anxiety disorders (Haver and Dahlgren, 1995).

Alcohol problems and post-traumatic stress disorder (PTSD) commonly occur together, and the course of the combined disorder is more severe than that of either disorder alone (Brown *et al.*, 1995).

Social complications

Women with alcohol problems experience high levels of marital instability and are at increased risk of domestic violence. They are also more likely than their male counterparts to be divorced or living with partners who also have an alcohol problem.

TREATMENT ISSUES

Despite the clear dangers of alcohol misuse and dependence for women, they under-utilise treatment services as a result of both real and perceived barriers. These barriers are conceptualised as occurring in three main domains (Allen, 1994) as follows:

1   Individual characteristics (internal barriers)
2   Socio-cultural issues
3   Treatment programme characteristics.

Barriers relating to *individual characteristics* include ethnicity, marital status, the presence of children and also perceptions, beliefs and attitudes towards addiction. Women tend not to see drinking as their primary problem and they seek help in a roundabout way for physical problems, depression and anxiety (Thom, 1986). They typically put others first, often presenting for treatment only after they have developed significant alcohol-related physical problems. Feelings of shame, inadequacy and low self-esteem may lead them to think that they are not worthy of treatment. Women with histories of childhood trauma and sexual and physical abuse find it particularly difficult to seek help, because for them alcohol offers a certain solace and dampens terrifying memories. The social stigma associated with alcohol dependence leads to intense feelings of guilt and shame (Reed, 1987; Copeland and Hall, 1992). This is particularly relevant to pregnant women, for whom alcohol withdrawal poses a serious risk to the developing foetus as a result of withdrawal seizures and oxygen deprivation. Mothers with alcohol problems have genuine concerns about leaving or losing their children.

Barriers related to *socio-cultural and environmental factors* include opposition of family and friends, the social costs of family disruption, lack of access to childcare, lack of knowledge and location of treatment services. These barriers make it difficult for women to seek help for their alcohol problem. A common scenario is failure to refer to specialist treatment services because of lack of information on the part of the primary health care team. Once in treatment women often receive little support from their partners, and this can be misconstrued as lack of motivation on their part.

Treatment programme characteristics are a very significant barrier to engaging and remaining in treatment. Existing services are usually male-dominated. Appropriate women-centred treatment facilities may not be available or may be too far away for the woman to attend on a regular basis. Sadly, attitudes of treatment staff may be negative, and the setting an inappropriate one for children. Often treatment is not individually tailored to women's needs. It is extremely difficult for a woman to cope in an inpatient or residential unit where she is the only woman. Health professionals may be inadequately trained to manage the complex problems with which women present. Confrontational techniques may compound fears of anxiety, low self-esteem and depression (Beckman, 1994). Often the vagaries of funding mean that treatment agencies cannot take a long-term view.

TREATMENT OUTCOMES

Women are underrepresented in treatment outcome studies, but overall seem to do as well as, or even better than men (Vanicelli and Nash, 1984). Women may do better during the first year after treatment, whereas men have better results at follow-up after twelve months (Jarvis, 1992). There is also evidence to suggest that women may be better than men at using self-help material to reduce heavy or problem drinking (Sanchez-Craig *et al.*, 1989). Robust treatment of co-morbid phobic anxiety and depression is central to improving drinking outcomes (Haver and Gjestad, 2005).

COMPONENTS OF A WOMEN-ORIENTED ALCOHOL TREATMENT PROGRAMME

Many of the treatment issues discussed above could be solved if there were a greater sensitivity to women's needs within existing services. Most services should be able to provide access to women counsellors and women-only groups within existing resources. A woman-centred approach should also include family support services, help with parenting skills, training to develop self-esteem, childcare, support groups, health care and supportive aftercare. Treating staff should be aware of and be sensitive to women's problems.

Certain women-specific needs must be addressed during treatment. These include:

- reproductive health and sexual problems
- childhood sexual and physical abuse
- psychiatric co-morbidity
- polydrug use.

REPRODUCTIVE HEALTH AND SEXUAL PROBLEMS

Treatment programmes should try to uncover any gynaecological and psycho-sexual problems and ensure access for appropriate assessment and treatment. This might be done in liaison with primary care (general practitioner, practice nurse) or with other specialist clinics. Treatment agencies should aim to set up networks with other specialist services and facilitate attendance by the client, perhaps by accompanying her, at least to the first appointment. Referral for appropriate treatment and adequate support throughout this process are potentially strong motivating factors for tackling the alcohol problem itself. One aspect of this work is the offering of support to grieving women who have lost children or who will never have children because of an early menopause.

Pregnancy offers a real opportunity for change. Women with alcohol and drug problems are more likely to present late in pregnancy and do not avail of antenatal care. They are at a higher risk of obstetric complications and FAS is obviously an important issue. Sadly, giving birth to one child with FAS does not preclude it happening again. A minority of women who have lost children to local authority care or through death continue to become pregnant to new partners in the vain belief that they will be able to hold on to at least one child.

Most women with alcohol problems reduce their consumption considerably during pregnancy, or manage to abstain. An integrated approach is important. Communication between alcohol services, antenatal clinics and primary care must be facilitated, with mutual education and attendance to basic issues such as housing and income maintenance, arrangements for delivery and postnatal care and preparation for parenthood. A balance needs to be struck to ensure that these women receive additional special help and are not written off because of an assumption that they will be incapable of successful parenting.

CHILDHOOD SEXUAL AND PHYSICAL ABUSE

This is a very sensitive area. Many women (and men) who have experienced sexual and physical abuse as children begin to use alcohol and drugs at an early stage to cope with the trauma and subsequent memories. Memories re-emerge when these individuals become alcohol- and drug-free, and this often leads to relapse. Such individuals need ongoing support in a trusting relationship, preferably with an experienced therapist. It may not be possible for them to engage in mainstream PTSD services, because this treatment in itself may precipitate relapse. Nevertheless they need to confront their past and learn relapse prevention strategies if they are to have any chance of abstinence and an improved quality of life.

PSYCHIATRIC CO-MORBIDITY/POLYDRUG USE

Paradoxically women with depression and alcohol dependence have better outcomes than women with alcohol dependence alone (Rounsaville *et al.*, 1987). Many women with alcohol problems also have significant drug problems and dependence. Older women may have problems with prescribed benzodiazepines. Illicit drugs such as cannabis, cocaine, other stimulants and hallucinogens are increasingly common, particularly in women under the age of 30. For a proportion of these women, facilitation of treatment for HIV and hepatitis C may be the first step in engagement with an alcohol treatment programme.

WOMEN-ONLY TREATMENT PROGRAMMES

There is considerable debate as to whether women are better served in women-only or mixed-sex treatment programmes. A Swedish study reported superior two-year outcomes on measures of alcohol consumption and social adjustment for a specialised women's programme, compared with a mixed-sex programme (Dahlgren and Willander, 1989). However, an Australian study showed no differences in outcomes when a women's service was compared with two traditional mixed-sex facilities (Copeland and Hall, 1992; Copeland *et al.*, 1993). The women attending the women-only service were more likely to have dependent children, to be lesbian, to have had a mother with a history of a drug or alcohol problem and to have suffered sexual abuse in childhood.

Women-only programmes may be able to attract women earlier or to attract women who are reluctant to enter mixed-sex programmes. Many women cite a preference for a mixed-sex programme with the proviso that it includes a nucleus of other women, one-to-one counselling with a woman counsellor and the option of a women-only group.

Conclusion

Women are not readily attracted into specialist alcohol services – they are more likely to approach generalist services, at least in the first instance. It is therefore vital that GPs, practice nurses, general psychiatrists, community psychiatric nurses, general physicians and health visitors are aware of and sensitive to the special needs of women, so helping to bridge the gap between generalist and specialist services. Such links are fundamental to early intervention. Women should have more choice in their treatment and have the option to be matched to appropriate levels and types of intervention. Specialist services should guarantee that certain women be seen by women counsellors and have access to women-only groups. Where possible, agencies should make it possible for all women to have the option to be seen, at least initially, by a women counsellor.

It must be remembered that the drinking may be only one facet of a larger problem. Psychological and physical complications need to be considered in an integrated treatment approach, together with housing, income maintenance and management and the needs of any children.

References

Aamon, E., Schafer, C., Hofmann, V. and Klotz, V. (1996) Disposition and first pass metabolism of ethanol in humans: is it gastric or hepatic and does it depend on gender? *Clinical Pharmacological Therapy* 59: 503–13.

Allen, K. (1994) Development of an instrument to identify barriers to treatment for addicted women, from their perspective. *The International Journal of the Addictions* 29: 429–44.

Anthony, J.C., Warner, L.A. and Kessler, R.C. (1994) Comparative epidemiology of dependence on tobacco, alcohol, controlled substances and inhalants: basic findings from the National Co-morbidity Survey. *Experimental and Clinical Psychopharmacology* 2: 244–68.

Beckman, L.J. (1978) Self esteem of women alcoholics. *Journal of Studies on Alcohol* 39: 491–8.

Beckman, J.L. (1994) Treatment needs of women with alcohol problems. *Alcohol Health and Research World* 18: 206–11.

Blume, S.B. (1992) Alcohol and other drug problems in women, in J.H. Lowinson, P. Ruiz and R.B. Millman (eds.), *Substance Abuse, a Comprehensive Textbook*, 2nd edn. Baltimore: Williams and Wilkins.

Brown, P.J., Recupero, P.R. and Stout, R. (1995) PTSD substance use co-morbidity and treatment utilization. *Addictive Behaviours* 20: 251–4.

Copeland, J. and Hall, W. (1992) A comparison of women seeking drug and alcohol treatment in a specialist women's and two traditional mixed-sex treatment services. *British Journal of Addiction* 87: 1293–302.

Copeland, J., Hall, W., Didcott, P. and Biggs, V. (1993) A comparison of a specialist women's alcohol and other drug treatment service with two traditional mixed-sex services: client characteristics and treatment outcome. *Drug and Alcohol Dependence* 32(1): 81–92.

Coulthard, M., Farrell, M., Singleton, N., Meltzer, H. (2002). Tobacco, alcohol and drug use and mental health: National Statistics. London: the Stationery Office.

Dahlgren, L. and Willander, A. (1989) Are special treatment facilities for female alcoholics needed? A controlled 2-year follow-up study from a specialised female unit (EWA) versus a mixed male/female treatment facility. *Alcoholism: Clinical and Experimental Research* 13: 499–505.

Edwards, G., Marshall, E.J. and Cook, C.C.H. (2003) *The Treatment of Drinking Problems*, 4th edn. Cambridge: Cambridge University Press.

Fillmore, K.M., Bacon, S.D. and Hyman, M. (1979) *The 27-year Longitudinal Panel Study of Drinking by Students in College*. 1979 Report to National Institute of Alcoholism and Alcohol Abuse. Contract no. ADM 281–76–0015. Washington DC: National Institute of Alcoholism and Alcohol Abuse.

Frezza, M., di Padova, C., Pozzato, G., Terpin, M., Baraona, E. and Lieber, C.S. (1990) High blood alcohol levels in women: the role of decreased gastric alcohol dehydrogenase activity and first-pass metabolism. *New England Journal of Medicine* 322: 95–9.

Haver, B. and Dahlgren, L. (1995) Early treatment of women with alcohol addiction (EWA): a comprehensive evaluation and outcome study. Patterns of psychiatric Co-morbidity at intake. *Addiction* 90: 101–9.

Haver, B. and Gjestad, R. (2005) Phobic anxiety and depression as predictor variables for treatment outcome. *Nord J Psychiatry*, 59, 25–30.

Helzer, J.E. and Pryzbeck, T.R. (1988) The co-occurrence of alcoholism with other psychiatric disorders in the general population and its impact on treatment. *Journal of Studies on Alcohol* 49: 219–24.

Helzer, J.E., Burnam, A. and McEvoy, L. (1991) Alcohol abuse and dependence, in L.N. Robins and D.A. Regier (eds.), *Psychiatric Disorders in America:The Epidemiological Catchment Area Study*. New York: Free Press, pp. 81–115.

Jarvis, T.J. (1992) Implications of gender for alcohol treatment research: a quantitative and qualitative review. *British Journal of Addiction* 87:1249–61.

Jones, M.C. (1971) Personality antecedents and correlates of drinking patterns in women. *Journal of Consulting and Clinical Psychology* 36: 61–9.

Kendler, K.S., Heath, A.C., Neale, M.C., Kessler, R.C. and Eaves, L.J. (1992) A population based twin study of alcoholism in women. *JAMA* 268: 1877–82.

Kendler, K.S., Neale, M.C., Prescott, C.A., Kessler, R.C., Heath, A.C., Corey, L.A. and Eaves, L.J. (1996) Childhood parental loss and alcoholism in women: a causal analysis using a twin-family design. *Psychological Medicine* 26: 79–95.

Lewis, C.E., Smith, E., Kercher, C. and Spitznagel, E. (1995) Assessing gender interactions in the prediction of mortality in alcoholic men and women: a 20 year follow-up study. *Alcoholism: Clinical and Experimental Research* 19: 1162–72.

Lindberg, S. and Agren, G. (1988) Mortality among male and female hospitalised alcoholics in Stockholm 1962–1983. *British Journal of Addiction* 83: 1193–200.

Maher, J. (1997) Exploring alcohol's effects on liver function. *Alcohol, Health and Research World* 21: 5–12.

Office for National Statistics (ONS) (2004). Living in Britain: results from the 2002 General Hosuehold Survey. London: the Stationery Office.

Plant, M. (1997) *Women and Alcohol: Contemporary and Historical Perspectives*. London: Free Association Books.

Prescott, C., Neale, M.C., Corey, L.A. and Kendler, K.S. (1997) Predictors of problem drinking and alcohol dependence in a population-based sample of female twins. *Journal of Studies on Alcohol* 58: 167–81.

Randall, C., Roberts, J.S., Boca, F.K., Carroll, K.M., Connors, G.J. and Mattson, M.E. (1999) Telescoping of landmark events associated with drinking: a gender comparison. *Journal of Studies on Alcohol* 60: 252–60.

Reed, B.G. (1987) Developing women-sensitive drug dependence treatment services : why so difficult? *Journal of Psychoactive Drugs* 19:151–64.

Ross, H.E., Glaser, F.B. and Stiasny, S. (1988) Sex differences in the prevalence of psychiatric disorders in patients with alcohol and drug problems. *British Journal of Addiction* 83: 1179–92.

Ross, H. and Shirley, M. (1997) Life-time problem drinking and psychiatric co-morbidity among Ontario women. *Addiction* 92: 183–96.

Rounsaville, B.J., Dolinsky, Z.S., Babor, T.F. and Meyer, R.E. (1987) Psychopathology as a predictor of treatment outcome in alcoholics. *Archives of General Psychiatry* 44: 505–13.

Sanchez-Craig, M., Leigh, G., Spivak, K. and Lei, H. (1989) Superior outcome of females over males after brief treatment for the reduction of heavy drinking. *British Journal of Addiction* 84: 395–404.

Thom, B. (1986) Sex differences in help-seeking for alcohol problems: I. The barriers to help seeking. *British Journal of Addiction* 81: 777–88.

Urbano-Marquez, A., Estruch, R., Fernandez-Sola, J., Niolas, J.M., Park, J.C. and Rubin, R. (1995) The greater risk of alcoholic cardomyopathy and myopathy in women compared with men. *Journal of American Medical Association* 274: 149–54.

Vannicelli, M. and Nash, L. (1984) Effect of sex bias on women's studies on alcoholism. *Alcoholism: Clinical and Experimental Research* 8: 334–6.

Walitzer, K.S. and Sher, J.K. (1996) A perspective of self-esteem and alcohol use disorders in early adulthood: evidence for gender differences. *Alcoholism : Clinical and Experimental Research* 20 and 1118–24.

Wilsnack, S.L. and Wilsnack, R. (1995) Drinking and problem drinking in US women, in M. Galanter (ed.), *Recent Developments in Alcoholism*, vol. 12. New York: Plenum Press.

Wilsnack, S.C., Wilsnack, R.W. and Hiller-Sturmhofel, S. (1994) How women drink: epidemiology of women's drinking and problem drinking. *Alcohol Health and Research World* 18: 173–84.

Winfield, I., George, L.K., Swartz, M. and Blazer, D.G. (1990) Sexual assault and psychiatric disorders among a community sample of women. *American Journal of Psychiatry* 147: 335–41.

Useful addresses

Alcoholics Anonymous – Head Office

PO box 1, Stonebow House, Stonebow, York, YO1 7NJ
Phone: Admin: 01904 644026   National helpline: 0845 769 7555
Website: www.alcoholics-anonymous.org.uk
Description: Head Office of national network of self help groups offering counselling and peer support to help members give up drinking.
Opening hours: Mon-Fri 9am-5pm
Referral: open access

Al-Anon Family Groups

61 Great Dover Street, London SE1 4YF
Phone: 0207 403 0888
Fax: 0207 378 9910
Email: alanonuk@aol.uk
Website: www.hexnet.co.uk/alanon
Description: national network offering advice and support to families and friends of problem drinkers, now or in the past. For details of local meetings throughout the UK and Ireland phone the main helpline number which is a confidential service.
Opening hours: daily 10am-10pm.
Referral: self or any other source
Criteria/catchment: families and friends of problem drinkers

Alcohol Recovery Project – Women's Alcohol Centre

Address: 66A Drayton Park, London N5 1ND
Phone: 0207 226 4581

Fax: 0207 354 8134

Website: www.arp-charity.demon.co.uk

Description: women-only alcohol service offering one-to-one counselling, group support, referral to detox and residential services, etc.

Special interest activities: daily drop in for women only, Mon-Fri 10am-12.30pm, access to complementary therapies.

Opening hours: Mon-Fri 9.30am-5pm

Referral: self or other agencies

Criteria/ Catchment: Londonwide project for women who want to change their patterns of alcohol use.

Drinkline

Address: 1st floor, Cavern Court, 8 Matthews Street, Liverpool L2 6RE

Phone: 0800 917 8282   Admin 0151 227 4150   Minicom: 0800 521361

Email: admin@healthwise.org.uk

Description: government-sponsored helpline providing information and advice to people concerned about sensible drinking habits. For people with an alcohol problem, their carers, friends and families. Range of information leaflets and posters available.

Opening hours: Mon-Fri 9am-11pm, Sat/Sun 6-11pm

Referral: open access

Alcohol Concern

The national agency on alcohol misuse (Alcohol Services Directory)

Address: Waterbridge House, 32–36 Loman Street, London SE1 0EE

Phone: 0207 928 7377

Fax: 0207 928 4644

Email: contact@alcoholconcern.org.uk

14 Treating women with drug addiction

Jennifer Bearn

Introduction

Women are less likely than men to enter treatment for substance misuse problems. The rate of illicit drug use is about half that of men and yet women only make up between 10 per cent and 30 per cent of most treatment samples. Perhaps women are underrepresented because most services are tailored to the needs of the male majority and do not appeal to women. This, in turn, suggests that there may be differences in the way women misuse drugs and the range of psychological and social problems that they suffer, compared to men, but is this indeed so?

Powis *et al.* (1996) compared men and women in a large community sample of heroin and cocaine users, both in and out of treatment. The women were younger, had started using drugs more recently and were using lower daily amounts. Despite this they were as severely dependent as men. Women were more likely to chase or inhale than inject; only a third of the heroin injectors were women compared to half of the chasers. Several strands of evidence suggested that the women's drug use was more profoundly influenced by their partner than vice versa. For example, there were interesting differences in the way men and women acquired money to pay for their habit. Men were more likely to finance themselves through theft and drug dealing, whilst women tended to be dependent upon their sexual partners. Not only were the women more likely to have a drug-using partner, who procured drugs on their behalf, they were also far more likely to have been given their first injection by a sexual partner (50 per cent of the women compared to 10 per cent of the men). Female cocaine users were less likely to seek treatment for their problems. Even though this did not apply to the heroin users, this is not to say that the treatment on offer was as well matched.

In another substantial study of women in treatment for drug and alcohol problems, Swift *et al.* (1996) interviewed a sample of women using a range of residential and community treatment services in Australia. Half of these women had a partner, the majority of whom also used drugs; 60 per cent had children but half of these were not living with their mother and were either being cared for by relatives or had been fostered or adopted. Many women said that worry about their children's welfare was a significant factor in seeking treatment. The study revealed that women carry a heavy burden of psychiatric co-morbidity. Half had received counselling for anxiety or depression, whilst a similar number had attempted suicide. Eating disorders were also common. Many women had experienced childhood sexual (37 per cent) or physical (21 per cent) abuse and the majority had been abused during adulthood usually when they or their partner were intoxicated.

Davis and DiNitto (1996) have attempted to address the issue as to whether some of these social and psychological problems are primarily gender- rather than substance misuse-related. This American study applied the Addiction Severity Index (a structured interview which elicits drug-related problems within a range of psychosocial domains) to a mixed-sex group of substance misusers and to men and women undergoing rehabilitation for disabilities due to a variety of physical and psychiatric problems. With the proviso that this was not a robust comparison group, the study did suggest that in the overall sample women were more troubled by family problems, were more likely to have parents with psychiatric problems and had more outpatient psychiatric treatment, whilst substance misusers were more likely to have problems controlling violence, have experienced divorce and other family problems, and have substance-misusing parents or siblings, independent of gender. Problems were compounded by being both a woman and a substance misuser, colourfully described by the authors as a 'double-whammy' effect.

There is a range of influences that may discourage women from seeking help for substance misuse problems (Powis *et al.* 1996). First, double standards enhance the stigma of drug misuse in women; in particular an intoxicated woman is perceived more negatively than a man. Also, the high frequency of psychiatric co-morbidity makes women more likely to seek help from general psychiatric services rather than those specialising in substance misuse. Women involved in an enmeshed relationship with a drug-using partner on whom they are dependent both emotionally and financially are likely to find it more difficult to present themselves independently for treatment. Many also fear the impact that revealing their drug problems and entering treatment may have on their children. Few treatment centres have childcare facilities and they are frightened that their children may be taken into care. Finally, women form a minority in mixed-sex treatment services. Indeed men may predominate not only amongst the client group but also the staff. Women may fear harassment and are vulnerable to forming exclusive relationships, which may sabotage their treatment.

Differences between men and women are also encountered during recovery (O'Connor *et al.* 1994). Female patients who have been abstinent from a range of drugs for a substantial period of time (mean 2.6 years) had higher depression scores than those for men and also scored higher on specific measures of self-blame and low self-esteem, particularly if they had a history of childhood sexual abuse. Men by contrast were more likely to blame others for their drug use and reported fewer emotional problems. Treatment programmes incorporating confrontation and challenging of beliefs, or a status hierarchy, whereby new members have low status and gain privileges and status as they progress through treatment, may selectively impede the recovery of women by reinforcing their low self-esteem.

Recognition of the specific difficulties expressed by substance-misusing women has led Finkelstein (1993) to formulate the key elements of a women-friendly treatment programme. First, it should be family-focused and should address specific issues in women-only groups, particularly dependence and assertiveness, low self-esteem and experiences of sexual abuse. It should be community-based and a multidisciplinary management team should be equipped to provide not only psychiatric and physical treatment but also parenting skills, support and paediatric care. Education and vocational training are also important components. They emphasise the need for flexible long-term support so that appropriate levels of service intensity can be offered at different times during treatment.

A particularly important time to engage a woman in treatment is when she is pregnant. Pregnant opiate-dependent women are at greater risk of a range of obstetric complications, particularly premature labour, eclampsia and placental insufficiency. Whilst opiates do not appear to be teratogenic, intrauterine growth retardation is common, rendering the new born more susceptible to infection and feeding problems; perinatal mortality rates are elevated. The foetus is also very sensitive to sudden opiate withdrawal, which is most severe when the mother is dependent upon injectable heroin, a consequence of the short half-life. The characteristic withdrawal syndrome seen in babies born with opiate dependence is more serious than in adults because of the significant risk of seizures and cerebral hypoxia. Babies born to stimulant users, whilst also prone to a specific withdrawal syndrome, are at increased risk of congenital anomalies as well.

In the face of these adverse effects, women drug users may be at their most reluctant to seek help for their addiction when they are pregnant and often present late to obstetric services. Sometimes a woman realises only late on that she is pregnant, because menstrual irregularity is common, but most often she is fearful of unsympathetic or judgemental attitudes of health care professionals. She may have particular concerns that her ability to look after her new baby as well as any existing children may be questioned. Many women therefore experience tension between their concerns about using drugs when pregnant and wanting to cut down or stop, and their fear of a hostile reception from treatment services.

It follows that treatment services developed for pregnant women need to take these difficulties into account. One such service was developed as a 'walk-in' health clinic based in two non-statutory drug agencies in South London (Dawe *et al.*, 1992). Antenatal care was shared between the general practitioner and the local hospital antenatal clinic. Women were offered a drug treatment programme with a hierarchical structure based on the principles of harm minimisation. Initially they were encouraged to substitute illicit drug use with methadone, then gradually reduce their methadone to low-dose maintenance, or complete abstinence. A particular feature was an outreach treatment component whereby women lost to the service were actively encouraged to return. Over half the women who started treatment remained in continuous contact for ten weeks or more and a quarter were drug free at delivery. Even so, about half the babies had signs of neonatal withdrawal which was related to the amount of methadone the mother was taking at the time of delivery. The study highlighted a gap in service provision for these women after they had delivered. Whilst several would have benefited from inpatient admission, no mother and baby facility was available for them.

In almost all cases there was a planned pre-birth case conference and a further case conference after delivery. Half the babies were not placed under statutory supervision, and 47 per cent were placed on the Child Protection Register, a significantly lower number than in previous studies, which might relate to the treatment, although follow-up was short.

In the United States there has been more attention to the problems of women using cocaine during pregnancy. One model treatment service for this group of women has been piloted at Bellevue Hospital in New York City by Egelko and colleagues (Egelko *et al.*, 1996). Treatment is delivered in an intensive day programme setting which is run as a modified therapeutic community based on the narcotics anonymous twelve-step approach to relapse prevention. Twenty-five per cent of the time is spent addressing perinatal issues, specifically parenting education, women's health, family reintegration and maternal bonding. Women were recruited into this specialised programme both antenatally and up to one year postnatally, after they had engaged for at least a month in the mainstream mixed-sex outpatient programme. However, the women who went into treatment postpartum were less successful in achieving abstinence than those who started treatment before the birth of their child. Those who were involved in child custody proceedings were also more likely to do well if they had started treatment before delivery. Postpartum women did not seem to respond to these motivational influences to stay drug free, in the same way.

In general the perinatal group stayed in treatment less time than a comparison group of non-perinatal women. These women had a heavy burden of social adversity including medical, child custody and housing problems. Not uncommonly the competing demands of the meetings needed to address these issues disconnected women from the treatment programme, rather than necessarily reflecting treatment failure. The authors acknowledged that such activities should be considered a legitimate part of relapse-prevention treatment rather than being incompatible with the formal treatment programme.

Recently there has been an increased interest in the treatment needs of pregnant and perinatal women with substance misuse problems (Howell *et al.* 1999). However, less attention has been paid to the needs of these women as their children get older. These women have often experienced disturbed relationships with their own parents including family disruption, violence and abuse. Moreover high levels of psychopathology including depression and anxiety also increase the risk of disruption in their relationship with their children. One specific problem that has been highlighted in substance-abusing mothers is a perception that they have been deprived of psychological parenting by their own mothers. This may lead to a role reversal in the relationship that they have with their own children; they overestimate their maturity and expect them to provide emotional gratification and support.

Luther and Walsh (1995) have described specific aspects of parenting education and training of particular relevance to mothers with drug and alcohol problems. Since they often have very low self-esteem and feel insecure about their parenting abilities they may be put off by critical feedback and practical help; they are more likely to respond to discussions about parenting using motivational rather than didactic approaches. They need encouragement to address their children's feelings and experiences of parental drug use and to minimise their direct exposure to this. Other aspects include recognition of the concept of role reversal and the 'parental' child and enhancement of the mother's ability to support and guide her children appropriately alongside realistic expectations of their behaviour in a maturational context. The concepts of harm minimisation can be applied to parenting as a factor in preventing and treating the adverse effects of maternal substance misuse on children. Helping the mother recognise appropriate levels of supervision and enabling her to help her own children resist drug involvement or use can improve the children's physical safety. Promoting insight into specific difficulties will help to determine if the child needs specific treatment interventions from either psychiatric or social services. The success of treatment programmes developed for substance-misusing mothers and babies appears to be enhanced by provision of onsite childcare, parenting classes and vocational training (Howell *et al.*, 1999), although there are very few reports of outcome studies in women with older children.

In summary, women have overlapping but also distinctive problems related to their drug use compared to men, and so it may be unrealistic to expect that women will gain equal benefit from a treatment programme largely populated and driven by the needs of a male majority. Recognition that women have specific needs must impact on the design of treatment programmes so that they are relevant and attractive to women.

References

Davis, D.R. and DiNitto, D. (1996) Gender differences in social and psychological problems of substance abusers: a comparison to non-substance abusers. *Journal of Psychoactive Drugs* 28: 135–45.

Dawe, S., Gerada, C. and Strang J. (1992) Establishment of a liaison service for pregnant opiate-dependent women, *British Journal of Addiction* 87: 867–71.

Egelko, S., Galanter, M., Edwards, H. and Marinelli, K. (1996) Treatment of perinatal cocaine addiction: use of the modified therapeutic community. *American Journal of Drug and Alcohol Abuse* 22: 185–202.

Finkelstein, N. (1993) Treatment programming for alcohol and drug-dependent pregnant women. *International Journal of the Addictions* 28: 1275–309.

Howell, E.M., Heiser, N. and Harrington, M. (1999) Review of recent findings on substance abuse treatment for pregnant women. *Journal of Substance Abuse Treatment* 16: 195–219.

Luther, S. and Walsh, K. (1995) Treatment needs of drug-addicted mothers. *Journal of Substance Abuse Treatment* 12: 341–8.

O'Connor, L., Berry, J., Inaba, D., Weiss, J. and Morrison, A. (1994) Shame, guilt and depression in men and women in recovery from addiction. *Journal of Substance Abuse Treatment* 6: 503–10.

Powis, B., Griffiths, P., Gossop, M. and Strang, J. (1996) The differences between male and female drug users: community samples of heroin and cocaine users compared. *Substance Use and Misuse* 31: 529–43.

Swift, W., Copeland, J., and Hall, W. (1996) Characteristics of women with alcohol and other drug problems: findings of an Australian national survey. *Addiction* 91: 1141–50.

Useful addresses

Adfam National Helpline

Waterbridge House, 32/36 Loman Street, London SE1 0EH

Phone: Helpline: 020 7928 8900   Admin: 020 7928 8898

Description: national helpline for families and friends of drug users offering confidential advice and support. Range of info booklets for parents, partners and families, various training courses for professionals working in related areas.

Special interest activities: some language services available, support for families of imprisoned drug users, including visits to various prison visitors' centres in Greater London area by arrangement.

Opening hours: helpline: Mon-Fri 10am–5pm, Tues till 7pm 0207 928 9800

Referral: self or any other source.

Criteria/catchment: national organisation for families and friends of drug users

Families Anonymous

Phone: Duddington and Rollo Community Association, Charlotte Despard Avenue, London, SW11 5JE

Phone: 020 7498 4680

Fax: 020 7498 1990

Email: office@famanon.org.uk

Website: www.famanon.org.uk

Description: national network offering support for partners, friends and families of people with a drug problem. Regular weekly meetings held

across the UK. Phone for details of your local group. Free voluntary service based on the twelve-step programme pioneered by Alcoholics Anonymous.
Opening hours: office Mon–Fri, 1–4pm. Answerphone with contact numbers at other times
Referral: open access
Criteria/catchment: national network

Narcotics Anonymous

Phone: Helpline: 10am–10pm 0207 730 0009   UK Service Office: 0207 251 4007
Website: www.ukna.org
Description: fellowship of men and women who help each other stay off drugs. Phone for details of meetings in your local area.
Additional info: UK Service Office deals with enquiries from other organisations and distributes publicity material. Phone during office hours.
Opening hours: helpline: 10am–10pm every day including weekends. Answerphone if nobody immediately available.
Referral: open access

Release

Address: 388 Old Street, London EC1V 9LT
Phone: 020 7729 9904
Fax: 020 7729 2599
Email: info@release.org.uk
Website: www.release.org.uk
Description: 24-hour Drug and Legal Advice Helpline for anybody having problems with illegal or prescribed substances, people with legal problems, or anybody else in need of a 24-hour legal advice service. Can arrange representation, advise on criminal proceedings, etc.
Opening hours: 24-hour telephone advice service only. Office not open to the public.
Referral: open access
Criteria/ Catchment: national organisation

15 Treatment of post-traumatic stress disorder

Judith Erskine

Introduction

This chapter focuses on women who experience trauma in adulthood and go on to develop post-traumatic stress disorder (PTSD). Psychiatric disorders that women may suffer as a result of childhood trauma are covered elsewhere in this volume. It must be noted that men also suffer from PTSD. The theory, diagnosis and treatment of PTSD remains a developing and expanding field; this chapter hopes to provide a basic overview of the topic, with suggested further reading around this field. I have used various terms to describe the sufferer of PTSD, i.e. woman, person, patient or client.

WHAT IS POST-TRAUMATIC STRESS DISORDER?

Post-traumatic stress disorder (PTSD) can develop as a result of an event or events that would be distressing to almost anyone (e.g. rape, domestic violence, road traffic accidents and childhood abuse). Many people who suffer a significantly traumatic event are distressed for a while but recover reasonably quickly (within a few weeks). However, for some their symptoms persist and develop into PTSD, lasting for many months or years, which can be very disabling and affect all facets of the client's life including work, social, family and personal life.

Who gets PTSD?

Each one of us reacts to life events differently; however PTSD does not distinguish between age, gender, race, class, sexuality or cultural background. It is difficult to say how many people suffer or who have suffered with PTSD, probably due to both under-diagnosis and spontaneous recovery. Formal criteria for the diagnosis of PTSD can be found in the Diagnostic and Statistical Manual of Mental Disorders, Fourth Edition, (DSM IV).

Why do some people appear to have more/worse symptoms than others? It is impossible to say whether one person's traumatic experience is worse than someone else's; however, women who develop 'simple' PTSD will usually have suffered a single or circumscribed trauma. Women who have experienced repeated and/or prolonged exposure to trauma, i.e. domestic violence, childhood abuse, war may develop 'complex' PTSD where the picture may be complicated with personality difficulties, such as *borderline personality disorder*, and *dissociative disorders*. Many women presenting with 'complex' adult PTSD have had significant childhood trauma.

Borderline personality disorder (BPD) is defined by DSM IV as 'a pattern of instability in interpersonal relationships, self image and affect, and marked impulsivity beginning by early adulthood'. Although BPD can co-exist with PTSD especially in those women with a history of childhood trauma it is a distinct disorder and not necessarily linked with post-traumatic stress disorder.

Dissociation is a complex defence mechanism in which the person attempts to protect their psyche from painful and distressing events. This is characterised by, amnesia (forgetting), absorption (losing oneself in another activity) and by depersonalisation (a sense of detachment from the world). This mechanism usually develops in childhood as a result of prolonged abuse.

The core symptoms of post-traumatic stress disorder are:

- *Avoidance phenomena* – Avoidance of people, places, and situations that remind them of the trauma;
- *Intrusive phenomena* – Flashbacks to the trauma, unwanted images and thoughts of the trauma. Distressing dreams and nightmares;
- *Hypervigilance* – Being excessively aware of the environment; some describe it as having a red alert system or radar in their head;
- *Hyperarousal* – Being excessively sensitive to external stimuli (being 'jumpy');
- *Irritability*;
- *Sense of detachment from the world*;
- *Numbness* – in a psychological sense.

PTSD may also co-exist with other psychological disorders, the most common ones being depression, alcohol abuse, drug abuse and eating disorders.

Further symptoms common to both PTSD and other linked disorders are:

- *A sense of helplessness or powerlessness*;
- *Anhedonia* – loss of interests in hobbies, etc.;
- *Anxiety* – both the physical (palpitations, sweating, etc.) and psychological (fear, dread) symptoms;
- *Feelings of guilt, humiliation, shame and blame* – often in relation to surviving the trauma or feeling that they invited the trauma in some way;
- *Low mood and depressive symptoms* – including loss of libido, poor appetite, poor concentration and poor energy levels;

- *Poor sleep* – including initial insomnia, early morning wakening and nightmares;
- *Somatic symptoms* – common ones being headaches and abdominal discomfort.

As well as enquiring about the core symptoms of PTSD it is very important to be aware of and enquire into the disorders and symptoms that can also be present (noted above). To aid this there are a number of different questionnaires that can be used to measure the presence and severity of symptoms of the various disorders, for example the Revised Impact of Events Scale and the Becks Depression Inventory.

Treatment options

The range of treatments offered to women with PTSD fall into broad categories: educative, psychodynamic and behavioural. The preferred treatment option should be dictated by the needs of the woman, but is often determined by what is available in the local area.

The basics of treatment often start with education, explaining the symptoms of the disorder or disorders to the woman and to a greater extent normalising their reaction to an abnormal event or events. Many people feel that they are 'going mad' or 'being stupid', which is often compounded by friends and family saying such things as 'pull yourself together' or 'it happened ages ago, just forget about it'. For effective treatment it is often necessary to include partners in the treatment and to explain to them the nature of the disorder and associated difficulties, and to include them as much as possible in the treatment. Both the client and the partner should be encouraged to ask questions to ensure that they understand what is happening in their lives.

Medication

Some women, having experienced significant trauma, will develop psychological symptoms and disorders that will need pharmacological treatment under the supervision of a doctor, e.g. depressive episodes, anxiety reactions or sleep disturbances.

Debriefing

Debriefing is a contentious issue, with some feeling that it can be more damaging than helpful to the individual but the basic premise is that it helps the woman process the trauma, and is undertaken as soon as possible after the trauma has occurred.

Cognitive behavioural therapy

Cognitive behaviour therapy works on the premise that the individual has not been able to process the trauma. It directly confronts the symptoms relating to the trauma by using exposure and cognitive restructuring. The aim is to challenge the woman's behaviour and ways of thinking, by directly confronting the symptoms of avoidance, intrusion and maladaptive coping strategies. These techniques help the person modify their reactions to the trauma within a specific framework.

Eye movement desensitisation and reprocessing therapy (EMDR)

This is a relatively new technique developed in the United States which helps the woman to re-process traumatic memories by using bilateral brain stimulation. As yet no one is absolutely sure how it works, but it has been seen to be hugely beneficial in helping to reduce flashbacks and assisting people to move on from the trauma. EMDR practitioners will have had extensive training in using this technique.

Supportive counselling

This gives the person space and time to explore the trauma and its subsequent effect on their life. This does not specifically look at previous life events that may have affected the person's response to the current trauma.

Psychodynamic psychotherapy

This technique also gives space and time to explore the presenting trauma, but will also look at earlier life events. This form of psychotherapy takes into account and works with the psychodynamics between the therapist and client. The woman hopefully learns from the psychotherapeutic experience and is then able to use that experience in other areas of their lives including their reactions to trauma.

Treatment can often involve a mixture of these various techniques and some have found relief by using alternative treatments, such as acupuncture, meditation, aromatherapy and homeopathy.

Some women benefit from individual treatment, whilst others gain benefit from group treatment in which they can explore their experiences in a group setting. This setting also confronts feelings of isolation and the feelings of being the only person to suffer from PTSD, but for some this approach is too confronting and difficult. It is also possible to combine group and individual treatment approaches.

As with all therapeutic relationships, successful treatment is dependent upon the development of a safe and secure attachment relationship between the therapist and client. Attachment is defined by Bowlby (1969) as:

To say of a child that he is attached to, or has an attachment to, someone means that he is strongly disposed to seek proximity to and contact with a specific figure and to do so in certain situations, notably when he is frightened, tired or ill.

Within the secure attachment relationship the therapist is able to empower the patient to begin the recovery process and to sustain progress made. However, for some patients the development of a safe and secure attachment relationship is progress in itself.

Safety is a basic requirement of treatment, which can be thought of and maintained using the Bloom (1997) 'SAGE' model within the treatment. In brief the components of this model are:

*S*afety: physical, psychological, social and spiritual.
*A*ffect modulation: covers managing difficult feelings and experiences such as flashbacks, dissociation, aggression and mood disorders without resorting to self-injury or substance abuse to cope.
*G*rief: recognition of losses incurred because of traumatic events, the appreciation of the seductive nature of familiar responses (addiction to trauma) and a commitment to the process of mourning together with the development and use of social and interpersonal resources.
*E*mancipation: encompasses successful management of thoughts and feelings, and being able to identify and use a sense of empowerment and move through the recovery process.

Some difficulties women encounter when in treatment

Women needing treatment often come up against practical difficulties, namely childcare arrangements, running the home, psychosexual issues, to name but a few and these need to be taken into account when offering treatment.

Women with children, who present with PTSD need to have additional social support, which can come from friends, family and in some cases from social services. This additional support can be used for childcare for appointments, etc.; however, this needs to be done with sensitivity, as some women may fear that telling their therapist how they really feel will lead to their losing their children. For many women it is caring for and loving their children that actually keeps them going. However, the needs of the children also need to be taken into account and the therapist needs to maintain alertness to any effects that the mother's symptoms may be having on the children, especially her increased level of irritability, and possible dissociative symptoms.

Supervision issues

It is imperative that clinicians receive adequate supervision when working with this client group as there is a risk of secondary re-traumatisation for the clinician, which can lead to psychological damage and also significantly effect the treatment of the client.

As previously stated this is a very brief overview of the topic and further reading is suggested below. It is hoped that the following case studies will give the reader a flavour of the sorts of difficulties encountered when working with someone with a trauma history.

Susan

Susan, a 36-year-old married woman with three children all of school age, went to her general practitioner's surgery complaining of whiplash following a car accident a few weeks ago. The GP referred her to the practice's physiotherapist. During her consultation with the physiotherapist, Susan complained of not being able to sleep properly saying that she could not get off to sleep and when she finally dropped off she kept waking up. The physiotherapist attributed her poor sleep to her physical discomfort due the neck injury. However, despite treatment, Susan still complained of poor sleep and made an appointment with her GP, asking for sleeping tablets. Upon further questioning it transpired that Susan was having nightmares relating to the accident. The GP asked if Susan was having thoughts about the accident when she did not want to. Susan reluctantly admitted that she was. Susan also admitted to having flashbacks and avoiding the road where the accident occurred. Susan also told the GP that she felt 'really ratty' all the time, was shouting at her husband and children at the slightest thing and that she felt that she was going 'mad'. The GP told Susan that he thought that she was suffering from a traumatic stress reaction and referred her to the practice counsellor.

The counsellor explained that Susan's symptoms were normal after a trauma such as this and helped Susan to talk through the accident in minute detail. She also suggested that, with the help of her husband, she resume driving by using a graded exposure approach: first sitting in the car with her husband in their driveway, and then moving through a gradual process to achieve her stated goal of being able to drive alone along the stretch of road where the accident happened.

Over the course of a few weeks Susan's sleep pattern improved and she found that she stopped thinking about the accident and that she was much less irritable with her family.

When to refer on?

Penny

Penny, 29 years, had disclosed to her midwife, one month before the birth of her first child that she had been raped at the age of 14. The midwife was the first person whom Penny had told about the abuse, as she was very worried about the process of giving birth. Penny was adamant that she did not want to talk about the rape, saying that she was more concerned about the birth.

The midwife discussed the issue with Penny and they agreed to concentrate on the birth itself and to think about a referral to psychological services after the birth if Penny wanted that. The midwife also discussed this with her own 'line manager'. Their joint conclusion was that the birth had to be safe, but that they would agree to Penny's requests if at all possible

The agreed plan was that there would be as little medical intervention as necessary, but all agreed that the physical health and safety of mother and child was paramount. It was also decided that students would not be permitted to examine Penny and only required staff would be in the delivery room. Penny also requested that only female staff be present; this was agreed with the understanding that this might not be ultimately possible given the constraints of the NHS. The midwife spent time individually with Penny and her husband explaining the usual process of labour and answering their questions. Penny said she felt that during the birth of her child she would feel helpless, very vulnerable and 'out of control'. It was acknowledged that Penny's thoughts and feelings were normal given her experiences, and that this was a common fear for any new mother-to-be.

The birth of Penny's child proceeded uneventfully, and Penny felt safe throughout, and subsequently had two more children. However, following the final birth, of her daughter, Penny felt that she needed help with coping with the rape. Her GP referred her to local psychiatric services where during the assessment it became clear that Penny also suffered from an eating disorder. Her symptoms of PTSD included daily flashbacks to the rape, finding herself thinking about it when she did not want to, poor sleep and distressing, frequent nightmares. She also described feeling very jumpy when not in her own home and having a fear of doors being locked and not being able to get out. Penny was also able to say that given the choice she would rather not talk about the rape at all, but knew that in order to fully recover she had to talk about it, but that she had never felt safe enough to do so. She also expressed concern that if she revealed how she felt then she would have her children taken into care. In short she fulfilled the criteria for PTSD and a co-morbid diagnosis of severe depression.

Penny was then referred to a specialist service where she was successfully treated after three years of intensive treatment. With help from primary health care professionals, she was able to cope with the birth of her children and all the reminders of the rape that were triggered by that. She also said that being involved in all aspects of her care left her feeling empowered and that she had as much control over the process as was possible.

References

Bloom, S. (1997) *Creating Sanctuary: Toward an Evolution of Sane Societies*. London: Routledge.

Bowlby, J. (1969) *Attachment and Loss*, Vol. 1, *Attachment*. Harmondsworth: Penguin.

Suggested further reading

Bowlby, J. (1988) *A Secure Base*. London: Routledge

American Psychiatric Association (1994) *The Diagnostic and Statistical Manual of Mental Disorders*, 4th edn (DSM IV). Washington: American Psychiatric Association.

Greenwald, R. (1999) *EMDR-Eye Movement Desensitization and Reprocessing in Child and Adolescent Psychotherapy*. New York: Aronson.

Herman, J. (1992) *Trauma and Recovery*. New York: Basic Books.

Kinchin, D. (1994) *Post Traumatic Stress Disorder: A Practical Guide to Recovery*. Thorsons Health Series. London: Harper Collins

Parnell, L. (1997) *Transforming Trauma: EMDR the Revolutionary New Therapy for Freeing the Mind, Clearing the Body and Opening the Heart*. New York: Norton and Company.

Parnell, L. (1999) *EMDR in the Treatment of Adults Abused as Children*. New York: Norton and Company.

Shapiro and Silk Forest (1997) *EMDR: The Breakthrough Therapy for Overcoming Anxiety Stress and Trauma*. New York: Basic Books.

Yule, W. (ed.) (1999) *Post-Traumatic Stress Disorders: Concepts and Therapy*. Chichester: John Wiley & Sons.

de Zulueta, F. (1993) *The Traumatic Root of Destructiveness: From Pain to Violence*. Chichester: John Wiley & Sons.

Useful addresses

Women's Aid Federation of England

PO Box 391, Bristol, BS99 7WS

Phone: Helpline: 0345 023468   Admin: 01179 444411

Fax: 01179 241703

Email: wafe@wafe.co.uk

Website: www.womensaid.org.uk

Description: runs Women's Aid National Helpline for women experiencing domestic violence, provides advice and support on support on related issues, can refer to women's refuge and other relevant services. National network of local groups, range of info booklets. Phone for details.

Opening hours: helpline: Mon–Fri 10am–8pm, Sat 10am–5pm

Referral: self or any other source

Criteria/catchment: women only

16 Treatment of psychosexual problems

Penny Mostyn

Introduction

Sexuality can be defined as our physiological capacity for desire, arousal and orgasm. This capacity is exquisitely responsive to social and psychological forces and has its own biological evolution throughout our life cycle (Levine, 1995). Healthy sexuality enhances our psychological well-being and satisfies our reproductive urge. Although not always a linear sequence of events the female sexual response cycle can be simply depicted starting with sexual desire and ending with orgasm (Figure 1). Other theoretical models of sexual response cycles are being considered and researched (Basson 2003) which may better represent the complexity and heterogeneity of women's sexual responses.

Sexual problems arise when there are disturbances within the sexual response cycle. The common problems women complain of are low desire, lack of arousal, inability to achieve orgasm and pain with intercourse (Box 16.1). Classification and definitions are from a consensus classification system (Basson 2000) which is built on the existing frameworks provided by the International Classification of Diseases (ICD10) and the Diagnostic and Statistical Manual of Mental Disorders (DSM IV).

Box 16.1 Female sexual problems

Sexual desire disorders
    Hypoactive sexual desire disorder
    Sexual aversion disorder
Sexual arousal disorder
Orgasmic disorder
Sexual pain disorders
    Dyspareunia
    Vaginismus

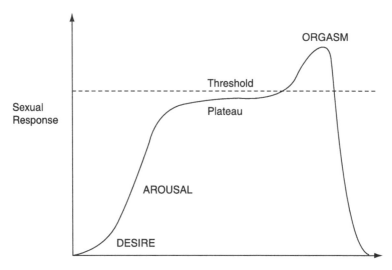

Figure 16.1 A sexual response cycle
Source (Adapted from Masters and Johnson, 1966)

PREVALENCE OF SEXUAL PROBLEMS

Female sexual dysfunction is common. The National Survey of Sexual Attitudes and Lifestyles (NATSAL) showed that 53.8 per cent of women in the general population in Britain reported at least one sexual problem in the previous year and 15.6 per cent reported problems lasting at least six months (Mercer 2003). The prevalence of sexual problems in women within specific populations has been shown to be 40% per cent in a general practice population (Nazareth 2003) and 44 per cent in non-acute psychiatric outpatients (Kockott and Pfeiffer, 1996).

GENERAL MANAGEMENT

Diagnosis

Few doctors ask patients regularly about sexual problems and few patients tell doctors about their problems. An important step in treating sexual problems is the physician-initiated discussion (Halvorsen and Metz, 1992). Open questions such as 'how do you feel about your sex life?' give the patient permission to open up and discuss any problems. Closed questions such as 'do you have any problems with sex?' will not encourage discussion as the answer can only be yes or no (Table 16.1). More focused questions can follow to obtain details. It is not necessary to have the answers but giving the patient time to talk can be invaluable. Doctors who are comfortable talking about sex

Table 16.1 Examples of open questions compared to closed questions

Open	Closed
How has your illness/medication affected your sex life?	Has it affected your sex life?
How do you feel about your sex life?	Do you feel good/bad about your sex life?
How does your partner respond?	Is your partner supportive?

and ask regularly about sexual difficulties are more likely to see patients with sexual problems (Burnap and Golden, 1967).

Assessment of causation

Sexual problems are caused by physical, psychological and social factors of which a number of factors may be involved. A woman may have pelvic adhesions and dyspareunia from pelvic inflammatory disease but her sense of pain may be exacerbated by the fact that it started after a termination of pregnancy which her religious upbringing forbade. Sexual problems do not exist in isolation as they are closely interrelated (Figure 17.2). Lack of desire can be caused by, and lead to, inadequate arousal which can lead to dyspareunia. Thus a woman can present with dyspareunia where the actual problem is in the desire phase. In assessing causality this link between problems needs to be considered.

Physical factors

Physical illness can effect sexual function in three ways (Bancroft, 1994:552):

1 the direct physical effects of the condition;
2 the psychological effects of the condition such as embarrassment, loss of self-esteem and anxiety;

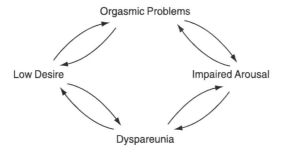

Figure 16.2 The interrelationship of sexual problems

3　the effect of treatment for the condition such as medication, surgery or radiotherapy.

Table 16.2 shows some common physical illnesses that can effect desire, arousal and a women's capacity to reach orgasm. Table 16.3 shows the possible causes of painful intercourse segregated into those that cause superficial pain and those that cause deep pain. Table 16.4 shows various drugs that may effect sexual function. Drug effects on female sexuality have been

Table 16.2 Organic causes of sexual dysfunction

Medical condition	Desire	Arousal	Orgasm
Endocrine			
Diabetes		+	+
Hypothyroid	+		+
Hyperthyroid	+		
Hyperprolactinaemia	+	+	+
Oestrogen deficiency		+	+
Neurological			
MS		+	+
Epilepsy	+		
Infection			
Vaginitis		+	
Psychiatric			
Depression	+		
Psychosis	+		+
Anorexia	+		+

Note: + indicates a negative effect.

Table 16.3 Common pathological causes of painful penetration

	Superficial pain		Deep Pain
vulval	allergies	*bladder*	cystitis
introital	atrophy	*bowel*	constipation
vaginal	bartolinitis		inflammatory bowel
	candida	*uterus*	endometritis/myometritis
	herpes		fibroids
	trichomonas	*adnexae*	endometriosis
	warts		pelvic inflammatory disease
	eczema		ovarian cysts
	psoriasis		
	vulval vestibulitis		
urethra	cystocoele		
	urethral caruncle		

far less studied than effects on male sexuality and are generally less acknowledged and understood. In psychiatric illness, there is the added difficulty of distinguishing between the effect of the illness and the effect of the medication on sexual function (Barnes and Harvey, 1993). For women taking conventional antipsychotic medication hyperprolactinaemia is the main cause of sexual dysfunction (Smith 2002).

Pregnancy and the menopause are key stages of the biological evolution in a woman's life cycle. Pregnancy can lead to a decline in desire and arousal, dyspareunia and painful uterine contractions with orgasm. Breastfeeding women report less sexual desire than non-breastfeeding women (Hyde *et al.*, 1996). This may be a result of the negative effect of raised prolactin levels on libido. Physical factors associated with sexual difficulties include discomfort, tiredness, pelvic congestion and increased candida infections. Women undergoing the menopause may complain of inadequate arousal and dyspareunia due to reduced vaginal lubrication and genital atrophy, reduced sexual desire and a reduced ability to attain orgasm. The last problem can be a result of clitoral hyposensitivity or hypersensitivity (Riley, 1991). Physiologically these symptoms are related to oestrogen deficiency. Many drugs can interfere with sexual function in women (see Table 16.4).

Psychological factors

The psychogenic factors causing sexual problems include intrapersonal issues and interpersonal issues. The *intrapersonal issues* can range from poor sex

Table 16.4 Drugs that affect sexual function

	Desire	Arousal	Orgasm
Psychotropic			
Antidepressants			+
Antipsychotics	+		+
Benzodiazepines	+		+
Lithium	+		
Antihypertensive			
Thiazide diuretics		+	
Labetolol		+	+
Spironolactone		+	
Clonidine			+
Methyldopa	+		+
Others			
Anticonvulsants	+		
Opiates	+		+
Alcohol – high dose	+		+

Note: + indicates a negative effect.

education and a restrictive family upbringing to poor self-esteem and a high level of anxiety. A vicious cycle can be set up between sexual failure and fear of sexual failure (Stanley, 1981). The more a woman fears being unable to feel sexual or be aroused, the more likely she will tense up and the problem be perpetuated.

In any sexual problem there are often psychological sequelae for the partner, who can feel angry and rejected. Over time unexpressed feelings turn to resentment, physical contact may be avoided in case it leads on to sex and the sexual problem becomes the focus of the couples' ills. These current *interpersonal issues* are helped with sex therapy. Similarly past relationships may be relevant to the presentation of single women.

Social/cultural factors

Social factors include current vogues for what is acceptable or expected sexual behaviour. An example is the expectation for post-1960s women to be homemakers, mothers, lovers and workers as well as to experience multiple orgasms. These pressures can cause anxiety and a sense of failure when expectations are not reached. Religious factors might cause unconscious conflicts about pre-marital sex such that the woman presents with a sexual problem such as vaginismus which effectively stops her having pre-marital sex. In many non-western cultures female sexual pleasure is secondary to procreation and duty. A woman may present only in crisis when pain or lack of interest in sex is preventing this. An example is where unexpressed anger at the pressure to procreate presents as a lack of sexual interest.

Psychosexual assessment

Problems can be subdivided as to when they started and in what situation they occur. A dysfunction can be *lifelong* or *acquired* over time after apparent normal sexual functioning. The dysfunction can also occur in all situations and be *total*, or occur only at certain times, in certain places or with certain partners and therefore be *situational* in nature. These further descriptions are useful in establishing the likely aetiology of the problem. An example is acquired total anorgasmia which is more likely to have a physical cause.

An assessment of the women and her problem involves taking a full sexual, relationship, medical, psychological, social and family history. A formulation of the problem can then be made with the client (Hawton, 1985:122). The formulation is made up of predisposing, precipitating and perpetuating factors which contribute to and maintain the sexual problem (Box 16.2).

Identifying all the possible factors helps the therapist and client in their understanding of the problem and its management.

Box 16.2 Examples of factors causing sexual dysfunction

Predisposing factors	poor sexual knowledge
	distressing childhood sexual experiences
	restrictive religious beliefs
	poor self-esteem
Precipitating factors	physical illness/aging
	childbirth/termination of pregnancy
	genital infection
	loss of employment
Perpetuating factors	relationship difficulties
	partners sexual problem
	fear of infection, pain or letting go
	stress and anxiety
	confused sexual identity

SPECIFIC MANAGEMENT

Desire disorders

Hypoactive sexual desire disorder

Low desire or hypoactive sexual desire is defined as the persistent or recurrent deficiency or absence of sexual fantasies/thoughts, and/or desire for or receptivity to sexual activity which causes personal distress (Basson 2000).

It is the commonest presentation in sex therapy, often the most difficult to treat and has the poorest outcome. This may well be due to the complexities of a women's sexual response which has yet to be fully understood. The typical sexual response cycle (Figure 17.1) begins with 'spontaneous' desire or interest. Ongoing research into other models of the female sexual response (Basson 2003) suggests that women especially in longer term relationships often do not 'spontaneously' have sexual desire. Motivation to be intimate combined with an ability to be aroused both physically and emotionally may however lead to a 'responsive' desire if approached by a partner. Normalisation of this 'responsive' desire as well as 'spontaneous' desire is important and assessment of motivation for sexual contact and the ability to be aroused need to be made. Low desire may therefore only be present when both spontaneous and responsive desire is absent.

There is a great variability in the sexual desire of women and the problem usually arises when there is a mismatch of desire within a relationship. A typical presentation is a woman who has chronically lost all her sexual interest within a steady relationship following childbirth. Causes are usually psychogenic, with anger at the partner and relationship problems as the commonest factors (Kaplan, 1985:13). Low sexual desire can be due to stress, anxiety and low mood.

The key to management is a detailed assessment. Factors surrounding the onset give clues to feelings that might be building up and inhibiting sexual desire. It is important to involve the partner to focus on the relationship rather than on sex (Box 16.3). Helping the woman explore what motivates or increases her desire can bring up simple solutions such as the need to have time for herself or the need for more non-sexual intimacy with her partner. Fanatasy development can be aided with books such as those by Nancy Friday which detail women's sexual fantasies (Friday, 1991).

Box 16.3 Specific management for low desire

1   Focus on relationship
    *   spend time together
    *   talk about how they feel
    *   be affectionate without being sexual
2   Explore ways of increasing desire as individual
3   Fantasy development

Sexual aversion disorder

Sexual aversion disorder is the persistent or recurrent phobic aversion to and avoidance of sexual contact with a sexual partner which causes personal distress (Basson 2000). Specific phobias can be generalised to any sexual sensations, feelings, thoughts or opportunities or may be limited to a specific aspect of sex such as secretions or kissing. Twenty-five per cent of patients with sexual aversions and phobias have an associated panic disorder for which Kaplan advocates a combination of tricyclic antidepressants and sex therapy (Kaplan, 1987).

Sexual desire, arousal and orgasm can be normal. Management involves systematic exposure to the feared situation.

Hyperactive sexual desire disorder

Hyperactive sexual desire disorder is not a classified sexual dysfunction but is worth mentioning for completeness.

The term nymphomania is still used, usually judgementally, to describe this problem but it is outdated and unhelpful as it does not distinguish between women enjoying and choosing multiple partners, and women who are in an addictive sexual cycle in need of support. In the latter case, women may benefit from specialised therapy dealing with addictive behaviour (Carnes, 1989).

Sexual arousal disorder

Sexual arousal disorder is the persistent or recurrent inability to attain or maintain sufficient sexual excitement, causing personal distress, which may be expressed as a lack of subjective excitement, or genital (lubrication/swelling) or other somatic responses (Basson 2000). Women with sexual arousal problems may present with low desire, orgasmic problems or dyspareunia. It is important to distinguish between subjective arousal and objective genital arousal. They might both be absent or one may be present with out the other such that a women may have proven genital vasocongestion but does not actually feel aroused or vice versa (Lieblum 2003). Organic causes need to be ruled out especially where there is a lack of objective arousal. Common non organic causes are lack of adequate stimulation, relationship tensions, stress and anxiety.

Management involves taking time sexually and learning how to relax.

Self-pleasuring exercises can increase sexual awareness and help focus on sensations rather than on distracting thoughts or anxieties (Box 16.4). Pelvic floor muscle contractions help increase vaginal sensations and in some women aid arousal and orgasm (Heinman and LoPiccolo, 1988). Sildenafil (Viagra) has been shown to increase genital blood flow, but not necessarily subjective arousal and may be useful where objective genital arousal is absent or diminished. It has been shown to counteract the sexual side effects of antidepressants (Nurnberg 1999).

Box 16.4 Specific management for arousal and orgasmic disorders

1   Graduated self-pleasuring exercises
2   Pelvic floor muscle contractions
3   Fantasy and erotica development
4   Self-help books, e.g. Heinman 1988; Friday 1991

Persistent Sexual Arousal Disorder

Recently a syndrome of persistent sexual arousal disorder has been described which comprises intrusive, spontaneous and unwanted genital arousal when sexual desire is absent. The symptoms may persist for days or months and are unrelieved by orgasm (Lieblum 2003). The causes and management are unclear.

Orgasmic disorder

Orgasmic disorder is the persistent or recurrent difficulty, delay or absence of attaining orgasm following sufficient sexual stimulation and arousal, which causes personal distress (Basson 2000). Women require variable psychological and physical stimuli for orgasm, but with the required positive inputs most women are capable of physiologically responding. Some 10 per cent of women have never experienced orgasms in any situation whereas 14 per cent are multiorgasmic (Kinsey *et al.*, 1953). Only 30 per cent of women are able to experience orgasm through penetration alone (Hite, 1976). These figures illustrate the many 'norms' within female sexual function. Orgasmic disorders are usually psychogenic in origin especially if lifelong and situational. Drug-induced anorgasmia is a common cause of acquired orgasmic problems. Psychogenic causes include excessive spectatoring or self-observation, fear of letting go or losing control and inappropriate or inadequate physical stimulation. Women describe being stuck on the plateau phase of the sexual response cycle (See Figure 16.1).

The goal of treatment for a woman who has never had an orgasm is attaining the first orgasm (usually through masturbation). If a woman can attain orgasm with masturbation but not with intercourse, the aim of treatment is to heighten sexual arousal so that the woman is close to orgasm before penetration. Similar management can be used as for arousal disorders aiming to increase arousal over the threshold required for orgasm (Box 16.4).

Sexual pain disorders

Dyspareunia

Dyspareunia is recurrent or persistent genital pain with sexual intercourse which can be described as being superficial or deep in nature. Superficial dyspareunia is felt near the introitus or vaginal barrel and deep dyspareunia is felt near the cervix or lower abdominal area. There are many possible causes of dyspareunia which need to be ruled out by a gynaecological examination and sexual infection screen (Table 16.3).

An important cause of psychogenic dyspareunia is inadequate sexual arousal. Superficial pain is caused by lack of vaginal lubrication and deep pain from the incomplete ballooning of the upper two-thirds of the vagina which should move the cervix and uterus away from the penetrating object and prevent coital buffeting (Figure 16.3). Once pain is experienced a vicious cycle can be set up whereby the fear of pain leads to further anxiety and inhibition of arousal leading to more pain. Management of psychogenic dyspareunia includes an explanation of the physiology of arousal and a bimanual and digital examination to pinpoint the pain. The vicious cycle can be broken by stopping the painful stimulus and the woman can try gentle self exploration with a focus on arousal (Box 16.5).

Vaginismus

Vaginismus is the recurrent or persistent involuntary spasm of the musculature of the outer one third of the vagina that interferes with vaginal pene-

---

Box 17.5 Specific management of psychogenic dyspareunia

1   Explanation of physiology of arousal
2   Examination to pinpoint the pain
3   Stop the painful stimulus
4   Self-exploration focusing on arousal

---

tration and causes personal distress (Basson 2000). Women with total lifelong vaginismus may present with non-consummation of a relationship.

Vaginismus can be situational and the pain can be localised to one side or site. Vaginismic women usually have normal desire, arousal and orgasmic capacity.

Vaginismus and dyspareunia are closely linked as vaginismus is a cause of superficial dyspareunia and repeated dyspareunia can result in the protective vaginismic reflex. The same organic and non-organic factors that can cause dyspareunia can thus cause vaginismus, although what predisposes the vaginal muscles to develop spasm in some women and not others is unknown (Bancroft, 1994:382). For some women there has been a single physical and psychologically scarring event such as rape, childhood abuse or trauma but for many this is not the case. Often it is the fear of pain rather than actual pain that perpetuates the vicious cycle.

An explanation of the problem and reassurance of physical normality at the woman's request are important. Digital pressure on the pelvic floor

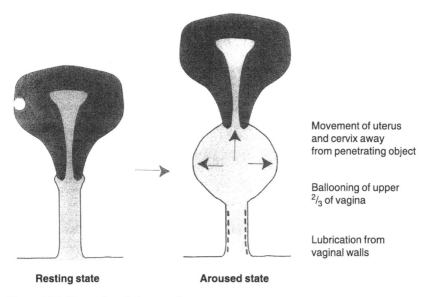

Resting state   **Aroused state**

Movement of uterus
and cervix away
from penetrating object

Ballooning of upper
$2/3$ of vagina

Lubrication from
vaginal walls

Figure 16.3 Normal genital arousal
Source (Adapted from Masters 1966:76)

muscles around the introitus imitates the pain and confirms the diagnosis. However, enforced examinations and speculum insertions can perpetuate if not exacerbate the problem, and are best avoided until the woman has embarked on sex therapy. There are three key pieces of advice which help break the vicious cycle and desensitise the spasm (Box 16.6). Pelvic floor contractions help take control of the spasm in that active contraction is followed by relaxation.

Box 16.6 Three key management points for vaginismus

1   Stop painful penetration to break vicious cycle
2   Non-painful self-exploration to desensitise the spasm
3   Pelvic floor muscle contractions to control the spasm

Referral to a psychosexual service

Referral to a psychosexual therapist has just as much to do with the availability of an appropriate service as it has to do with when a woman might benefit (Box 16.7). NHS service provision is sporadic and underfunded and is provided in psychiatry, psychology, gynaecology, family planning or sexual health departments. Professionals providing this service within the NHS or privately are ideally members of the British Association of Sexual and Relationship Therapists (BASRT), the Institute of Psychosexual Medicine, Relate or the Tavistock Centre for Couple Relationships. Advice about training and referrals can be obtained from these organisations.

Box 16.7 Indications for referral to psychosexual therapy

1   The problem is causing marked distress
2   Self-help measures are not helping
3   There are complex underlying issues
3   There are significant relationship problems
4   The women is requesting expert help
5   The referrer does not feel confident helping

Psychosexual therapy

Present-day psychosexual therapy incorporates a number of treatment strategies, which are adapted for the presenting client. Therapy can be for the couple or the individual and involve regular weekly or fortnightly sessions. Education and allaying anxieties may be all that is required and sometimes there is so much associated distress that initial counselling is crucial.

The components of psychosexual therapy

Education
Counselling/listening
Behavioural therapy
Cognitive therapy
Relationship therapy
Psychodynamic input
Stress management

The core of the work is often behavioural. Sensate focus exercises based on Masters and Johnson's work comprise a series of graded exercises for the individual or couple in conjunction with a ban on intercourse (Masters and Johnson, 1970). These homework exercises start with mutual non-genital touching, moving in stages to whole body touching including sexual arousal. They open up issues of intimacy and help separate sensual awareness from sex. The exercises can be adapted for particular sexual complaints to include systematic desensitisation for vaginismus and sexual aversion, and activity scheduling for impaired desire.

Cognitive work helps in understanding how assumptions and beliefs can cause and maintain the problem. Interventions confront the negative assumptions such as those minimising the good aspects of the sexual experience or those personalising the failures, such that one partner assumes full responsibility for sexual enjoyment of the other. Psychodynamic input looks at the underlying conflicts and family background, referring on to psychotherapy when appropriate.

Couple therapy using a behavioural systems approach is of key importance for many sexual problems (Crowe and Ridley, 1990). Sessions help the couple with communication, problem-solving and scheduling of time together.

Communication skills are useful for dealing with underlying resentments and unexpressed emotions. It is surprising how difficult couples find exercises such as one partner listening to the other one talk about how they feel for 10–15 minutes without the listener saying anything.

The therapist has to take account of the cultural and religious background of the client. Sex therapy is based on western values where a key principle is that one's sexuality is the responsibility of oneself. Therapy aims to enhance choice and responsiveness within oneself. Self-stimulation, masturbation, women taking the initiative or the female superior position can be a problem for women whose culture disapproves of such behaviour (da Silva 1999).

Outcome of psychosexual therapy

Moderate or better outcome is achieved in two-thirds of sex therapy requiring an average of nine sessions for female presenters (Warner *et al.*, 1987). Vaginismus has the best outcome with over 85 per cent achieving and maintaining resolution. Impaired sexual desire has the poorest outcome with a 69 per cent post-treatment resolution but only 34 per cent long-term resolution (Hawton *et al.*, 1986). High success rates are implied by failure rates of less than 20 per cent in orgasmic disorders (Masters and Johnson, 1970). There is little substantive outcome data for arousal disorders and dyspareunia.

Conclusions

Sexual problems are common. Few women seek help and when they do there is a paucity of secondary referral sources. However, at primary care level physical reassurance, listening and practical advice can be a starting point before secondary referral is made. The key to managing sexual problems is being aware of the heterogeneous nature of women's sexuality, the multifactorial origins and the close interrelationship of the various problems.

References

Bancroft, J. (1994) *Human Sexuality and its Problems*. Edinburgh: Churchill Livingstone.

Barnes, T.R.E. and Harvey, C.A. (1993) Psychiatric drugs and sexuality, in A.J. Riley, M.Peet and C. Wilson (eds.), *Sexual Pharmacology*. Oxford: Clarendon.

Basson, R., Berman, J., Burnett, A., et al (2000) Report of the International Consensus Development Conference on Female Sexual Dysfunction: Definition and Classifications. *Journal of Urology* 163, 3: 888–893

Basson, R. (2003) Biophysical model's of women's sexual response: application to management of 'desire disorders'. *Sexual and Relationship Therapy* 18,1: 107–115

Burnap, D.W. and Golden, J.S. (1967) Sexual problems in medical practice. *Journal of Medical Education* 42: 673–80.

Carnes, P. (1989) *Contrary to Love: Helping the Sexual Addict*. Minneapolis: CompCare.

Crowe, M. and Ridley, J. (1990) *Therapy with Couples: A Behavioural Systems Approach to Marital and Sexual Problems*. Oxford: Blackwell.

Da Silva, P. (1999) Culture and sex therapy. *Sexual and Marital Therapy* 14, 2:105–7.

Friday, N. (1991) *Women on Top*. London: Arrow.

Halvorsen, J.G. and Metz, M.E. (1992) Sexual dysfunction, Part II: Diagnosis, management and prognosis. *Journal of the American Board of Family Practice* 52: 177–92.

Hawton, K. (1985) *Sex Therapy: A Practical Guide*. New York: Oxford University Press.

Hawton, K., Catalan, J., Martin, P. and Fagg, J. (1986) Long term outcome of sex therapy. *Behaviour Research and Therapy* 24(6): 665–75.

Heinman, J.R., LoPiccdo, L. and LoPiccolo, J. (1988) *Becoming Orgasmic*. London: Piatkus.

Hite, S. (1976) *The Hite Report*. London: Pandora.

Hyde, J.S., DeLamater, J.D., Ashby Plant, E. and Byrd, J.M. (1996) Sexuality during pregnancy and the year postpartum. *The Journal of Sex Research* 33(2): 143–51.

Kaplan, H.S. (1985) *Comprehensive Evaluation of Disorders of Sexual Desire*. Washington: American Psychiatric Press.

Kaplan, H.S. (1987) *Sexual Aversion, Sexual Phobias, and Panic Disorder*. New York: Brunner/Mazel.

Kinsey, A.C., Pomeroy, W.B., Martin, C.E. and Gebhard, P.H. (1953) *Sexual Behaviour in the Human Female*. Philadelphia: Saunders.

Kockott, G. and Pfeiffer, W. (1996) Sexual disorders in nonacute psychiatric out-patients. *Comprehensive Psychiatry* 37(1): 55–61.

Leiblum, S.R. (2003) Arousal disorders in women:complaints and complexities. *The Medical Journal of Australia* 178,12: 638–640

Levine, S.B. (1995) What is clinical sexuality? *The Psychiatric Clinics of North America* 18(1): 1–6.

Masters, W.H. and Johnson, V.E. (1966) *Human Sexual Response*. Boston: Little, Brown.

Masters, W.H. and Johnson, V.E. (1970) *Human Sexual Inadequacy*. London: Churchill.

Mercer, C.H., Fenton, K.A., Johnson, A.M., Wellings, K., Macdowall, W., McManus, S., Nanchalal, K. and Errens, B. (2003) Sexual function problems and help seeking behaviour in Britain: national probability sample survey. *British Medical Journal* 327: 426–427.

Nazareth, I., Boynton, P., and King, M. (2003) Problems with sexual function in people attending London general practitioners: cross sectional study. *British Medical Journal* 327: 423–426.

Nurnberg, H.G., Laruiello, J., Henlsey, P., Parker, L., and Keith, R.S. (1999) Sildenafil for Sexual Dysfunction taking Antidepressants. *American Journal of Psychiatry* 156(10): 1664

Riley, A.J. (1991) Sexuality and the menopause. *Sexual and Marital Therapy* 6(2): 135–46.

Smith, S., O'Keane, V., and Murray, R. (2002) Sexual dysfunction in patients taking conventional antipsychotic medication. *The British Journal of Psychiatry* 181(1): 49–55.

Stanley, S. (1981) Non-organic causes of sexual problems. *British Medical Journal* 282: 1042–4.

Warner, P., Bancroft, J. and Members of the Edinburgh Human Sexuality Group (1987) A regional clinical service for sexual problems: a three-year survey. *Sexual and Marital Therapy* 2(2): 115–26.

Useful addresses

The British Association of Sexual and Relationship Therapy (BASRT)

Website: www.basrt.org.uk Telephone 020 8543 2707.

Institute of Psychosexual Medicine

Website: www.ipm.org.uk Telephone 020 7580 0631

Relate

Website: www.relate.org.uk Telephone 01788 573241
The Tavistock Centre for Couple Relationships
Website: www.tccr.org.uk Telephone 020 7435 7111

.

Part V

Managing the sequelae of trauma

17 The management of borderline personality disorder, a possible sequelae of childhood trauma

Catherine Smith

Introduction

The term 'childhood trauma' encompasses a vast array of different experiences ranging from single traumatic events to systematic long-term abuse. What is traumatic for one individual isn't necessarily so for another. Individual characteristics, the nature of the trauma and the surrounding environment all influence the eventual outcome. Not surprisingly the range of outcomes following on from the original trauma are extremely varied. I am going to concentrate on the management of borderline personality disorder (BPD), one possible outcome following childhood trauma especially pertinent to women, as most individuals who meet the criteria for BPD are female. There is strong, accumulating evidence showing that childhood abuse and neglect plays an important role in the onset of personality disorders (Johnson *et al.*, 1999). The risk for sexual abuse is two to three times greater for females than for males (Finkelhor, 1979) and the prevalence of sexual abuse in the childhood histories of women with BPD is such that it cannot be ignored as an important possible aetiological factor. Not all women with BPD experienced childhood trauma and not all childhood trauma results in BPD in adult life, but the association between the two is undeniable. The reason for concentrating on this group of women is two-fold. Firstly, they present with severe problems that are difficult to manage successfully. Secondly, they represent a sizeable proportion of individuals involved with mental health services and tend to utilise a large amount of time and resources. Eleven per cent of all psychiatric outpatients and 19 per cent of psychiatric inpatients are estimated to qualify for a diagnosis of BPD (Wideger and Frances, 1989).

WHAT IS BPD?

The idea of personality disorders does not fit easily into the medical model. Everyone has a personality and defining precisely where in the continuum abnormality begins is arbitrary. The dividing line is usually taken as being when the personality disturbance results in impaired relationships and disturbed social or occupational functioning. Personality tends to be stable over time; disorders are usually recognisable in adolescence or early adult life and persist until middle age when they seem to become less prominent. Personality disorders defy exact definition; however the World Health Organisation (1992) gives a comprehensive overview, which states: 'These types of condition comprise of deeply ingrained and enduring behaviour patterns manifesting themselves as inflexible responses to a broad range of personal and social situations. They represent extreme deviations from the way that the average individual in a given culture perceives, thinks, feels and particularly relates to others. Such behaviour patterns tend to be stable and become multiple domains of behaviour and social functioning. They are frequently, but not always, associated with various degrees of subjective distress and problems in social functioning and performance'.

Borderline personality disorder is one specific type of personality disorder (PD), the essential features of which are (according to DSM IV), a pervasive pattern of instability of interpersonal relationships, self-image and affects, coupled with marked impulsivity, present in a variety of contexts (American Psychiatric Association, 1994).

Understanding BPD

BPD characteristics can lead to significant distress for the sufferer and management problems for mental health workers, who often perceive borderline patients as being 'manipulative' and 'attention seeking'. It is essential that the difficult behaviour of these patients be understood to try to avoid management becoming reactive and punitive.

Several theories of BPD development and behaviours have been postulated. It is not possible in this short text to go into any detail; however, the reader will find more detailed texts referenced below.

Generally, over the last twenty years or so BPD is increasingly being seen as a disorder of psychological development. Many of the characteristics of BPD can be understood in terms of damage to the attachment system (De Zulueta, 1999). Healthy interactions between infant and primary caregiver lead to the development of a secure attachment. This promotes a sense of self as separate from the 'other' (a significant attachment figure), an ability to think coherently about one's own thoughts and feelings as well as those of others and to the development of internal psychic representations which allow one to keep the 'other' in mind during separations. Disruption to this developmental process in childhood trauma can lead to insecure attachments.

Separation becomes devastating and every effort will be made to avoid abandonment. The early attachment pattern tends to be replayed throughout an individual's subsequent relationships, and an associated lack of reflective capacity impairs relationships between the individual and the world. BPD has been linked with PTSD (Herman, 1992). Patients with BPD often have a history of severe early trauma and present with many symptoms of PTSD, including dissociative symptoms and pervading feelings of terror. It is believed that PTSD results from a violent disruption to attachments (De Zulueta, 1993) and that BPD represents a complex form of PTSD, with the attachment system being disturbed at a very early stage.

The biosocial model of BPD is based on the premise that BPD is primarily a dysfunction of the emotion regulation system and borderline characteristics are sequelae of this dysregulation. Invalidating environments fail to teach the child how to label and regulate arousal, how to tolerate emotional distress, and when to trust her own emotional responses as reflections of validm interpretations of events (Linehan, 1993).

In traditional psychoanalytic thinking, the borderline condition is a result of poor personality integration, excess hostile affect and ego weakness (Kernberg, 1975). The lack of a coherent sense of self is linked to the mental process of splitting, where the internal and external world is split into good and bad, and ambivalent feelings towards themselves or others are vigorously avoided. If good and bad are allowed to co-exist, the fear is that the bad will destroy anything good and any sense of 'loving' will be annihilated. 'Splitting', traditionally considered a primitive defence mechanism, is an understandable response to abuse by a figure that is also a caregiver, an initially adaptive mechanism for dealing with a traumatic experience which allows the abusive caregiver to be preserved as separate to the abuse in the mind of the child, thereby maintaining some sense of a good figure for the child to rely on (Calverley *et al.*, 1994).

Projective mechanisms also powerfully colour the borderline world, i.e. personal thoughts and feelings get attributed to external sources and feelings are conveyed not by words or symbols but by direct transfer into the 'other's' world: the 'other' is made to feel the emotions of the borderline patient. The despair often felt when working with these patients can be a direct reflection of the despair these patients feel themselves.

SELF-HARM AND SUICIDE

These women have around a 9 per cent mortality rate from suicide (Stone, 1989), and between 70 per cent and 75 per cent have a history of at least one self-injurious act (Cowdry *et al.*, 1985). Self-harming behaviour is difficult to manage safely and staff can feel 'manipulated' by patients when it is threatened. Patients themselves, however, report that their self-harming is often in response to very difficult feelings, intense suicidal ideation and ambivalence regarding living. A 'manipulative' interpretation may well be a fundamental invalidation of their feelings.

Self-harm is not always in response to actual suicidal ideation, but sometimes an attempt to lessen psychological pain. These patients have poor internal resources to modulate distressing feelings and therefore attempt to create a visible wounding to deflect from the more unmanageable psychological wounding and / or to 'self-medicate' by causing a release of 'soothing' endogenous opiates through re-traumatisation, cutting themselves, binge eating or resorting to abuse of alcohol and drugs.

MANAGEMENT

Engagement

The first clinical task in management is to engage the patient successfully, enabling sufficient information to be gathered to make a reliable diagnosis, and to allow the development of a therapeutic alliance.

When considering a diagnosis, one needs to consider all aspects of personal functioning and to utilise as many sources of information as possible. Many patients often have characteristics of more than one personality disorder subtype and there is often co-existence of a major psychiatric disorder complicating management. Successful engagement should result in a productive relationship between patient and professional, within which relatively clear and relevant goals concerning diagnosis and treatment are set. It is vital not to take for granted the ability of these women to play the role of 'patient' successfully. They often lack the capacity to present a complaint or symptom directly and do not expect to receive appropriate professional help.

Difficulties in engagement and treatment

Engaging these patients is fraught with difficulties. Some have unrealistic expectations of professionals (too high, too low) and will make inappropriate demands. It is crucial to educate them about what is realistically available and not try to be 'all providing'. Many have insecure attachments and thus expect professionals to fail them (as did their parents) whilst secretly hoping that someone will come along and provide 'perfect care'. Any help that is provided, however, is often perceived as insufficient, falling short of 'perfect care', causing disappointment. Professionals can feel in a no win situation. Consequently, patients' unfamiliarity with secure attachments and their ambivalence towards treatment need to be assumed and directly addressed as part of ongoing engagement (Norton, 1996).

Professionals can find themselves in conflict with each other when managing patients with borderline personality disorder, either due to differing patient behaviour towards different staff members, or unresolved staff disagreements about the best treatment strategies. This can echo the patient's ambivalence about receiving care and/or the use of unconscious mechanisms including splitting. A subsequent lack of communication between those involved in the patient's care can lead to damaging inconsistencies in treatment. Good communication between staff and involved agencies is vital for a coordinated treatment delivery.

Patients need to experience something other than the control and neglect that historically shaped their personalities in order for them to start questioning their habitual maladaptive attitudes, behaviours, cognitions and accompanying emotions (Norton and Dolan, 1995). They need to question their basic mistrust and try working together with staff to allow for a novel experience. This in turn necessitates staff trying to understand difficult behaviours, not just condemn or condone. Hopefully this leads to a more flexible approach, whereby staff can condemn certain behaviours whilst at the same time understanding their origin, validating the associated feelings and facilitating the consideration of more adaptive alternatives. Patients are helped to feel that they are more than just their behaviour and that condemnation of certain behaviours is not a personal attack. The aim is to help the patient to be able to think and feel rather than just act.

Support for staff is vital. Difficult, often dangerous, behaviours can cause significant anxieties. The countertransferance can be challenging and therapists must be wary of being drawn into acting out 'patterns of old' within the therapy. A staff forum is needed which offers supervision and containment.

SPECIFIC TREATMENT STRATEGIES

Treatment contracts

Negotiating and implementing treatment contracts with borderline patients can be helpful, as clinical interactions tend not to be straightforward. They are essentially a formalised agreement between patient and professional which states clearly the boundaries and specific achievable goals of therapy.

They should be mutually agreed by all parties and make clear the specific responsibilities, including what can be reasonably expected from the therapist and what patient behaviours will not be tolerated. If established early, they can help to anchor the treatment goals, minimise interference from insecure attachment patterns and help foster a therapeutic alliance (Norton, 1996).

Unrealistic fears about treatment can be addressed and difficult behaviours hopefully contained. Alternative strategies for managing intolerable feelings must be provided if behaviours previously used by the patient to cope with psychological distress are no longer 'allowed'. It may be useful to involve people from the woman's wider social network, especially if they are likely to be directly affected by the implementation of the contract.

In practice, contracts are not always easy to negotiate and implement. It involves time and tact, exploring the woman's mistrust, her ambivalence regarding treatment and her destructive impulses. Commonly, treatment contracts fail if they are unduly restrictive, become a substitute for therapy or are used as a means of defence or punishment (Miller, 1989).

PHARMACOTHERAPY

Psychological approaches represent the mainstay of treatment for women with borderline personality disorder. Medication is generally of limited benefit; however, it is useful in some instances. Particular major psychiatric diagnoses (including affective and anxiety disorders) often co-exist in patients with borderline personality disorder and may require medication in their own right.

Prescribing

There is no general consensus as to the most effective medication regime for these women. It is essential when prescribing to bear in mind the high risk of overdose and the tendency to become dependent on medication both physically and psychologically. Medication should therefore be dispensed in small quantities. The patient should be engaged as an ally in studying medication effects, to try and diminish both unrealistic expectations and conflict around prescribing. As it is impossible to predict which drug regime will be individually beneficial, it is advisable to adopt a pragmatic, symptomatic approach. Targeting medication at particular symptoms will enable the medication to be tailored to the individual's needs. An additional systematicm approach, offering drugs in succession (not together), so that the most suitable one can be selected, is also helpful. Drug 'cocktails' should be avoided and doses carefully titrated against benefit and side-effects.

Medication can be used inappropriately to alleviate staff anxieties or as an indirect expression of anger. It can also contradict the therapeutic goal of teaching patients to manage feelings with words, or be seen by patients as a signal that staff's own interpersonal resources are used up. These factors need to be kept in mind when prescribing.

Specific medications

For overviews of pharmacotherapy in BPD see Markovitz (2004) and Raj (2004).

Neuroleptic medication

Low-dose neuroleptic medication may benefit several of the symptoms of BPD. It can help with brief paranoid states, ideas of reference, depersonalisation, derealisation, anxiety, hostility, anger and importantly can also reduce impulsivity and associated acts of self-harm. The depression associated with BPD also responds to neuroleptic medication in some instances.

Patients with BPD tend to benefit from low doses of neuroleptic medication as they are generally less tolerant of side-effects and dose titration is essential.

The atypical antipsychotics may be more beneficial in this population as they tend to be better tolerated.

Antidepressants

Depression in BPD responds poorly to tricyclic antidepressants. This coupled with their toxicity in overdose makes their usefulness limited. Some patients respond well to the monoamine oxidase inhibitor (MAOI) group of anti-depressants. They are however dangerous in overdose and the newer reversible MAOIs, that are less likely to trigger hypertensive crises, may be preferable.

Studies looking at the serotonin uptake inhibitors suggest that some are effective in reducing impulsivity/aggression, depression and affective instability. Their additional, relative safety in overdose makes them an attractive treatment option.

Mood stabilisers

Lithium helps some women with affective instability and both lithium and carbamazepine may help with impulsive-aggressive behaviour. It may be worth a few months' trial treatment to investigate individual response.

Benzodiazepines

These drugs are generally unhelpful due to their addictive potential and their disinhibiting effects, which can lead to serious episodes of dyscontrol. If used, it should be for short periods of time, where the use of alternative medication is not permissible.

Electroconvulsive Therapy (ECT)

Patients who have comorbid depression and BPD often show a good initial response to ECT, but there is often an early relapse. Using ECT in this population is complicated, the presentation of depressive symptoms is not typical and underlying depression is often missed, especially if sedative doses of neuroleptics are used. Patients may be unable to comply with anti-depressant medication and ECT may be the only antidepressant remedy they can utilise. See Part VI, Chapter 20.

Fatty acids

Recently omega-3 fatty acids have been found to be safe and useful in the treatment of women with moderately severe borderline personality disorder (Zanarini, 2003).

PSYCHOLOGICAL TREATMENTS

Psychotherapy often presents the only hope of improvement for patients with borderline personality disorder. Maladaptive traits are deeply ingrained and are difficult to change; thus therapy has typically been of long duration, with small, slow improvements (Waldinger and Gunderson, 1984).

Most women suffering with borderline personality disorder, if receiving psychiatric help, will be receiving 'non-specific, supportive psychotherapy'; however, specialised psychotherapeutic techniques are usually needed to produce beneficial change.

Most therapies applied to BPD emphasise the 'here and now' rather than the 'distant past', as the aim is to change current behaviour patterns and ways of relating.

Treatment goals should be realistic, a total change of character is very unlikely yet a change to more adaptive coping strategies, with a reduction in distress, may be possible.

No specific psychotherapeutic technique has currently been shown to be superior and therefore the technique utilised will depend on patient and clinician preference together with local availability and resources.

Outpatient Treatment: individual therapies

Psychoanalytical psychotherapy

Psychoanalytical therapy has long been used in the treatment of BPD. The limited data on its effectiveness suggests that only a minority of BPD patients benefit from it in its traditional form (Waldinger and Gunderson, 1984). A modified approach that concentrates on the present, with the therapist taking a more active role, is usually more suitable. The aim is to facilitate integration of the immature personality via resolution of intrapsychic conflicts. This is hopefully achieved through the development of a transference–countertransference relationship and the use of modified interpretations with the patient being seen one or more times a week. A modified form of brief analytical psychotherapy, designed for use with patients with BPD has been described (Stevenson and Meares, 1992). Patients were seen twice weekly for a year and therapy could be delivered by trainee therapists using a treatment manual. The results reported that 30 per cent of patients at the end of treatment no longer met DSM III-R criteria for BPD.

Clarkin et al (2001) have developed a transference focused psychodynamic treatment for patients with BPD, which has shown promising results. They have described an ongoing randomized controlled trial of their transference based psychotherapy compared to DBT and a more supportive psychotherapy; the outcome of this study is awaited Clarkin *et al.* (2004).

Interpersonal therapies

These approaches aim to modify dysfunctional interpersonal behaviour. Benjamin (1996) has developed a technique for analysing patterns and ways of modification of interpersonal behaviour , which utilise a range of techniques including: role play, free association, dream interpretations and educational tasks. Brief interpersonal therapy (IPT) (Klerman *et al.*, 1984), originally designed for the treatment of depression, has now been adapted for the treatment of BPD. IPT is a time-limited, structured therapy that focuses on the relationship between symptoms and interpersonal difficulties. These approaches have yet to be evaluated fully in BPD.

Cognitive psychotherapy

Cognitive psychotherapy focuses on a patient's underlying cognitive distortions and schemas. Schemas are: 'broad pervasive themes regarding oneself and one's relationship with others, developed during childhood and elaborated throughout one's lifetime and dysfunctional to a significant degree'. Cognitive therapy looks at the effect these have on the individual's life and how these distortions are maintained. Investigation and reality testing of these maladaptive processes is aimed at replacing them with more self-affirming, adaptive measures.

Schema-focused cognitive therapy, aimed at BPD is now in use (Young, 1994). Core schemas are identified and activated; they are then modified using cognitive reconstruction, behavioural and experiential techniques.

Cognitive-analytical therapy (CAT)

Developed by Ryle *et al.* (1997), CAT is a time-limited, integrated therapy using both psychoanalytic and cognitive principles. When applied to BPD, CAT therapy focuses on identifying different self-states, which resist integration into a whole. Rapid shifts between these self-states and their accompanying interpersonal styles are thought to cause the instability that borderline patients display. In therapy the patient is helped to identify different self-states, their accompanying cognitions and maladaptive behaviours, and to link these with their early experiences. The collaborative nature of the therapeutic relationship also gives the patient an experience of a more healthy way of relating. A recent update of the contribution of CAT to the treatment of borderline personality disorder can be found in Ryle (2004).

Dialectical behaviour therapy (DBT)

DBT (Linehan, 1993) is based on the biosocial model of BPD which emphasises dysfunctional emotional regulation and interpersonal skills. Emotional regulation and interpersonal skills are taught in both weekly group and individual sessions. Patients have a high level of support, their feelings are validated but their destructive or maladaptive behaviours are challenged and alternative, more adaptive behaviour encouraged. Under ordinary circumstances, the patient and therapist make a one-year agreement, renewable annually.

DBT has shown mixed results in follow-up studies that have had methodological difficulties (Linehan *et al.*, 1993; 1994).

Non-individual therapies

Family therapy

Family therapy tends to be under-utilised as a treatment in personality disorders. This may reflect the common absence of an intact family or ambivalent relationships with family members. In families that have seperation or enmeshment difficulties, family therapy may well be beneficial if family members and treatment resources permit (Norton, 1996). It is seldom sufficient on its own and the aim should be to combine it with individual treatment.

Group therapy

For patients with BPD who can tolerate group therapy, the peer group can give useful insights into their maladaptive traits. This can be highly effective and conveyed by group members in language that couldn't be used by individual therapists. The peer group can also provide a field of study of others' maladaptive and adaptive coping strategies, together with providing support for new relationships in and out of the group. Provided there is some degree of cohesiveness, groups appear to have a containing role for the patient with a borderline personality disorder without resulting in damage to other members. There is controversy over whether to have more than one personality-disordered patient per out-patient group.

Groups that specialise in treating patients with histories of childhood sexual abuse can be successful, as they help to decrease the feelings of isolation and shame (Hall, 1992).

It has been recommended that group therapy can be a useful addition to individual therapy, but in order to avoid splitting, it is better for the same therapist to be involved in both therapies (Higgit and Fonagy, 1992).

Inpatient treatment

General setting

Admission to a general inpatient setting should ideally be planned and have clear aims which are agreed by the patient and their team. Admission, however, is often unplanned during a crisis. In this situation it is important to establish therapeutic goals early to give the best chance of a helpful admission. There is no overall consensus on indications for hospitalization, however, several scenarios can warrant short-term hospitalisation in a general psychiatric setting: facilitation of diagnosis and treatment planning; crises with potentially dangerous consequences; stabilisation and re-establishment of a therapeutic alliance; and psychotic episodes that cannot be resolved in an outpatient setting. The risks of admission to both patient and hospital setting must be considered in the decision to admit either to a general or specialist setting. Patients risk hospital-induced regression with loss of their already reduced coping mechanisms, as well as a potential anti-therapeutic experience with 'sicker' patients. There is also the possible interruption of outpatient psychotherapy and disruption to social and occupational roles.

There is a staff risk of becoming drawn into acting out the patient's internal dramas which can lead to feelings of anxiety, anger, helplessness and exhaustion. Also the treatment milieu as a whole can suffer as containment becomes the pervasive treatment modality, or as staff time is usurped so that patients must compete for staff attention. There is still no general consensus regarding the most appropriate theoretical basis for inpatient management of BPD. There is thus the potential for conflict between staff ambitions, with some wanting structural change via interpretive psychotherapy and others wanting to avoid intensive therapy and merely provide support. These types of clashes are more likely with treatment in a non-specialist setting.

Specialist inpatient setting

Referral to a specialist inpatient unit may be appropriate following failure of outpatient and general psychiatric inpatient treatment or in response to an escalation in hopelessness and destructiveness. Referral needs discussion with the patient to try and avoid it being seen as rejection or confirmation of their badness.

Basic educational achievement, a period of stable employment, maintenance of interpersonal stability in an intimate relationship for longer than six months and a recall of a positive enduring relationship during childhood may be positive prognostic factors for specialist inpatient treatment (Healey and Kennedy, 1993).

One of the advantages of the specialist setting is its ability to select its patients and to deliver a coordinated treatment strategy with expert staff all utilising the same treatment methods. The usual therapy basis is psychodynamic and units vary as to what extent they use the peer group therapeutically. Treatment usually lasts between 6 and 18 months and requires voluntary and motivated participation. There is evidence for the effectiveness of therapeutic communities, both in terms of psychological improvement and cost-offset following treatment (Dolan *et al.*, 1996; 1997).

Other specialist treatments

More recently studies have found that 'hybrid' treatments involving shorter inpatient admissions coupled with outpatient treatments can lead to an encouraging outcome in borderline personality disorder. Chiesa *et al.* (2004)found that a 'step-down' specialist psychosocial programme including a brief residential stay and an outpatient component was more effective than both long-term residential treatment and general psychiatric treatment.

Bateman and Fonagy(1999, 2001) found that partial hospitalisation was superior to standard psychiatric treatment in borderline personality disorder and that these results were sustained at eighteen months follow up. They have also shown that partial hospitalization treatment is no more expensive than treatment as usual and shows considerable cost savings after treatment (2003).

Following specialist treatments many patients will still require aftercare which may need to last for several years. This realistic time frame needs to be conveyed to the patient early on to avoid unrealistic expectations, and sensitively to avoid extinguishing optimism.

Long-term outcome and future developments

Several studies have shown that the long-term outcome in BPD is significantly better than previously thought and a large proportion of patients improve over time. Two large studies of BPD patients confirmed that two-thirds of the patients treated had a good outcome when followed up 10–15 years after the index admission (Stone, 1990), (McGlashan, 1986).

With more treatment options available for BPD, the relative merits of each needs to continue to be assessed. The briefer therapies need long-term follow-up to assess whether their benefits persist or whether they need complementation with longer-term work. As aetiological understanding of BPD increases, the possibility of prevention by early intervention for high-risk groups needs to be considered.

Despite many unanswered questions, the therapeutic potential for this group of women seems more optimistic as we increase our understanding and start to evaluate a growing population of therapies.

References

American Psychiatric Association (1994) *Diagnostic and Statistical Manual of Mental Disorders IV*. Washington: American Psychiatric Association.

Bateman, A. and Fonagy, P. (1999) Effectiveness of partial hospitalization in the treatment of borderline personality disorder: A randomized controlled trial. *American Journal of Psychiatry* 156: 1563–1569.

Bateman, A. and Fonagy, P. (2001) Treatment of borderline personality disorder with psychoanalytically oriented partial hospitalization: an 18-month follow-up. *American Journal of Psychiatry* 158 (1): 365–42.

Bateman, A. and Fonagy, P. (2003) Health service utilization for borderline personality disorder patients treated with psychodynamically oriented partial hospitalization versus general psychiatric care. *American Journal of Psychiatry* 160: 164–171.

Benjamin, L.S. (1996) *Interpersonal Diagnosis and Treatment of Personality Disorders.* New York: Guilford Press.

Calverley, R.M., Fischer, K.W. and Ayoub, C. (1994) Complex splitting of self representations in sexually abused adolescent girls. *Development and Psychopathy* 6: 195–213.

Chiesa, M., Fonagy, P., Holmes, J. and Drahorad, C. (2004) Residential versus community treatment of personality disorders: a comparative study of three treatment programs. *American Journal of Psychiatry* 161(8): 1463–70.

Clarkin, J.F., Foelsch,P.A., Levy, K.N., Hull, J.W., Delaney, J.C., Kernberg,O.F. (2001) The development of a psychodynamic treatment for patients with borderline personality disorder:A preliminary study of behavioural change. *Journal of Personality Disorders* 15(6):487–495.

Clarkin, J.F., Levy, K.N., Lenzenweger, M.F. and Kernberg, O.F. (2004) The Personality Disorders Institute/Borderline Personality Disorder Research Foundation randomized control trial for borderline personality disorder: rationale, methods, and patient characteristics. *Journal of Personality Disorders* 18(1): 52–72.

Cowdry, R.W., Pickar, D. and Davies, R. (1985) Symptoms and EEG findings in the borderline syndrome. *International Journal of Psychiatry in Medicine* 15(3): 201–11.

De Zulueta, F. (1993) *From Pain to Violence: The Traumatic Roots of Destructiveness.* London: Whurr Publishers.

De Zulueta, F. (1999) Borderline personality disorder as seen from an attachment perspective: a review. *Criminal Behaviour and Mental Health* 9: 237–53.

Dolan, B. Warren, F., Menzies, D. *et al.* (1996) Cost-offset following specialist treat-ment of severe personality disorders. *Psychiatric Bulletin* 20: 413–17.

Dolan, B., Warren, F., Menzies, D. *et al.* (1997) Change in borderline symptoms one year after therapeutic community treatment for severe personality disorders. *British Journal of Psychiatry* 171: 274–9.

Finkelhor, D. (1979) *Sexually Victimised Children.* New York. Free Press.

Hall, Z.M. (1992) Group therapy for women survivors of childhood sexual abuse. *Group Analysis* 125: 463–75.

Healey, K. and Kennedy, R. (1993) Which families benefit from in-patient psychotherapeutic work at the Cassel Hospital? *British Journal of Psychotherapy* 9: 394–404.

Herman, J.L. (1992) *Trauma and Recovery: The Aftermath of Violence – from Domestic Abuse to Political Terror.* New York: Basic Books.

Higgit, A. and Fonagy, P. (1992) Psychotherapy in borderline and narcissistic personality disorder. *British Journal of Psychiatry* 161: 23–43.

Johnson, J.G., Cohen, P., Brown, J., Smailes, E.M. and Bernstein, D.P. (1999) Childhood maltreatment increases risk for personality disorders during early adulthood. *Archives of General Psychiatry* 56: 600–6.

Kernberg, O.F. (1975) *Borderline Conditions and Pathological Narcissism.* New York: Aronson.

Klerman, G.L., Weissman M.M., Rounsaville, B.J. *et al.* (1984) *Interpersonal Therapy of Depression.* New York: Basic Books.

Linehan, M.M. (1993) *Cognitive-Behavioural Treatment of Borderline Personality Disorder*. New York: Guilford Press.

Linehan, M.M., Heard, H. and Armstrong, H.E. (1993) Naturalistic followup of a behavioural treatment for chronically parasuicidal borderline patients. *Archives of General Psychiatry* 50: 971–4.

Linehan, M.M., Tutek, D., Heard, H. *et al.* (1994) Interpersonal outcome of cognitive behavioural treatment of chronically suicidal borderline patients. *American Journal of Psychiatry* 151: 1771–6.

McGlashan, T.H. (1986) The Chestnut Lodge follow-up study III: long-term outcome of borderline personalities. *Archives of General Psychiatry* 43: 20–30.

Markovitz, P.J. (2004) Recent trends in the pharmacotherapy of personality disorders. *Journal of Personality Disorder* 18(1): 90–101.

Miller, L.J. (1989). Inpatient management of borderline personality disorder: a review and update. *Journal of Personality Disorders* 3: 122–34.

Norton, K.R.W. (1996) Management of difficult personality disorder patients. *Advances in Psychiatric Treatment* 2: 202–10.

Norton, K.R.W. and Dolan, B. (1995) Acting out and the institutional response. *Journal of Forensic Psychiatry* 6: 317–32.

Raj, Y.P. (2004) Psychopharmacology of borderline personality disorder. *Current Psychiatry Reports* 6(3): 225–31.

Ryle, A., Leighton, T. and Pollock, P. (1997) *Cognitive Analytical Therapy of Borderline Personality Disorder*. Chichester: John Wiley.

Ryle, A. (2004) The contribution of cognitive analytic therapy to the treatment of borderline personality disorder. *Journal of Personality Disorder* 18(1): 3–35.

Stevenson, J. and Meares, R. (1992) An outcome study of psychotherapy for patients with borderline personality disorder. *American Journal of Psychiatry* 149: 358–62.

Stone, M.H. (1990) *The Fate of Borderline Patients*. New York: Guilford Press.

Stone, M.H. (1989) The course of borderline personality disorder. *Review of Psychiatry* 8: 103–22.

Waldinger, R.J. and Gunderson, J.G. (1984) Completed psychotherapies with borderline patients. *American Journal of Psychotherapy* 38: 190–202.

Wideger, T.A. and Frances, A.J. (1989) Epidemiology, diagnosis and co-morbidity of borderline personality disorder. *Review of Psychiatry* 8: 8–24.

World Health Organisation (1992) *The ICD-10 Classification of Mental and Behavioural Disorders*. Geneva: World Health Organisation.

Young, J.E. (1994) *Cognitive Therapy for Personality Disorders: A Schema-Focused Approach*, (2nd edn). Sarasota, FL: Professional Resource Press.

Zanarini, M.C. and Frankenburg, F.R. (2003) Omega-3 fatty acid treatment of women with borderline personality disorder: a double-blind, placebo-controlled pilot study. *American Journal of Psychiatry* 160(1):167–9.

18 Management of deliberate self-harm (DSH) and parasuicide

Ulrike Schmidt, Joanne Godley and Cathy Cox

Introduction

Different forms of deliberate self-harm have been present throughout history and across all cultures, dictated by religion, society or fashion, including such diverse practices as self-flagellation, foot-binding and body piercing (Johnstone, 1995). Self-harm also occurs in the context of almost any psychiatric or brain disorder, for example in psychosis, severe depression, dementia and severe learning disability. The present chapter will not consider the needs of these cases. Instead we will focus on the majority of cases presenting to psychiatric services or to Accident and Emergency Departments, who do not suffer from severe mental illness or mental impairment. In these cases self-injurious behaviour often is an expression of psychological distress at a time of life-crisis in vulnerable individuals.

It has long been accepted that there are important differences, other than outcome, between the majority of self-injuring acts, attempted suicide and suicide (Overstone and Kreitman, 1974). These differences include such dimensions as intent, willingness to die, seriousness of the injury incurred and the methods employed. Clinicians, the general public and people who engage in self-injurious behaviour are usually of the opinion that deliberate self-injury can be clearly distinguished from suicide or attempted suicide on the grounds that, despite some similarities, self-injurious behaviour is not about dying, it is about trying to cope and carry on with life (Hawton, 1986; Arnold, 1996). In practice it can often be extremely difficult to establish whether an individual who has self-injured was trying to take their own life or was self-harming for other reasons, and they may report different and conflicting motivations at different times. Likewise, there are occasions where self-injury has 'gone wrong' and the individual has died apparently without the intention to do so (Lloyd, 1990). For the purposes of the present chapter, we will adopt the umbrella term of deliberate self-harm defined by Kreitman, Smith and Eng-Seong (1970) as: 'any non fatal act of self-injury or taking a substance (excluding alcohol) in excess of the generally recognised or prescribed therapeutic dose'.

The size of the problem

Statistics on the incidence rate of deliberate self-harm are unreliable due to the fact that many individuals do not report their injuries or seek medical attention. Looking at figures from hospital referrals alone there are at least 142,000 presentations of DSH in England and Wales every year and 'best estimates' give a figure of 400 incidences of DSH per 100,000 of the population per annum (NHS Centre for Reviews and Dissemination, 1998). Deliberate self-harm is most common in young women, with episodes of female deliberate self-harm currently outnumbering male episodes by a ratio of 1.5:1 (Samaritans, 1999). Deliberate self-harm remains one of the most common causes of emergency admissions to hospital. There are no detailed UK data relating to the costs of providing DSH services. An estimation of the general hospital costs of DSH services at 1998 prices suggests that they are around £45–50 million annually (NHS Centre for Reviews and Dissemination, 1998). These costs are relatively low due to the fact that admissions tend to be short.

In industrialised countries women carry out the majority of non-fatal suicidal acts (Weissman, 1974; Wexler, Weissman and Kasl, 1978; Kessler and McRae, 1983; Jack, 1992), although the gender gap seems to be narrowing (NHS Centre for Reviews and Dissemination, 1998). In the UK the commonest method of DSH is overdosing with analgesics such as Paracetamol, followed by cutting (NHS Centre for Reviews and Dissemination, 1998). Unsurprisingly, there are cross-cultural differences in the methods employed in DSH, due to differences in familiarity with particular substances and methods and different accessibility of substances (Canetto and Lester, 1995). Thus in countries such as Ghana (Safa-Dedeh and Canetto, 1992), and Malaysia (Maniam, 1988) women most commonly use household or agricultural poisons to self-harm.

Individuals who engage in DSH are at an increased risk of repeating DSH and of completed suicide. In the year following DSH, 1 per cent will kill themselves (Fremouw, de Perczel and Ellis, 1990), which is a rate 100 times higher than in the general population.

Understanding self-harm

Reasons for self-injurious behaviour are complex, and vary from one individual to another. It is clinically important to attempt to tease out what the reasons and motives for a particular act of deliberate self-harm are, in order to understand its meaning for the person concerned (Arnold, 1996), and for the formulation and implementation of assessment, treatment and prevention packages. It has been suggested that self-injury almost always occurs in response to painful and difficult events occurring in an individual's life (Arnold, 1996). Leibenluft, Gardner and Cowdry (1987) suggest that there are five stages to self-injurious behaviour: a precipitating event (such as loss of a significant relationship); an escalation of dysphoria; attempts to forestall the self-injury; self-mutilation; and the aftermath (for example relief from tension). Likewise, Shneidman (1980) suggested that typically self-injurious behaviour is accompanied by: sudden and recurrent intrusive impulses to harm oneself without the perceived ability to resist; a sense of existing in an intolerable situation which one can neither cope with nor control; increasing anxiety, agitation and anger; constriction of cognitive-perceptual processes resulting in a narrowed perspective on one's situation and personal alternatives for action; and a sense of psychic relief after the act of self-harm.

CHARACTERISTICS OF WOMEN WHO SELF-HARM

It is beyond the scope of this chapter to describe in detail the demographic, psychiatric and psychological characteristics of individuals who harm themselves (for detailed review see Hawton, 1997). We will focus here on those characteristics that have implications for the treatment and services needed for these women.

Psychological and psychiatric characteristics

As mentioned, acute interpersonal life events are common precipitants of self-harm, but these often occur against the background of long-standing interpersonal difficulties. Often the person's problem-solving skills are impaired and underlying psychiatric disorders, especially depression, substance misuse or dependency (Kessel and Grossman, 1961) and personality disorders are common. Alcohol or drugs may serve to both deepen feelings of hopelessness and helplessness and remove inhibitions about engaging in DSH, i.e. by increasing impulsivity and altering perceptions.

Scott and colleagues (1997) specifically looked at what distinguishes repeaters from those who do not repeat and found that compared with 'single DSH' subjects, those who repeated within three months were more depressed and hopeless, less likely to have a confiding friend, more likely to say that they wanted 'to communicate desperation' through their DSH and less skilled at problem solving. Additionally, those who are repeaters are likely to repeat again in a much shorter time period than those who are first-time self-harmers (Gilbody *et al.*, 1997).

Childhood factors

The links between childhood experiences of sexual, physical and emotional abuse or neglect and later deliberate self-harm have been amply documented (Finkelhor, 1986; Van der Kolk *et al.*, 1991; Arnold, 1995, 1996). In one survey of women who self-injured 49 per cent had been sexually abused as children, 43 per cent had been emotionally abused and 25 per cent had experienced physical abuse during childhood (Arnold, 1995). Gil (1988) proposed a number of psychological mechanisms as factors in adult survivors of childhood sexual abuse engaging in self-injurious behaviour. (1) Survivors often dissociate from traumatic childhood experiences in order to cut off from and avoid the effects of physical and emotional pain. Self-injurious behaviour can then become a method of proving that survivors are alive, are 'flesh and blood' and confirms that they have feelings of pain. (2) Pain and love become linked in the mind of the victim. This association may have the effect of the survivor inducing pain in an attempt to recreate the love they felt towards the perpetrator of the abuse. This is especially common if the perpetrator of the abuse was a parent. (3) Self-punishment: survivors of sexual abuse may internalise negative feelings about themselves. This can lead to feelings of being bad, resulting in attempts to destroy their body and mind through self-injurious behaviour. (4) During childhood the individual may not have received any acknowledgement from any source that sexual abuse was indeed taking place. In these cases self-injurious behaviour may function to alert others to their trauma and invisible scars.

However, an alternative view is that self-harm in victims of childhood abuse is biologically driven, as there is evidence to suggest that childhood abuse re-sets brain biology in a number of different ways (Van der Kolk *et al.*, 1991).

Apart from backgrounds that are obviously abusive, childhood neglect and absence of emotional support may also account for self-injury in later life (Arnold, 1996). The following quote provided by a woman with a history of self-injury illustrates her attempt to deal with feeling unnoticed and unloved during childhood:

> I went into Care when I was 6, after my mother died and my father remarried – they had a new family and made it completely obvious they didn't want me. I had loads of foster parents but it never worked out. As far as I'm concerned they just did it for the money. I always felt like rubbish. I never felt loved or wanted. I think I thought if I hurt myself someone would look after me, but then I was usually too scared to show them what I had done.
>
> (Woman X; cited in Arnold, 1996: p. 5).

Marital difficulties and abusive relationships in adulthood

Marital disharmony and breakdown are common immediate precipitants of self-harm attempts (Kessel, 1965; Kreitman and Casey, 1988). Women who are divorced or separated show higher rates of self-injurious behaviour than those who are single, married or widowed. It has been suggested that divorce or separation is a repetition of a disrupted, disorganised life pattern experienced in childhood (Bruhn, 1963; Roberts and Hooper, 1969).

Women who self-harm are often involved in abusive relationships during adulthood (Romans *et al.*, 1995). A number of studies have shown that women in heterosexual relationships who present to services following a suicide attempt report battering, physical or emotional abuse, sexual infidelity by their partner and emotional neglect within their relationship (Arcel *et al.*, 1992; Stark and Flitcraft, 1995; Kaslow *et al.*, 1998). In a Swedish study, Bergman and Brismar (1991) found that battered women were eight times more likely to be admitted for an act of DSH than women who suffered no domestic abuse. Stark and Flitcraft (1995) propose that self-harm and suicidality among battered women is evoked by the 'entrapment' women experience when they are subject to 'coercive control' by abusive men.

Poor educational attainment

One study reported an inverse relationship between level of education and self-injurious behaviour in later life, that is the lower the level of education reached by the individual, the greater their rate of self-injurious behaviour is likely to be (Wenz, 1977). This association may result from the fact that individuals from very disturbed backgrounds are likely to have had more limited scholastic achievements. However, poor educational attainment may contribute to and perpetuate a cycle of disadvantage by being associated with more limited work opportunities, greater financial hardship, less status in society and poorer self-esteem.

SPECIAL GROUPS

Women from ethnic minorities

Three studies from the UK have found that rates of attempted suicide in Asian women are higher than in white women and in men (Merrill and Owens, 1986; Glover *et al.*, 1989; Bhugra *et al.*, 1999a). Merrill and Owens (1986) suggest that unmarried adolescent girls face cultural conflict around family discord over Asian versus western life-styles. Bhugra *et al.* (1999b) compared Asian women who attempted suicide with female Asian GP attenders. The former group were more likely to have a history of previous suicidal behaviour, to have a psychiatric diagnosis and to be unemployed. They were also more likely to have been in an interracial relationship and to have changed religions. Their parents were more likely to have arrived in the UK at an older age. These findings are likely to be only the tip of the iceberg, especially in Muslim Asian women, as there are strong religious sanctions against suicide in Islam and many Islamic countries have punitive laws against attempted suicide, leading to both suicide and attempted suicide being under-diagnosed and under-reported (Khan, 1998).

Women prisoners

Studies show that women prisoners have a higher prevalence of DSH, but only when self-harm outside prison is taken into account (Maden, 1996). When deliberate self-harm in custody is considered alone, 5 per cent of female and male prisoners report this behaviour at least once during the present or previous times in custody. Women prisoners with a history of self-cutting are more likely to have been in care, have a history of violent offending and drink excessively (Maden, 1996).

WHAT TREATMENTS WORK?

The answer to this question depends on what the goal of treatment is. The goal from the public health perspective is to reduce the population rate of suicide and DSH; population-based measures aimed at reducing the availability of methods commonly used for committing suicide (e.g. selling Paracetamol in small quantities, catalytic converters, the change to North Sea Gas) help towards this goal (Lewis *et al.*, 1997); however, effective interventions to help high-risk populations are also needed. From a user's perspective a highly desirable goal might be the reduction of distress which may lead to a reduction in the likelihood of repetition. Most of the early intervention studies in parasuicide patients (including psychiatric, psychosocial and multifaceted interventions) either have shown very little effect on repetitions or completed suicide, or have been too small-scale to detect genuine differences.

Over the last few years, however, there have been some promising new developments in the treatment of deliberate self-harm. A systematic review of the effectiveness of psychosocial and drug treatments of DSH identified twenty randomised controlled trials in which repetition of self-harm was reported as an outcome (Hawton *et al.*, 1998). Whilst cautioning that the limited numbers of patients prevented firm conclusions, the review identified some interventions which showed promise. These included help with problem-solving (Hawton *et al.*, 1987; Salkovskis *et al.*, 1990; McLeavey *et al.*, 1994) and provision of a card to allow patients to make emergency contact with services (Morgan *et al.*, 1993), although the effect of this intervention may be limited to first-time self-harmers (Evans *et al.*, 1999).

Additionally, Marsha Linehan's seminal work on the treatment of chronically suicidal female borderline patients showed that DSH repetition rates are reduced in this population by dialectical behaviour therapy (DBT) (Linehan *et al.*, 1991; 1993). DBT consists of a one-year treatment package including both individual and group sessions. The main emphasis of DBT, unlike in brief crisis interventions, is on teaching the client skills to manage their emotions, thoughts and relationships in more adaptive ways than through self-harm (see Box 18.1). Yet how can a cash-strapped NHS

Box 18.1 Dialectical behaviour therapy

Individual psychotherapy sessions	*Group psychotherapy sessions*
Weekly – lasting for 1 hour Focus is on • alternative coping strategies • contingency management • cognitive modification • exposure to emotional cues • enhancing capability • emotional regulation	Weekly lasting for 2 1/2 hours Uses a psychoeducational approach. Focus is on • Problem-solving skills • Interpersonal skills • Emotional regulation • Distress tolerance
Every episode of DSH or suicidal threat that occurs over the course of treatment is examined in great detail to elicit a step by step chain of behavioural and emotional events that preceded the behaviour. This aims to: • Provide the client with alternative solutions and coping strategies that could have been used and could be used in the future • Enable the client to view the episode from other perspectives	Clients do not have telephone access to their group therapist Any problems or crisis that arise concerning an individual are referred back to the client's individual therapy sessions
Therapist actively reinforces adaptive behaviour and withholds reinforcement for any behaviour that has been highlighted for change	
Clients have telephone access to the therapist between sessions.	

---

introduce this type of treatment to the thousands who might be eligible? How applicable is the treatment to patients who present in crisis needing some form of immediate help rather than referral to a highly specialised service?

A number of important negative findings also emerged from Hawton *et al.*'s (1998) review. For example, there was no evidence that long-term treatment was better than short-term treatment in terms of preventing repetition in patients with a history of self-harm (Torhorst *et al.*, 1988), nor was there any evidence that intensive intervention plus outreach was superior to standard aftercare (e.g. Van der Sande *et al.*, 1997). No conclusions could be drawn about whether keeping the same therapist was better than changing to a different therapist after initial assessment (Torhorst *et al.*, 1987). Lastly, inpatient admission to a general psychiatric ward did not seem to confer any advantage over outpatient treatment (Waterhouse and Platt, 1990).

The review identified only one drug study which showed a reduction of repetition rates: flupenthixol depot medication compared to placebo (Montgomery *et al.*, 1983). The potentially serious long-term side-effects of neuroleptic medication, however, would need to be taken into account here. Studies using antidepressants (mianserin or nomifensine) indicated no apparent benefit regarding repetition of DSH. However, since the systematic review was conducted, Verkes *et al.* (1998) published a study showing that paroxetine, one of the serotonin reuptake inhibiting antidepressants (SSRI), reduces repetition rates significantly for patients who are 'minor' repeaters (less than five previous attempts of deliberate self-harm). The patients included in the study were not depressed, but the majority of them had Cluster B personality difficulties. The general conclusion from the systematic review is that there is an urgent need for large trials of promising therapies for this clinical population.

New developments in treatment

Manual-assisted cognitive therapy (MACT), a new approach to treatment of DSH, combines five to seven therapist-aided sessions with the use of a patient manual. The MACT treatment approach was developed as a tool for treating patients with deliberate self-harm within the confines of NHS practice. It is an approach which is simple enough and yet solid enough to be delivered to patients by a wide range of health workers without the highly specialised skills and training needed for DBT. MACT was evaluated in a preliminary study with promising results (Evans *et al.*, 1998). Patients who had received MACT showed a trend for a reduction in the rate of repeat episodes of DSH over six months after the index episode. They also were significantly less depressed and somewhat less anxious than treatment-as-usual patients. In contrast to patients who received standard care, patients receiving MACT showed an increase in positive expectancies for the future at six months. This is a potentially very important finding given that hopelessness about the future is an important predictor of repetition of deliberate self-harm and suicide.

A large-scale multi-centre study funded by the Medical Research Council evaluating the manual-based approach against treatment has now been evaluated and has found that brief cognitive behaviour therapy is of limited efficacy in reducing self-harm repetition, but it is more cost-effective than treatment as usual (Tyrer *et al.*, 2003). This study found that the manual can help to reduce self-harm cost-effectively, but only in those who do not have borderline personality disorder. This is important as the majority of people presenting with BPD are female.

SERVICES FOR DELIBERATE SELF-HARM PATIENTS

Whilst some excellent, well-coordinated DSH services exist, in many parts of the UK the typical service still consists of assessment in Accident and Emergency with at best a follow-up appointment by a junior psychiatrist a few weeks later (Leeds Consensus Conference, 1992). The time pressures faced by already overburdened casualty staff or junior psychiatric staff undoubtedly contribute to making this an often unsatisfactory exercise. User groups like Survivors Speak Out have strongly criticised existing DSH services in their publications (Pembroke, 1994; Bristol Crisis Service for Women, 1997).

The marked differences in the management of deliberate self-harm episodes between centres were highlighted in a study comparing services in four teaching hospitals. Despite similar clinical characteristics of the populations seen across centres there were huge variations in discharge rates from accident and emergency departments, and in the proportions of subjects receiving specialist psychosocial assessments (Kapoor *et al.*, 1998).

At the coal face of clinical practice, women who harm themselves are widely regarded as a low medical and psychiatric priority and often fall between two stools. Health professionals of all disciplines bend over backwards to avoid taking responsibility for these patients and try to get others to take on the task. The physicians will point out that the patient is no longer physically at risk and therefore is wasting a medical bed, whereas the psychiatrist will point out that their beds are reserved for those with severe mental illness, a term which is not taken to include most cases of self-harming behaviour (Kapoor *et al.*, 1998). Health professionals of any speciality view these patients as difficult, unrewarding and even as undeserving of help. General nurses in particular are often afraid of saying the wrong sort of thing to these patients (Bailey, 1994). Several recent papers (Hawton *et al.*, 1998; Kapoor *et al.*, 1998) have emphasised the need for the development of effective aftercare strategies. The recent NICE guidelines have outlined the best practice when caring for people who self-harm. They have particularly emphasised the importance of training for all clinicians who may encounter those who self-harm, starting at the point at which they first present to services (NICE, 2004).

WORKING WITH WOMEN WHO SELF-HARM

Parasuicide assessment

A good parasuicide assessment should consist of a full mental state examination, an assessment of the patient's current suicide risk and intent at the time of the act (see Box 19.2) and a full psychosocial assessment. All of this should form the basis of the case formulation, which ideally should be shared

---

Box 18.2 Assessment of suicide risk and intent post-DSH act

During the actual act itself:

WHAT WAS THE IMMEDIATE PRECIPITANT?

Why now? If no obvious precipitant, why?

ISOLATION	Anyone present or in contact
TIMING	Likelihood of someone coming
PRECAUTIONS AGAINST DISCOVERY	Locking the door, hiding
GAINING HELP	Contacting and telling someone
FINAL ACTS	Making plans for after death, e.g. a will
SUICIDE NOTE	Whether present and content
PATIENT'S VIEW OF LETHALITY	Belief regarding likelihood of death from act
INTENT	Stated intent of act, the wish to die
PREMEDITATION	Length of time planning the act
REACTION	Feelings regarding being alive

---

with the patient. The second task of the initial assessment is to engage and prepare the patient for psychological work and deal with any obstacles to help-seeking.

Engaging self-harm patients in psychological work

The first contact the patient has will be with the police, ambulance crew or the Accident and Emergency nurses and doctors. All these people will influence the patient's view of health care professionals and will therefore influence their decision to engage or not with psychological help. Many women who present to hospital services following an act of deliberate self-harm, are looking to be taken care of medically. They have not necessarily come wanting psychological help. In fact, many find it impossible to look at, and think about, their difficulties and instead harm themselves as a way of blocking out painful thoughts and feelings. They may also feel that the self-harm has successfully drawn a line under what was an emotionally difficult situation or has provided them with a solution to a problem, i.e. has brought back a partner who had threatened to leave them. The relationship with the person conducting a psychosocial assessment therefore is initially one which is imposed on the patient. The mental health professional may be concerned about the risk of recurrence of self-harming behaviour but the patient may not be. There may thus initially be some hostility towards the professional for the uninvited intrusion into the patient's 'private affairs'. One of the assessor's tasks therefore has to be to help the patient move towards acknowledging and accepting that they are in some difficulty and to encourage them to become concerned about themselves. The techniques of motivational interviewing (Miller and Rollnick, 1991) are useful here as they are especially designed to help ambivalent, reluctant and hostile patients to move towards change. Rather than the assessor providing the arguments for change, the emphasis has to be on eliciting whether the patient herself has any concerns about the effect of the self-harm on herself and close others. Acknowledging the 'good and the not so good' about the self-harm episode is also a useful exercise. Once patients feel that the assessor has fully understood the advantages conferred by an episode of self-harm they may be much more ready to discuss the disadvantages. For example, for some women, getting them to consider the effect their self-harm or suicide might have on their children can be used as a motivating factor for accepting help.

Some women will be deeply embarrassed about having harmed themselves and may try to play down the seriousness of the act. The assessor can help by talking frankly and normalising their feelings of shame, embarrassment and humiliation. Others will be worried that if they really thought about their life's predicaments, and did express what are seemingly unbearable feelings, they would become so overwhelmed that they might become even more suicidal. It may be helpful for the assessor to point out that 'bottling up' and suppressing difficult thoughts and feelings needs as much emotional energy – if not more than – to express them (Kelly and McKillop, 1996), and that emotional expression and processing will reduce the likelihood of another impulsive act.

For some women the psychosocial assessment following an overdose may be the first time in their life that they feel they have been listened to and have been allowed to tell their story. This can lead to the health professional feeling overwhelmed, confused and under a lot of pressure 'to make up for and sort out' a lifetime of neglect and abuse. It is important for the assessor to help the patient focus on the DSH act and not get lost in an overwhelming amount of information. This will help the patient make sense of what otherwise may feel rather uncontained and chaotic.

Many patients will have had contact with the 'caring professions' in the past. They may have been in care and have had an experience of having been passed around from one person to another as they become more difficult and challenging. This is sometimes done under the guise of seeking others' opinions, etc. but can be experienced by patients to be a passing on of the problem and of them as a person. In these cases it is helpful if the person conducting the assessment can be the one who takes on the DSH-counselling. If that is not possible it will be very important that the assessor points out that there is a link between their work and that of the therapist, e.g. that they will speak personally to the therapist to hand the patient over.

There are many practical reasons also why self-harming women find it difficult to accept help. Having small children at home and little support may be one of them. Likewise, women who are carers for elderly or disabled relatives may find it difficult to come for help and see it as yet another burden imposed on them. Another common reason is disapproval by a controlling, abusive partner who may fear her becoming alienated from him. Women from different ethnic backgrounds may be prevented by their families from seeking psychological help. Contact with psychiatric services might be thought to affect marriage prospects, with the family believing that they should deal with their daughter themselves. It will therefore be important to sensitively enquire about potential obstacles to help-seeking.

Given the many practical and emotional reasons why women who self-harm find it difficult to engage in follow-up treatment, each assessment must be viewed as potentially the only contact and window of opportunity for helping her to change. It is therefore imperative that a good attempt is made to reach an understanding of the self-harm act and that the assessing health professional gives the patient an experience of being listened to and feeling understood. On occasions, painful, difficult messages may need to be given about the danger the patient is in, e.g. if they are denying the seriousness of a violent relationship or of a substance abuse problem.

WORKING WITH THE PATIENT IN A THERAPEUTIC SETTING

Most designated deliberate self-harm services offer brief psychological work/ counselling. The aim usually is to develop a fuller understanding of the DSH, and the crisis leading up to it, to help the patient mobilise supports (practical and emotional), to begin to address the patient's skills deficits and also help the patient think about their longer-term difficulties and assess whether they may need additional help later. Irrespective of the particular type of psychological treatment or counselling used, there are a number of issues that need to be taken into account to ensure that the treatment is effective and beneficial to the patient.

- Clear boundaries and explanations of what patients can expect from treatment are important to help the patient feel safe and contained.
- Negotiation of appointment time needs to take into account any reservations the patient may have. She may say that she cannot attend on a regular basis due to her work commitments. The therapist needs to appreciate the reality of this whilst at the same time continuing to impress on her the importance of taking the DSH act seriously.
- Patients must be told how long the sessions will be and how often they will be seen. It is difficult to talk about painful issues if you have no idea how long a session will last. The reliability and predictability experienced in the therapeutic relationship may be the only stable part of the patients' lives.

One of the main roles of the therapist in DSH treatment is to sensitively keep alive the importance of the act and concern about the patient's difficulties, without lecturing or getting into an argument with the patient. McGinley and Rimmer (1992), in an excellent paper describing the psychodynamic factors that affect the assessment and treatment of patients presenting following DSH, point out that patients may use a variety of defences, including rationalisation, dissociation, splitting and projection or 'defensive focussing' on the past to keep the focus away from their self-harm. It is important that the therapist is sensitive to the patient's state of mind so he/she can think about what is going on for them and why they are dealing with their difficulties in the way that they do. A good DSH therapist needs to be able to talk with the patients about their fragility in a way that does not leave them feeling attacked and belittled but understood and supported. The work of understanding the DSH act within the context of the patient's experiences and personality can then be undertaken. Understanding in itself may not be enough and given the skills deficits many of these patients have, basic cognitive and behavioural strategies including problem-solving, self-monitoring and challenging of difficult thoughts and feelings may be helpful. Practical measures such as developing a jointly agreed crisis plan which contains contact numbers of family friends and professionals and coping strategies to be used in case the patient should feel like harming herself again may also be very useful.

McGinley and Rimmer (1992) make the important point that 'teaching on suicide in psychiatry tends to focus on depression and despair as the main driving forces behind suicidal acts'. However, depression and a helpless/ hopeless stance may mask underlying feelings of anger and aggression. The apparent 'depression' may be a way in which the patient protects herself and others from these feelings which may seem totally unacceptable and frightening to her. Patients may also be worried that, given a voice, their angry impulses may become so overwhelming that they will lose control, resulting in some terrible, violent outburst.

It can be tempting for the therapist to go along with this cleaned-up version of the patient's pathology as it is more palatable than to begin to identify and name the anger and aggression. However, many patients feel relief at having this scary, 'dangerous' side of themselves addressed and understood. If it is not, then it remains unpalatable and the patient remains in danger of DSH acts when overwhelmed and frightened by these impulses again in the future.

It is extremely important to address feelings surrounding the ending of the therapeutic contact, to help the patient anticipate and verbalise the painful reality that they may well feel rejected, abandoned, let down and angry about the ending of their sessions. If these feelings are not talked about the patient may precipitate an early end to the sessions to avoid feelings about the ending or take another overdose in an attempt to 'cling on' to the therapist.

Some patients will rubbish the sessions to avoid confronting their feelings regarding the loss of something good. If the sessions become useless in their mind there is no loss to cope with and therefore no feelings of sadness or anger. It is important that the therapist does not collude with the patient that the loss of the sessions is not a problem. It can be tempting to do so as the therapist may also feel guilty about leaving the patient at a time when they are obviously attached to them and would benefit from more help. The therapist has to help the patient recognise and deal with the pain of this loss and help model coping with difficult feelings.

The need for supervision

Working with deliberate self-harm patients is difficult work which will arouse difficult thoughts and feelings in the therapist. For example, when working with a patient who presents as extremely helpless and vulnerable the therapist may find him/herself under immense pressure to put things right and provide the patient with solutions to their dilemmas. This can then leave the therapist feeling helpless and then angry with the patient for putting them in this position. The patient may then be seen as difficult or unpleasant because the therapist hates his or her own helplessness. Alternatively, the therapist may initially enjoy being put in the position of being helpful, needed and idealised, but then end up feeling extremely guilty for being unable to fulfil the patient's expectations and for letting them down.

With chaotic disorganised patients the therapist may be drawn into acting rather than thinking. With some patients the therapist may be persuaded to ignore the seriousness of the risk of further self-harm by the patient's dissociation or rationalisation of events. It is thus vital in this kind of work to have regular supervision and support to be able to reflect on the work and to avoid burnout.

SELF-HELP AND USER GROUPS

Increasingly users themselves are beginning to gain a voice in addressing shortfalls in existing services and presenting suggestions and standards for service development. The Bristol Crisis Service is an organisation developed by women with personal experience of self-injury and mental health services. Its aims are to improve understanding of, and responses to, self-injury. Their findings (published on their website http://www.users.zetnet.co.uk/BCSW) reveals key differences between users and professionals in understanding self-harm and gives helpful insights for improving clinical approaches to women who self-injure. Users described the following problems with services: negative attitudes of staff to self-injury, failure on the part of professionals to look at the causes of the underlying distress and failure to provide an adequate response at times of crisis. Women who self-injured found the following valuable in services: respect; accepting and positive attitudes; being listened to; staff giving time to exploring the underlying causes of self-injury; staff giving time to assisting people to develop alternative coping strategies and putting in extra support during crisis periods.

An important implication emerging from this is the need for providers of services to review policies of excluding people who self-injure from services because they are considered to be manipulative and not in real need of help. Policies and practices based on this understanding of self-injury can deny many people in extreme distress the help and treatment they need.

Bristol Crisis Service suggest that agencies should adopt the following:

1   Involvement of service users in planning and management of services.
2   Individuals to be encouraged to define their own needs and offered choices in treatment and support.
3   People who self-injure should be treated with respect, sensitivity and kindness by staff in all agencies.
4   Treatment of people who self-injure should be based on an understanding of the meanings of self-injury to individuals, and the emphasis should be on addressing the individual's distress rather than on controlling their self-injury.
5   Professionals working with people who self-injure must be provided with thorough training, and good supervision and support.
6   Agencies serving people who self-injure should draw up practice guidelines in consultation with users to ensure services are delivered in accordance with these principles.

The recent NICE guidelines about the management of self-harm are an excellent guide for all professionals involved in treating patients who self-harm. Readers are referred to this evidence-based guidance in order to optimise the care they provide to these women (NICE, 2004).

There are also a great many websites dedicated to deliberate self-harm, giving information and support for sufferers, carers, relatives, and professionals. The following sites will give helpful information and provide links to other resources and websites:

http://www.self-injury.net/resources/uk.htm
http://www.self-injury.net/resources/internet.htm
http://crystal.palace.net/~llama/psych/intro.html

Summary and conclusions

Deliberate self-harm is a common problem in women and the boundaries between what is suicidal and what is a cry for help or a coping strategy are often blurred. Women who present to services following an episode of deliberate self-harm often have histories of past and/or current physical sexual and emotional abuse and the presenting crisis usually is the culmination of much more long-standing difficulties. Women from some ethnic minority backgrounds may be at a particularly high risk of self-harm. Services around the country remain patchy with poor-quality care, especially in those areas where there are no designated deliberate self-harm services. Increasingly, research is focusing on developing better treatments for this patient group. Increasing involvement of users in service planning and development and training of health professionals will be vital in improving the quality of their care and in giving a voice to this silent, ignored or even disliked group whose needs have so often remained unaddressed.

References

Arcel, L.T., Mantonakis, J., Petersson, B., Jemos, J. and Kaliteraki, E. (1992) Suicide attempts among Greek and Danish women and the quality of their relationships with husbands and boyfriends. *Acta Psychiatrica Scandinavica* 85: 189–95.

Arnold, L. (1995) *Women and Self-Injury; A Survey of 76 Women*. Bristol: Bristol Crisis Services for Women.

Arnold, L. (1996) *Self-Help for Self-Injury; Women and Self-Injury Information Booklet 2*. Bristol: Bristol Crisis Services for Women.

Bailey, S. (1994) Critical care nurses' and doctors' attitudes to parasuicide patients. *Australian Journal of Advanced Nursing* 11: 11–17.

Bergman, B. and Brismar, B. (1991) Suicide attempts by battered wives .*Acta Psychiatrica Scandinavica* 83: 380–4.

Bhugra, D., Desai, M. and Baldwin, D.S. (1999a). Attempted suicide in west London: I. Rates across ethnic communities. *Psychological Medicine* 29: 1125–30.

Bhugra, D., Baldwin, D.S., Desai, M. and Jacob, K.S. (1999b). Attempted suicide in west London: I. Rates across ethnic communities. *Psychological Medicine* 29: 1131–9.

Bristol Crisis Service for Women (1997) *Mental Health Foundation Briefing No. 2*, Online. Available HTTP: http://www.mentalhealth.org.uk/brief002.htm

Bruhn, J.G. (1963) Comparative study of attempted suicides and psychiatric out-patients. *British Journal of Preventive and Social Medicine* 17: 197–201.

Canetto, S.S. and Lester, D. (eds) (1995) *Women and Suicidal Behaviour*. New York: Springer Publishing Company.

Evans, K., Tyrer, P., Catalan, J., Schmidt, U., Tata, P., Dent, J., Davidson, K. and Thornton, S. (1998) Manual-assisted cognitive-behaviour therapy in the treatment of deliberate self-harm: a randomised controlled trial. *Psychological Medicine* 29: 19–25.

Evans, M.O., Morgan, H.G., Hayward, A. and Gunnell, D.J. (1999) Crisis telephone consultation for deliberate self-harm patients: effects on repetition. *British Journal of Psychiatry* 175: 23–7.

Finkelhor, D. (1986) 'Abusers: special topics', in D. Finkelhor, *A Source Book on Child Sexual Abuse*. Beverly Hills: Sage.

Fremouw, W.J., de Perczel, M. and Ellis, T.E. (1990) *Suicide Risk: Assessment and Response Guidelines*. New York: Pergamon Press.

Gil, E. (1988) *Treatment of Adult Survivors of Childhood Abuse.* Walnut Creek, CA: Launch Press.

Gilbody, S., House, A. and Owens, D. (1997) The early repetition of deliberate self harm. *Journal of the Royal College of Physicians* 31: 171–2.

Glover, G., Marks, F. and Nowers, M. (1989) Parasuicide in young Asian women. *British Journal of Psychiatry* 154: 271–2.

Hawton, K. (1986) Suicide and attempted suicide amongst children and adolescents, London: Sage, cited in A. Liebling (1992) *Suicides in Prison.* New York: Routledge.

Hawton, K. (1997) 'Attempted suicide', in D.M. Clark, and C.G. Fairburn (eds.), *Science and Practice of Cognitive Behaviour Therapy.* Oxford: Oxford University Press.

Hawton, K., Arensman, E., Townsend, E., Bremner, S., Feldman, E. *et al.* (1998) Deliberate self harm: systematic review of efficacy of psychosocial and pharmacological treatments in preventing repetition. *British Medical Journal* 317: 441–7.

Hawton, K., McKeown, S., Day, A., Martin, P., O'Connor, M. and Yule, J. (1987) Evaluation of out-patient counselling compared with general practitioner care following overdoses. *Psychological Medicine* 17: 751–61.

Jack, R. (1992) *Women and Attempted Suicide.* Hillsdale, NJ: Erlbaum.

Johnstone, L. (1995) 'Self-Injury and the Psychiatric Response', in Bristol Crisis Services for Women (1995), *Cutting Out the Pain: National Conference on Self-Injury.* Bristol: Bristol Crisis Services For Women.

Kapoor, N., House, A., Creed, F., Feldman, E., Friedman, T. and Guthrie, E. (1998) Management of deliberate self poisoning in adults in four teaching hospitals: descriptive study. *British Medical Journal* 316: 831–2.

Kaslow, N.J., Thompson, M.P., Meadows, L.A., Jacobs, D., Chance, S. *et al.* (1998) Factors that mediate and moderate the link between partner abuse and suicidal behaviour in African American women. *Journal of Consulting and Clinical Psychology* 66: 533–40.

Kelly, A.E. and McKillop, K.J. (1996) Consequences of revealing personal secrets. *Psychological Bulletin* 120: 450–65.

Kessel, N. (1965) Self-poisoning I–II, in: J. Roberts, and D. Hooper (1969) The natural history of attempted suicide in Bristol. *British Journal of Medical Psychology* 42: 303–12.

Kessel, N. and Grossman, G. (1961) Suicide in alcoholics. *British Medical Journal* ii: 1671–2.

Kessler, R.C. and McRae, J.A. (1983) Trends in the relationship between sex and attempted suicide. *Journal of Health and Social Behaviour* 24: 98–110.

Khan, M.M. (1998) Suicide and attempted suicide in Pakistan. *Crisis* 19: 172–6.

Kreitman, N. and Casey, P. (1988) Repetition of parasuicide: an epidemiological and clinical study. *British Journal of Psychiatry* 153: 792–800.

Kreitman, N., Smith, P. and Eng-Seong, T. (1970) Attempted suicide as language: an empirical study. *British Journal of Psychiatry* 116: 456–73.

Leeds Consensus Conference (1992) The general hospital management of adult deliberate self-harm: a consensus statement on minimum standards for service provision. Leeds, 5 November.

Leibenluft, E., Gardner, D.L. and Cowdry, R.W. (1987) The inner experience of the borderline self-mutilator. *Journal of Personality Disorders* 1(4): 317–24.

Lewis, G., Hawton, K. and Jones, P. (1997) Strategies for preventing suicide. *British Journal of Psychiatry* 171: 351–4.

Linehan, M.M., Armstrong, H.E., Suarez, A., Allmari, D. and Heard, H.L. (1991) Cognitive-behavioural treatment of chronically parasuicidal borderline patients. *Archives of General Psychiatry* 48: 1060–4.

Linehan, M.M., Heard, H.L. and Armstrong, H.E. (1993) Naturalistic follow-up of a behavioural treatment for chronically parasuicidal borderline patients. *Archives of General Psychiatry* 50: 971–4.

Lloyd, C. (1990) *Suicides in Prison: A Literature Review*. Home Office Research Study 115. London: HORPU.

McGinley, E. and Rimmer, J. (1992) The trauma of attempted suicide. *Psychoanalytic Psychotherapy* 7: 53–68.

McLeavey, B.C., Daly, R.J., Ludgate, J.W. and Murray, C.M. (1994) Interpersonal problem-solving skills training in the treatment of self-poisoning patients. *Suicide and Life Threatening Behaviour* 24: 382–94.

Maden, T. (1996) *Women, Prisons and Psychiatry: Mental Disorders Behind Bars*. Oxford: Butterworth Heinemann.

Maniam, T. (1988) Suicide and parasuicide in a hill resort in Malaysia. *British Journal of Psychiatry* 153: 222–5.

Merrill, J. and Owens, J. (1986) Ethnic differences in self-poisoning: a comparison of Asian and white groups. *British Journal of Psychiatry* 148: 708–12.

Miller, W. and Rollnick, S. (1991) *Motivational Interviewing: Preparing People to Change Addictive Behaviours*. New York: Guilford Press.

Montgomery, S.A., Roy, D. and Montgomery, D.B. (1983) The prevention of recurrent suicidal acts. *British Journal of Clinical Pharmacology* 15 Suppl 2: 183S–188S.

Morgan, H.G., Jones, E.M. and Owen, J.H. (1993) Secondary prevention of non-fatal deliberate self-harm: the green card study. *British Journal of Psychiatry* 163: 111–12.

NHS Centre for Reviews and Dissemination (1998) Deliberate self harm. *Effective Health Care* 1(6). University of York.

National Institute for Clinical Excellence, NICE (2004) Self-harm: the short-term physical and psychological management and secondary prevention of self-harm in primary and secondary care. CG16. www.nice.org.uk

Overstone, I. and Kreitman, N. (1974) Two syndromes of suicide. *British Journal of Psychiatry* 124: 336–48.

Pembroke, L.R. (1994) *Self-Harm: Perspectives from Personal Experience*. London: Survivors Speak Out.

Roberts, J. and Hooper, D. (1969) The natural history of attempted suicide in Bristol. *British Journal of Medical Psychology* 42: 303–12.

Romans, S.E., Martin, J.L., Anderson, J.C., Herbison, G.P. and Mullen, P.E. (1995) Sexual abuse in childhood and deliberate self-harm. *American Journal of Psychiatry* 152(9): 1336–42.

Ross, R.R. and McKay, H.B. (1979) *Self-Mutilation*. Boston, MA: Lexington Books.

Safa-Dedeh, A. and Canetto, S.S. (1992) Women, family and suicidal behaviour in Ghana, in U.W. Gielen, L.L. Adler and N. Milgram (eds), *Psychology in International Perspective*. Amsterdam: Swets and Zeitlinger.

Salkovskis, P.M., Atha, C. and Storer, D. (1990) Cognitive-behavioural problem solving in the treatment of patients who repeatedly attempt suicide: a controlled trial. *British Journal of Psychiatry* 157: 871–6.

Samaritans (1999) *Suicide in the UK and Ireland*. Samaritans Web Page, Online. Available HTTP: http://www.samaritans.org.uk

Scott, J., House, R., Yates, M. and Harrington, J. (1997) Individual risk factors for early repetition of deliberate self-harm. *British Journal of Medical Psychology* 70: 387–93.

Shneidman, E. (1980) *Voices of Death*, cited in Pattison, E.M., and Kahan, J. (1983) The deliberate self-harm syndrome. *American Journal of Psychiatry* 140(7): 876–2.

Stark, E. and Flitcraft, A. (1995) Killing the beast within: woman battering and female suicidality. *International Journal of Health Services* 25: 43–64.

Torhorst, A., Möller, H.J., Bürk, F., Kurz, A., Wächtler, C. and Lauter, H. (1987) The psychiatric management of parasuicide patients: a controlled clinical study comparing different strategies of outpatient treatment. *Crisis* 8: 53–61.

Torhorst, A., Möller, H.J., Kurz, A., Schmid-Bode, K.W. and Lauter, H. (1988) Comparing a 3-month and a 12-month-outpatient aftercare program for parasuicide repeaters in H.J. Möller, A. Schmiedke and R. Welz (eds.), *Current Issues of Suicidology*. Berlin: Springer Verlag.

Tyrer, P., Thompson, S., Schmidt, U., Jones, V., Knapp, M., Davidson, K. *et al.* (2003) Randomized controlled trial of brief cognitive behaviour therapy versus treatment as usual in recurrent deliberate self-harm: the POPMACT study. *Psychological Medicine* 33(6): 969–76.

Tyrer, P., Tom, B., Byford, S., Schmidt, U., Jones, V., Davidson, K., Knapp, M., MacLeod, A. and Catalan, J.: POPMACT Group (2004) Differential effects of manual assisted cognitive behavior therapy in the treatment of recurrent deliberate self-harm and personality disturbance: the POPMACT study. *Journal of Personality Disorder* 18(1): 102–16.

Van der Kolk, B.A., Perry, J.C. and Herman, J.L. (1991) Childhood origins of self-destructive behaviour. *American Journal of Psychiatry* 148: 1665–71.

Van der Sande, R., van Rooijen, L., Buskens, E., Allart, E., Hawton, K., van der Graaf, Y. and van Engeland, H. (1997) Intensive in-patient and community intervention versus routine care after attempted suicide: a randomised controlled intervention study. *British Journal of Psychiatry* 171: 35–41.

Verkes, R.J., Vander Mast, R.C., Hegeveld, M.W., Tuyl, J.P., Zwinderman, A.H. and Van Kempen, G.M. (1998) Reduction by paroxetine of suicidal behaviour in patients with repeated suicide attempts but not major depression. *American Journal of Psychiatry* 155: 543–7.

Waterhouse, J. and Platt, S. (1990) General hospital admission in the management of parasuicide: a randomised controlled trial. *British Journal of Psychiatry* 156: 236–42.

Weissman, M.M. (1974) The epidemiology of suicide attempts, 1960 to 1971. *Archives of General Psychiatry* 30: 737–46.

Wenz, F.V. (1977) Ecological variation in self-injury behaviour. *Suicide and Life-Threatening Behaviour* 7(2): 92–9.

Wexler, L., Weissman, M.M. and Kasl, S.V. (1978) Suicide attempts 1970–75: updating a United States study and comparisons with international trends. *British Journal of Psychiatry* 132: 180–5.

Useful addresses

Bristol Crisis Service for Women

PO Box 654, Bristol, BS99 1XH

Phone: 0117 925 1119

email: bcsw@womens-crisis-service.freeserve.co.uk

Website: www.users.zetnet.co.uk/BCSW/

Description: helpline service for women in emotional distress, particularly for women who harm themselves. Range of literature on self-harm, training for professionals and other organisations on self-harmers. Phone for further details.

Opening hours: helpline: Fri and Sat, 9pm–12.30am

Referral: self or any other source

Criteria/catchment: national organisation for women only

National Self-harm Network

PO Box 16190, London NW1 3ND

Email: nshn@talk21.com

Description: campaign for the rights and understanding of self-harmers. Can provide a range of info leaflets and a resource lack. Also offer training to voluntary and statutory services on issues surrounding self-harm.

Opening hours: letter or email service only

Referral: self or any other source

Nottingham Crisis Line for Women

Address: Room 218, Vernon House, 18 Friar Lane, Nottingham NG1 6DQ

Phone 0115 958 3399

Email: nclw@ukonline/index.html

Website: http://web.ukonline.co.uk.nclw/index.html

Description: a user-led service providing a telephone helpline for women in emotional distress with an emphasis on self-harm. Provide training for professionals and other organisations on issues surrounding self-harm.

Special interest activities: weekly self-help group for women with direct experience of self-harm. Mutually supportive unfacilitated meetings.

Additional info: member of the telephone helplines association

Opening hours: helpline: Fri and Sat, 9pm–12 midnight

Referral: open access

Criteria/Catchment: women only but literature can also be sent to men

Part VI

Therapies

19 Biological therapies

Shubulade Smith and
Claire Henderson

Introduction

Since this is a vast area we have selected issues particularly relevant to women with respect to drug treatments, electroconvulsive therapy and psychosurgery. We shall also discuss hormonal treatments for psychiatric problems. The appendix at the end of the chapter describes particular factors that should be borne in mind when prescribing psychotropic medication to women.

DRUG TREATMENTS

The legacy of inappropriate prescribing

Overuse of benzodiazepines and professionals' lack of knowledge about dependence and withdrawal in the 1970s have resulted in wariness about taking psychotropic medications in general. Many patients have direct or indirect experience of adverse effects resulting from inappropriate use of psychotropic drugs, particularly benzodiazepines. They may also have ideas about medication based on stigmatising stereotypes of psychiatric patients. This means there are a number of concerns commonly associated with taking psychotropic drugs:

- Being made an addict
- Being turned into a zombie
- Permanent side-effects
- Brain damage
- Used to suppress normal reactions to stress/bereavement
- Fobbed off instead of talking about problems
- Used to thwart their ambitions
- Benzodiazepines as a political band-aid
- Medication is for dangerous and violent people.

These concerns should be taken seriously by the prescriber as they may adversely affect the therapeutic relationship as well as willingness to take medication. Doctors are often poor at discussing side-effects with patients due to their fear of lack of compliance but such fears are unfounded (Howland *et al.*, 1990). However, some psychotropic drugs do cause problems that are particular to women, such as menstrual dysfunction, infertility and teratogenesis. These need to be known about and discussed with the patients. As well as the above common concerns, prescribers should also bear in mind a number of patient- and prescriber-level factors that influence practice.

Prescribing practices: patient-level factors

It has been consistently found throughout Europe and America that women receive twice as many prescriptions for psychotropic medication as men. This may be because medication is needed for true pathological states, which occur more frequently in the female sex. In favour of the above is the finding that rates of depression in women are twice as high as those in men (Jenkins *et al.*, 1997). Depression is the psychiatric disorder most commonly associated with suicide; however, men have three times higher rates of completed suicide than women (Charlton *et al.*, 1992). Might this indicate a more frequent failure of the therapist to detect and treat underlying psychiatric disturbance in men compared with women? Is women's depression more frequently identified and treated?

There do appear to be sex differences in illness behaviour. Horwitz (1977) found that women were more likely to report psychological distress, accept a label of psychiatric illness, enter treatment more willingly and accept the role of patient more readily than men. Men were more likely to be coerced into treatment. Hohmann (1989) states that women can accept illness at a lower social cost than men, because of the different societal expectations that exist for men and women. She suggests that women are more likely to ask for medication and to persuade their doctor of their need. Men on the other hand may manifest underlying distress by aggressiveness or abuse of alcohol.

Prescribing practices: prescriber-level factors

Doctors prescribe medication usually because it is felt it is necessary in order to combat a particular illness. This perception of need may be influenced by prescriber attributes as well as those of the patient.

It seems likely that doctors look for psychological disturbance more in women; not only do they expect it more, they are more likely to treat it with psychotropic medication. It is notable that one of Hohmann's (1989) most compelling findings was that women with the same presenting complaints and psychiatric diagnosis as men were significantly more likely to receive prescriptions for anxiolytics and antidepressants.

Pharoah and Melzer (1995) found that in general practice the psychotropic drugs prescribed in greatest amounts were hypnotics (sleeping tablets) and that highest prescribing was associated with being female and being aged 65 years and over. King *et al.* (1982) and Hohmann (1989) describe similar findings. It is not clear how much of this prescribing is appropriate, since it has been shown convincingly that detection rates for psychological disturbance in general practice are poor, with a significant proportion of patients with depression being missed (Goldberg *et al.*, 1976). It is possible then that hypnotics may be being prescribed for depressive symptoms (Olfson and Klerman, 1992).

Time or lack of resources may result in the prescriber feeling compelled to give a tablet as a way of responding to expressed psychological disturbance that he/she cannot deal with more appropriately, i.e. prescribing as a panacea. In certain areas where there is marked social deprivation the rates of benzodiazepine prescribing are very high (King *et al.*, 1982). It may be that doctors prescribe anxiolytics and hypnotics because they feel that the woman has to face psychosocial stressors which cannot be addressed at an individual level, as the causes are located within the family, community or wider society.

Physiological sex differences affecting drug handling

Throughout Europe and America, women receive twice as many prescriptions for psychotropic medication as men do. These are drugs that, in the most part, have been developed from research in young healthy male subjects. How relevant are the findings from drug trials to the female consumers of these medications?

Women differ from men in terms of their physiology, and thus differ in the way that they handle drugs. Physiological mechanisms showing sexual differences include

- total blood volume
- absolute percent body fat
- gastric emptying
- small intestine absorption
- hepatic metabolism
- renal clearance.

These all tend towards increased blood levels of a drug after ingestion and decreased renal clearance compared with men. This is especially true for those drugs that are mainly metabolised by the liver, as most psychotropic medications are. These effects are not simply countered by dosing on an mg/kg basis because the effects of gender affect multiple mechanisms underlying the pharmacokinetics. Thus a man of the same body weight will clear a drug more quickly and have lower plasma levels than a woman. Women may therefore be more at risk of adverse effects because the drug stays in the body for longer.

For women there exist particular physiological states which do not occur in men. The menstrual cycle, pregnancy and menopause all represent physiologically normal processes that may affect drug handling.

- Menstrual phase changes may affect drug distribution and metabolism. Plasma concentration of drugs tends to fall in the late luteal phase because of dilutional effects. This means that, for example, variable dosing of antidepressants and lithium is needed in some patients to control symptoms during the different stages of the menstrual cycle.
- Oral Contraceptive Pill – these exogenous steroids can interact with psychotropic medication, e.g. to decrease clearance of benzodiazepines.
- Pregnancy – large changes in drug kinetics and dynamics may be expected. In addition there is the presence of the foetus and the added risk of teratogenicity (see above).
- Menopause – following menopause, women are physiologically more similar to men. However, the little research that has been done seems to indicate that the effect of gender on drug metabolism may vary for different drugs. Thus in post-menopausal women some drugs are metabolised more slowly, others more quickly, than in men of the same age. It is hard to disentangle the effects of age and the menopause in women on drug handling because many studies use arbitrary age categories. This means that pre- and post-menopausal women are combined in the same group, although they may have widely differing physiological states. Ninety-five per cent of natural menopause occurs between 42 and 58 years of age, thus it may be more informative to use these ages as cut-off points for grouping female research subjects (Jensvold *et al.*, 1996).

Women are frequently excluded from drug trials, but there is a growing body of research that indicates the need for specific sexual differences to be taken into account when drug research is being done, including:

- cytochrome P450 metabolism (differs in men and women);
- the prolactin response to neuroleptics is increased in women compared to men;
- women respond better to smaller doses of neuroleptics than men do, but are more likely to get tardive dyskinesia later in life.

Despite all the above, women are still excluded from drug research trials. This increased as a result of Thalidomide-induced foetal abnormalities and diethylstilboestrol (DES)-associated vaginal neoplasia (increased incidence of vaginal cancer in the daughters of women treated with DES to reduce the risk of spontaneous abortion). Researchers thus became reluctant to use women of childbearing age in research. It was also thought by some researchers that hormonal fluctuations experienced by women might interfere with consistent kinetic results (Dawkins and Potter, 1991). This is the very reason why women's response to medication needs to be studied as part of any clinical trial.

From this brief synopsis, it is clear that as doctors and mental health practitioners it is important to be aware of the factors that motivate our patients to present and the factors that motivate us to prescribe. It is also important to remember that women's physiology is different to men's and that many of the medications we are prescribing have not been tested in women; thus the therapeutic response to the drug and the side-effects experienced may not be as expected.

HORMONES AS THERAPIES FOR MENTAL DISORDERS

Premenstrual syndrome (PMS)

There is little evidence that a mood disorder specific to the premenstrual phase exists. Women may ascribe an erratic mood to being premenstrual, but keeping a mood diary often shows little connection with the menstrual cycle. It is important to remember that a woman presenting with PMS may have an underlying psychiatric problem. Further, patients with major mental illness such as schizophrenia and bipolar illness sometimes have premenstrual exacerbations of their illness. This may in part be related to changes in fluid balance, especially for drugs such as lithium. The control of lithium levels in certain patients may be extremely difficult at this time.

Various treatments for PMS have been tried, including:

* progesterone vaginal suppositories were found to have no better effect than placebo;
* oestrogen has had little success, the fears about endometrial hyperplasia severely curtailing widespread use of this method;
* the oral contraceptive pill has not been very effective, its use being implicated in the onset of depression in certain women.

Other treatments range from changing diet, exercise, vitamin B6 and Evening Primrose oil, to more drastic interventions such as GnRH agonists, Danazol and even surgical ablation. Recently attention has been paid to the SSRIs, which have been found to significantly relieve symptoms of PMS in women (Young *et al.*, 1998).

Postnatal depression

Both progesterone and oestrogen have been tried as treatments for postnatal depression. A recent systematic review of such studies identified two randomised placebo-controlled trials, one of each hormone type (Lawrie *et al.*, 2000). The trial of a progesterone, norethisterone enanthate, showed it was associated with an increased risk of postnatal depression (Lawrie *et al.*, 1998). Sichel *et al.* (1995) hypothesised an 'oestrogen withdrawal state' resulting from the sudden reduction in oestrogen after delivery after finding that high-dose oral oestrogen was effective in preventing relapse in women at high risk of puerperal depression. While the trial by Gregoire (1996) suggests it may be of use at a late stage, its side-effects (including deep vein thrombosis, endometrial hyperplasia and suppression of lactation) mean that further research is unlikely.

Hormone replacement therapy

No real association between any psychiatric illness and the menopause has been found. The main predictors of depression during the menopause are psychosocial and do not differ from those risk factors associated with depression occurring at other times of life, i.e. past history of depression, stressful life events and unemployment (for review see Nicol-Smith, 1996). Thus, many women developing psychiatric symptoms around the time of the menopause also appear to develop symptoms in response to other stresses. These women have been found to be more likely to attend clinics than matched controls.

HRT is found by many women to improve their mood as well as physical symptoms. However, evidence of improvement in psychological symptoms has been found only in those women who have undergone surgical menopause. When sexual symptoms are the main complaint, HRT seems to be more effective. Women presenting with psychological symptoms should be treated with interventions specifically for the disorder, as the response to HRT has been found to be no better than placebo.

ELECTROCONVULSIVE THERAPY

Electroconvulsive therapy is an emotive topic that seems to form a flashpoint for debate on the practice of psychiatry. Like psychosurgery, it brings connotations of political repression and brain damage; unlike psychosurgery, it continues to be in routine use although many psychiatrists use it much less often then in the past. It is also unlike psychosurgery in that it can currently be given involuntarily to patients admitted on a treatment section of the Mental Health Act 1983. The proposals for consultation on the reform of the Mental Health Act 1983 (Department of Health, 1999) highlight the compulsory use of ECT as a subject requiring further discussion, but state that it should be recognised as a treatment that can at times save lives. This section will explore the reasons for both the negative press ECT has received and its continued use.

Positive aspects of ECT

While ECT was once widely used for a variety of psychiatric conditions, its use is now largely limited to the treatment of severe depression, where the evidence for its effectiveness is strongest. It has been shown to be very effective in the treatment of severe depression in the short term and appears to be more effective over this timeframe than pharmacotherapy (UK ECT Review Group, 2003). Readers wishing to find out more about its use for other conditions may consult the National Institute for Clinical Excellence (NICE) guidance on ECT (NICE, 2003). According to this guidance, ECT may be indicated in these situations:

- severe depressive illness
- catatonia
- a prolonged or severe manic episode.

The guidance states that 'ECT should be used to achieve rapid and short-term improvement of an individual's severe symptoms after an adequate trial of other treatment options has proven ineffective and/or when the condition is considered to be potentially life threatening.'

The introduction of newer antidepressants that are, for many, more tolerable than the pre-existing ones potentially reduces the frequency with which ECT is likely to be felt necessary. In some hospitals, the use of ECT has indeed diminished significantly over this time period, but as with many medical therapies there is wide variation in its prescription among hospitals.

Negative aspects of ECT

Two audits by the Royal College of Psychiatrists have been highly critical of the standard in many hospitals of all aspects of ECT, including the lack of written information for patients, the facilities, equipment, nursing and medical procedures. The Royal College of Psychiatrists has published standards for administration of ECT and these are recommended for any reader with patients undergoing ECT (Caird and Worrall, 2003).

However well the procedure is carried out, one of the unappealing aspects of ECT is that it is a procedure done to rather than with the patient. Even with pharmacotherapy, the patient must decide herself to take medication; for oral medication, this requires an active commitment to taking it regularly to see whether it will help. With ECT the patient plays no part as she is anaesthetised; this passivity can make people feel helpless and vulnerable. Many surgical patients have a fear of assault while anaesthetised; this is likely to be at least as common in psychiatric patients since a disproportionate number have suffered physical or sexual abuse. This passivity may make it more difficult for people to try and take control of their problems, particularly as the procedure implies faulty brain chemistry as their root

(Cobb, 1993). Further, the induction of a generalised seizure seems a grossly blunt instrument in a society which is becoming ever more educated about the complexity of the mind. We are thus culturally at odds with ECT and no amount of evidence for its effectiveness will change this.

Because ECT was introduced before muscle relaxants, the image of people being restrained during violent tonic-clonic seizures is a powerful one that has stayed in the popular memory. This image is like one of torture, indeed 'unmodified' ECT has been used as torture in some countries where torture is practised. Thus it has been easy for ECT to symbolise the function of psychiatry in social control, particularly the control of women, as they are more frequently treated with ECT than are men.

While explanation about the procedure may allay fears based on the vision of unmodified ECT, psychiatrists do not seem to be able to persuade people that there is no risk of permanent cognitive deficits, particularly memory loss. It seems that while many people complain of permanent memory loss and attribute it to having had ECT, research provides evidence for only short-term deficits. There are several possible reasons for this. It may be that current methods of testing are insufficiently specific or sensitive to pick up what people subjectively experience. There is evidence that depression itself causes memory loss (Baldwin, 1999) and further that depression and anxiety prevent registration of new information, so that memories are never laid down in the first place, let alone lost. Last, concurrent use of alcohol, benzodiazepines or cannabis will also impede registration and retention of information.

Unfortunately, statements by researchers that there is no evidence for permanent brain damage can easily be interpreted as defensive falsehoods by patients who feel assaulted and damaged by ECT. Whatever the apparent benefits of ECT and despite the lack of evidence regarding cognitive damage, psychiatrists must weigh against these the possible impact of the negative connotations of ECT on the self-image of the patient as well as on the therapeutic relationship.

PSYCHOSURGERY

This is rarely used as a psychiatric treatment. In the past it was used widely for a variety of disorders including schizophrenia, bipolar illness, severe depression, anxiety states, obsessional compulsive disorder and personality disorders. It is still used occasionally, but there is no agreement about its efficacy or effectiveness. This is because all the studies that have been done were uncontrolled, that is there was no comparison group of patients who were not given surgery. It is also clear that the sheer complexity of neuronal configuration precludes accurate interruption of neural pathways. Even with modern stereotactic techniques, which greatly reduce the side-effects seen when psychosurgery was first introduced, the same pattern is seen of apathy, weight gain, disinhibition and epilepsy.

Very rarely, patients may request psychosurgery for relief of long-term intractable illness. Some psychiatrists would always consider such a request as inappropriate, because of lack of evidence about its efficacy and the availability of other treatments. Patients seeking such drastic measures may have a desire to self-harm, which should be thoroughly explored. However, if a decision is made that psychosurgery may be appropriate, then the following conditions must be fulfilled under the Mental Health Act 1983:

- The patient must have a treatable mental disorder as defined under the Act;
- The patient's responsible medical officer (consultant) must make a recommendation to the Mental Health Act Commission;
- A second recommendation must be made by an independent doctor;
- The independent doctor and two more independent people must find the patient capable of giving consent.

APPENDIX: GUIDELINES FOR PRESCRIBING TO WOMEN

Hypnotic/anxiolytic drugs

Benzodiazepines

- Tolerance/withdrawal: these should not be prescribed for more than 2–4 weeks. (Zopiclone and zolpidem are newer drugs less likely to produce withdrawal, but they can still induce tolerance.)
- Pregnancy: avoid in early pregnancy due to possible foetal malformations (e.g. cleft lip and palate). Use in late pregnancy may cause neonatal withdrawal syndrome.
- Breastfeeding: should not be prescribed as significant amounts enter breast milk.

Antidepressants

Tricyclic antidepressants

Specific serotonin reuptake inhibitors

- Women may need smaller doses than men but, as for men, adequate doses for at least 4–6 months should be used.
- Reports of hyperprolactinaemia in patients on higher than average doses of SSRIs have occurred. This can result in menstrual dysfunction and lactation in non-parturient women.
- Pregnancy and breastfeeding: these drugs should be avoided if possible, but can be used if there are compelling reasons to do so. No clear causal association with congenital malformations have been found in studies of both types of drug (Kulin *et al.*, 1998; Simon *et al.*, 2002).

Mood stabilisers

Lithium salts
Carbamazepine
Sodium valproate

- Doses of lithium may need to be varied during differing phases of the menstrual cycle
- The OCP may become ineffective when taken with carbamazepine as its metabolism is accelerated. Another method of contraception should be considered.
- Pregnancy: all these drugs are associated with major congenital abnormalities. If lithium is restarted at the end of pregnancy, the increase in maternal blood volume must be allowed for. At childbirth, diuresis occurs leading to increased risk of lithium toxicity.
- Breastfeeding: lithium and carbamazepine should not be prescribed as significant amounts enter breast milk. Valporate enters breast milk but at much lower levels.

Antipsychotics

- Increased risk of hyperprolactinaemia in women, with subsequent menstrual dysfunction, suppression of ovulation, infertility and lactation in non-parturient women.
- Pregnancy: no clear evidence for congenital abnormalities, but few drugs have been studied. Chlorpromazine given in late pregnancy may cause neonatal jaundice. In addition antipsychotics may produce extrapyramidal side-effects in the newborn (restlessness, stiffness, tremor and muscle spasms).
- Breastfeeding: enter breast milk but no gross motor abnormalities have been observed as a result. However, Yoshida (1998) advises caution in their use after finding cognitive decline over time in infants breastfed by mothers on antipsychotics.

References

Baldwin, R. (1999) Aetiology of late-life depression. *Advances in Psychiatric Treatment* 5: 435–42.

Caird, H. and Worrall, A. (2003) *The ECT Accreditation Service: Standards for the administration of ECT*. London: Royal College of Psychiatrists Research Unit.

Charlton, J., Kelly, S., and Dunnell, K. (1992) Trends in suicide deaths in England and Wales. *Population Trends* 69: 10–16.

Cobb, A. (1993) *Safe and Effective? MIND's Views on Psychiatric Drugs, ECT and Psychosurgery*. London: MIND publications.

Dawkins, K. and Potter, W.Z. (1991) Gender differences in pharmacokinetics and pharmacodynamics of psychotropics: focus on women. *Psychopharmacology Bulletin* 27(4): 417–26.

Table 20.1 Receptor binding profiles of new atypical antipsychotics compared with conventional antipsychotics

Receptor	Conventional antipsychotic	Risperidone	Quetiapine	Olanzapine	Amisulpiride	Clozapine
Dopamine (D2)	Yes	Yes	Yes	Yes	Yes	Yes
Dopamine (D3)	No	No	No	Yes	Yes	Yes
Serotonin (5HT)	No	No	Yes	Yes	No	Yes
Muscarinic	Yes	No	No	Yes	No	Yes
Histaminic	Yes	No	Yes	Yes	No	Yes
α adrenergic	Yes	Yes	Yes	Yes	No	Yes

Table 20.2 Side-effects of different antipsychotic medications

Side-effect	Conventional antipsychotic	Risperidone	Quetiapine	Olanzapine	Amisulpiride	Clozapine
Extrapyramidal side-effects	Yes	Occasionally	No	Rare	Yes	No
Sedation	Varies	Slight	Yes	Yes	No	Yes
Anticholinergic (blurred vision, constipation, etc.)	Varies	Occasionally	Yes	Yes	No	Yes
Weight gain	Varies	Occasionally	Occasionally	Yes	Yes	Yes
Raised prolactin	Yes	Yes	No	transiently	Yes	No
QTc prolongation	Yes	Yes	Yes	Yes	Yes	Yes

Department of State for Health (1999) *Reform of the Mental Health Act 1983: Proposals for Consultation.* London: HMSO.

Goldberg, D., Kay, C. and Thompson, L. (1976) Psychiatric morbidity in general practice and the community. *Psychological Medicine* 6: 565–9.

Gregoire, A.J.P., Kumar, R., Everitt, B., Henderson, A.F. and Studd, J.W.W. (1996) Transdermal oestrogen for the treatment of severe postnatal depression. *Lancet* 347: 930–3.

Hohmann, A. (1989) Gender bias in psychotropic drug prescribing in primary care. *Medical Care* 27(5): 478–90.

Horwitz, A. (1977) The pathways into psychiatric treatment: some differences between men and women. *Journal of Health and Social Behaviour* 18(2): 169–78.

Howland, J.S., Baker, M.G. and Poe, T. (1990) Does patient education cause side effects? A controlled trial. *Journal of Family Practice* 31(1): 62–4.

Jenkins, R., Lewis, G., Bebbington, P., Brugha, T., Farrell, M., Gill, B. and Meltzer, H. (1997) The National Psychiatric Morbidity surveys of Great Britain: initial findings from the household survey. *Psychological Medicine* 27(4): 775–89.

Jensvold, M., Halbreich, U. and Hamilton, J. (1996) *Psychopharmacology and Women: Sex, Gender and Hormones.* Washington, DC: American Psychiatric Press.

King, D., Griffiths, K., Reilly, P. and Merret, J. (1982) Psychotropic drug use in Northern Ireland 1966–80: prescribing trends, inter and intra-regional comparisons and relationships to demographic and socioeconomic variables. *Psychological Medicine* 12(4): 819–33.

Kulin, N.A., Pastuszak, A., Sage, S.R., Schick-Boschetto, B., Spivey, G. *et al.* (1998) Pregnancy outcome following maternal use of the new selective serotonin reuptake inhibitors: a prospective controlled multicenter study. *JAMA* 279(8): 609–10.

Lawrie, T.A., Hofmeyr, G.J., de Jager, M., Berk, M., Paiker, J. and Viljoen, E.A. (1998) Double blind randomised placebo controlled trial of postnatal norethisterone enthanate: the effect on postnatal depression and serum hormones. *British Journal of Obstetrics and Gynaecology* 105: 1082–90.

Lawrie, T.A., Herxheimer, A. and Dalton, K. (2000) Oestrogens and progestogens for preventing and treating postnatal depression. *Cochrane Database Systematic Review* (2): CD001690.

National Institute for Clinical Excellence (NICE) (2003) *Guidance on the Use of Electroconvulsive Therapy.* Technology Appraisal 59. London: NICE.

Nicol-Smith, L. (1996) Causality, menopause and depression: a critical review of the literature. *British Medical Journal* 313: 1229–32.

Olfson, M. and Klerman, G.L. (1992) The treatment of depression: prescribing practices of primary care physicians and psychiatrists. *Journal of Family Practice* 35(6): 627–35.

Pharoah, P. and Melzer, D. (1995) Variation in prescribing of hypnotics, anxiolytics and antidepressants between 61 general practices. *British Journal of General Practice* 45(400): 595–9.

Sichel, D., Cohen, L., Robertson, L. *et al.* (1995) Prophylactic oestrogen in recurrent postpartum affective disorder. *Biological Psychiatry* 38(120): 814–18.

Simon, G.E., Cunningham, M.C. and Davis, R.L. (2002) Outcomes of prenatal antidepressant exposure. *American Journal of Psychiatry* 159(12): 2055–61.

UK ECT Review Group (2003) Efficacy and safety of electroconvulsive therapy in depressive disorders: a systematic review and meta-analysis. *Lancet* 361(9360): 799–808.

Yoshida, K., Smith, B., Craggs, M. and Kumar, R. (1998) Neuroleptic drugs in breast-milk: a study of pharmacokinetics and of possible adverse effects in breast-fed infants. *Psychological Medicine* 28(1): 81–91.

Young, S., Hurt, P., Benedek, D. and Howard, R. (1998) Treatment of premenstrual dysphoric disorder with sertraline during the luteal phase: a randomised, double-blind, placebo-controlled crossover trial. *Journal of Clinical Psychiatry* 59(2): 76–80.

Useful addresses

ECT Anonymous

Address: 33/34 Caroline Street, Hull, HU2 8DY
Phone 01482 585244
Fax: 01482 320525
Information and advice on all issues surrounding the use of electroconvulsive therapy (ECT). For people who have had ECT or others who want to find out more about ECT before accepting treatment. Well-established campaigning organisation.
Special interest activities: involvement in occasional demos, meetings, etc.
Opening hours: Mon–Fri 10am–2pm
Referral: open access
Criteria/Catchment: national catchment

Medication helpline

Phone: 020 7919 2999
Description: telephone helpline offering confidential information and advice on all aspects of psychiatric medication. Run by qualified psychiatric pharmacist.
Opening hours: Mon–Fri 11am–5pm. Not bank holidays
Referral: open access
Criteria/catchment: national helpline

MIND – Pharmacist

Phone: 020 8215 2274
Description: confidential and impartial information and advice on psychiatric medication. This line is currently open on Thursday mornings only.
Opening hours: every Thursday 9.15–11.45am

20 Psychodynamic psychotherapies

Dr Sarah Majid

INTRODUCTION

This chapter aims to give a brief overview of psychodynamic psychotherapy. I will look very briefly at the underlying theory and what psychodynamic psychotherapy involves in practice. I will consider some of the specific issues in relation to women. Various forms of psychodynamic psychotherapy are described, as are some broader applications of psychoanalytical ideas. The chapter ends by looking briefly at some of the feminist criticisms of early psychoanalytical theory and subsequent developments in theory and practice.

Women often prefer to explore their difficulties with another and to opt for a 'talking therapy'. Psychotherapy in its broadest sense is a talking treatment, and involves the consideration of psychological influences on the presentation of problems (emotional/behavioural/ physical) and the use of the doctor / patient relationship as a therapeutic tool.

The psychodynamic (or psychoanalytic) psychotherapies, to varying degrees, are rooted in the theory and utilise the techniques of psychoanalysis, originally defined by Freud and developed by subsequent analysts such as Anna Freud, Jung, Klein, Fairburn, Winnicott, Bion and others. Psychoanalytical concepts of personality development, psychopathology and symptom formation all inform psychodynamic psychotherapy.

A full explanation of these concepts is beyond the scope of this chapter. Key concepts include:

- The concept of the **unconscious** as a part of the mind containing repressed material (feelings, anxieties, memories) that finds expression through dreams, parapraxes (slips of the tongue) and symptoms.
- Understanding the mind in terms of **basic instincts** and **conflict**. Unacceptable instinctual wishes are repressed, with unconscious conflict giving rise to symtpoms
- A **structural model** of the mind divided into 3 components; **Id** - irrational and concerned with inborn drives and impulses; **Superego** - internal representation of aspired to ideals (conscience) and **Ego** – the rational

and executive aspect that negotiates the demands of external and internal reality.

- **Defences** – unconscious, habitual mental procedures that enable the ego to manage intrapsychic conflict e.g. between instinctive needs (Id) and internalized prohibitions (Super-ego) or, between internal wishes and external reality. They can be normal and adaptive or pathological. (For further details see Bateman and Holmes 1995).
- **Enactment** – action as a substitute for remembering. This includes acting out as the direct behavioural expression of an unconscious impulse that avoids awareness of the accompanying affect.
- A **talking treatment**, with reconstruction of a narrative and catharsis providing relief from symptoms in making the unconscious conscious. Techniques of free association and transference and dream interpretaion.
- **Transference**–"the experiencing of feelings, drives, attitudes, fantasies and defences towards a person in the present, which do not befit the person but are a repetition of reactions originating in regard to significant persons of early childhood, unconsciously displaced onto figures in the present" (from Greenson, 1967) originally described by Freud in 1895.
- **Countertransference** – the therapist's attitudes and emotions towards the patient that may originate from either the therapists own unresolved problems (inappropriately transferred on to the patient), or be evoked in the therapist, by the patient, through projective processes.

PSYCHCOANALYTICAL PSYCHOTHERAPY IN PRACTICE

Psychoanalytical psychotherapy aims to understand the woman's difficulties in relation to unconscious conflicts or deficits and to alleviate these using interpretations. Symptoms are understood as arising from the unconscious and carrying symbolic meaning. Unconscious conflicts are uncovered through the use of free association and through the systematic use of the therapist–patient relationship, including the transference relationship and countertransference experiences. Psychodynamic therapists use techniques common to a variety of psychological treatments such as empathic listening, reflection, clarification and confrontation (drawing attention to repeated behaviour, of which the patient may be unaware). There is however an emphasis on the experience of the therapeutic / transference relationship, which enables an understanding of how the patient relates to others which is in turn determined by significant childhood relationships. Over time a psychodynamic formulation is arrived at which links the current symptoms, childhood conflict or deficit and the transference situation.

The therapeutic relationship is seen as enabling exploration, insight and change. Within the sessions there is a lack of structure which aims to allow the anxieties and associated defences, arising from the patient's unconscious, to come to the fore relatively undistorted by immediate goals, questions or therapist preconceptions.

In the NHS, patients are usually seen individually once weekly for a up to a year, or offered group therapy for a longer period. Rarely, psychotherapy departments are able to offer twice or thrice weekly individual sessions for longer periods for patients with more severe difficulties who are considered able to make use of such intensive work. Patients may also be referred to a specialist psychotherapeutic day hospital or residential setting, as required.

Alternatively, patients may be redirected into the private sector (if feasible financially) or to one of a number of a non-statutory services where they can receive individual or group psychotherapy at a reduced fee. In London, the London Centre and The Women's Therapy Centre offer therapy on a means tested sliding scale. The British Association of Psychotherapists (BAP), the Lincoln Centre and the London Centre for Psychotherapy also offer low fee sessions with experienced clinicans currently in further psychoanalytic psychotherapy training. Similarly, the London Clinic of Psychoanalysis can offer affordable psychoanalysis.

Assessment for psychotherapy

Prior to being offered psychotherapy, a woman referred for psycho-therapeutic help will undergo an assessment. The assessor aims to empathic-ally understand the patient's current predicament, bringing together current difficulties, childhood issues and the transference situation in a tentative psychodynamic formulation. Ideally the interview provides an experience of psychodynamic therapeutic contact which can help the patient make an informed treatment choice. This will also enable the clinician to assess the patient's ability to use and benefit from psychoanalytic interventions, e.g. the patient's response to a trial interpretation. Features in the assessment interview associated with suitability for psychodynamic psychotherapy include the ability to form a good working alliance, the ability to work with interpretations, and the capacity to respond affectively in the session, such as to allow feelings of fear, sadness or anger to surface. (Orlinsky and Howard, 1986)

Stern (2000) has described certain key questions to consider in assessment for psychotherapy: Are the person's difficulties understandable in psycho-logical terms? Is there sufficient motivation for insight and change? Is per-sonal responsibility for difficulties denied and / or projected into others who are blamed? Has the patient the capacity to form and maintain relationships?

Does the patient have the requisite ego strength? The patient must be able to cope with the emotions stirred up by therapy without being overwhelmed, acting destructively or becoming psychotic i.e. maintaining contact with the therapist through an adult part of the self in the working alliance whilst being in sufficient contact with powerful feelings and a more childlike part to enable exploration of these.

There are also factors that may be contraindications to therapy, these include:

Repeated suicide attempts, gross deliberate self-harm and violence towards others. These suggest that the patient is unable to safely contain difficult feelings and resorts to dangerously acting out the feelings instead. This is likely to worsen in therapy with risk to the safety of the patient and others.

Addictions: The ongoing use of psychoactive substances to manage difficult feelings demonstrates the patient's inability to tolerate these sufficiently for therapeutic exploration and understanding. Patients are likely to use substances to blot out the feelings stirred up by therapy and addictions may worsen or relapse in treatment. However psychotherapy may be helpful and appropriate after a substantial period of stable abstinence, as part of longer- term relapse prevention.

Psychosis: Impaired boundaries and difficulty distinguishing fantasy from reality render these patients unable to distinguish their own thoughts from those of others and unable to use the 'as if' quality of transference work. However patients with psychotic illnesses (especially bipolar) may benefit from psychodynamic work in remission. This should be done in close liaison with their community psychiatric team.

Somatisation: Women who suffer from chronic somatisation (physical symptoms as an expression of psychic pain) as an ongoing solution to unmanageable conflict, tend not to engage in psychodynamic work and it is not generally considered helpful. However, those with less ingrained somatisation, who are able to consider psychological causes, may be helped (Guthrie, 1996). Recent work by Guthrie et al (1991) has demonstrated the usefulness of dynamic therapy with patients with irritable bowel syndrome.

Similarly, patients with severe chronic obsessional or phobic disorders tend to respond poorly to psychodynamic approaches.

Request for a female therapist

Female patients not uncommonly request to see a female therapist. The sociocultural dynamic in which women feel disempowered in relation to men can be exacerbated by the power differential in therapy between the patient (struggling and asking for help) and the therapist (supposed to have answers or be in control). Women who have been abused by men may anticipate that they will feel safer and more easily trust a woman. Others anticipate finding it easier to discuss intimate issues and feel understood by someone of the same sex. Departments will usually try to meet such requests if possible, however it may affect waiting times. Patients are vulnerable in the therapeutic situation, however actual abuse of patients by therapists is extremely rare, and there is more variation between individual therapists than between the genders with regard to therapeutic integrity and skill. Previous experience of abusive males will inevitably powerfully influence the transference towards the male therapist. There is clearly much to be gained if the patient is able to tolerate this situation, work through their anxieties in the therapeutic situation and come to trust the male therapist. However this must be balanced with the need to form a working alliance in which such issues can be explored and resolved. For some patients the powerfulness of initial negative transference feelings may prevent them from engaging in therapy at all. In such cases it makes sense to offer a female therapist if possible. This may be particularly relevant in the context of the limited time available in NHS psychotherapy. During the course of treatment, transference feelings originating in experiences with both men and women will inevitably be revived and can be worked with, regardless of the gender of the therapist. However some psychotherapists believe that for women with certain problems such as reproductive issues, male sexual abuse as a child, or loss of mother before puberty it may be beneficial to see a female therapist (Raphael-Leff, 1997). Some services, such as the Women's Therapy Centre offer an exclusively female setting with all female therapists and an explicit interest in working with women's issues and experience of working with a wide range of issues including childhood sexual abuse, self-harm and violent relationships.

PSYCHODYNAMIC PSYCHOTHERAPY SUBTYPES

Brief focused dynamic Psychotherapies

These have developed more recently in the context of limited treatment duration available in the NHS. They are considered dynamic therapies because they use ideas from psychoanalysis, such as linking symptoms to childhood experience and working with the therapeutic relationship. Holmes (1994) defined Brief Dynamic Psychotherapy as a time limited psycho-analytically based psychotherapy lasting anything from 6–40 sessions. Specific adaptations include identifying a focus for treatment, focus on termination issues, a more active therapist role and follow up. Good indications include a circumscribed problem, motivation for change, at least one good relationship and the capacity for psychological mindedness.

Based on the work of Malan (1979), *focal psychoanalytic psychotherapy* for one year has been shown to be effective in the treatment of late onset (>19yrs) anorexia and bulimia compared with standard outpatient treatment. The symptom is linked to past relationships and understood in terms of its function in relationships to avoid interpersonal feelings and feared risks of being adult or sexual (Eisler, 1997). Guthrie ((1991) has demonstrated the use of brief dynamic therapy in work with patients with irritable bowel syndrome.

Cognitive Analytical Therapy (CAT) (Ryle, 1990)

This psychodynamic therapy also shares features with CBT in being struc-tured and explicitly collaborative with homework and the use of cognitive tools (CAT specific). Patients are usually offered 16–24 weekly sessions. Early sessions are spent identifying *target problems* for therapy (eg relationship difficulties) and *target problem procedures*, which maintain these. These include *traps* (vicious circles of thinking and behaving) *dilemmas* (actions based on false choices) and *snags* (ways in which the patient undermines their own fulfilment). These are understood as dysfunctional ways of coping with feelings that actually perpetuate the *core pain* and are thought to originate in early relationship experiences which form a blue print for subsequent relationships. These blueprints are conceptualised in terms of *reciprocal roles*, and may be based on experience ('neglecting – neglected') or on compensatory fantasy ('perfect caring – perfectly cared for') and are manifest in current relationships and the therapeutic relationship. The therapist's understanding of the patient is shared with the patient in the *reformulation letter*, which explicitly links target problems, target problem procedures and reciprocal roles to childhood experience. Current symptoms and maintaining behaviours are brought together diagrammatically in the *Sequential Diagrammatic Reformulation.* Therapy aims to promote recognition and revision of these, using a wide range of techniques including diary writing, imagery, no send letters, cognitive behavioural experiments and reciprocal role interpretations to promote insight and behavioural change. At the end of therapy, the therapy is reviewed explicitly in terms of problems addressed and those remaining through the exchange of *goodbye letters.*

CAT has been used with a variety of conditions including depression, eating disorders and borderline personality disorder.

Family therapy

In family therapy, an individual's symptoms are understood in the context of the family group in which the illness has arisen and is maintained. Families are seen in conjoint interviews, with the opportunity for additional separate sessions for individuals or parents if required.

In this country family therapy has been largely influenced by systems theory, which states that a component can only be understood as a function of the total system. Problems are understood in terms of the ongoing interactions between family members, so that any causality is circular. This is useful in identifying processes that maintain the symptom and can be subject to change, rather than blaming an individual or symptom. The family is understood as a dynamic system that changes over time in interaction with the environment. Symptoms often occur at disruption or transition points in the family lifecycle such as birth, death etc, which require renegotiation of patterns of interaction and establishment of a new family equilibrium. (For further details see Stern, 2000).

Family systems therapy has been shown to be effective in the treatment of early onset (<19yrs), short duration (<3yrs) anorexia nervosa or bulimia nervosa in a series of controlled trials at the Maudsley Hospital (patients with late onset were helped more by individual focal psychoanalytic psycho-therapy) (Dare et al. 1990).

Family interventions have also been demonstrated as effective in pre-venting relapse of schizophrenia in families with high expressed emotion (Leff 1994).

Group therapy

Group therapy provides an interpersonal context in which individuals' feelings and problems can be shared and explored, and their difficulties doing this in relation to others can be understood. It can often be helpful for patients who feel threatened by individual work, who need to observe ways of relating other than their previous interpersonal experiences, or for patients with specific anxieties relating to others (eg social phobia). The group is also a setting in which pathological behaviour can be challenged by fellow group members more directly than in individual psychoanalytic psychotherapy.

Yalom (1985) emphasised certain therapeutic factors specific to groups including Universality, Altruism, Imitative behaviour, Interpersonal learning, Guidance, Cohesiveness, Catharsis, Development of socialising techniques, Insight, Instillation of Hope, Existential factors (including the recognition of responsibility) and Corrective recapitulation of the family group (ie early family processes can be repeated and recognized in the group, where less maladaptive responses can be worked out). Pairing, sub-grouping and idealisation of the therapist are seen as destructive.

Bion emphasised the primitive states of mind ("basic assumptions") that are activated whenever people come together as a group. These include dependence (expecting solutions to be solved by the group leader), Fight-flight (fleeing from or battling with adversaries especially outside the group) and Pairing (encouraging individuals in the group to couple in the hope of a person or idea that would provide group salvation). These may dominate the group and interfere with its "work task". (For further details see Brown and Pedder, 1991).

There are a variety of group therapeutic approaches available within the NHS. Psychotherapy Departments tend to offer small group work with 8–10 patients and a single or two co-therapists. The waiting lists are usually shorter than for individual work. Groups are usually time-limited (usually at least 18 months) but may be open ended.

Most therapy groups are mixed. Some centres offer women's only groups, which may be helpful for women with a fear of men based on previous experience. Clearly, however, issues in relationships with men need to be worked through in treatment. Recommendations regarding a mixed or single sex group for a particular woman need to weigh up the therapeutic value of being in a mixed situation which stirs up pertinent difficulties making them available for working through, and the need to offer something that the patient will be able to engage with and use helpfully.

Therapeutic communities

The Therapeutic Community was first described by Main as an institution in which the setting itself is designed to restore morale and promote the psychological treatment of emotional disturbance. The most well known example is the Henderson Hospital, whose structure and working strategy demonstrates the characteristic features of permissiveness, reality confrontation, democracy and communalism. The permissiveness encourages the expression and enactment of disturbed feelings and relationships, which can then be examined by staff and patients alike. Staff/ patient differences are minimized with patients having the majority vote in decision-making, in particular procedures regarding admission, disciplining and discharge. Patients are often those with severe personality disorders. They undergo small and large group psychotherapy as part of their participation in the residential setting. The treatment has been shown to be cost effective through reducing patients' deliberate self-harm, inpatient admissions, psychological distress and improving self esteem in the year post treatment. (Dolan and Norton, 1998). Main himself founded the Cassel Hospital, which offers individual psychoanalytic psychotherapy in addition to large and small group work in a residential setting.

There are also an increasing number of day services in which patients do similar work in a non-residential community. This has recently been shown to be effective in the treatment of borderline personality disorder. (Bateman and Fonagy, 1999)

Some of the principles of a therapeutic community are used in other settings such as residential drug rehabilitation units and supported accommodation for psychiatric patients. (For further details see Brown and Pedder, 1991: Stern, 2000)

BROADER APPLICATIONS OF PSYCHOANALYTIC IDEAS

Psychoanalytic ideas are useful in many areas outside formal Psychoanalytical Psychotherapy:

Psychodynamic formulations of psychiatric patients

An attempt to understand the development of the patients' difficulties and current relationships in the context of childhood experience should be made in all psychiatric assessments.

Working group dynamics

Group theory has been applied to understanding problems in staff teams and institutional settings. Some teams now have regular facilitated staff groups to explore and manage ongoing difficulties arising in the work context.

Transference and counter-transference in therapeutic relationships

Transference occurs in many situations, particularly with health professionals, who may be inappropriately feared, resented, idealised, or desired. The awareness of this and the recognition of counter-transference experiences in staff is crucial to avoid staff acting out towards patients and potentially re-enacting the patients earlier experiences e.g. of neglect or abuse.

Disruptive patients

There is an increasing emphasis on trying to understand such patients in terms of the dynamic between members of staff and the patient, e.g. a borderline patient (using primitive defences such as splitting) on an inpatient ward where staff are *split* between those who sympathise with the patient and wish to offer more protection and those who see the patient as bad and manipulative and call for immediate discharge. Where possible, it is important to try to contain these aspects of the patient within the team, think clearly about management and avoid acting out countertransference feelings in response to the patients' intense projective processes of anger or helplessness.

PSYCHOANALYSIS AND FEMINISM

As many women undergo psychoanalytical treatment, it is helpful to consider some of the feminist criticisms of psychoanalysis. Although Freud's concepts remain central to psychoanalysis some of his ideas, especially about women, have been increasingly questioned and revised as part of the evolution of theory and practice. In particular, Freud's ideas have come under attack from feminists as part of a wider sociocultural critique of universalist assumptions about human nature, perpetuated by scientific or medical theories; notably, his theories of male and female development and infantile sexuality. These are deconstructed as having evolved in the patriarchal context of turn of the century Vienna, and becoming part of a discourse which perpetuates male and female inequality through apparent scientific justification of cultural gender roles. Attention is drawn to his association with a number of writers of his time such as Hall, Fleiss and Deutsch who expounded deterministic theories of female psychology as dominated by reproductive physiology.

These are seen as justifying traditional female roles as passive, uncreative, non-competitive wives and mothers needing male protection and physically confined to a domestic world. Critics also emphaise the limited evidence for his theory, being based on his self- analysis, analysis of his daughter and a series of case studies.

For Freud, the Oedipus complex was key to understanding the development of an individual personality , with resolution resulting in healthy male and female development. In his view little boys love and wish exclusive possession of mother but fear retaliatory castration by father, with inevitable rivalry . The situation resolves when the boy gives up this wish in favour of an identificatory bond with father and the promise of true potency in the future. Freud assumed a similar scenario for girls, who love their fathers, wish to replace their mothers and lacking the essential organ of power and significance, feel powerless. In resolution, the girl identifies with the mother and believes that her lack of a penis will be compensated by her capacity to attract and 'have' a man and to produce a baby.

Freud's original theories of development and infantile sexuality have been significantly developed and altered over the years, in line with a more modern view of women as different but equal to men.

Many of the early influential analysts were women (Melanie Klein, Anna Freud) and there was much lively debate in the 1920's and 30's, particularly over the issue of femininity and female sexuality. Freud's theory was rejected as a phallocentric account of femininity as reactive, and constructed on a masculine foundation, with the wish for a baby as a secondary compromise formation. Klein emphasised instead primary femininity and the little girl's innate knowledge of a vagina. Horney, emphasised the wish to receive a penis and create a baby in its own right, rather than as a penis substitute. She attributed the notion of female deficiency (with inferior genitals) to 'masculine narcissism' and stressed fear of the archaic mother, with 'womb envy' and social denigration of mothering as accounting for male 'dread of women' and denial of the vagina (1932) (see Raphael-Leff, 1997)

More recently feminists have drawn on Lacan's emphasis on the phallus as symbolic of power, in a society structured by patriarchy in its language, thought and individual identity. They used Freud's ideas to explain the cultural construction of femininity and masculinity, with perceptions of women as inferior, powerless and marginalised underpinned at an unconscious level. In this way the oedipus complex has been used to offer an exposition of the sociocultural construction of gendered power relations and nuclear family norms, rather than a deterministic account of the normative route of development (Mitchell, 1974)

Freud's understanding of hysteria has come under particular scrutiny His initial understanding, based on the narrative accounts of Dora, the young woman he analysed, identified *actual* childhood sexual abuse as a crucial aetiological factor. He subsequently revised his theory, focusing on childhood sexual *fantasy* as being aetiologically important with her symptoms expressing repressed desires. Subsequently Freud's own lack of awareness of transference and counter transference factors have been highlighted in his (mis)understanding of her case. His retraction of his initial theory of actual sexual trauma and emphasis on Dora's memory as fantasy has also been understood as reflecting his inability as a conservative 19th century man to tolerate a belief in the existence of childhood sexual abuse as a social fact. This has been seen as contributing to the continuing lack of investigation and silence surrounding sexual abuse for much of the past century (Astbury, 1996).

Clearly the potential reality of sexual abuse is now well accepted and incorporated into psychoanalytical aetiological understanding. Socioculturally however, the fear persists of a psychoanalyst as someone with fixed beliefs, who imposes theory coercively and dismisses disagreement or distress as resistance and proof of validity, abusing the power of the therapeutic situation and the vulnerability of patients. For the overwhelming majority of psychoanalysts and psychoanalytical psychotherapists this is an unfortunate mistaken fear that may well prevent women accessing valuable, effective psychotherapeutic help.

Further developments in psychoanalysis

While Freud's concepts remain central to psychoanalysis and psychoanalytic psychotherapy today, therapeutic work in the UK has been increasingly influenced by object relations theory, in which individual psychology is dominated by very early relationships to others. Early women analysts, such as Klein (1977), moved away from the role of the father to a focus on the early mother–infant relationship. She described the *paranoid schizoid* position where the infant has a split experience of mother as either an idealised good object or a denigrated persecuting bad object. The crucial developmental move to the *depressive* position involves both the integration of the good and bad aspects of mother, and the infant's experience of itself and mother as separate, with associated feelings of loss, guilt and reparation. Failure of this results in the predominance of primitive defence mechanisms such as splitting. These early psychological processes are considered the same for male and female infants. The issues of the oedipal complex remain pertinent to the infants crucial developmental move from a two person (mother–infant) to a three person relationship (incorporating a relation to father). This involves the infant's painful acceptance of the reality of his/her position in relation to the sexual relationship of the parental couple. The negotiation of this is seen as having a profound effect both on our sexuality and on our ability to think and use symbols. It is seen essential for healthy development and interpersonal relations.

The influence of Klein and others such as Winnicott (1965), Fairburn and Bion (1962) on psychoanalytical developments is reflected in the emphasis, in current work, on the development and interpretation of the therapeutic relationship as a crucial component of change. There has also been increasing interest in the impact of external reality, such as adverse childhood experience, which represents a broadening of the initial focus on the fantasies and drives of internal reality. More recently there has been an interest in understanding, psychodynamically, issues of particular relevance to women such as pregnancy, abortion, perinatal loss and postnatal depression (Raphael-Leff, 1993; 1997). There has also been an increasing interest in investigating early attachment patterns to caregivers, and in joint mother–infant psychotherapy.

Psychodynamic psychotherapy can offer a woman the opportunity to gain more conscious awareness and understanding of her difficulties, and increase her capacity for more fulfilling relationships and enjoyment and engagement in life. This type of therapy is not suitable for all women, but is likely to benefit a significant proportion of women seeking help for emotional difficulties. Below is a list of references for those who wish to learn more about this mode of therapy.

References

Astbury, G. (1996) *Crazy for You – The making of Womens Madness*, Melbourne: Oxford University Press.

Bateman, A. and Holmes, J. (1995) *Intoduction to Psychoanalysis: Contemporary Theory and Practice*, London: Routledge.

Bion, W. (1962) Learning from experience. London: Heinman.

Brown, D. and Pedder, J. (1993) *Introduction to Psychotherapy: An outline of psychodynamic principles and practice*, 2nd (ed.) London: Routledge.

Dare, C., Eisler, I., Russell, G. and Szmukler, G. (1990) Family therapy for anorexia nervosa. Implications from the results of a controlled trial of family and individual therapy, *Journal of Marital and Family Therapy* 16: 39–57.

Fonagy, P. & Bateman, A. (1999) Effectiveness of partial hospitalisation in the treatment of Borderline Personality Disorder: A randomised controlled trial. *American Journal of Psychiatry* 156, 10: 1563–69.

Freud, S. (1895) *Studies in Hysteria*. Standard Edition. London: Hogarth.

Freud, S. (1914) *Introductory Lectures on Psychoanalysis*. Standard edition. London: Hogarth.

Freud, S. (1900) *The Interpretation of Dreams*. Standard Edition. London: Hogarth.

Freud, S., (1856–1939). *On Sexuality: Three essays on the theory of sexuality, and other works*. A. Richards (ed) (1977) Harmondsworth: Penguin.

Greenson, R. (1967) *The technique and practice of Psychoanalysis*. London: Hogarth Press.

Guthrie, E. *et al.* (1991) A controlled trial of treatment for Irritable Bowel Syndrome. Gastroenterology 1991, 100, 450–7.

Guthrie, E. (1996).Psychotherapy for Somatization disorders. *Current Opinion in Psychiatry* 9: 182–7.

Holmes, J. (1994) Brief Dynamic Psychotherapy, *Advances in Psychiatric Treatment* 1, 1: 9–15.

Klein, M. (1977) *Envy, Gratitude and other works 1946–63*. New York: Delta Books.

Kryzowski, S. and Land, P. (1988) *In our experience: Workshops at the Women's Therapy Centre* – Women's Press.

Lawrence, M. and Maguire, M. (eds) (1997) *Psychotherapy with women – femisnist perspectives* Macmillan.

Lawrence, M. (1987) (eds) *Fed Up and Hungry: Women, Oppression and Food* Women's Press 1994 reprint.

Lawrence, M. (1984) *The Anorexic Experience*–Marilyn Lawrence The Women's Press 1998 reprint.

Orbach, S. (1978/82) *Fat is a Feminist Issue*. Arrow publications.

Orbach, S. (1998) *Fat is a Feminist Issue II*. Arrow publications.

Orbach, S. (1986) *Hungerstrike* Penguin. 1993 reprint.

Leff, J. (1994) Working with families of schizophrenic patients. *British Journal of Psychiatry* 164 (supp 23), 4: 71–76.

Malan, D. H. (1979) *Individual Psychotherapy and the Science of Psychodynamics*, London: Butterworth.

Mitchell, J. (1974) *Psychoanalysis and Feminism*, Harmondsworth: Penguin.

Orlinsky, D. and Howard, K. (1986) 'Process and outome in psychotherapy' in S. Garfield and A. Bergin (eds) *Handbook of Psychotherapy and Behaviour Change*, London: Wiley.

Powell, A *et al* (1997) *Moving from the Margins – Psychotherapy and black women's experiences.* Women's Therapy Centre.

Raphael-Leff, J. and Perelberg, R. (1997) Female Experience. *Three Generations of British Women Psychoanalysts on Work with Women*, Routledge: London.

Raphael-Leff, J. (1993) *Pregnancy: The inside story*, Sheldon Press: London.

Ryle, A. (1990) *Cognitive Analytic Therapy: Active Participation in Change*, London: Wiley.

Ryle, A. (1997) The structure and development of Borderline personality disorder: a proposed model. *British Journal of Psychiatry* 170: 82–87.

Sandler J., Dare, C. and Holder, A. (1992) *The Patient and the Analyst*, London: Karnac.

Stern, J. (2000) 'Psychotherapy – individual, family and group', in P. Wright, J. Stern, and M. Phelan, (eds) *Core Psychiatry*, WB Saunders: London.

Sutton-Smith, D (1994) *Groups for Incest Survivors:* A Handbook based on practice at the Women's Therapy Centre . The W T C.

Swift, C (1998) *Supporting Women in the community* – report of the women's therapy centre community care project . The WTC.

Treasure, J. L. and Ward, A. (1997) Cognitive Analytic Therapy in the Treatment of Anorexia Nervosa. *Clinical Psychology and Psychotherapy* 4: 62–71.

Yalom, I.D. (1985) *The Theory and Practice of Group Therapy*, New York. Basic Books.

Winnicott, D.W. (1965) *The maturational process and the Facilitating Environment.* London: Hogarth Press.

Useful Addresses

Women's Therapy Centre

Address: 10 Manor Gardens, Islington, London N7 6JS
Phone: 0207 263 6200

Fax: 0207 281 7879

Ema   Opening   hours: Mon-Thurs   9am-9pm,   Fri   till   2.30pm   il: info@womenstherapycentre.co.uk

Website: www.womenstherapycentre.co.uk

This is an exclusively female setting that offers individual and group psychotherapy with female therapists. There is an explicit interest in thinking about links between women's internal worlds and their external circumstances and experience of working with a wide range of issues including eating disorders, childhood sexual abuse, self-harm and violent relationships. The centre runs various self-help groups, and has a database of relevant services. Therapy is offered in Turkish, Greek, Spanish and Portuguese to make therapy available to a wide range of women whose needs might otherwise not be met. The centre also offers consultancy and training service for professionals, including workshops to explore working with women's issues from a feminist perspective. This work has formed the basis of a number of publications including self help literature.

Referral: Self referrals only

Criteria/catchment: women aged 18 plus, Londonwide catchment

21 Cognitive behavioural therapy

Ruth Williams

Introduction

Cognitive Behavioural Therapy (CBT) is a type of psychological therapy that has made a rapid rise to prominence in both professional and public arenas over the past thirty years. It is now widely recognised as an evidence-based treatment approach with application to a range of mental health problems (Roth and Fonagy, 1996). It is best established as a treatment for depression, anxiety disorders and eating disorders. However, exciting developments are emerging in fields as diverse and challenging as psychosis and personality disorder, such that at the present time there seems to be almost no limit to the possibilities for therapy that the cognitive behavioural model offers. Some studies have yielded outcomes of up to 90 per cent recovery in selected randomised controlled trials (Clark *et al.*, 1994). Whilst this section can only provide a brief discussion of theory and therapy with special attention to the needs of women, the reader will find many recent texts which present more detail on the approach in general and on its application to specific problem areas (Beck, 1995; Fowler, Garety and Kuipers, 1995; Clark and Fairburn, 1997; Wells, 1997). There are also a number of excellent self-help books available for use by the patient alone or in combination with individual therapy (Burns, 1990; Gilbert, 1997; Greenberger and Padesky, 1995).

The plan for this section is to briefly outline the features of the cognitive behavioural model and relate these to the phases and techniques of treatment. The model and therapy for depression will be selected as an example, although many of the features of the approach described will be similar for other problems. In the third part some discussion of who responds best to CBT is followed by consideration of the particular applicability of CBT to female patients.

THE COGNITIVE BEHAVIOURAL MODEL

The model upon which CBT is based can be stated very simply as the proposition that the way a person feels is largely determined by the nature of their perceptions or interpretations of themselves and their situations and by the way they behave. This statement has been considerably elaborated as a result of research and clinical activity in the past thirty years such that the details of cognitions and behavioural responses associated with differing emotional problems have been specified and consistent patterns have been observed. In depression, for example, the central theme of loss is associated with helpless and hopeless connotations which engender a sense of defeat and an abandonment of constructive behavioural responses which might otherwise restore a sense of meaning and hope. The depressed person can thus become trapped in a vicious circle linking cognitions, emotions and behaviours which acts to *maintain* an emotional state and prevent recovery. In depression the circle is often between negative thinking (e.g. 'I'm a failure. Nothing I do works out') and behavioural inactivity or social withdrawal. Inactivity or social withdrawal tends to confirm or fail to disconfirm such negative thoughts and the state of inaction itself tends to provide fertile conditions for further negative rumination (e.g. 'I'm so lazy. I can't even get myself to do the housework'). Drawing out these *maintenance* systems (recurrent cycles between self-defeating thoughts, feelings and behaviours) forms an important part of the cognitive behavioural model for problematic mental states.

In addition, one of the notable contributions of A.T. Beck, arguably the foremost innovator in CBT, was to posit an *aetiological* cognitive behavioural model which explains the origins of disorders, distally in early life experiences and, more proximally, in life events which impinge upon areas of personal vulnerability. Beck (1976) proposed that as a part of normal development in early life, cognitive structures, or schema, are laid down as the means by which reactions to environmental stimuli can occur automatically or with minimal attentional resources. Some of these meaning structures can be dysfunctional in that they may distort information processing. When a relevant life event trigger occurs (e.g. a loss or disappointment), they may become activated and result in specific thoughts which are biased and emotion-laden. For example, a child who learns in the family that they must always do their best in all circumstances or else they will be criticised and subject to disapproval (dysfunctional schema) may become anxious about the possibility of failure ('what will mum think?') and depressed and guilty in the face of it ('It's my fault I should have tried harder'). These *dysfunctional assumptions* or underlying rules and attitudes may be similar in content for many people but in vulnerable individuals they are more primitive and extreme. They are also more rigidly and inflexibly applied – hence the importance of terms such as 'always' or 'never' in the formulation above. The principle components of the longitudinal model are illustrated in Figure 21.1.

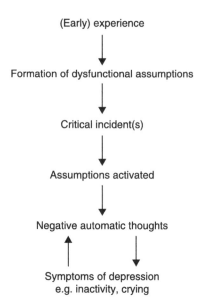

Figure 21.1 Cognitive behavioural model for depression

COGNITIVE BEHAVIOURAL THERAPY (CBT)

CBT is a short-term, problem-focused treatment aimed at symptom relief and the restoration of functioning but also the acquisition of generalisable skills to help the patient make further progress after termination of therapy and deal successfully with adverse events in the future. The therapy proceeds in a sequence of phases each of which is associated with different types of technique and skills to be learned. These phases map onto the components of the model outlined above.

Beginning therapy

In the first phase, the emphasis is problem-oriented assessment and, upon applying the CBT model to the individual's particular difficulties: drawing up a problem list, setting short-term goals and introducing the maintenance model, exploring the links between cognitions, affect and behaviour. This phase is often regarded as a *socialisation* period in which a person is introduced to the main features of the therapy including the model and concepts but also to the structure of the therapy session and its business-like, action-oriented style. Whilst being vigilant and attentive to the content of the patient's personal material, the therapist is active, educational and explicit in introducing procedures and techniques. She is systematic in seeking feedback from the patient about their reactions to therapy in order to deal with misperceptions on both patient's and therapist's parts. In effect this phase can also have considerable cognitive, affective and behavioural consequences, as the patient begins to see their problems in chunks that can be tackled step-by-step. At the same time they will get some greater distance from and understanding of how their thoughts may have tied them into a trap from which it has been difficult to escape on their own.

Preliminary interventions

Following the assessment session the CBT therapist wastes no time in introducing homework activities to take the therapeutic agenda forward. Early interventions may be to some extent informational, e.g. reading pamphlets or chapters selected for relevance to the patient's problems. Wherever possible the therapist will also seek out some elements of behavioural change in order to test out the application of the maintenance model's hypothesis and obtain symptomatic relief. In the case of a depressed patient this could be, for instance, checking out the cognition: 'I'm so lazy. I can't even get myself to do the housework' with a behavioural monitoring task to explore in detail what housework or other productive activities the individual may be doing. This could often be combined with graded task assignment in which a problem that has been left to accumulate is tackled in manageable sections (e.g. spend twenty minutes each day ironing). The completion of an activity monitor is likely to lead to some re-evaluation of their deficiency. It can also lead to interesting discussions about how the patient is spending their time, what they would like to be doing more of, what has led them into their current pattern and its consequences for their mood and well-being.

Core interventions

Typically the third and often core stage of intervention once some mood restoration and symptomatic control has been achieved is the detailed monitoring and challenging of specific negative thoughts associated with problems. The patient is now introduced to noting their specific 'hot' emotion-laden thoughts that occur in response to day-to-day activities and to ways of examining them as part of their homework tasks. Session work then becomes devoted to further work to challenge or test out these cognitions where the patient is having difficulty.

   Challenging negative automatic thoughts is a therapist skill requiring considerable practice. The concept is not to supply the patient with the therapist's own responses or answers nor, and this is crucial, to imply that the person *should* not think in a negative way. Rather the skill is to ask questions that guide the patient to their own new conclusions by requiring them to think about contextual information and previous experiences. This process, called *Socratic questioning*, aims to open up the patient's mind to other interpretations and explanations which can then be subjected to further testing.

For example, the depressed woman who attributed her difficulties in completing her housework to laziness could be engaged in thinking about the experiences she had had in the past that supported such an explanation. Such an exploration could reveal specific experiences of criticism that had fuelled her painful self-doubt. In addition, however, the exploration could also reveal how many instances of activity had not attracted such criticism and bring to memory times in the woman's life when she had felt more energetic and able to get things done without such effort. This discussion can then lead to thinking about how one might make sense of these apparently conflicting pieces of information: is it that she is lazy or is there some other explanation? Could it be that when low in mood she experiences lower levels of energy and motivation? Attributing such states to laziness could then compound the problem by intensifying low mood. In addition it would appear that 'I'm lazy' is an *overgeneralisation*, a common information-processing error encountered in depressed mood whereby one problem or mistake comes to take the shape of a general personal trait. What could be done to test these ideas out further? Such a discussion could then lead to homework experiments aimed at learning which experiences lead to improved mood and energy (as well as, of course, to additional negative thoughts that might block such activity: 'I can't do this when the housework isn't done'). A different course of discussion could take the therapy down the avenue of considering more precisely what 'lazy' means. This could start with asking friends and colleagues, and then evaluating the self and others on *continua* for the more concretely defined criteria. Alternatively it could take the form of an experiment, with being more kind to the self and finding out whether this helped or hindered in getting on with things, or even perhaps to experiment with being temporarily and non-guiltily 'lazy'.

Final stages of therapy

The detailed discussion and discovery of information-processing biases inherent in many specific negative thoughts, as well as the previously explored details of personal history, leads the therapist and patient to consider the themes underlying specific thoughts and the verbal formulation and challenging of dysfunctional assumptions. This further layer of exploration frequently happens spontaneously as a result of the distancing consequences of monitoring and challenging thoughts. For example, the depressed woman may announce that she feels low whenever she is criticised, 'as if I should never do anything wrong or that everyone should always approve of me!' Use of the *downward arrow* technique exploring the implications of a specific negative thought can be useful to arrive at *the bottom line* basic assumptions that drive specific thoughts, e.g. Figure 21.2 shows a downward arrow line of questioning from 'I'm lazy' to arrive at a dysfunctional assumption.

Challenging underlying assumptions involves the patient in processes of rational challenging, exploring childhood origins and considering the context

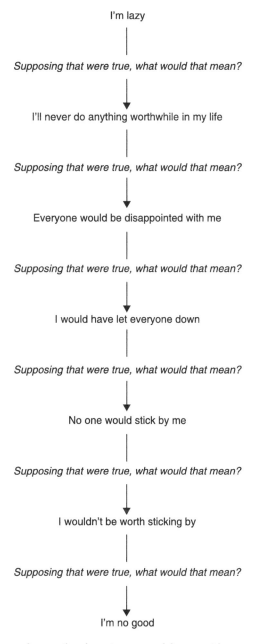

Figure 21.2 Example of a 'downward arrow'

of any such crucial developmental experiences and ultimately of voluntarily contravening them in order to test out the consequences in the context of adult life and relationships. The aim of these techniques is not to radically alter the patient's attitudes and value systems but to crucially increase the band-width of their self-imposed criteria for self-evaluation so that they are not so subject to unnecessary stress in their attempts to meet unrealistic standards. As a result the techniques tend to push the individual up against their vulnerability issues and strengthen their coping techniques or else reveal areas where further work is needed.

CBT is a multi-level therapy which is perhaps more complex than the simplicity of its underlying model would suggest. It requires a great flexibility on the part of the therapist to conceptualise the material the patient brings, to utilise levels of intervention appropriate to the patient's problem intensity and the stage of therapy, and to devise homework tasks with a good fit between patient skills and problems. Relatively little is known at the present about how to select therapists for training and how best these skills are learned. Few therapists have adequate training and, furthermore, therapists with some skills are frequently required to work unsupported by supervision with the complex cases often seen in the secondary services.

Suitability for CBT

Some considerable research interest has been shown in the predictors of a good outcome in CBT in order that therapy can be directed to those who are most likely to benefit from it. However, the findings have not yet yielded clinically useful guidelines. Some findings have not been replicated and others have been seen to reflect more service-related issues, such as the number of sessions available, rather than strong theoretical principles relating to the power of the model. The following combines 20+ years' clinical experience from a service setting and some recent research work as yet unreplicated.

The minimum requirements for CBT are to do with the applicability of the model:

1   The person must have a focal problem(s) that is relatively stable over time rather than highly diffuse and variable.
2   The existence of an identifiable life event trigger, prior to which the individual can recall not having the problem, rather than the problem being lifelong, also makes the problem more easily conceptualised within current Axis 1 CBT models. (Treatments for Axis 2 disorders have not yet been evaluated systematically and are likely to entail more lengthy duration of therapy.)
3   The patient's problem must have identifiable cognitive and behavioural components.

Other issues have to do with the processes of CBT:

4   There must be some minimal interest in pursuing a psychological type of intervention and preferably not a competing wish to pursue some other therapy or medication not yet tried.
5   The patient must accept some personal responsibility for change and their active involvement to promote change through engagement in homework assignments.
6   The patient must be reasonably able to relate to the therapist so that vital information is made known in a relatively short period of time.

This may seem quite a big deal and to be somewhat at odds with the widely held reputation of CBT as an effective treatment for many problems. However, from the point of view of an assessor for CBT, if only point 1 above was considered more often by referrers, the therapy services would be less overloaded by persons on waiting lists who are unlikely to gain significant benefit.

HOW SUITABLE IS CBT FOR FEMALE PATIENTS?

The literature on CBT specifically for women is scant. The CBT models and therapy approaches that have been advanced and studied in trials to date have not often considered gender to be central to the understanding of the disorders studied and to the processes by which individuals change. This is perhaps surprising in view of the differences in incidence between men and women for many problems, although perhaps it is also an advantage in that psychological problems are not attributed to factors that are in principle gender-related and not easily changed.

One researcher (Nolen-Hoeksema, 1987) has suggested that there may be a difference between the typical coping styles of males and females, whereby women are more likely to ruminate on the causes and consequences of emotional distress, whereas men are more likely to distract themselves and do something practical in response to such problems. In this way then, the model of CBT for depression might be particularly applicable to the way some women tend to dwell on their subjective experiences and get immersed in unproductive attempts to make sense of them.

A feminist discussion of therapy approaches (Worell and Remer, 1992) also commends some aspects of CBT as being consistent with the main principles of feminism. The 'collaborative relationship' is particularly consistent with the value placed upon equality in adult relationships. Collaboration is the relationship hallmark of CBT and one that receives much emphasis in training of therapists. Collaboration is essential to the core processes of CBT in which, in a short timeframe the client and therapist must identify and make important changes related to the client's internal world. It is simply not possible to do this if the client holds back, does not reveal their thoughts and feelings and does not tell the therapist when they are off track. In CBT the client's role is to be the expert on their own experiences and an important part of the therapist's role is to create the conditions in which the client can learn that this is expected and valued. The experience of a collaborative relationship of this kind may be a vital aspect of the therapy and perhaps particularly for women who have been used to being treated as if their views and reactions are less significant than those of male peers in family, friendship or work groups. The direct communication required for collaboration could then be a positive and growth-enhancing experience for female patients. But, in some cases, women's experiences may have given them such poor models of adult relationships that there may be severe difficulties in participating in this way over a short therapy timeframe.

Worell and Remer (1992) also point to the 'messages' that women receive from society about being feminine in personal attributes and in relating to men and family responsibilities. They suggest that self-sacrifice, putting others' needs first and taking responsibility for family matters are female themes that could take extreme and rigid forms consistent with Beck's concept of a dysfunctional assumption. This view has been developed in Jack's 'self-silencing' model of female depression (Jack, 1991). However, it must be recognised that some feminist writers do not endorse CBT approaches which focus upon personal meanings but would rather act to change political realities that foster the personal experiences of women (Kitzinger and Perkins, 1993).

More research which investigates the particular themes of content and process in relation to gender and gender roles would be very welcome as an addition to this fertile field of therapeutic activity.

References

Beck, A. T. (1976) *Cognitive Therapy and the Emotional Disorders*, New York: International Universities Press.

Beck, J. S. (1995) *Cognitive Therapy: Basics and Beyond*, New York: Guilford.

Burns, D. D. (1990) *The Feeling Good Handbook*. New York: Plume.

Clark, D.M., Salkovskis, P.M., Hackmann, A., Middleton, H., Anastasiades, P. and Gelder, M. (1994) A comparison of cognitive therapy, applied relaxation and imipramine in the treatment of panic disorder. *British Journal of Psychiatry* 164: 759–69.

Clark, D.M. and Fairburn, C.G. (eds.) (1997) *Science and Practice of Cognitive Behaviour Therapy*. Oxford: Oxford Medical Publications.

Fowler, D., Garety, P. and Kuipers, E. (1995) *Cognitive Behaviour Therapy for Psychosis*. Chichester: Wiley.

Gilbert, P. (1997) *Overcoming Depression*. London: Robinson.

Greenberger, D. and Padesky, C.A. (1995) *Mind Over Mood: A Cognitive Therapy Treatment Manual for Clients*. New York: Guilford Press.

Jack, D.C. (1991) *Silencing the Self: Women and Depression*. Cambridge, MA: Harvard University Press.

Kitzinger, C. and Perkins, R. (1993) *Changing our Minds: Lesbian Feminism and Psychology*, New York: New York University Press.

Nolen-Hoeksema, S. (1987) Sex differences in unipolar depression: evidence and theory. *Psychological Bulletin* 101: 259–82.

Roth, A. and Fonagy, P. (1996) *What Works for Whom? A critical Review of Psychotherapy Research*. New York, London: Guilford Press.

Wells, A. (1997) *Cognitive Therapy for Anxiety Disorder*. Chichester: Wiley.

Worell, J. and Romer, P. (1992) *Feminist Perspectives in Therapy: An Empowerment Model for Women*. Chichester: Wiley.

Useful address

UK Council of Psychotherapy

Address: 167 Great Portland Street, London W1N 5FB

Phone: 0207 436 3002

Fax: 0207 436 3013

Description: maintains a register of qualified professional psychotherapists; contact lists of practitioners in your area free of charge.

Opening hours: office: Mon–Fri, 9am–5.30pm

Referral: open access

22 Complementary therapies

Jo Evans

Introduction

At least 40 per cent of General Practice surgeries now offer alternative treatments, according to a recent Department of Health survey. Complementary medicine has much to offer the treatment of women's mental health problems. Some alternative treatments may be sought as a viable alternative, others will complement conventional treatment. People who present with psychotic behaviour, and who could be a danger to themselves or others, will generally be referred, or treated in conjunction with a conventional practitioner.

This chapter provides an introduction to the principles of medicine shared by alternative therapies in their approach to psychiatric treatment and then describes a selection of therapies individually. The constraints of space mean that only the most readily available therapies are mentioned, and the description is necessarily brief.

Alternative medicine offers a model of treatment which suits many cases, covers body and mind, and is based upon a particular philosophy of health and disease, making its processes and treatment differ from conventional medicine. Alternative therapies do not make a division in the treatment of mental and physical disease; they are *holistic*, treating the mental symptoms or pathology as part of a broader picture which includes the physical, emotional, environmental and spiritual life of the patient.

DEFINING HEALTH AND DISEASE

For an alternative holistic practitioner, mental health is the ability to live with all aspects of the body and mind in harmony, providing clarity, coherence, self-knowledge and creativity. Mental health means the ability to feel the whole range of human emotions without becoming stuck in a particular emotional mode, and to be able to return to a point of balance, or *homeostasis*. In health we have the flexibility and potential to experience life to the full, and are able to reach our full potential as individuals, as well as in groups, in society, in our environment and on a spiritual level.

Disease on the mental and emotional level includes any symptoms or patterns of behaviour which restrict the individual, preventing them from achieving a state of balanced health, as described above. This may include anything from poor memory, phobias and fears, to suicidal depression and delusional states.

This definition of health and disease may be similar to that of conventional medicine. The common aim is to restore the patient to health. However, where the two models diverge is on the *causes* of disease, the *interpretation* of symptoms and the *approach* to treatment.

ENERGY MEDICINE

Reductionist and materialist versus quantum and holistic? The terms used to describe the opposition between conventional and alternative medicine can be confusing. Simply stated, *energy medicine*, which includes, for example, acupuncture, Reiki and homeopathy, bases its practice largely on Einstein's science, where conventional medicine is based largely upon Newtonian principles.

A Newtonian scientist sees the body as an intricate machine. Its components and biological processes can be analysed and recorded in a material way, according to fixed scientific principles. Einstein's equation $E = mc^2$ states that energy and matter are dual expressions of the same universal substance. Applying Einstein's theory to the human mind and body, one can view the individual as being made up of complex energy fields which interface with the physical and cellular systems. This is the principle of alternative medicines. *Energy medicine* works on the principle that when we are sick (mentally or physically), it is the energy fields in the individual's body that are disturbed first. This then manifests in mental and physical symptoms, according to our individual susceptibility (inherited predisposition to disease, environmental factors, etc.).

One person may be susceptible to humidity which always undermines their system, producing an illness, another to sadness and depression. Each individual reacts differently given the same external stimulus.

Energy medicine works by affecting the energy first, e.g. inserting acupuncture needles along meridian lines in the body, or administering homoeopathic potencies, or the laying on of hands. These treatments stimulate healing in the electromagnetic energy fields of the body, which, when correctly applied, then create a resolution and balance on a material or physical level. Once this return to homeostasis is achieved, the symptoms disappear and the person becomes well.

PHYSICAL THERAPIES FOR PSYCHOLOGICAL WELL-BEING

Another important category of alternative treatments is physical therapy such as yoga, meditation and osteopathy. In many cases, there is no fixed philosophical dividing line between physical and energy medicine, as they are working on the same principle of an *energy field* or vital force.

The advantage of the 'physical' therapies is that they have an immediate effect on the mind as well as the health of the body. When this inner calmness is enjoyed by the patient, it helps to create hope and optimism about recovery, as well as encourage a significant change in lifestyle.

It could be argued that these therapies would benefit any psychological symptoms. Physical therapies are useful in 'stress' and 'depression', and 'anxiety' states, as well as in chronic cases where psychological symptoms are combined with musculoskeletal injury or pain. Physical therapies help to re-balance the chemical changes in the body that are often the result of chronic stress, such as rise in basal metabolic rate or lowering of the immune responses.

SCIENTIFIC EVIDENCE AND RESEARCH

As a result of the different philosophical positions taken by conventional and alternative medicine, it is sometimes difficult to prove the effects of alternative medicines according to the conventional Newtonian scientific model. These inherent problems have been documented (Heron, 1986; Lewith and Aldridge, 1993).

Alternative medicine begins with an alternative viewpoint which, while it may be seen as controversial by some, has historical weight centuries older than the beginnings of modern medicine. Long before Einstein's theory, more than 4,000 years ago, the Chinese and Tibetans were successfully using energy medicine (acupuncture, Reiki) in this way.

Quantum physics holds the key to explaining why alternative energy medicines have been so successful for thousands of years. Though there are accepted research studies, much rests still on anecdotal evidence but this tends to indicate many years of successful treatments. Stephen Fulder's *Handbook of Alternative and Complementary Medicine* is an excellent source for information on medical research into the area, and provides the detail which space precludes here.

HOLISTIC: WHAT IT MEANS IN RELATION TO MENTAL HEALTH

Holistic practitioners believe that *every* symptom has a psychological content *and* expresses itself in the body, hence the often-quoted phrase: 'we treat the person, not the disease'. This means that no single part can be understood except in its relation to the whole. The alternative practitioner is looking for 'patterns of disharmony' by examining physical as well as mental and emotional symptoms, even in a psychiatric case, rather than compiling a list of separate symptoms to treat as separate entities (Kaptchuk, 1983).

Woody Allen, in the film *Deconstructing Harry*, creates a character who is a film actor suffering from being permanently out of focus, both on and off camera. His disease is 'being blurred' and everyone else can see it too; it is not just a subjective state of being. Later in the film, when Woody Allen becomes anxious himself, he too becomes blurred, while all around him remains in focus. Despite the comedy of the situation, and for the purpose of analogy, we can say this was a metaphor for a 'pattern of disharmony'. It is both physical and psychological. In looking at disease in this way, alternative medicines blend art and science. This analogous and symbolic way of viewing the body and its processes is explained in detail under the heading 'The Meaning of Symptoms'.

Because the blurring is material and visible, a conventional doctor might diagnose this as a physical symptom aiming to eradicate the blurring, and then to treat the anxiety separately. An alternative practitioner would treat the physical and psychological symptoms as one disorder. For the alternative practitioner, assessing symptoms from a holistic point of view, it is the degree and quality of blurring of the energy that is looked at, instead of the isolated symptoms in physiological systems.

Physical pain and illness on the mental and emotional plane cannot be seen as clearly as a blurred man's predicament. The human body can show the material effects of disease (tumours, skin eruptions, swellings) but despite scientific research into the chemistry of the brain and endocrine system, the subtler aspects of health, especially mental and emotional problems, are sometimes less easy to pin down in a material way.

Whatever the model for the interpretation of symptoms (e.g. Qi energy, vital force, the elements) or the therapeutic process (needles, massage, herbs, laying on of hands), for alternative practitioners there is no separation between the energy, the individual and their disease picture, whether the disease is predominantly physical or mental.

INDIVIDUALITY

An important principle shared by alternative medicines is that of individuality. Medicines and treatments are not prescribed under disease categories (as with conventional medicine) but under patient categories. Five patients with panic attacks and IBS may be given five completely different treatments or prescriptions. This will depend on the background of their symptoms, concomitant symptoms, medical history, psychological state as a whole, their constitutional type and the triggers to their symptoms. So there is no 'panic attack medicine', only a number of medicines which can be used to treat different kinds of panic attack symptoms, and this will depend upon the rest of the patient's symptom picture.

The function of symptoms

The next principle of energy medicine is that symptoms manifest for a reason, and the alternative therapist works *with*, not against the symptoms. Disease is viewed as manifestation of the energy acting to remove obstructions to the normal functioning of organs and tissues. However, the body and mind's natural self-defence systems cannot always shake off illness completely. Symptoms are viewed as signs of the body's attempt to heal itself, and thus physical and psychological symptoms are perceived as the patient's *defence posture*.

The symptoms are the clues towards the cure of any individual case. However subjective a symptom may be, it is still valid, because it is part of the patient's perception of their dis-ease. Rather than suppressing the body's expression of the symptoms at all costs, alternative therapies generally work with the symptoms, seeing them as the clue to that individual's cure: analysis of symptoms will include a broad picture with mind, body, environment, social and spiritual dimensions.

The meaning of symptoms

Sometimes the two models, conventional and alternative, seem to have different ways of talking about the same thing. In conventional medicine, the liver plays an important part in excreting wastes, neutralising poisons and manufacturing (or processing) new chemicals. It provides energy from food, and defence against toxins.

In Chinese medical philosophy the liver's function is to store blood and ensure smooth flow of Qi (vital energy) through the body. In Chinese medical texts, the liver is compared to an army general, and is seen as the seat of courage and resoluteness when healthy. Furthering the analogy of the army general, who deals in the strategies of war, the liver influences the capacity we have to plan our life. This can be equated with the liver as a defender against toxic invaders, and as a regulator of many of the chemicals in the body. Flow of liver Qi is said to have a deep influence on the emotional state, particularly in terms of anger, suppressed anger and frustration (war).

If the 'Liver-Blood' is weak, we may be lost souls, with no direction in life, unable to make plans. Or we may be prone to violence. This is an example of how the psychological symptoms are inseparable from the organs, and vice versa, and how their binding force is the energy, Qi.

Therefore if a patient presents with deep depression and apathy (lost all hope, can't make any plans for life) and listlessness (no energy), or alcoholism (damaging the liver) with aggressive tendencies (war), it may well mean that the liver Qi meridian points will be the points worked on. This will depend upon the rest of their symptoms and the 'bigger picture' of the patient's state of ill-health.

The meaning of symptoms comes from a view of the body as an integrated whole where, for example, organs have affinities with emotions, and the ruling principle of the body and mind's functioning is vital energy. Psychological and physical symptoms are seen as expressions of the same pattern of disharmony.

Empowering the patient

No health practitioner would underestimate the healing dynamic, in which the patient feels heard, and is given time and attention in order to overcome their illness. Alternative treatments offer the patient the time to focus on themselves and think about their problems in a reflective environment. Treatments generally last a minimum of thirty minutes, often up to ninety minutes. Some of them are, by their nature, physically relaxing: such as yoga, meditation, reflexology, aromatherapy.

By enquiring into the 'bigger picture' of the patient's life, alternative medicine facilitates self-knowledge and understanding, and encourages the patient to take responsibility for their own well-being. This is viewed as part of the healing process. The practitioner acts as the catalyst to bring an understanding of the patient's illness to light. The patient may come to understand the patterns of their behaviour and why they became ill, and are encouraged to take appropriate steps to remain well, without becoming dependent on the treatment. In this way the patient takes an active responsibility for their illness and health.

THE THERAPIES

Homeopathy

The word homeopathy is derived from the Greek meaning 'similar suffering' and is based upon the principle of 'like cures like'. The medicines are tested on healthy people to see what kind of physical, mental and emotional symptoms they produce. Homeopathic medicines cure the symptoms in a person who is unwell which are most similar to those produced when testing the remedy on people who are healthy. The results of this test, called 'proving' are combined with botanical, toxicological, clinical and other information to provide a detailed picture of the action of a remedy on the mental and physical levels. The medicines are highly diluted and then 'potentised' by a form of shaking, which releases their healing powers. High dilutions act upon the 'energy' systems of the body, as explained in the introduction to this chapter. The medicines are derived from animal, mineral and botanical sources.

Homeopathy is well suited to the treatment of mental illness. Prescriptions are based upon a complete picture of the 'pattern of disharmony' experienced by the patient. Treatment with homeopathic medicine involves the practitioner taking a detailed case history which will include the patient's family history, personal medical history and current problems, but also a lengthy enquiry into the personality and 'constitutional type' of the patient. This means enquiring about reactions to food, weather, environment, as well as fears, anxieties, dreams, relationships, sexuality and anything which triggers mental or emotional 'stress'. The homeopath will record everything the patient says, in the patient's own words, as each detail, reaction and even the use of language may provide clues to the remedy that will resolve their inner disturbance.

A fundamental difference between homeopathy and conventional medicine in, for example, the treatment of a patient who presents with anxiety as their main problem, is that instead of a tranquilliser being prescribed, which might well palliate, a remedy will be prescribed with the aim of a deep cure, or resolution of the symptoms. It will work with the exact thoughts, feelings and physical symptoms of the individual patient, rather than chemically supressing them. Homeopaths often work alongside the patient's General Practitioner, where it is thought appropriate to reduce conventional medications.

It is the aetiology of the presenting problems and *the exact manner in which the individual reacts* to a given situation that are most important in prescribing a remedy. The homeopath looks for patterns in the case history which represent the central disturbance of the patient, and prescribes a similar remedy accordingly.

A 35-year-old woman presents with suicidal depression and alcoholism some months after losing her highly paid job. This individual has become claustrophobic for the first time in her life. She cannot even travel in a car as she fears the confinement so much. All of her mental problems, particularly the suicidal thoughts, are much worse at the time of menstruation. At this time she fears that she will actually become insane and has visions that a black cloud envelops her head, sees dark figures in the room and in her bed at night, and has a sense of suffocation and entrapment. Physically she experiences electric-shock-like cramps. These combined symptoms indicate the remedy *Cimicufugia* (Black Cohosh), a plant of the Ranunculacea family.

Another woman, aged 35, has been made redundant from her highly paid job where she held a high position. In the following months she has reached the stage of suicidal depression and has problems with alcohol abuse. How does she react? What is the totality of this individual's picture? The individual who requires the remedy made from a preparation of gold, *Aurum Metallicum*, presents with anxiety in the chest and stomach, and palpitations. She is primarily anxious about her failure, and feels she will never succeed in life. She may have attempted suicide by jumping from a height or through a window, or talks of this method of suicide. She dreams of and fears falling from high places. The depression of *Aurum Metallicum* is severe and involves much self-loathing, a strong aversion to any company whatsoever (even aversion to family) and complete loss of joy. The issues of the patient are their failure, and failed duty in particular; they often feel betrayed by friends. They were once ambitious and tended to be leaders in their work. They have a history of glandular problems and blood pressure instability and a family history of heart disease.

Both of the above examples are much simplified but attempt to show how each case is *individualised* as far as possible. The repertory of mental and emotional symptoms produced by homoeopathic medicines is vast and covers hundreds of symptoms as wide-ranging as the examples below:

- *Delusion: defend themselves against imaginary attacks and insults* (one remedy: Lyssin);
- *Mania for cleanliness* (four remedies have this symptom: Arsenicum Album, Sepia, Silicea, Sulphur);
- *Striking, knocking his head against the wall* (fourteen remedies);
- *Mental affections in puberty* (twenty-seven remedies);
- *Refuses to eat* (thirty-two remedies).

However, it is the *combination* of mental, emotional and physical symptoms as well as the general constitutional type of the patient that will be used to attain a homeopathic solution to any mental health problem.

Acupuncture

Practised in China for 3,500 years, this is based on an understanding of three principles: Chi, Yin and Yang, and the five elements, in relation to the body and mind. According to traditional Chinese philosophy, our health is dependent on the body's motivating energy, called Qi ('chi'), which moves along a system of twelve meridians or channels, internally. There are approximately 365 major acupoints along the meridians where Qi is concentrated and through which it can enter or leave the body. By inserting fine needles, the flow of Qi is affected.

Qi is made of equal and opposite forces called Yin and Yang, and when these are imbalanced the person becomes sick. In balance, the person remains well.

The five elements are fire, earth, metal, water and wood. Each element has a yin and a yang organ and is associated with a particular taste, emotion and season.

By inserting fine needles, energy flow along blocked Qi channels can be stimulated to flow more easily. The flow of Qi can be disturbed by anxiety, stress, anger, shock, poor nutrition, weather conditions, hereditary factors, infections, poisons and trauma. The physical and emotional symptoms of the patient are seen as one, and the imbalance is corrected by insertion of the needles at the correct points to suit the whole picture, rebalancing the energy and thereby having an effect on the physical and emotional balance of the body.

Acupuncture is recommended for anxiety, depression, addictions, eating disorders, sexual problems, post-traumatic stress disorder, manic depression and combined physical/emotional disorders.

THERAPIES RELATED TO ACUPUNCTURE

Acupressure

This uses finger pressure at meridian points instead of needles, and is used more often in first aid situations or in cases where needles cannot be used.

Shiatsu

This is Japanese pressure point stimulation combined with massage, working on the same principles as acupuncture, but applying pressure on meridian points with massage and finger pressure. In this way it is non-invasive compared to acupuncture, and is considered to be a gentler, albeit perhaps less deep-acting therapy. Certain acupressure points will affect the mood; however, there will be a concentration on overall balance and relaxation in the treatment. In one research project 74 per cent of people improved in tests of coordination, communication, emotional and physical well-being.

Chinese herbalism

Another aspect of the philosophy of Traditional Chinese Medicine is herbalism, where the treatment is mainly derived from plants, but some mineral and animal substances are also used. This is based on the principles of holism, yin and yang and the five elements. Qualities belonging to the same element are said to support one another, e.g. the element wood has the following affinities: the taste is sour; emotion is anger; season is spring; and organs are gall bladder, liver, tendons and eyes. Fire's taste is bitter, emotion is joy, season is summer and organs are heart, small intestine, tongue and blood vessels. Therefore to treat a heart disorder or depression (lack of joy), a Chinese herbalist might use bitter-tasting herbs, as bitterness is associated with fire.

Western herbalism

This strengthens the body's natural ability to heal itself. Remedies are prescribed for the individual not the disease. St John's wort is the most well known example of a herb that is effective at treating mental illness, but it has been prescribed in a non-individualistic way, and therefore doesn't help everyone. Prescriptions can be of a single herb or combination of herbs. Their efficacy has been ascribed to their ability to stimulate helpful defensive reactions in the body, to adjust body processes (e.g. ginseng root improves the ability of the adrenal cortex to respond to stress, and to eliminate toxins and waste and valerian, passion flower and hops have a sedative effect). Herbal medicine is most often prescribed in tinctures or capsules.

Reflexology

This therapy involves working on the 'pressure points' (similar to acupuncture points) of the feet, to affect the health of the body. There is evidence of it being used 5,000 years ago in China, India, Japan and Egypt. The therapy is called reflex-ology because the foot serves as a 'reflection' of the whole body. Imagine a blueprint corresponding to the body and all its organs and systems which is mapped out on the foot. Pressure points stimulated on the foot will have an effect on the organ corresponding to that pressure point. This is another way of stimulating vital energy, accessing meridian lines through the foot rather than the whole body, as in acupuncture. The general effects have been found to be relaxation, better sleep, and increased ability to deal with life's ups and downs. It is recommended in medical practices for dealing with long-term chronic cases; cases involving tension or stress; cases where there is a need to reduce reliance on drugs; people who need more support than consultation time allows; and patients who produce symptoms for which there appears to be no underlying pathology. It was also found to reduce anxiety and depression amongst a group of patients in a geriatric unit. Research at Worthing MIND found that participants who had reflexology as well as counselling achieved a significantly more balanced physical and psychological state than those who had just counselling. The Association of Reflexologists has several research reports available relating to the effects of reflexology on patient dependency ratings; premenstrual syndrome; neurosis; women with need for emotional support; and children with behavioural problems and hyperactivity.

Naturopathy

This promotes health by stimulating and supporting the body's inherent power to regain balance, and rests on belief in the vital force, the higher energy of the body. Disease is seen as a manifestation of the vital force applying itself to remove obstructions to the normal functioning of organs and tissues. Treatment involves an investigation into whether the basic cause of the illness is chemical (diet, bad excretion, poor circulation); mechanical (musculoskeletal); or psychological. Whatever the cause, the disease affects the whole person, not an isolated organ or system. Emphasis is on education of patients, encouraging them to take more responsibility for their health, and be aware of nutrition, rest, exercise and lifestyle. Devised treatments may involve nutritional programmes, fasting, osteopathy, chiropractic, exercise, hydrotherapy, homeopathy, herbalism and nutritional biochemistry.

Healing

Healing is the channelling of healing energy by the laying on of hands, or by thought, or prayer. Many practitioners believe that God, or a divine presence, is behind their healing power. Healing has its roots in shamanism and magic. Extensive modern studies have been carried out in the USA to record the effects on heart and circulatory problems as well as tension headaches, post-operative healing and wound healing. It has also been positively tested on animals and seeds, which are not susceptible to the power of suggestion. Brainwave patterns of healers were found to be similar to those of clair-voyants and yogis, and it was found that brainwave patterns for healer and recipient changes in a similar pattern during healing. Healing results in an increase in vitality and well-being, enabling the recipient to more easily overcome their mental or physical problems.

Reiki (pronounced *ray-key*) is an ancient Tibetan healing art, based on the belief in a Universal Life Force 'Qi' or 'Chi', which flows through all things, inside us, as well as around us. During treatment, the practitioner is channelling and focusing energy into the body of a subject by the laying on of hands, on or near the body of the patient. It is a relaxing, meditative process. Emotional and physical 'blockages' are released by focusing on the chakras (energy centres) of the body. There are seven major chakras in the body, lying along the cerebrospinal axis, and each corresponds to particular organs and emotions.

Transcendental meditation (TM)

The main purpose of TM is to enable the subject to attain a deep level of relaxation, where mind and body become one, aware of each other on a profound level, and to access more energy and peace of mind. The state achieved by this method has been termed 'restful alertness'. It is an easily learned technique and is ideally practised 15–20 minutes a day. It has been found to trigger a drop in levels of cortisol, decrease muscle tension and to normalise blood pressure. Scientific research studies have shown that, compared to other relaxation and meditation methods, TM is effective in reducing anxiety, alcohol, cigarette and drug intake, and improving psychological health (Shafil *et al.*, 1975; Monahan, 1977; Eppley *et al.*, 1989). Its effects may be cumulative. It has been used in criminal rehabilitation programmes in the USA, and shown to reduce aggression and improve mental illness, as well as lowering reoffending rates. The British Association for the Medical Application of Transcendental Medicine has successfully lobbied the UK government for the right to prescribe TM.

Osteopathy

This is light massage, stretching and manipulation of the body framework. It is based on the principle that the musculoskeletal system plays a vital role in maintaining health, so that if there is a problem anywhere in this system there will not only be localised pain and inflammation, but an adverse effect on the vital organs, and all other systems including the nervous system and endocrine system. Osteopaths will talk to their patients about their emotional symptoms as well as their medical history and the physical symptoms they experience. In the USA osteopaths have been licensed as medical practitioners since 1972, and in the UK the 1993 Osteopathy Act granted osteopaths official recognition.

Cranial osteopathy

This gentle manipulation of the cranial and spinal bones helps to rebalance disturbances in the cerebrospinal fluid. It is often used for babies after birth, but is also useful for adults experiencing emotional states which may be a result of accidents and injuries, especially to the spine and head.

Yoga

Yoga means 'union' in Sanskrit. Yoga has its origins more than 5,000 years ago in India. The most popular form of yoga in the western world is hatha yoga, which does not involve spiritual training or the adoption of a dietary regime, as do some kinds of yoga practice. Hatha means balance, signifying the beneficial effects of uniting and balancing mind and body. Slow movements and stretching the body with coordinated breathing have been found to result in mental calmness, as well as having a positive effect on blood pressure and the endocrine system. The Yoga Biomedical trust has been working with NHS patients for over five years.

Clinical aromatherapy

Differentiation is necessary here from its use by the beauty market, which has hi-jacked the term to include almost anything perfumed. In its medical application aromatherapy is the use of pure aromatic volatile essences or 'essential oils' extracted from plants, flowers, grasses, fruits, leaves, roots, trees. Many of them are active ingredients in conventional drugs. Small amounts of essential oils are diluted in a carrier oil (e.g. almond oil) and massaged into the skin of the patient. Absorbed through the skin and by inhalation, the oils have definite psychological effects in addition to the pharmacological action of the oils. The biological actions of pheromones are a good example of the power of the sense of smell to trigger physiological and psychological response. Each essential oil is made up of more than a hundred components which can be chemically analysed, e.g. terpenes, esters, alcohols, ketones. The essential oils trigger reactions in the receptor cells of the nose, leading to a chain reaction in the olfaction bulb and the limbic system, seat of emotions, sexual feelings, memory and learning. The Egyptian priests used essential oils for treating psychological disorders such as mania, anxiety and depression. In depression, for example, the choice of oils (they are often used in combinations) would depend upon whether the depression was listless and lethargic, hysterical, anxious or restless.

Aromatherapists are employed by GPs and hospitals in the NHS (Cannard, 1996). At Worcester Hospital in Hereford, a six-month trial showed that simply vaporising lavender through the air caused patients to sleep in a more natural pattern and caused them to be less aggressive during the day. In addition, some patients were able to discontinue their tranquilliser, due to lavender's calming effects. Aromatherapy massage has been found to significantly reduce psychological distress (anxiety and depression) in patients with cancer (Kite *et al.*, 1998).

References

Cannard, G. (1996) The effect of aromatherapy in promoting relaxation and stress reduction in a general hospital. *Complementary Therapies in Nursing & Midwifery* 2(2): 38–40.

Dethlefsen, T. and Dahlke, R. (2004) *The Healing Power of Illness: Understanding what Your Symptoms are Telling You.* (?)USA: Vega Books.

Eppley, K.R., Abrams, A.I. and Shear, J. (1989) Differential effects of relaxation techniques on trait anxiety: a meta-analysis. *Journal of Clinical Psychology* 45(6): 957–74.

Gerber, R. (2001) *Vibrational Medicine: The Number 1 Handbook of Subtle Energy Therapies.* (?)USA: Bear and Company.

Heron, J. (1986) Critique of conventional research methodology. *Complementary Medical Research* 1: 12–22.

Kaptchuk, T. (1983) *The Web that Has No Weaver.* New York: Congdon & Weed.

Kite, S.M., Maher, E.J., Anderson, K., Young, T., Young, J., Wood, J., Howells, N. and Bradburn, J. (1998) Development of an aromatherapy service at a cancer centre. *Palliative Medicine* 12(3): 171–80.

Lewith, G.T. and Aldridge, D. (eds.) (1993) *Clinical Research Methodology for Complementary Therapies.* London: Hodder & Stoughton.

Monahan, R.J. (1977) Secondary prevention of drug dependence through the transcendental meditation program in metropolitan Philadelphia. *International Journal of the Addictions* 12(6): 729–54.

Shafil, M., Lavely, R. and Jaffe, R. (1975) Meditation and the prevention of alcohol abuse. *American Journal of Psychiatry* 132(9): 942–5.

Further reading

Dethlefsen, T. and Dahlke, R. (1990) *The Healing Power of Illness*. Element.

Fulder, S. (1996) *The Handbook of Alternative and Complementary Medicine*. Oxford: Oxford Medical Publications.

Gerber, R. (1988) *Vibrational Medicine*. (?)New York: Bear & Co.

Kaptchuk, T. (1983) *The Web that Has No Weaver*. New York: Congdon & Weed.

Maciocia, G. (1989) *The Foundations of Chinese Medicine*. London: Churchill Livingston.

Vithoulkas, G. (1980) *The Science of Homeopathy*. (?) London: Thorsons.

Vithoulkas, G. (2000) *The Science of Homeopathy*. New York: Grove Press/Atlantic Monthly Press.

Whitmount, E. (1993) *The Alchemy of Healing: Psyche and Soma*. Berkeley, CA: North Atlantic Press.

Woodham, A. and Peters, D. (1997) *The Encyclopedia of Complementary Medicine*. London: Dorling Kindersley.

Worwood, V.A. (1997) *The Fragrant Mind: Aromatherapy for Personality, Mind, Mood and Emotion*. London: Bantam.

Useful addresses

The British Acupuncture Council, Park House, 206–208 Latimer Road, London W10 6RE

Phone: 020 8964 0222

Fax: 020 8964 0333

Email info@acupuncture.org.uk

Website www.acupuncture.org.uk

British Medical Acupuncture Society (www.users.aol.com/acubmas/bmas/html).

Aromatherapy Organisations Council, 3 Latymer Close, Braybrooke, Market Harborough, Leicestershire, LE16 8LN.

The British Association for the Medical Application of Transcendental Meditation, telephone: 08705–143733 for information.

Confederation of Healing Organisations, 113 High Street, Berkhamsted, Herts HP4 2DJ, tel. 01442 870660.

The Register of Chinese Herbal Medicine, PO Box 400, Wembley, Middlesex HA9 9NZ.

National Institute of Medical Herbalists, 56 Longbrook St, Exeter EX4 6AH.

General Council and Register of Consultant Herbalists, 18 Sussex Square, Brighton, E. Sussex BN2 5AA.

The Society of Homoeopaths, 4 Artizan Road, Northampton, NN1 4HU.

Tel. 01604 621400

Email: societyofhomoeopaths@btinternet.com

Jo Evans (RSHom) Registered Homeopath, London WC1, 07973 764 026, www.likecureslike.org., email; jo@likecureslike.org

General Council and Register of Naturopaths, Frazer House, 6 Netherhall Gardens, London NW3 5RR, tel. 020 7435 8728.

General Council and Register of Osteopaths, 56 London Street, Reading, Berkshire, RG1 4SQ.

Association of Reflexologists, 27 Old Gloucester Street, London WC1N 3XX.

The Reiki Association, Cornbrook Bridge House, Clee Hill, Ludlow, Shropshire SY8 3QQ.

The Yoga Biomedical Trust, PO Box 140, Cambridge, CB4 3SY, tel. 01223 67 301.

Part VII
The future

23 Implications for training, research and service provision

Claire Henderson, Shubulade Smith,
Catherine Smith and Angela Stevens

For many women, both the prevention and treatment of mental ill-health is inadequate. Gender inequalities may place women at risk of developing common mental disorders, e.g. depression or anxiety. It may also lead to therapies and services that are ill-designed to meet their needs.

The chapters in this book outline some of the difficulties faced by women in need of psychological treatment and suggest a variety of solutions that, if put in place, could improve care. A practical and realistic approach is to consider how the National Service Framework (NSF) for mental health (Department of Health, 1999) can be used to improve both prevention and treatment for all adults with mental health problems. The NSF is a ten-year strategy for adult mental health services in England. It gives guiding principles for treatment and standards covering all aspects of services. The standards include:

1. HEALTH PROMOTION

Public policy should recognise the epidemiological finding that being female is associated with potential victimisation from childhood abuse, domestic violence and single parenthood, with the associated poverty, low pay and unemployment. All of these are risk factors for mental illness. Further, there may be other aspects of the female gender role that put women at risk of mental ill-health but which have received little attention from researchers, for example sexual exploitation in adulthood.

2. PRIMARY CARE

The majority of women using mental health services do so within the primary care system. It is vital to expand the evidence base for what works within primary care rather than simply applying secondary care-based evidence, as the populations and resources are different. This means a lot more research on interventions in primary care. This should include research on appropriate prescribing of antidepressants and anxiolytics, and on the different forms of psychotherapy currently grouped together under the umbrella of counselling.

Primary care is an ideal setting for screening for postnatal disorders, alcohol and drug misuse, depression and anxiety disorders; at the moment this happens in a patchy manner. The routine visits made postnatally and that women make with children, e.g. for immunisations, provide access for health professionals to screen for these common mental disorders. These visits are already used to good effect to detect other problems, but could be made more effective by the inclusion of such screening procedures. Similarly, cervical and breast cancer screening and family planning visits provide opportunities for screening for mental disorder. Depression, with its resulting economic impact on society and adverse impact on children and other dependants, will affect a significant proportion of women during their lifetime. Given the growing problem among women of alcohol misuse and the resultant physical ill-health, an argument could be made for routine screening for both depression and alcohol misuse in their own right. For both problems, screening procedures and treatments are both acceptable and cost-effective. The Beck Depression Inventory and the CAGE questionnaire (alcohol screening questionnaire) are quick and easy screening questionnaires to administer and have well-established psychometric properties.

3. ACCESS TO SERVICES

Women frequently complain that they are given treatments that are inadequate for their needs. For example, access to talking therapies is very limited, due to a shortage of staff trained in such techniques. It is of note that the most common mental health problems seen in women are known to be helped significantly by psychotherapeutic intervention. More recently, research on innovative therapy for borderline personality disorder has had significant implications for training and service provision. In addition, the settings within which these treatments might take place are often felt to be stigmatising, hostile and non-therapeutic. As mentioned in preceding chapters, linguistic barriers and mixed-sex wards can make women reluctant to get involved with psychiatric services.

4 AND 5. SEVERE MENTAL ILLNESS

Women with severe mental health problems are more likely to: be exposed to sexual exploitation; have children who are in the care of statutory services; have physical health problems; and commit suicide, compared with other women.

Standard four of the NSF states that patients with severe mental illness should receive care which optimises engagement, anticipates or prevents a crisis and reduces risk. Clearly women are telling us that the services they receive make it hard for them to engage in psychiatric services.

Rates of severe mental illness in women are no different to those in men. However, the factors that make the 'well' woman vulnerable in society may be doubly difficult for psychotic women. Women with severe mental illness are more likely to need support with housing, finances, work and relationships (including those with children as well as partners). Research on problems that provoke relapse, e.g. financial problems, would be invaluable and could inform clinical practice.

Acute care settings

Innovations such as home treatment services and women's crisis houses, run by Community Mental Health Team (CMHT) staff with operational input from service users from the point of inception and throughout, are currently under way in certain areas. Evaluation of these services will give an indication of their use and acceptability to female users. To speed dissemination of these models of care, training will need to be provided for mental health professionals in appropriate community settings so that they can gain confidence in working out of the hospital setting.

Physical health care

Evidence is cited in the book that physical health needs of women with severe mental illnesses are not being met. Assessing these physical needs is generally agreed to be the role of the GP. In practice consultations are often too brief to include physical problems, preventive or health promotion interventions and mental health complaints. Those with depression or chronic psychotic illnesses may have little motivation to address preventive health issues in particular. Since CMHT staff have greater contact in many cases, better training would enable them to identify physical problems in their clients and ensure that they seek treatment.

Pharmacotherapy

There is little research on how female physiology affects drug handling. Such research is vital to create a solid evidential base for prescribing to women. Similarly, sex-specific side-effect profiles are needed in order to improve the acceptability of medication. The important effects of oestrogen on D2 receptors leads to many research questions, including the role of oestrogen in the pathogenesis of and possible protection against psychoses. Furthermore, the effect of antipsychotics in lowering oestrogen status may increase the risks of heart disease and osteoporosis in later life.

6. CARERS AND FAMILIES

Women form the majority of carers in society. Thus:

1   as carers they have higher than average levels of both mental and physical problems;
2   they are more likely to care for someone with a mental health problem; and
3   when they become mentally ill themselves, the impact on others is greater.

Service providers must take account of this to ensure that women as patients are able to access services, for example providing creche facilities, and that as carers of mentally ill relatives they are given the information and support that they need.

7. SUICIDE PREVENTION

As in the case of men, most women who kill themselves have a mental illness, most commonly depression. While rates in women are generally lower than those for men, young Asian women in Britain have a markedly elevated rate of completed suicide. This suggests that there is a high level of unmet need in this group. Changes in social policy, health promotion, primary and secondary mental health care, as well as research and training would help to address these needs.

Conclusion

In the course of writing this book, the foundations for a different type of service delivery have been laid down:

* A number of women's crisis houses have been set up around the country.
* Many inpatient units have been segregated such that they are/have single-sex areas.
* New child and adolescent teams are being developed (this will have a secondary effect on their female carers).
* A ruling has been passed which will allow greater openness with clinical case notes. This may help to foster an understanding of how NHS processes work and give reassurance that help is being provided.
* Recent advances in pharmacotherapy mean greater availability of less stigmatising drugs.
* The ongoing integration of health and social services should mean more effective delivery of holistic care.

It appears that things are beginning to change. All of these initiatives mean that women's needs may be better catered for within mainstream psychiatry in the future. We hope that the government in partnership with statutory health services will be able to build on these initiatives, thus providing a solid foundation for delivery of good mental health services, not only for women, but for the population as a whole.

The aim of this book is to make available a practical guide for mental health workers looking after women with psychiatric illness. Despite the inevitable limitations of the setting in which they work, we hope that this book will help practitioners to provide continually improving care to their female patients, capitalising on the skills, diagnostic and therapeutic, that they already possess.

Reference

Department of Health (1999) *National Service Framework for Mental Health: Modern Standards and Service Models*. London: HMSO.

Index

For Product Safety Concerns and Information please contact our EU representative GPSR@taylorandfrancis.com Taylor & Francis Verlag GmbH, Kaufingerstraße 24, 80331 München, Germany

T - #0011 - 270225 - C0 - 234/156/19 [21] - CB - 9780415213943 - Gloss Lamination